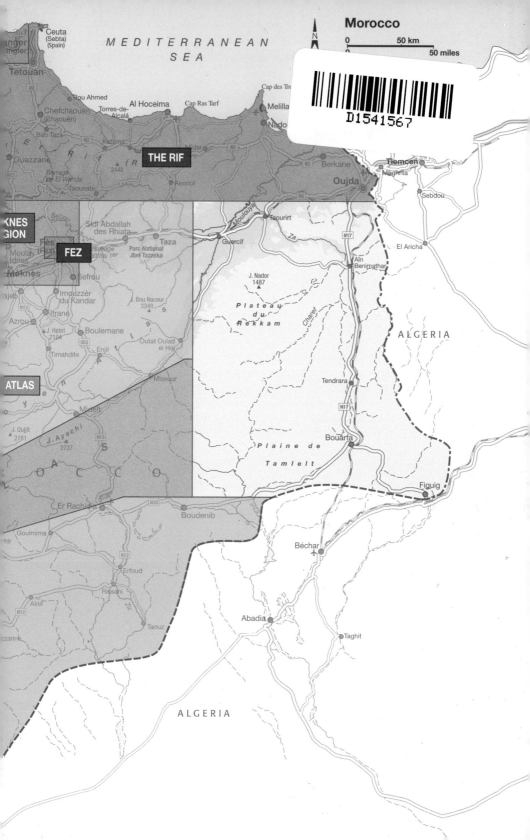

INSIGHT GUIDES
MOROCCO

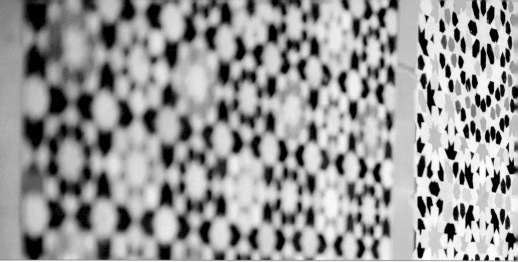

Contents

THE BEST OF MOROCCO: TOP ATTRACTIONS

From north to south, desert to coast, here are
the top 10 must-see places in Morocco.

△ **Marrakech**. Both African and Arab, eastern and western,
Marrakech is an exotic and exciting city. Join the nightly spectacle on
the Jemaa el Fna. See page 231.

▽ **Essaouira**. This windswept, fortified coastal town has been
inhabited since Phoenician times, and is now popular with artists
and kite- and windsurfing enthusiasts. See page 175.

▽ **The South**. Saharan dunes, nomad tents, the Anti-Atlas, Souss
Valley and stunning beaches of Mirleft and Tan Tan make this one
of Morocco's most exciting, though least-visited, regions. See
pages 263 and 285.

△ **Meknes**. Imperial Meknes was
built by the extravagant Sultan
Moulay Ismail. See page 203.

△ **Fez**. Step back in time to the old city of Fez el Bali – a golden-hued, mysterious labyrinth of medieval markets, palaces, mosques and medersas. See page 183.

△ **Chefchaouen and the Rif**. Nestled amidst the peaks of the Rif Mountains, blue-washed Chefchaouen is a vibrant arts and crafts centre with a relaxed Spanish feel. A great base from which to explore the Rif massif. See page 133.

△ **The Dadès and Drâa valleys**. These lush, palm-filled, kasbah-studded valleys plunging south and east from Ouarzazate present one of the archetypal images of Morocco and are gateways to the great desert expanses of Merzouga and M'Hamid. See pages 269 and 266.

△ **The High Atlas**. Majestic snowcapped peaks, breathtaking valleys, dizzying mountain passes, remote Berber villages, trekking, hiking, skiing: the Atlas has it all. This is Morocco untouched by the modern world. See page 248.

▽ **Tangier**. Iconic hangout for writers and artists, Tangier is one of Morocco's best-loved cities, with a great medina, an elegant corniche and beaches nearby. See page 115.

△ **Volubilis**. The ruins of this Roman town lie scattered in a fertile plain near Meknes. Archways, pillars and mosaics are remarkably preserved. See page 212.

THE BEST OF MOROCCO: EDITOR'S CHOICE

Wild adventures, laid-back beaches, soaring mountains and vibrant souks... here, at a glance, are our top recommendations for the best places to see and things to do.

Legzira beach, Agadir.

BEST BEACHES AND SEASIDE TOWNS

Asilah. Favoured by artists, this whitewashed town south of Tangier is known for its vibrant arts festival, fish restaurants and pretty painted houses. See page 142.

Tangier. There are dozens of beaches around this city. To the east are the beaches of the calm Mediterranean and to the west, long stretches of the Atlantic coast. See page 124.

Agadir. A magnificent bay, year-round high temperatures and a good choice of hotels make Agadir

Morocco's top seaside resort. See page 277.

Oualidia. This pretty holiday resort, located between Casablanca and Essaouira, is famous for its oyster beds and popular for its calm, crescent-shaped lagoon. See page 172.

El Jadida. Historic Portuguese coastal enclave bounded by beautiful Atlantic beaches, including the hedonistic Mazagan tourist complex. See page 170.

Essaouira. Beautiful whitewashed town with an endless expanse of pristine Atlantic beach stretching south towards the villages of Diabat and Sidi Kaouki. See page 175.

Berber man.

BEST MONUMENTS

Koutoubia Mosque. Marrakech's magnificent 12th-century mosque and minaret is the model for the Hassan Tower in Rabat and the Giralda in Seville, Spain. See page 233.

Hassan II Mosque. One of only two mosques in Morocco that can be visited by non-Muslims, this is the largest mosque in Morocco and the fifth-largest in the world. See page 166.

Volubilis. The remains of this Roman town are some of the best preserved in the world and illuminate Morocco's ancient past. See pages 213 and 212.

Saadian Tombs. These golden tombs date back to the 16th century and

house the remains of several sultans of the Saadian dynasty. See page 240.

Jemaa el Fna. A living monument, the Jemaa el Fna is the cultural soul of Marrakech and the heart of Morocco's storytelling tradition. See page 234.

Kairaouine Mosque and University. The nation's second-largest mosque and what claims to be the world's oldest university. See page 193.

Hassan II Mosque, Casablanca.

BEST ADVENTURES

Hiking. Hike up and around Jebel Toubkal, the highest peak in North Africa, explore Aït Bouguemez or the Rif Mountains, or trek through the Jebel Siroua. See pages 253, 258, 134 and 273.
Whitewater rafting and kayaking. Raft or kayak down the wild N'Fiss, Ourika and Ahansal rivers as they tumble down out of the mountains of the High Atlas. See page 324.
Mountain biking. This is still being developed, but the *pistes* are ideal, especially around Jebel Siroua and in the Dadès

and Drâa valleys. See page 102.
Rock climbing. The Todra Gorge and the area around Tafraoute are best for this. See page 281.
Kite- and windsurfing. These sports are increasingly popular, and there are near-perfect conditions in and around Essaouira and further south, in Dakhla. See page 290.
Camel-trekking. Explore the Sahara on camel and sleep under the stars in a Bedouin tent: a quintessential Morocco experience. See page 323.

The dunes of Erg Chebbi Desert.

BEST SOUKS

Marrakech. Be dazzled by the Aladdin's cave-like array of shoes, lanterns, leather bags, kaftans, carpets, spices and jewellery in Marrakech's colourful souks. See page 235.
Taroudant. This walled town, a mini-Marrakech, is famous for its Berber souks, filled with wares from across the south. See page 273.
Tiznit. The souk here is best known for its ethnic

Berber silver jewellery. See page 282.
Essaouira. A more peaceful (and less expensive) experience than the souks of Marrakech, full of local thuya-wood handicrafts and the paintings and sculptures of local artists. See page 178.
Fez el Bali. Ancient, labyrinthine souks, crammed with leather work, fine silks and ceramics. See page 187.

BEST ARTS AND CRAFTS

Leather work. Bags, shoes, belts and pouffes are made in softest camel or goatskin, coloured in a multitude of shades and often finely tooled or embroidered. See page 86.
Carpets and kilims. Laboriously handmade, styled according to each region and often exorbitantly priced, a Moroccan carpet or kilim is something you'll keep for life. See page 83.
Jewellery. Vintage amber necklaces, silver rings, coral and turquoise cuffs – Moroccan tribal jewellery is impossible to resist. See page 86.
Pottery. Handmade, brilliantly coloured pottery from Fez, Meknes, Salé and Safi, whether antique or new, is much sought after. See page 85.
Woodwork. Cedar and walnut from the Rif and thuya from Essaouira are

painstakingly carved by skilled craftsmen into intricate doors, windows, jewellery boxes and wedding chests. See page 86.
Textiles. Silk-embroidered kaftans, finely woven jellabas, brightly coloured curtains and cushions – Moroccan textiles are lavishly beautiful, but won't come with a high price tag. See page 85.
Metalwork. Moroccan lanterns, crafted from copper, brass or iron and hammered, inlaid and cut into lacy Aladdin's lamps are irresistible. See page 86.

Bangles from Tiznit, Agadir.

Bellows for sale in Marrakech medina.

A Fez souk.

GATEWAY TO AFRICA

The ancient, mysterious and beautiful country of Morocco has lured foreign visitors for millennia, and remains one of the world's most popular tourist destinations to this day.

In a Marrakech riad.

Morocco, Land of the Setting Sun or 'El Maghreb el Aqsa' (the Farthest West), is one of the world's most dramatic, exotic and compelling countries. Its strategic position on the border zone of Africa and Europe, East and West, has long attracted conquerors and colonialists – from the Phoenicians and Romans of antiquity to the Arabs and French of more recent times. Morocco has always adapted and absorbed these many influences, but the country's wild hinterlands and rugged mountain regions have also sheltered and preserved a unique indigenous Berber culture. The result is a country of powerful extremes, where the traditional and the modern thrive side by side, and the lifeblood of the country is a vibrant intermingling of dozens of cultural and social elements.

For centuries, Morocco's breathtaking landscapes and unique heritage have inspired some of the most famous Western artists, from Delacroix to Matisse; writers, from Edith Wharton to William Burroughs; musicians, from Bob Marley to the Rolling Stones, and filmmakers from Orson Welles to Ridley Scott. Iconic cities such as Tangier and Marrakech also became hip places both for weekend visitors and long-term expats, their romantic riad palaces and villas the scenes of decadent parties and all manner of expat intrigues, particularly from the 1920s to the 1970s.

Timbuktu sign in Zagora.

Today, Morocco has become one of the world's most fashionable destinations once again. Budget flights from across Europe deposit thousands of tourists every month, eager to dive into the many experiences that the country has to offer: whether shopping in Marrakech, hiking in the High Atlas, camping in the desert or surfing on the Atlantic Coast. The king, Mohammed VI, is seen to be a liberal reformer, and the country's economy is rapidly growing. Yet, beneath all the shiny newness, the old Morocco – a land of ancient customs and compellingly untouristy regions – remains. You may have to search a little harder to find it, but that is half the adventure of exploring this magical country.

A LAND OF CONTRASTS

Morocco's contradictions can baffle the first-time visitor, but they are all part of the country's unique appeal and reward those who explore further.

Ancient and modern, Arab and Berber, European and African, religious and secular – Morocco really is the proverbial land of contrasts and captivating extremes. This is a country that cannot be easily defined or neatly explained, and where it's best to leave all assumptions behind you the moment you arrive.

Despite a turbulent history shaped by warring tribes and punctuated by waves of foreign involvement, Morocco today has developed into one of the region's most stable and prosperous countries. It is by no means without problems, of course – unemployment, poverty, corruption and illiteracy all present major challenges – but the country as a whole is full of hope for a future spearheaded by the popular king, Mohammed VI.

Morocco has its roots in Africa, but its face turned firmly towards Europe. It is uniquely African, uniquely Arab, profoundly Berber and, in its main cities at least, thoroughly Westernised. It is also an Islamic country that has a deep-rooted respect for and tolerance of other religions. This rich and eclectic mix and unique cultural heritage and way of life are endlessly fascinating and vary dramatically from region to region.

Erg Chebbi dunes.

Regions and places to visit

Essentially, Morocco can be divided into seven distinct geographical and cultural regions: the Mediterranean Coast and the Rif mountain region; the Middle Atlas, encompassing the Imperial Cities of Fez and Meknes and the ancient Roman city of Volubilis; the northern Atlantic Coast, including the economic and commercial capital, Casablanca, and the national capital, Rabat; Marrakech and the High Atlas; the southern oases and desert, from Ouarzazate to the border with Algeria; the central Atlantic Coast, from El Jadida to Agadir; and the Deep South, from Agadir to the Western Sahara and inland to the Souss Valley.

> '"There are men", say the Moors, "who have come from islands far away... to see Morocco. Like all the world, they know that there is no other land to compare to it... "'
> Walter Harris

Exploring all these various regions properly would take several months or more – a magnificent journey, if you are able to find the time. Most travellers, however, come on weekend breaks to one of the main cities – usually Marrakech or Fez – or one- or two-week tours of a particular region: Marrakech and the High Atlas; Marrakech and Essaouira; the High Atlas and the desert; Agadir and the Deep South; the Imperial Cities of Marrakech, Fez, Meknes and Volubilis; Tangier and the Mediterranean and Rif regions. The great cities alone could keep you busy for weeks, while enthusiasts. For those in search of the traditional rural Moroccan way of life, the valleys of the Souss, Tafilalt, Drâa and Ziz offer the traveller glimpses of a way of life that has changed little in centuries and of an iconic landscape of desert, mountains and sprawling oases dotted with ancient mudbrick villages, kasbahs and forts.

Romantic geographies

Morocco's diverse geography is a major part of the country's appeal. In the far north, the Mediterranean region is a land of rolling

Morocco's southwest coast.

trekking in the High Atlas, Middle Atlas and mountains of the Rif is fast becoming one of Morocco's major draws, with thousands of enthusiasts flooding in during the season, which runs from October to May, and with an ascent of Jebel Toubkal as the literal pinnacle of their trip.

In addition to these relatively well-trodden routes, independent travellers are hiring their own transport and taking to Morocco's roads to explore off the beaten track. For beach-lovers, the stretch of coastline between Essaouira and Agadir and the wild expanses between Tiznit and Dakhla are exceptionally beautiful, blissfully empty and a paradise for wind- and kitesurfing hills, dotted with olive groves and white-washed villages, with windswept cliffs dipping into emerald coves and the soaring peaks of the Rif in the distance. Here Spain is always on the horizon, both physically and culturally, exemplified by the anachronistic Spanish enclaves of Ceuta and Melilla, which still cling to Morocco's Mediterranean shore.

The Middle Atlas, from Fez to Midelt, is a relatively untravelled region, and thinly populated. A wildlife paradise, where species such as the Barbary ape and Golden eagle are found, the area's landscapes range from mountain peaks (snowcapped in winter), reaching heights of 3,400 metres (11,150ft), to verdant cedar and pine-forested foothills and scrubby lowland plains. All present endless opportunities for those wanting to explore either on foot or by bike.

The High Atlas is much more extreme and, in parts, more remote. This is the highest mountain range in North Africa, with peaks soaring to over 5,000 metres (16,400ft), offering some of the finest trekking anywhere on the continent. Culturally, the mountains are the domain of various warrior-like Berber tribes, who live here, isolated from the rest of the country, in their

> *Sleeping in a tented camp under the stars in one of Morocco's two spectacular dune deserts – the Erg Chigagga or the Erg Chebbi – is top of many visitors' Moroccan wishlists.*

with lush palm oases and time-warped villages of crumbling mudbrick, this part of the country offers a huge variety of things to see and do, from the thrills of surfing, desert camping and dune-boarding through

Snow-covered peaks of the High Atlas.

pisé and stone villages clinging impossibly to high mountainsides. Life remains hard to this day. Electricity has only recently reached many areas and in the winter months much of the range is completely covered in snow, and the high mountain passes and villages are cut off for days.

At the other end of the spectrum, much of the southern half of the country is covered with dry coastal plains and vast tracts of desert. These are wild and historically rich areas in which to travel – from the windy expanses of the Atlantic Coast, battered by huge waves and scattered with long stretches of golden beach, to the deserts south of the High Atlas and in the Saharan region. Laced

to exploring winding oases and labyrinthine kasbahs.

Unique identities

From the Riffians of the north to the Berbers of the Atlas and the Arab nomads of the south, the people of Morocco are as distinct as its landscapes. Their individuality is reflected in their traditional dress and local customs, which remain remarkably unaffected in most places by the modern world. The music of Morocco, too, is a vibrant mix of old and new, with a wealth of eclectic influences: Algerian raï, Saharan sounds from Mali and Senegal, the hypnotic rhythms of Gnaoua and Western-inspired hip-hop and rap.

All of these elements – dress, music, customs and dialects – are further demarcated by the pronounced, and ever-widening, urban–rural divide which separates those living in Morocco's cosmopolitan cities from the country's rural inhabitants.

Climate

Climate-wise, the north and Mediterranean Coast are largely cool and wet in winter and spring and comfortably warm in the summer. The Atlas regions can be bitterly cold during winter, but blissfully cool in the summer, when the rest of the country swelters. The plains around Marrakech probably see the most extreme temperatures. The summers are scorching, with temperatures exceeding 45°C (113°F). In winter the nights are cold, but daytime temperatures are warm in the sun. The Deep South and desert region south of the High Atlas have similar, albeit more pronounced, extremes. Generally, the best time to visit most regions in Morocco is during the spring months, between February and late May, with periods such as Christmas and New Year and Easter especially popular.

A Marrakech souk.

TOURISM IN THE 21ST CENTURY

Morocco has always been popular with foreigners – from ancient Phoenician traders to contemporary artists, celebrities and hippies. But since the turn of the millennium, tourism in Morocco – both in terms of numbers of visitors and tourist-related development in the country itself – has risen to new levels. Soon after he came to power in 1999, King Mohammed VI announced his 'Vision 2010' plan, with the goal of attracting 10 million tourists to the country by 2010, backed up by the 'Plan Azur', aimed at developing six major new resorts around the coast. In the event, Vision 2010 missed its target, but not by much, and King Mohammed subsequently launched the, perhaps even more ambitious, 'Vision 2020', aiming to bring 20 million visitors to Morocco by 2020, as well as establishing it as one of the world's top-20 tourist destinations (it currently lies 25th). Dozens of European budget airlines now fly into Morocco, while new roads are opening up previously remote parts of the country and plans for a high-speed rail link between Tangier and Casablanca will slash travel times in the north. Meanwhile, standards of accommodation and choice of things to see and do improve every year. Growing numbers of five-star international hotel chains are arriving, while riads in the medina of Marrakech are being bought and renovated by expats.

DECISIVE DATES

8000 BC
Neolithic cultures spread through the region, leaving rock drawings in the northeast of Morocco.

12th century BC
Phoenicians establish trading posts along Morocco's coast.

146 BC
Carthage falls to Rome. Roman influence spreads west through North Africa. Volubilis becomes the capital of the Roman province of Mauretania Tingitana, ruled by Berber kings.

AD 24
Direct Roman rule under Emperor Caligula.

429
Vandals conquer the north of the country. They are followed by the Visigoths and

Mosaic tiling.

Byzantines in 535, who introduce Christianity.

684
First Arab raids under the command of Oqba ibn Nafi.

711
Berbers embrace Islam and invade Spain under the Arab leader Tarik ibn Ziad.

Idrissid dynasty

788
Idriss I, exiled from Baghdad, is welcomed by Berber tribes in Volubilis and establishes Morocco's first Islamic and Arab dynasty.

807
Idriss II founds Fez. Refugees arrive from Kairouan, Tunisia, establishing the important Kairaouine University.

Almoravid dynasty

1060–1147
The Berber Almoravid dynasty sweeps up from the south. Youssef ibn Tashfin makes Marrakech his capital in 1062.

1106
Almoravid power is at its peak. Youssef ibn Tashfin dies.

Almohad dynasty

1147–1269
The Almohad dynasty rises from Tin Mal. At its peak, the Almohad Empire stretches from Spain to Tripoli.

Merinid dynasty

1248–1465
The Berber Beni Merin tribe oust the Almohads, establishing the Merinid

Moulay Ismail, who made Meknes the capital.

dynasty with its capital in Fez.

1269
Abu Yusuf Yaqub captures Marrakech and takes control of most of the Maghreb.

The Wattasids

1465–1549
The Wattasids, hereditary viziers of the Merinids, usurp the Merinids, but control only northern Morocco.

1492
Fall of Muslim Spain, heralding the decline of Moroccan power and influence abroad.

Saadian dynasty

1554–1669
The Saadians reign (the first Arab dynasty since the Idrissids) having defeated the Wattasids at the battle of Tadla.

1578–1603
Reign of Ahmed el Mansour, 'the Golden One'.

Alaouite dynasty

1664
The present Alaouite dynasty is founded by Moulay Rashid.

1672–1727
Moulay Ismail, the 'warrior king', moves the capital from Fez to the new imperial city of Meknes, built using thousands of slaves.

1873–94
Moulay el Hassan is the last of the notable pre-colonial sultans.

1894–1908
Moulay Abd el Aziz incurs foreign loans, leaving Morocco open to European encroachment.

1906
The Act of Algeciras recognises France's 'privileged position' in Morocco.

1912
The Treaty of Fez. Morocco is carved up between France and Spain. Tangier becomes an international zone.

1920–6
Abd el Krim el Khattabi leads a large-scale resistance

Green March, 1975.

movement against Spanish and French rule in the north of the country.

1927
The beginning of the reign of Sultan Mohammed Ben Youssef – Mohammed V.

1953
Mohammed V goes into exile.

1956
The French Protectorate ends.

1961
Accession of Hassan II.

1975
The Green March: 350,000 unarmed Moroccans claim the Western Sahara for Morocco.

1976
The Polisario liberation movement, aided by Algeria, disputes Morocco's claims on the Western Sahara.

1999
Hassan II dies and is succeeded by his son, Mohammed VI, who establishes the Equity and Reconciliation Commission to look into abuses of power during his father's reign.

Morocco under the French Protectorate.

2004
Mohammed VI reforms the *mudawana*, or family code, granting unprecedented rights to women. Morocco signs free trade agreements with the EU and US and becomes a non-NATO ally.

2006
Morocco holds the first direct talks about Western Sahara with the Polisario in 11 years, but nothing is resolved.

2010–11
The Arab Spring. Peaceful protests are held across the country, although most Moroccans remain supportive of the king. Elections in late 2011 see the moderate Islamist Justice and Development Party (JDP) securing a majority of seats.

2011
Nail bomb detonated in Jemaa el Fna in Marrakech, with 17 people killed. No one claims responsibility.

2013
The Istiqlal party, the second-largest in government, resigns from the JDP-led government coalition.

The Roman outpost of Volubilis.

BEFORE ISLAM

Little is known of the early Berbers until their land became part of the Roman Empire. The Romans built a number of important towns, including Volubilis, whose remains now form Morocco's most impressive monument from the pre-Islamic period.

Morocco is steeped in myths and legends, many of them Western in origin. Atlantis is said to have sunk into the sea to the west of Spain and Morocco. Legend has it that Hercules forced apart Europe and Africa to create the Straits of Gibraltar, a feat remembered in the Caves of Hercules near Tangier, and in the 'Pillars of Hercules' – the rocks of Gibraltar and Jebel Musa, near Ceuta. Some say that the idyllic Garden of the Hesperides was also in Morocco, somewhere between the Atlas and the ocean, and that the golden apples Hercules had to collect from it were in fact oranges.

The factual basis for such legends (if any) remains inconclusive, however. What is known is that Neanderthal man was already living in Morocco over 50,000 years ago. A specimen of his remains was found in caves at Tamara beach near Rabat in 1933. This so-called 'Rabat man' seems to have been a boy of about 16 years old. He lived when the region was physically very different from the way it is today. Engravings on flat slabs of rock – some can be seen near Tafraoute, southeast of Agadir – show that the area was densely forested and populated by lions, panthers, giraffes, ostriches, elephants and antelopes, besides prehistoric people.

Bronze head of Juba II from Volubilis.

Phoenician traders

The discovery of rock carvings representing a ram with a solar disc between its horns, similar to the god Ammon Ra of Thebes in Egypt, suggests that a civilisation of sorts existed here as far back as 5,000 years ago, although archaeological evidence remains slight. We know slightly more about Morocco's history from the 12th century BC onwards, thanks to the Phoenicians who set up trading posts along the coast. Punic remains have been found at Melilla (Russadir), Tetouan (Tamuda), Ceuta, Tangier (Tingis), Larache (Lixus), Mehdia, near Kenitra (Thymiaterion), Rabat (Sala) and Essaouira (Karikon Telichos). These were probably not permanent settlements, although a number of Punic tombs have been found near Tangier and Rabat.

The Roman period

The Romans dominated the area for over four centuries (AD 24–429) but found the Berbers, or the Barbarians as they called them, an intractable race who attacked the Roman legions as they established permanent settlements.

Among these outposts of the Roman Empire were Tingis, Zilis (Asilah), Lixus, Valentia Banasa on the Sebou River near Kenitra, Sala Colonia and Volubilis.

Ruins can be seen today in Rabat at Chella, the Roman Sala Colonia. The name survives in Salé, Rabat's sister town on the other side of the river, still called Sala in Arabic. The most impressive remains are at Volubilis.

The most remarkable local figure of the Roman period was King Juba II, who ruled Mauretania Tingitana for half a century until his death, in his seventies, in AD 23. Juba mar-

Tafraoute, where evidence of Neanderthal man has been found.

ried Cleopatra Selene, daughter of Antony and Cleopatra, and was one of the most prolific writers of his time in Latin, Greek and Punic, He also re-established the Phoenician process of making the legendary purple dye, created from shellfish on the Iles Purpuraires (modern Essaouira), that was so important to the senators of Rome (see box).

The Romans also established factories in Morocco to make *garum*, a salty fermented fish paste used in cooking. The remains of two *garum* factories can be seen at Lixus near Larache and at Tangier close to the Caves of Hercules, where the Romans used to quarry millstones.

In the 3rd century, Christian evangelisation of Rome's African provinces began. It seems that many Berbers embraced the new religion as there were numerous bishoprics, including four in Morocco. In some cities the Latin and Christian ways of life survived the fall of the Western Roman Empire. Latin inscriptions in Volubilis date from as late as the 7th century.

It was during this period that Jewish communities, established after the Exodus from Egypt, also evolved in Morocco. Judaism is the oldest religious denomination in the country to have survived without interruption to the present day, though many Jews left following the founding of Israel in 1948. Reminders of their presence can be seen in the Jewish quarters, or *mellah*, which survive in virtually every medina in Morocco up to this day.

The dark age

The Vandal invasion of AD 253 wiped out what was left of Roman Christian civilisation. King Genseric of 'Vandalusia' in southern Spain set out from Tarifa with 80,000 people, including 15,000 troops, who swept through Morocco and along the North African coast, destroying everything in their path in an orgy of looting and burning that culminated in the sack of Rome in 455. Yet, in spite of their heavy presence during these years, very little remains of their time in Morocco.

The history of the following century in Morocco, and indeed in most of North Africa, is obscure to say the least. That is until, 4,800km (3,000 miles) away in the east, a fire of religious fervour swept along the Mediterranean coast, bringing Islam to Morocco.

PURPLE DYE FOR CAESAR

On the islets off the coast of Essaouira, deep deposits of murex shells are thought to be evidence of the dye-making industry that supplied the imperial purple robes of the Caesars. The highly prized purple dye was extracted from the shellfish, each of which, it was said, had a drop 'no bigger than a single tear'. Ptolemy of Mauretania, the son of Juba II and Cleopatra Selene and the last Roman client king, came to grief because of the dye. Apparently a vain man, on a visit to Rome he wore a magnificent robe of imperial purple that aroused the jealousy of Emperor Caligula, who had the upstart executed.

A painting of Sultan Abderrahman (1822–59) outside Meknes, by Eugène Delacroix.

ISLAM AND THE DYNASTIES

In the 7th and 8th centuries Arabs introduced Islam to Morocco, and the great Arab dynasties began to rule over vast swathes of the Maghreb and Spain.

El Maghreb el Aqsa (The Farthest West), as Morocco is known in Arabic, was seen in Arabia, the birthplace of Islam, as a land of misguided infidels who needed to be converted to the new faith *besiff* (by the sword). The first of these military missions was led by one of the greatest of North African heroes, Sidi Okba ibn Nafi.

Inspired by fervent dedication to the teachings of the Qur'an, Okba left Arabia in AD 666, at the head of an Arab cavalry force, 34 years after the death of the Prophet Mohammed. By all accounts, admittedly written by Arab historians centuries after the event, the expedition was a magnificent sight as it rode westwards, the curvetting steeds and their scimitar-wielding warriors sweeping through deserts and mountains to spread the 'divine revelation.'

Converting pagans

In fact, Okba made three expeditions, apparently covering over 8,000km (5,000 miles) on horseback to convert pagans, Christians and Jews. He paused for a time to found the city of Kairouan in Tunisia and finally arrived in Morocco on his third thrust westwards in the year 684. Arab chroniclers say that in the Souss Valley near Taroudant, Okba defeated a Berber army so big that 'Allah alone could count them' – an oriental hyperbole frequently used to describe the exploits of the Arab invaders. Later, perhaps on the curving sands of Agadir Bay, he rode his charger into the waves and cried: 'Allah! If this sea did not stop me, I would go into distant lands to Doul Karnein (where the sun sets), forever fighting for your religion and slaying all who did not believe in you or adored other gods than you!'

Tarik ibn Ziad killing Roderic, the last Visigoth king of Iberia, in 711.

Okba made no attempt to rule Morocco, but quickly withdrew, only to be slain in a battle with Berbers in Algeria, where his tomb is still revered. Thirty years later another Arab conqueror, Musa ibn Noseir, arrived to subjugate Moroccan tribes between Tangier and the Tafilalt oases in the name of the Umayyad Caliph of Damascus.

The commander of Musa's forces was a Berber chieftain, Tarik ibn Ziad, a glorious hero enshrined in history and literature as the man who led the Muslim invasion of Spain. With an army of Berber warriors he routed the Visigoths in 711 to begin seven centuries of civilisation at a time when the rest of Europe was still sunk in the Dark Ages.

Zealous Berbers

Tarik's army landed on the bay of Algeciras, near the limestone pinnacle that was named after him, Jebel Tarik or Tarik's mountain, today known as Gibraltar. From this foothold his armies spread with spectacular speed across Spain and into France, where they were finally halted at the battle of Poitiers in 732.

It seems certain that Tarik's armies were composed almost entirely of Berbers rather than Arabs. The Berbers had voluntarily embraced Islam and, like many recent con-

The Idrissids

Harun el Rashid, the Caliph of Baghdad, was unwittingly responsible for the creation of Morocco's first Muslim dynasty, the Idrissids. Idriss ibn Abdullah, a descendant of the Prophet Mohammed, was among a group of rebels who disputed the legitimacy of the Abbasid caliphs, of whom Harun el Rashid was the fifth. The revolt was one of many, for the Prophet did not designate a successor and had no surviving son. Consequently Islam was plagued for centuries by discord over the legitimacy of its rulers. The lack of a clear-cut

The court of Harun el Rashid, the Caliph of Baghdad who sent an emissary to murder Idriss I.

verts, were the most fervent supporters of the faith, whose simplicity and conquering spirit suited their temperament. In Morocco they revolted against various attempts at Arab domination and the exactions of the eastern caliph's tax collectors.

The Berbers founded several independent Muslim kingdoms of the Kharijite sect, which emerged following one of numerous schisms caused by bloody quarrels in the east over succession to the caliphate after the Prophet's death. The heretical kingdoms had already established themselves by the time another Arab hero arrived in 788, accompanied only by an ex-slave, to establish what became the first orthodox Muslim dynasty in Morocco.

tradition, such as primogeniture, to establish succession, and the fact that polygamous rulers often had numerous sons, were often a cause of anarchy in Morocco, as rival pretenders fought for the throne.

Harun el Rashid sent his army to crush the rebels, who were defeated and massacred near Mecca in 786. However, Idriss escaped, eventually reaching in Morocco after a two-year journey in which he was accompanied by

Harun el Rashid, the legendary Caliph of Baghdad, was immortalised in the epic Thousand and One Nights.

only a faithful ex-slave, Rashid. Taking refuge in Walili, the former Roman town of Volubilis, Idriss so impressed the local Berbers by his erudition and piety that they made him their leader.

Hearing that the rebel had set up a kingdom, Harun el Rashid sent an envoy, who killed Idriss with a poisonous potion in 791. But two months later Idriss's Berber concubine Kenza gave birth to a son. Nurtured by Kenza and the faithful Rashid, the boy became Sultan Idriss II and the Idrissid dynasty was established.

Idriss II re-founded the city of Fez, which

The Almoravids

Youssef ibn Tashfin was part of a tribe of nomadic Berbers whose leader invited a holy man to preach the Islamic faith to his people and established a fortified camp or *ribat*. The 'People of the *ribat*' or El Murabetun (altered by Europeans into Almoravids) became the first of three Berber dynasties.

In a very short time, the Almoravid sultans forged a Berber empire that covered Northwest Africa as far east as Algiers and incorporated southern Spain. While Macbeth was king of Scotland, the Normans were invading Eng-

Arabs migrating from the east.

became under his rule a great centre of enlightenment and learning focused around the Kairaouine University, which is considered to be the oldest continuously functioning university in the world. On the death of Idriss II in 828, his wife divided the small state between their 10 sons. This led inevitably to the decline of the dynasty, and it expired in 974.

Moulay Idriss, the holiest city in Morocco, shelters the tomb of Idriss I, who is venerated now as a holy man. His son's shrine in Fez is also the object of pious devotion. Each year a *moussem* (pilgrimage) is made to their tombs to honour the founders of Muslim Morocco and the only dynasty that did not have to impose itself by force.

land and the First Crusade took Jerusalem, the Almoravids, led by Tashfin, founded Marrakech in 1060, captured Fez in 1069 and then pushed on across the Mediterranean into Spain.

Muslim Spain, in the time of the romantic *Cid Campeador* 'El Cid', was divided into 23 *taifas*, or petty principalities. The Almoravids had little difficulty in dominating them on the pretext of helping to defeat Christian armies, as they did at Zallaqa near Badajoz in 1086. They took Granada, Cordoba and Seville in the south, and Badajoz, Valencia and Saragossa in the north, although they were unable to hold them for long.

Tashfin's son Ali ruled the empire from 1120 to 1143, and in his time the fierce and austere Almoravids abandoned the veil to become luxury-loving potentates in Andalusia. The Almoravid dynasty disappeared almost as quickly as it had risen out of the desert, but not before spreading the influence of Andalusian culture throughout the Maghreb.

The Almohads

Ibn Toumart (The Son of Happiness) was another radical religious reformer who emerged at the beginning of the 12th century to preach a unitarian *(tawhid)* doctrine. His followers became known as El Mowahhadidoun, or the Almohads. By the time the fiery Toumart died

A Moroccan emir.

grandson, Youssef Yacoub, consolidated Almohad power and won the title El Mansour (the Victorious) when he crushed the Christians under King Alfonso VIII of Castile at the battle of Alarcos, on 18 July 1195.

At the height of their power between 1160 and 1210, the Almohads built a number of famous landmarks (see box), as well as the unfinished Tour Hassan in Rabat, the Giralda in Seville and

Among the Almoravids' few remaining monuments are the mosque at Tlemcen in Algeria, the ramparts around Fez and the Koubba Baroudiyn in Marrakech.

the Koutoubia Mosque in Marrakech. But, like their predecessors the Almoravids, they sank, perhaps inevitably, into silken decadence. In their time Alicante boasted 800 looms for weaving silk cloth and minted fine gold coinage, and paper was manufactured in Ceuta and Fez.

Towards the end of the dynasty, in 1230, Sultan el Mamoun was reduced to accepting 12,000 Christian cavalrymen from King Ferdinand of Castile and Leon in order to retake Marrakech from local dissidents. As part of the bargain he allowed the construction of a Catholic church in the city. A Marrakech bishopric subsisted until the 14th century to serve foreign mercenaries.

Merinids and the Black Sultan

The Beni Merin were a nomadic Berber tribe from the Sahara, pushed westwards by Hilali invaders. They settled northeast Morocco in

at Tin Mal in 1128, he had gathered numerous Berber tribes around his banner.

Abd el Moumin, Toumart's able warrior chieftain, kept Toumart's death a secret for two years, while he established his power base and then proclaimed himself Caliph and Amir el Mumineen (Commander of the Faithful). Moumin seized Marrakech and Fez, defeated the Almoravids and controlled all Morocco by 1148. He later moved into Spain and raged across North Africa, defeating the Hilali Arab hordes at Sétif. By the time he died, Moumin had forged an empire even larger than that of the Almoravids, extending eastwards as far as Tripoli. Most of Muslim Spain was reduced to vassaldom under his son Yacoub Youssef. His

YACOUB'S GOLDEN AGE

The reign of Yacoub el Mansour was the zenith of the Almohad dynasty, a golden age for Morocco. He surrounded himself with distinguished poets and brilliant philosophers, such as the Jewish thinker Maimonides, the court physician Ibn Tofail, and Ibn Rushd (Averroes), the father of European secular thought and of the school of philosophy known as Averroism. Yacoub's enlightened building projects included Rabat el Fath (The Camp of Conquest), a vast ramparted enclosure where troops for military expeditions into Spain were assembled, and Rabat's monumental Bab er Rouah (Gateway of Souls).

The bloody excesses of the Inquisition were matched by Moroccan xenophobia provoked by the presence of infidels on the soil of Dar el Islam – 'the sacred House of Islam'.

the period when King John was forced by the English barons to sign Magna Carta (in 1215) and the Spanish Inquisition began to persecute Muslims and Jews.

The Beni Merin tribesmen took part in the battle of Alarcos of 1195, so they were well

He reorganised the empire between the Atlantic and the Gulf of Gabes in Tunisia, and held it with an iron hand. However, he was less successful in Spain, where his army was beaten at the battle of Rio Salado near Tarifa in October 1340.

Hassan died an embittered man and was buried within the Chellah necropolis in Rabat. His own son Abou Inan had rebelled against him to rule until 1358, when he was strangled by a vizier in favour of a five-year-old pretender. Inan had lost control of what is now Algeria and Tunisia, the Maaqil Arab invaders started to move in, the Spanish connection was finished,

Jewish Wedding in Morocco by Eugène Delacroix.

aware of the potential rewards of the *jihad* (holy war) that they began waging – with the help of Christian mercenaries – against the Almohads. By taking Fez on 20 August 1248, their leader Abou Yahya established the Merinid dynasty.

His son Abou Youssef crossed the Straits of Gibraltar four times to help the Muslims reconquer lost territory, notably after one memorable battle on 8 September 1275, in which the army led by the Christian hero Don Nuno Gonzales de Lara was routed – a black day for the Cross.

Abou el Hassan was the son of an Abyssinian mother and became known as the Black Sultan. He ruled the Merinid Empire from 1331 to 1351 (during the Hundred Years War in Europe) and was a prodigiously powerful and active man.

and the Christians began their encroachments. The gangrene of anarchy set in under various infant sultans.

Although their political achievements could not be compared with those of the Almohads, the Merinids left a substantial cultural legacy in the shape of *medersas* in delicate Hispano-Moorish style, which can be seen in Fez, Meknes and Salé. The Medersa Bou Inania in Fez, finished in 1357, is one of the most remarkable, with a clepsydra water clock in the narrow street outside that at one time told the time with 13 brass gongs.

Christian encroachments

At the beginning of the 15th century, rampant piracy directed at European vessels off the coast

The El Badi Palace in Marrakech was built of Italian marble bought kilo for kilo in exchange for sugar produced in the Souss Valley.

of North Africa provided the perfect excuse for Spain to intervene in Morocco. The Spanish kings were perhaps motivated also by a spirit of revenge after seven centuries of Muslim domination, which would not finally end until the fall of Granada in 1492.

As Muslim and Jewish refugees began flood-

Saadian Tombs, Marrakech.

ing into Morocco to escape the Inquisition, Spanish and Portuguese kings sent armies and navies after them. Henry III of Castile took Tetouan and massacred the population in 1399, Portugal grabbed Ceuta in 1415 and, after three attempts, finally took Asilah and Tangier with a fleet of 477 ships and 30,000 men in 1471.

After *Los Reyes Católicos* – Ferdinand II of Aragon and Isabella I of Castile – ousted Morocco from Granada, Spain occupied Melilla in 1497 with a fleet originally intended to take Columbus on his second voyage of discovery. Meanwhile the Portuguese established fortresses on the Atlantic Coast at Agadir, Azemmour and Safi, and the Ottoman Turks arrived on Morocco's doorstep at Tlemcen.

These were dark days for Morocco, enfeebled for a century by anarchy under the Wattasid dynasty (1465–1549), but they were a prelude to another glorious era.

The Moroccan renaissance was the result of a reaction against Christian intolerance. The spirit of *jihad* coalesced around the great Saadian dynasty, who overthrew the last of the Wattasids in 1557 and then astounded Europe by annihilating a Portuguese army of 20,000 at the Battle of the Three Kings on 4 August 1578.

The Saadians

Members of the Arab tribe of Beni Saad had arrived in the 12th century to settle in the Drâa Valley near Zagora. Claiming descent from the Prophet Mohammed, they were supported by the resistance movement fighting Spanish and Portuguese occupation in parts of Morocco. They retook Marrakech, which became their capital, in 1525, and Fez in 1548. After being driven out of Agadir in 1541, the Portuguese also abandoned the ports of Safi and Azemmour. Only El Jadida, Tangier and Ceuta remained in European hands.

These crushing defeats inspired 24-year-old King Sebastian of Portugal to embark on a crusade to retake Portugal's lost territory. He was aided in his crusade by Mohammed II Saadi, who had ruled as sultan for a brief period but had fled to Portugal after being overthrown by his uncle Abd el Malik I Saadi.

Everything was lost, however, at the battle of the Three Kings in 1578, where all three 'kings' – Mohammed, Sebastian and Abd el Malik – were killed.

Ahmed el Mansour

Abd el Malik was succeeded by Ahmed el Mansour, undoubtedly the greatest of the 11 Saadian sultans, during whose reign the Saadians reached the pinnacle of their power and wealth. Since Spain was too powerful for him to attempt any exploits on the Iberian peninsula, Ahmed instead set out to conquer the salt and gold mines of the Songai Empire, on the banks of the Niger River. A ragtag army of 3,000 Christians, Kabyles, Ottomans and black African slaves, led by the Spanish renegade Jouder and trained by Turks, trekked across the Sahara Desert.

Half the troops died of thirst and exhaustion on the way. The rest arrived at Timbuktu after marching for 135 days in probably one of the most gruelling forced marches of all time. An offer, made by the local emperor Ishaq Askia, to buy them off with 100,000 pieces of gold and 1,000 slaves, was spurned by Ahmed as 'insulting.'

The Songai Empire was destroyed and Ahmed appointed unscrupulous pashas to rule it. Goaded by greed, the pashas' unruly troops massacred the population or sent them into slavery in caravans carrying gold back to Marrakech. Laurence Maddock, an English trader in Marrakech, counted 30 mule loads of gold dust

of the Ottoman Turkish-style court ceremonies, the result of Ahmed's youthful days spent in Constantinople. Ahmed also organised the *makhzen* government, which survives with little change into the 21st century. Of his other achievements little remains. The El Badi Palace was razed by the next dynasty, the Alaouites. Among the few notable relics are the Saadian Tombs in Marrakech, built by Ahmed's son, Moulay Zidan, which were walled up by his successors and not revealed again until the French came to Morocco.

Ahmed died in August 1603. Three of his

Bombarding Tripoli, the centre of piracy.

The Saadian sultan, Ahmed el Mansour (1578–1603), wrote to England's Queen Elizabeth I, proposing an Anglo-Moroccan alliance against Spain, after the defeat of the Spanish Armada by Sir Francis Drake.

sons fought over the succession for seven years, and for a time Morocco was divided into two Saadian states, ruled from Fez and Marrakech. A third state, proclaimed in Rabat-Salé, was an independent corsair republic led by converted Catholics expelled from Spain. These were the infamous 'Salle Rovers' (see box).

The Alaouites

The next remarkable sultan was Moulay Ismail, whose 55-year reign (1672–1727) was one of the longest and most brutal in Moroccan history. He was a cruel and profligate megalomaniac reputed to have had a harem of 500 women and to have fathered over 700 sons and uncounted daughters.

arriving in the city in a single day. The historian El Ifrani said court officials were paid in gold and there were 1,400 hammers at the palace to strike gold ducats. Ahmed and his court's notoriety spread throughout Europe.

To match his great wealth, Ahmed built himself a sumptuous palace, El Badi in Marrakech. Foreign visitors marvelled at the magnificence

Ismail was the brother of Moulay Rashid, the founder of the Alaouite dynasty and the scion of an Arab family that had emigrated from Arabia to the Tafilalt oasis in the 13th century. The family was descended from El Hassan, son of Ali and the Prophet's daughter Fatima.

Ismail's reign is well documented by Arab historians and also by European diplomats, monks and the slaves they came to redeem from captivity at the hands of the corsairs. Some 2,000 Christian slaves and 30,000 other prisoners were employed for half a century in

a frenzy of building in Meknes, which Ismail made his capital.

A hotchpotch of gigantic structures was built, mostly of adobe, but also with some marble looted from Volubilis and Ahmed el Mansour's palace in Marrakech, which Ismail had razed to the ground. The city was ringed by ramparts 25km (15 miles) long and included palaces with vast colonnaded courtyards, huge gardens, a zoo, stables for hundreds of horses, granaries, barracks for large numbers of troops and, of course, a harem where his wife the Sultana Zidana, a giant negress, cracked the whip

Moulay Ismail.

Princess Conti, a daughter of Louis XIV.

THE SALÉ CORSAIRS

In 1619, the 'Salé Corsairs' established the pirate Republic of Bou Regreg, an independent state free from the influence of the Sultan of Morocco. These pirates were immortalised as the 'Sallee (or Salé) Rovers', who captured Robinson Crusoe in Daniel Defoe's eponymous novel. The heart of the republic was the naturally fortress-like harbour of Rabat-Salé, home to a government of 14 pirate leaders serving under a president. Made up of Moroccans, exiled Spanish Moors, Dutch, German and English, the pirates created their own language, based on Spanish mixed with French, Italian, Portuguese and Arabic. The buildings in their new medina also displayed

Spanish architectural influences. Over the course of 40 years, the Salé pirates launched brilliant and daring raids on European harbours and merchant vessels, capturing gold, silver, silks and, most notoriously, thousands of white slaves taken from the southern coasts of England and Ireland. It is estimated that their total wealth exceeded £2 billion in today's terms. In 1624, the ruling sultan, Zidan Abu Maali, tried to recapture Rabat-Salé, but was fiercely repelled. It was not until 1666 that Sultan el Rashid was able to seize the republic, forcing it to submit to his rule and ending one of the most extraordinary periods of Moroccan history, a golden age of piracy.

over hundreds of concubines. Each time Ismail granted his favours to one of them, she was paraded through the palace on a litter accompanied by singers and dancers.

A brutal king

When Ismail inspected the building sites, he would personally run his lance through slave labourers if he thought they were shirking,

> In 1777, Sultan Mohammed ibn Abdullah was the first world leader to recognise the infant United States of America. Washington called him a 'great and magnanimous friend'.

or crush their skulls with bricks if he considered their work to be substandard. The French diplomat Pidou de Saint Olon saw him dripping with blood after slitting a slave's throat. It is said that the walls of Meknes are filled with the bones of those who died building the city. The French remember the sultan for his plan to marry Princess Conti, the illegitimate daughter of the Sun King Louis XIV, a proposal that caused hilarity in the Palace of Versailles and not a little bemusement in Meknes when Ismail was turned down.

Ismail's power rested on an army of black soldiers, the Abids, formed from the remnants of slaves brought to Morocco by the Saadians. They were placed in a compound at Meshra er Remel on the Sebou River and their male offspring were then pressed into military service at the age of 15. Considered more reliable than Arab or Berber warriors, the Abids were garrisoned in kasbahs built at strategic points around the country. They were also used to retake Larache and Asilah from the Portuguese, to lay siege for years to Ceuta and Melilla, and to evict the Turks from Tlemcen in Algeria. The English left Tangier of their own accord after occupying it from 1662 to 1684.

Ismail's death at the age of 81 in 1727 was followed by a period of chaos. His numerous sons and the Abids fought over the succession for 30 years. One was proclaimed and dethroned six times, and in a single generation there were 12 sultans. A contemporary wrote that in this period of instability, 'the hair of babes in arms turned white' with terror.

In contrast, Sultan Mohammed ibn Abdullah (1757–90) was a pious and peaceful man. He built Mogador (Essaouira), designed by the French architect Cornut of Avignon and finished by an English renegade named Ahmed el Inglesi. The Portuguese were forced out of their last stronghold at Mazagan, which was renamed El Jadida, but Moulay Abdullah failed to reclaim Melilla from Spain, which continues to hold it to this day.

There was a bloody two-year interlude under Abdullah's son, Moulay Yazid, a bloodthirsty man who had Jews crucified in Fez by nailing

Sultan El Hassan.

them to the doors of their houses. He was followed by his brother Moulay Slimane (1792–1822) and Moulay Abderrahman (1822–59), who were pious and benign.

Decline of the realm

In the second half of the 19th century, Morocco isolated itself, lost much of its wealth and strength, and was plagued by unrest in the Bled es Siba (Land of Lawlessness), the parts of the country outside the Bled el Makhzen (Land of Government). The Alaouite sultan El Hassan (1873–94) spent most of his reign trying to subdue rebellious tribes, while European imperialists began gnawing at the country's fragile fabric.

BIG STICK

MOROCC
(VIA ALGECIRAS)

W.A.

EUROPEAN ENCROACHMENT

With France and Spain's occupation of Morocco,
resentment of foreign rule simmered for 40 years
until the country's independence was regained.

In the 'last scramble for Africa' at the beginning of the 20th century, Britain, France, Germany and Spain vied with one another to dominate Morocco, one of few remaining parts of the continent outside the colonial grasp.

Morocco had escaped colonialism not because it was considered worthless, but because it was a sovereign nation with a relatively organised government and society more capable of resisting foreign interference than the fractured tribal regions of the rest of Africa. In addition, the country had a long history of dynastic rule, its own distinct culture and civilisation, established ancient cities such as Fez, Marrakech and Rabat and a record of fierce resistance to invasion.

Until the turn of the century, Morocco had survived by playing one European power off against another. But gradually the rivals were eliminated. In return for a free hand in Morocco, France – which already had a presence in Algeria and Tunisia – agreed to allow Italy to colonise Libya; as part of the Entente Cordiale, France then struck a similar deal with Britain, which was given carte blanche in Egypt.

This left France with just two other claimants to contend with: Germany, whose Kaiser Wilhelm landed in Tangier in 1905 and later sent a gunboat to Agadir to demonstrate its 'interests'; and Spain, which, because of its centuries-long occupation of the Ceuta and Melilla enclaves on the north coast, maintained 'historic rights' in Morocco.

When European plenipotentiaries met in Algeciras, Spain, in January 1906 to decide upon Morocco's future, Britain and Italy supported France. The subsequent Treaty of Algeciras recognised France's 'privileged position' in Morocco. Germany withdrew as World War I loomed, after receiving from France the 'gift' of part of

European visitors in the 1920s.

Cameroon in West Africa, while Spain signed a secret accord with France delimiting their respective 'spheres of influence' in Morocco.

The prodigal son

All of this coincided with a crisis in Morocco. Moulay el Hassan, a strong monarch who spent most of his reign fighting rebellious tribes, had died suddenly in 1894. He was succeeded by his son Abd el Aziz, a weak ruler who emptied the treasury with extravagant spending on frivolous pursuits. Unscrupulous Europeans sold him solid gold cameras, pianos no one at court knew how to play, a German motorboat with its own engineer, and a gilded state coach even though there were then no roads in Morocco.

To solve the resulting financial crisis, large loans were contracted with a French bank consortium. To repay them, Morocco had to forfeit its customs dues, which led to revolts against the growing influence of the 'infidels' and encroachments by French troops into areas bordering Algeria. One revolt, backed by powerful tribal chiefs of the south, resulted in the overthrow of Abd el Aziz in 1908 by his brother, Moulay Hafid. But the new ruler was unable to assert his authority over a debt-ridden country assailed by external pressures and internal dissent. He was forced to sign the

'international zone' in December 1923, under the joint administration of France, Spain and Britain. For some time foreign diplomats had been extending their influence in Tangier; they had been responsible for the building of the Cap Spartel lighthouse and had established a sanitation programme. Good works, they believed, would foster good relations, and no one wanted Spain to control both sides of the Straits of Gibraltar – particularly not Britain. Each nation represented in the international zone had its own currency and ran its own post offices and banks.

Marshal Lyautey meets a Saharan tribe.

Treaty of Fez on 30 March 1912, which made Morocco a protectorate of France. Hafid immediately abdicated in favour of his half-brother, Moulay Youssef.

Carving up the country

As a result of the Treaty of Fez, France and Spain effectively partitioned the country. France took over the 'useful' parts of Morocco, the main cities on the central plains and the territories bordering Algeria. Spain received most of northern Morocco – the rugged Rif region next to its enclaves of Ceuta and Melilla and the southern enclaves of Ifni, the Tarfaya strip and Western Sahara. Because of its strategic location, Tangier and its immediate vicinity became an

The Rif War

The Treaty of Fez and the dividing up of Moroccan territory resulted in the Rif War of 1920–26. In 1920, the Spanish commissioner attempted to occupy the lands of the *Jibala* tribes, east of Melilla. He was unsuccessful, and in 1921 the Spanish army was defeated by the guerrilla forces of the Riffian hero, Abd el Krim (see box). Increasingly desperate, the Spanish adopted many of the tactics of the French Foreign Legion and formed the Spanish equivalent, whose second-in-command was none other than General Francisco Franco. In 1924, the Riffian army attacked a line of French soldiers and in retaliation the French intervened on the side of Spain and a full-blown war commenced. Finally, in the face of superior manpower and weapons, Abd el Krim surrendered to the French and in 1926, 'Spanish Morocco' was restored.

Lyautey's way

Marshal Lyautey, the first French Resident-General, was an experienced soldier but also an idealist who loved Morocco. He believed the protectorate concept should be respected and that all actions must be taken in the name, and with the consent of, the Sultan in cooperation with the *makhzen* government, or traditional Moroccan elite.

protectorate into a virtual colony, with direct administration that sidelined the traditional ruling classes and left few outlets for ambitious young Moroccans. As one commentator remarked, the sultan was reduced to reading the French press to find out what was going on in his own country.

As Lyautey had predicted, intellectuals formed a nationalist movement in Fez to spearhead resistance just as the 'pacification' of Morocco ended in 1934. Some of them were French-educated and inspired by '*Liberté, Egalité et Fraternité*'; others, trained in Fez's old

Outside Abd el Krim's headquarters during the Rif War.

From the start, he realised the importance of preserving Moroccan culture and ensured new French-built towns were located away from the traditional medinas. He also insisted that younger Moroccans should take an active part in all stages of the country's modernisation in order to prevent them becoming frustrated and rebellious.

After Lyautey left in 1925, succeeding resident-generals (14 in 44 years) turned the

Lyautey's maxims are still current in independent Morocco: for instance, 'Not a drop of water should reach the ocean,' and 'Morocco is a cold country with a hot sun.'

RIFFIAN HERO

Spain's occupation of northern Morocco was marked by the 1920 revolt of the 'Emir' Abd el Krim, whose Berber warriors routed a Spanish army of 60,000 at the battle of Annual; a remarkable achievement. Abd el Krim set up an independent republic in the Rif, with an education programme, a state bank and much of the administrative infrastructure of a modern country. He was defeated by a combined Spanish and French army commanded by the Marshal Philippe Pétain, and he surrendered to the French rather than face Spanish execution. He was exiled to the French Indian Ocean island of Réunion and later died in Cairo.

> *After independence, the Berber Glaoui family was left disgraced and dispossessed, and their leader, Thami el Glaoui, died of natural causes soon after. His great ruined kasbah at Telouet is a reminder of his former glory.*

Kairaouine University, were strongly influenced by Middle Eastern politicians.

The movement was amply fuelled by resentment over two grievances. First, the influx of French settlers (which Lyautey had opposed),

The French Consul and Thami el Glaoui in Marrakech, 1912.

who took over the best farmland and monopolised the economy. Second, a heavy-handed bureaucracy – which had a mania for regulating everything, right down to the profession of snake charmer – made sure that Moroccans were given only subordinate jobs.

Desirable property

While development of the Spanish zones was minimal because of Spain's civil war and the poor shape of the Spanish economy under Franco, France poured resources into Morocco: building roads, railways and ports, laying out modern, efficient farms, opening up mines, and setting up education, public health and justice systems on the French

pattern. Ironically, in nationalist eyes, the French protectorate made Morocco even more worth fighting for than before.

When Sultan Moulay Youssef died in 1927, he was replaced by his third son, Mohammed BenYoussef, who was just 18 and had led a cloistered life. The French thought he would be more amenable to their interests. This was to prove a grave miscalculation. The publication by the French of the Berber *Dahir* (decree) in 1930, to which the young and inexperienced monarch set his seal, was later seen as a serious political mistake. The decree was intended to apply tribal custom law to the Berbers instead of traditional Islamic law. Instead, it incensed the Berber tribes, who claimed that its underlying purpose was to convert the Berbers to Christianity, and divided the country.

Unrest broke out, and the main nationalist leaders, including Allal el Fassi, Mohammed BenHassan Wazzani, Ahmed Balafrej and Mohammed Mekki Naciri, were arrested. Along with many others, they were in and out of jail or in exile for the next 25 years.

In the Spanish zone, meanwhile, nationalists were tolerated – more to exasperate the French than out of idealism, since Madrid was still angry at being given the poorest parts of the country. The Franco regime also encouraged rivalry and infighting between four nationalist groups to divert attention from the fact that Moroccan troops had been recruited for the 'anti-communist crusade' in the Spanish Civil War.

The Glaoui

To counter nationalist agitation, the French enlisted the support of the *grands caïds*, the Berber tribal chiefs of the south, led by the charismatic Thami el Glaoui, the pasha or governor of Marrakech, whose name means 'Lion of the Atlas'. El Glaoui acquired great wealth during his years as pasha of Marrakech and was a sophisticated and influential man who often entertained European luminaries such as Winston Churchill and Charlie Chaplin. He was also ruthless in his political machinations and never more so than in his dealings with the French.

World War II and the Istiqlal

With the outbreak of World War II, the arrival of Allied forces in North Africa and the US-British Atlantic Charter, which advocated that all citizens should have the right to choose their own form of government, the Moroccan nationalists doubled their efforts for freedom. Sultan Mohammed BenYoussef began espousing the nationalist cause shortly before the newly formed Istiqlal (independence) Party issued a 'manifesto' in January 1944, demanding, for the first time, not just reforms but outright independence. The Sultan's support for the cause was said to have been inspired in part by President Franklin D. Roosevelt's support for him when they met at the Anfa conference, near Casablanca in 1942.

As agitation grew, the French reacted by arrest-

The plot thickens

In May 1953 General Guillaume, accompanied by Marshal Alphonse Juin, a former Resident-General born in Algeria, inspected tens of thousands of Berber tribesmen assembled near Azrou in the Middle Atlas Mountains. Many were French army veterans who had served valiantly under Guillaume and Juin in the final stages of World War II. They were generally seen by settlers as 'good Moroccans', in contrast to the 'bad' ones represented by the urban nationalists. The latter considered the Azrou parade as a dress rehearsal for a march by massed Berber tribesmen on Fez

Moroccan soldier waving a Spanish flag, 1936.

ing the ringleaders. Riots and demonstrations followed, and finally the Sultan went 'on strike' by refusing to sign or endorse protectorate decrees.

When General Augustin Guillaume, the 10th French Resident-General, took over in Rabat in July 1951, he found an uncooperative sultan and seething unrest among the nationalists. He also inherited a protectorate apparatus that was ready to defy the government in Paris and give in to the demands of the diehard leaders of settlers, who by then had grown to nearly half a million.

By March 1953, Thami el Glaoui, Kettani and other Moroccan 'collaborators' led a rebellion to depose Sultan Mohammed. The idea received active support from settlers and their lobby in Paris.

and Rabat to force the Sultan off his throne.

But the French Foreign Minister, Georges Bidault, in April had informed Guillaume in no uncertain terms: 'The French government will not accept being placed by anyone before a *fait accompli*. I ask you to oppose without hesitation any new progress towards a situation in which we shall have no choice but to depose the Sultan and use force against our friends.'

Nevertheless, El Glaoui and 300 of his followers convened in Marrakech on 13 August – while Guillaume was in Vichy – and drew up a proposal to depose the Sultan and proclaim Sidi Mohammed BenArafa – an obscure 70-year-old relative of the Sultan Mohammed – as sultan in his place.

Despite another Bidault message warning of the 'incalculable consequences' of such a pronouncement, contingents of tribes began to march on Fez and Rabat, many of them supposedly under the impression that they were on their way to attend the Muslim feast day ceremonies of Aid el Kebir, due to start on 21 August that year (when the Sultan would perform in public the traditional sacrifice of a ram).

The French government capitulated: Sultan Mohammed BenYoussef was duly deposed and replaced by the elderly BenArafa.

On 20 August 1953, the Sultan and all his sons and daughters were whisked away in a fleet of black cars to the airport in Rabat and flown into exile, first in Corsica and later in Madagascar.

The victory celebrations of El Glaoui and the French settlers were short-lived. Only three weeks later, on 11 September, the puppet-sultan BenArafa narrowly escaped death when an assailant named Allal BenAbdallah crashed an open car into the royal procession on its way to the mosque in Rabat, then tried to knife BenArafa. This signalled the start of violent

Sultan BenArafa being escorted to a plane in Rabat.

Crisis at the palace

In an atmosphere of hysteria whipped up by the conspirators and echoed in the colonial press, French Prime Minister Joseph Laniel gave the green light for the Sultan's deposition, apparently believing that the only alternative would be civil war in Morocco. His interior minister, and future French president, François Mitterrand, did not agree and resigned in protest.

> People swore they could see the face of their exiled sultan, Mohammed V, in the moon, or they would say he was 'chez Madame Gascar' on that faraway island in the Indian Ocean.

popular protests against the exiling of the legitimate sultan. They quickly snowballed into an urban terrorism campaign that joined with the emergence of a liberation army in the Rif and Middle Atlas Mountains.

A bloody end

Resistance fighters – often small independent groups of patriots operating outside the control of the nationalists, – shot French leaders and Moroccan 'collaborators' and set off bombs in crowded cafés and markets. On Christmas Eve 1953, in Casablanca's central market, Mohammed Zerktouni planted a bomb in a shopping basket that killed 20 people and wounded 28. The choice of the Christian holiday was symbolic: the Sultan had been exiled on a Muslim feast day.

The resistance fighters enjoyed the tacit support of the population at large, but extremist French settlers reacted by organising terrorist campaigns of their own, at times shooting indiscriminately from cruising cars and murdering those French that they suspected of pro-nationalist sympathies.

The campaign reached a climax on the second anniversary of the Sultan's departure into exile, on 20 August 1955, when tribesmen descended on the small farming town of Oued

on 1 October, when the Moroccan Liberation Army attacked three French outposts on the border of the Spanish zone.

The surprise U-turn

The Aix-les-Bains conference was designed to form an interim Moroccan government and hammer out a compromise solution to the dynastic problem. But the proposed formula was contested by none other than Thami el Glaoui himself, who astounded everyone by announcing on 25 October that the solution was to restore Mohammed BenYoussef to his throne.

Jubilant Moroccans celebrating the imminent return of the reinstated Sultan Mohammed BenYoussef on the streets of Casablanca in 1955.

Zem, southeast of Casablanca, and savagely butchered 49 French people, including eight women and 15 children.

The French Foreign Legion was sent in; according to Moroccan sources, some 1,500 tribespeople were slain by the Legion, raising tension in the country to boiling point at a time when the latest Resident-General, the liberal civilian Gilbert Grandval, had been trying to solve the crisis.

In Paris, Prime Minister Edgar Faure called a conference of nationalist leaders in Aix-les-Bains amid fears that a *jihad* was about to be launched against France in Morocco and Algeria. The feared uprising broke out in the Rif

In the circumstances, France could hardly do otherwise. The legitimate sultan was flown back to Rabat on 16 November 1955 to receive a hero's welcome, with his son, Hassan, beside him. He announced to massed crowds assembled in front of the palace that the protectorate had come to an end, which it did formally in 1956.

For independence workers in the French and Spanish zones, post offices in the international zone of Tangier proved useful sources of uncensored news of what was going on in the rest of Morocco.

SINCE INDEPENDENCE

The elation felt at independence soon gave way to rivalries, insurrection and the repressive reign of Hassan II. This lasted until 1999, and the crowning of the young Mohammed VI, signalling a new era of hope and change.

Sultan Sidi Mohammed BenYoussef changed his title to King Mohammed V in 1956 when Morocco regained its independence. The change symbolised the additional prestige he had acquired as 'The Liberator' of the country. His great popularity, together with his religious prestige as Emir el Mumineen (Commander of the Faithful), enabled him to rule with uncontested authority during the crucial period when an elite had to be assembled to run a modern nation.

Though he had been humiliated by the French, Mohammed V proved a moderate and magnanimous monarch. Foreigners were kept on to advise inexperienced Moroccan officials to smooth the transition. Many French settlers fled, but others ran farms and industries until as late as 1973, when 'Moroccanisation' measures were taken.

Morocco joined the Arab League, was a founder member of the Organisation of African Unity (OAU), and cultivated relations with France and Spain, who helped create the Royal Armed Forces and supply aid for economic development. New industries sprang up based on agriculture and phosphates. The number of schoolchildren grew from a few thousand to over 3 million in 25 years; at the same time, improved health conditions stimulated rapid population growth coupled with the emergence of a restive urban proletariat. Providing work, housing and social services became (and remains) an arduous task.

Crisis management

A crisis erupted in October 1956 when the French in Algeria forced down the aircraft carrying Algerian nationalist leader Ahmed Ben Bella and his associates from Rabat to Tunis.

Mohammed V.

Rioters attacked French settlers in a violent protest organised by nationalists in support of the Algerian Front de Libération Nationale. Relations with France were strained further because Morocco was channelling arms to the Algerian revolution.

The former Spanish and French protectorate zones and the Tangier international zone were abolished in 1958, but it took several years to convince Spain to evacuate the Tarfaya strip and the enclave of Ifni in the south, in the latter case only after local tribes staged a revolt.

The king's main domestic problem was dealing with the old-guard Istiqlal Party, whose leaders considered themselves the real architects of Moroccan independence and thus entitled to monopolise power in what they called 'homogeneous governments' excluding other political parties.

Istiqlal pretensions sparked revolts by other nationalist groups who felt deprived of the fruits of victory. One of the most serious insurrections broke out in 1958 in the Rif Mountains after the Istiqlal ordered the arrest of Abd el Krim and Mahjoubi Aherdan, two Moroccan Liberation Army (MLA) leaders who had led guerrillas against the French but also contested the Istiqlal Party's ascendance.

Although Mohammed V ordered the

Prince Moulay Hassan, future King Hassan II of Morocco, hunting in 1956.

release of Aherdan and Abd el Krim, the rebels defied Rabat until February 1959. There were heavy casualties when 20,000 troops commanded by Crown Prince Moulay Hassan were sent in to wipe out resistance. Nevertheless, the king espoused the Istiqlal's claims to large tracts of Algeria, the Spanish Sahara and Mauritania.

At the same time he tried to thwart Istiqlal attempts to dominate the government. Aherdan and Khatib were allowed to create a rival party, the People's Movement, representing the rural majority, which held office in all later governments, while by the end of 1962 the Istiqlal was eased out of power and into opposition.

> *Hassan II's 38-year rule (1961–1999) was often known as 'The Years of Lead'. Dissidents were arrested, tortured and 'disappeared', protests were banned and freedom of the press curtailed.*

Hassan's accession

King Hassan II ascended the throne in February 1961 on the death of his father. By this time the Istiqlal Party had split. A radical left wing, led by Mehdi Ben Barka, emerged with distinctly republican leanings regarded by the palace as a serious threat to the throne. Ben Barka's breakaway faction, which came to be known as the Union Socialiste des Forces Populaires (USFP), agitated for radical political and economic reforms, attacking Hassan II's 'personal power' and accusing the monarchy of being feudal – views shared by the socialist regime in Algeria.

In 1963 newly independent Algeria rejected Moroccan claims to parts of its territory and a brief war broke out. Moroccan and Algerian troops fought over oases in a disputed area where the frontier had never been formally drawn. The conflict was halted by the Organisation of African Unity, but Mehdi Ben Barka was sentenced to death *in absentia* for treason for taking Algeria's side in the dispute.

Just before the border war, Morocco's first constitution was promulgated. It outlawed the one-party regime, guaranteed basic democratic freedoms and provided for an elected parliament, but Hassan II retained substantial powers.

The first parliament elected in May 1963 comprised five parties. Hassan II dissolved the parliament in June 1965 because of the 'contradictory and irreconcilable demands of the parties' and declared a 'state of emergency', ruling himself by decree for the next five years .

Plots and coups

Faced by Hassan II's autocratic rule and oftensinister abuses of power, left-wing militants resorted to violence. Many were arrested in connection with five plots against the monarchy between 1963 and 1977; on two occasions, in 1965 and 1973, armed infiltrators entered the country from Algeria; in 1965, 1981 and 1984 there were serious street riots fomented by leftists.

The agitation was severely repressed and there were mass trials resulting in death sentences. Mehdi Ben Barka, who had been living in exile and was suspected of inciting the agitation, disappeared in Paris in mysterious circumstances on 29 October 1965. General Mohammed Oufkir, the Moroccan Minister of the Interior, who had been in Paris at the time of the incident, was convicted by a French court of masterminding Ben Barka's abduction, and sentenced to life imprisonment in his absence.

France recalled its ambassador in Rabat and for three years relations were frozen as Hassan entourage by pumping cannon shells into his aeroplane as it was flying home from France. Once again Hassan escaped unscathed, allegedly by radioing the attacking planes in a disguised voice to tell them 'the tyrant is dead', whereupon they called off the attacks.

General Oufkir's alleged suicide during the night after the attacks was at first thought to be the act of a dedicated officer who felt he had failed in his duty to protect his king. The official version revealed days later was that he had masterminded the attack and planned to rule Morocco using the king's elder son,

King Hassan II with his brother Abdullah, who is asleep on the reviewing stand during a military parade.

II refused to admit Oufkir's guilt. In an unsettled atmosphere, senior officers of the Royal Armed Forces staged an abortive coup d'état by storming the royal palace at Skhirat, near Rabat, on 10 July 1971 while Hassan II was celebrating his 42nd birthday. Nearly 100 guests were gunned down by 1,400 cadets, but the king escaped by hiding in a bathroom.

General Oufkir, now Defence Minister, had the rebels rounded up with the help of loyalist troops. Ten officers including four generals were summarily executed. Just over 1,000 of the troops stood trial in the following February, but only 74 were convicted.

On 16 August 1971, the pilots of three air force jets tried to assassinate Hassan II and his Crown Prince Sidi Mohammed, then aged nine, as a puppet.

Divine protection

The two abortive military coups convinced many that the Moroccan monarchy's days were numbered. This may help explain why, in the following year, on 3 March 1973, several hundred armed men infiltrated the country from Algeria with the intention of touching off a 'popular uprising' on the 12th anniversary of the king's accession.

The 'uprising' also failed, reinforcing the popular belief that the king enjoyed *baraka*, or divine protection. Perhaps misled by their own propaganda that claimed only a spark was needed to set off a revolution, left-wing USFP activists who led the infiltrators found that, instead of welcoming them as 'liberators', peasants in border areas telephoned local security forces. During the trials, at which 22 were sentenced to death, it was revealed that the plotters had also planted bombs at US offices in Casablanca and Rabat, and in the capital's theatre.

Taking possession

A sudden surge in the price of crude oil, when Morocco had to import at least 75 percent of its energy, combined with substantial increases

paid allegiance to Moroccan monarchs but that this did not constitute sovereignty, which should be decided by self-determination. The king interpreted this as vindication of Moroccan claims, arguing that in a Muslim society, and particularly in Morocco, allegiance to the monarch was sovereignty. In November 1975, with extraordinary speed and great efficiency, he organised the Green March, and some 350,000 Moroccans marched unarmed into the region, camped for three days under the guns of the Spanish Foreign Legion, which held its fire, and then withdrew when the

The Green March, 1975.

in dollar and interest rates and later a series of droughts which made it necessary to import millions of tons of grain, placed Morocco in an uncomfortable position. But these problems were overshadowed by the Western Sahara problem. When Spain announced plans to give its desert colony internal autonomy and hold a referendum in Western Sahara, the king revived Moroccan historic claims to the territory and launched a campaign to recover it for the 'motherland'.

West Saharan issue

Asked to decide whether the area was a *terra nullius* before Spain colonised it, the World Court found that West Saharan tribes had

king announced that they had 'accomplished their mission'.

The Green March succeeded mainly because Franco was very ill and, faced with the prospect of his imminent death, Spanish leaders were anxious to avoid a colonial war. So, on 14 November the administration of the disputed territory was transferred to Morocco and Mauritania.

The Algerian president, Colonel Houari Boumedienne, who until then had supported Moroccan and Mauritanian claims to Western Sahara, suddenly came out in support of the Polisario Front – a group of left-wing guerrillas led by a former member of the Moroccan Communist Party, Mustapha el Ouali, who began campaigning for independence of the Spanish colony.

Algeria trained, armed, financed and gave sanctuary to the guerrillas, who proclaimed the Saharan Arab Democratic Republic (SADR) just as the last Spanish troops withdrew at the end of February 1976.

The guerrilla war with Morocco dragged on for more than a decade. Aggressive Algerian diplomacy enabled the SADR to get official recognition from over 70 non-aligned or so-called 'progressive' states, among them Libya and the communist regimes of North Korea, Vietnam and Cuba, prompting Hassan II's supporters to say there was a 'worldwide communist conspiracy against Morocco.'

In the event, the war took on some of the aspects of an East–West conflict: the Polisario were armed with Soviet weapons, while pro-Western Morocco received military aid from France and the United States.

The Moroccan view was that Algeria was bent on creating a satellite state in Western Sahara which would give it access to the Atlantic Coast, that the Polisario believed its guerrilla war would bring Morocco to its knees, and perhaps that the monarchy would collapse. Algeria on the other hand maintained that it acted on the 'sacred principle' of self-determination and equated the Polisario's struggle with its own bloody independence war against France.

However, while the Algerian war became increasingly unpopular in France, and ultimately forced a political settlement, the war in the Sahara resulted in unprecedented cohesion within the country. Far from weakening King Hassan II, it actually created unity as all political parties from left to right rallied around him.

> Some 350,000 unarmed Moroccans were mobilised to claim the Western Sahara, and on 6 November they marched south across the frontier waving flags and copies of the Qur'an.

Eventually, however, the king had to restrain his armed forces, many of whose field officers believed that the quickest and most effective way to end the war would be to launch a major strike into Algeria and attack the Polisario Front's rear bases.

The turning point came in 1981 when Morocco began building defence lines studded with electronic sensors to give forewarning of guerrilla attacks. Gradually the lines were extended eastwards until they ran for 1,610km (1,000 miles) along the frontiers. The Moroccan army gained control of four-fifths of the territory and forced a military stalemate.

After mediation by King Fahd of Saudi Arabia, Algeria and Morocco restored their diplomatic relations in May 1988. Morocco and the Polisario Front accepted a peace plan drafted by the United Nations; the plan proposed a

A Moroccan soldier defends the country's new border against Polisario guerrillas.

ceasefire, to be followed by a self-determination referendum, under international control, to give the people of the thinly populated area a choice between independence or remaining part of Morocco.

Into the 1990s

Towards the end of the 1980s, reconciliation with Algeria paved the way for the realisation of an old North African dream of economic union: 'The Grand Arab Maghreb', comprising Algeria, Libya, Mauritania, Morocco and Tunisia. But many of the promises of the late 1980s failed to come to fruition. The Union du Grand Maghreb was abandoned in the face of Algeria's civil war, and in Western Sahara the promised referendum never took place, though the cease-fire still holds. Attempts at a vote were repeatedly postponed through the 1990s, initially due to US disquiet and Polisario objections when the Moroccan government moved 37,000 Moroccans into the region on the grounds that their families had originated in the area.

A new king, a new era

In July 1999 King Hassan II died at the age of 70. He had been the Arab world's longest-reigning monarch. His successor, Muhammad

Hassan II in 1997, flanked by his son, the future Mohammed VI.

Ben el Hassan, was crowned Mohammed VI in July 1999, ushering in a new era. Within a few months it was clear that Mohammed VI had a new vision for Morocco's future and was keen to nurture the small seeds of reform that Hassan had planted in the last years of his reign. Mohammed VI was reported as saying he wanted to reign over a state of law not of fear, referring to the years of his father's reign, which had become known as the 'Years of Lead'.

The new king was young, bright, modern and intent on implementing pioneering reforms. Days after he ascended the throne, Mohammed VI began a tour of Morocco, beginning in the historically rebellious Rif region. The tone of his reign had been set. Announcing his intention to combat poverty, fight corruption and create jobs, one of his first acts was to sack the country's much-hated Interior Minister, Driss Basri, who, as Hassan II's right-hand man, had run the country's reviled security forces for some 20 years and was known for his brutal suppression of dissent. At the same time, several leading dissidents were permitted to return from exile in France, including the communist leader Abraham Serfaty and the exiled family of Mehdi Ben Barka, the political opponent who had disappeared in Paris in 1965 (see page 46). Mohammed VI also freed many political prisoners, including Abdessalem Yassine, leader of the Islamic Justice and Spirituality Movement.

In 2004, Mohammed established the Equity and Reconciliation Commission to investigate human rights abuses during his father's reign. Hailed internationally as a major step towards transparency and reform in Morocco, the Commission aimed to rehabilitate and pay compensation to victims of rights abuses. Also in 2004, Mohammed VI instigated arguably his most meaningful reform to date by replacing the *mudawana*, or family code based on Islamic law, with a new version, which managed to retain traditional Islamic values. Considered progressive by regional standards, the reforms benefited women in particular by raising the minimum age of marriage to 18, limiting the allowances of polygamy, allowing men and women to petition for divorce and giving women more of a say in the negotiation of marriage contracts. Morocco's first new parliament after the accession of Mohammed VI had 30 seats retained for women. In 2009 Marrakech elected its first female mayor, Fatima Zahra Mansouri. In the same year, further legislation was passed granting women the right to divorce their husbands without the consent of their husbands.

Mohammed's visions

As well as looking to rectify things at home, Mohammed VI began to court foreign investment and tourism, establishing his 'Vision 2010', which aimed to boost visitor numbers to Morocco from 2 million to 10 million by 2010. Nine million euros were allocated towards building infrastructure, and 600,000 new jobs were created. In 2004, Morocco signed free trade agreements with the EU and the United States (only the third country in North Africa and the Middle East to have done so) and became a non-NATO ally. In 2008, in recognition of its 'raft of reforms', the EU granted Morocco advanced status, the first country in the region to benefit from this. In 2010, Mohammed VI announced his 'Vision 2020' which aims to make Morocco one of the top 20 tourism destinations in the world, investing nearly 16 billion euros to double the number of visitors to the country and create 147,000 new jobs by 2020.

fundamentalism, which has unquestionably slowed the early pace of reform. On the night of 16 May 2003, 12 suicide bombers attacked several locations around Casablanca. As well as the bombers, 33 civilians were killed and over 100 people injured. The Moroccan government acted swiftly. By May 2004, they claimed to have arrested 2,000 people linked to the attacks, and hundreds of other suspected Islamic militants have been imprisoned since then. On the whole, the king has been praised for managing to stem the rising tide of Islamic fundamentalism that is prevalent

King Mohammed VI (right) carries his father's coffin, July 1999.

One and a half decades after his coronation, Mohammed VI remains a popular and much-loved figure. Step into any shop, hotel or restaurant across Morocco and you will see a framed photograph of the monarch, dressed either in full royal Moroccan dress or in a sharp Gucci suit in front of one of his many classic cars. In spite of the obvious wealth gap between the king (the seventh-richest royal in the world) and his people, he is still hailed as 'King of the Poor'.

Setbacks

In spite of such groundbreaking reforms, Mohammed VI's reign has not been without problems, in particular the shadow of Islamic

across the rest of the Maghreb, as well as keeping home-grown Islamism from gaining any sort of power or voice in the country. In 2006, however, controversy erupted regarding supposed secret CIA detention centres, or 'black sites', in Morocco. And the threat of terrorism remains – another bomb was set off by extremists in Casablanca in 2007, while in April 2011 a bomb exploded in the heart of Jemaa el Fna in Marrakech, killing 17 people.

The western front

The issue of Western Sahara remains contentious, with continued deadlock despite UN attempts to broker an agreement between both sides. Between 2000 and 2003, several solutions were proposed, all based around autonomy for Western Sahara with a referendum a few years later, but still neither side could agree, and Mohammed VI openly rejected any proposals for a referendum on independence. 'We shall not give up one inch of our beloved Sahara, not one grain of its sand,' he asserted, and proposed instead an autonomous region within Morocco. In 2005, riots by those in favour of independence broke out in Western Sahara and demonstrations continued into 2010 when the Gadaym Izik Sahrawi protest camp in Laâyoune was vio-

Mohammed VI.

lently broken up by Moroccan security forces, causing international outrage. This complex and highly sensitive issue looks set to remain unresolved for some time to come.

Looking forwards

In late 2010 and 2011, the fire of revolution swept through North Africa. First the 23-year regime of Tunisia's Zine el Abidine Ben Ali came crashing down in the face of angry popular protests. Then, in January 2011, massive peaceful protests in Cairo's Tahrir Square led to the resignation of Hosni Mubarak, ending his 40-year grip on Egypt. Days later, violent demonstrations erupted in Libya. Morocco did not remain immune. Kick-started by a

pro-democracy group on Facebook called the February 20 Movement, peaceful protests demanding constitutional reform, more opportunities for the jobless young and an end to corruption were held across the country. Yet what was notable about these protests was that not a single group or individual criticised the king or called for him to step down. Mohammed VI remains popular. The reforms he made in the early years of his reign are not forgotten and, perhaps most importantly, as a descendant of the Prophet and 'Commander of the Faith-

> Western Sahara covers an area of 267,000 sq km (103,000 sq miles), but is one of the most sparsely populated regions in the world, with just half a million Sahrawis living in its capital, Laayoune.

ful', he is an important and greatly respected spiritual leader.

The king responded to protestors by announcing the creation of a new constitution devolving roughly half his powers to a prime minister elected by the Moroccan people. In addition, the Berber language would for the first time be recognised as an official language of Morocco alongside Arabic.

Fresh elections under the new constitution, scheduled for 2012, were brought forward to late 2011 in order to accelerate the speed of reform – although pro-democracy activists continued to argue that the king was giving up too little power and still exercised a disproportionately powerful grip over affairs of state. Despite the elections and constitutional concessions, protests orchestrated by the 20 February Movement continued into 2012 and 2013, with a series of mass rallies, sometimes erupting into violence in Casablanca and Rabat, demonstrating against unemployment, corruption, rising prices and the holding of political prisoners. Ongoing economic difficulties allied to tensions between rich and poor, and between traditionalists and reformers, are likely to create further problems in the years to come, although compared to many other countries in the region Morocco remains well advanced along the road to prosperity and stability, setting an example for the rest of the Maghreb, and indeed the Arab world.

Hassan II Mosque, Casablanca.

THE MOROCCANS

The true pulse of Morocco is to be found in its people, who are still as diverse and fascinating as the country itself, despite increasing urbanisation and Arabisation.

Morocco is a labyrinth of contradictions and complexities, and its people are no different. In the 21st century, they stand on the knife edge of change. Although they are proud of their heritage, the young in particular – and Morocco is a young country: 45 percent of the population are under 25 – are also increasingly worldly, outward-looking, modern and educated. With the world outside Morocco seemingly attainable at the click of a mouse, the question facing most Moroccans today is how to reconcile past and present and balance a deep love of their country with the social and economic challenges that confront them on a daily basis.

Contrasts are fundamental to the story of the Moroccan people, highlighted by the divides between the traditional and the modern, between rich and poor, male and female, urban and rural, Berber and Arab. Ever since the first invaders and colonisers swept through the country, influencing and merging with the indigenous culture, the Moroccan people have been characterised by their diversity. As you travel around the country, you will notice distinct differences in the way people look, dress, speak and behave.

Berbers and Arabs

The Berbers are the ancient indigenous race of Morocco who now account for roughly 60 percent of the population – although they face a battle to protect their traditional identity in the face of the dominant, but minority, Arab culture that spread throughout Morocco following the Islamic conquest in the 7th century. The native Berber language has now begun to be taught in schools, and has only just been recognised as an official language of Morocco, in

Mausoleum of Mohammed V and Hassan II, Rabat.

spite of the fact that most Moroccans speak a variant of it as their first language. The Berbers are made up of three main types (subdivided into countless tribes): the Riffians, or Tarifit, of the north, the Imazighen of the Middle Atlas and the Shilha of the High and Anti-Atlas. Their origins remain shrouded in mystery, with many theories including the possibility of European descent, probably based on the not-unusual occurrence of fair colouring and blue or green eyes.

Today most Moroccans are of mixed ancestry – Berber, Arab and black African (the last being mostly Haratin and Gnaoua, descended from black slaves imported from Mali during the Saadi dynasty) – as can be seen from the rich variety of faces, even within the same family. In the countryside, pockets of pure Arabs in mainly Berber regions – for example, Erfoud in the Tafilalt and Tamegroute in the Drâa – are unusual. In this part of the country the women are shrouded in heavy black *haik* and reveal only one eye to the world, in contrast to their brightly attired and unveiled Berber sisters.

Jews and Christians

Moroccan (Sunni) Islam is traditionally flexible and tolerant and Moroccan people are immensely proud of this fact, as they will

> The three main Berber languages spoken in Morocco – Tamazight, Taselhit and Tarifit (or Riffian) – are completely different from Arabic and totally incomprehensible to most Arabs, Moroccan or otherwise.

often delight in telling you. Moroccan Muslims recognise their fellow religions 'of the book', Judaism and Christianity, which have been established in Morocco for nearly 2,000 years, and in spite of the colourful accounts of

High Atlas shopkeeper.

Asilah fisherman.

TAKING A SOCIAL BATH

The public bath *(hammam)* is very much a part of Moroccan daily life, particularly in the medinas. Even families that have modern bathrooms occasionally visit their local hammam. Its function is as much social as practical. Cleanliness is also close to godliness, and ritual cleansing is important before prayer. Every town and most villages have a public *hammam* – sometimes there are separate male and female hammams or different opening hours for different sexes. There are an increasing number of luxurious hotel hammams. Non-Muslims are usually welcome – indeed some hammams in touristy areas are trying to boost their income by attracting overseas visitors

– although a few are unwilling to take foreigners. Inside you will find a changing area leading into a series of dim, misty chambers of varying temperatures, and be given a bucket for sluicing down. Women, for whom a visit to the hammam is a social occasion, take scrapers for exfoliation, henna and *savon noir* (a tar-like olive soap), items often happily shared with foreigners. The mood in a female hammam is animated and more sober in the men's, although a degree of modesty prevails throughout (at no point are underpants removed). Hammam attendants are available, who, for just a dollar or two, will scrub you down mercilessly and examine every pore.

Christian slavery in the 17th century and the departure of most Jews in 1948, at the founding of Israel, Morocco claims historical respect for both.

Jesus is an immensely important prophet of Islam, as the messenger of Allah, and Mary is the woman most frequently mentioned in the Qur'an. Similarly, the Jewish Abraham – under the name of Ibrahim – is one of Islam's most revered prophets, and it is in memory of Ibrahim's willingness to sacrifice his son that Muslims sacrifice a sheep every year to mark the festival of Aid el Kebir (or Eid al-

always built close to the palace so that it could benefit from royal protection. If you look hard enough, you can also find several old Christian churches and graveyards in various Moroccan towns, such as the Church of Saint Andrew in Tangier, where Walter Harris (see page 120), among others, is buried.

Social and economic divides

As Morocco forges ahead into the 21st century, the disparities between urban and rural life in the country widen ever further. It is common for first-time visitors to remark on the seem-

Children in Fez.

Adha as it's known elsewhere in the Islamic world). Many Jews emigrated to Morocco from Spain to escape the Inquisition, and before 1948 there were almost 200,000 living in the country, though today only around 6,000 remain. There is a Jewish quarter – or *mellah* – in every city, and so respected were the Jews in Morocco that this quarter was

> Conversion to another religion is unthinkable for a Muslim and deemed an act of treason by the State. It is illegal to take Arabic editions of the Bible into Morocco and to proselytise.

ingly timeless appearance of rural Moroccan villages, whose pisé (mud brick) houses meld into the harsh landscapes in which they are situated and whose inhabitants live, it seems, in a different era. Although there is now electricity in even the most remote villages in Morocco, water is still drawn by donkeys from wells, food is still cooked on a traditional hearth, children work in the fields or tend herds of goats and sheep and life is lived at subsistence levels, reliant on harvests and livestock. Life is hard, and most boys, when they reach their teens, will move to a town or city where there are better opportunities. Indeed, urbanisation is rapidly increasing, with 57 percent of the Moroccan population now living in a town or city.

The power of the Evil Eye (spells cast by those who wish people ill) and the presence of jinn (malicious spirits) are not taken lightly. Many parents give their children protective charms or line a newborn's eyes with kohl.

Major cities such as Casablanca, Tangier and Marrakech are a world apart from rural Morocco. Here virtually every inhabitant will own a mobile phone – and perhaps a car and satellite TV as well. Fancy boutiques and res-

below the poverty line. Although much less than it was when Mohammed VI came to the throne, unemployment remains high, at nearly 9 percent (although this figure is significantly lower than in other countries in the Maghreb). Groups of young men hanging around on street corners or in parks with nothing to do is an all too frequent sight in Moroccan towns, as are *bidonvilles* (shanty towns), and many educated Moroccans choose instead to emigrate to Europe or America – 4.5 million at the last count. The average household income in Morocco is around US$5000 per annum,

Kairaouine Mosque, Fez.

taurants line the streets, patrolled by cashed-up teenagers and upwardly mobile twenty-somethings flaunting the latest fashions, their plunging necklines and skimpy skirts offering an almost surreal contrast to the older generation of Moroccan ladies, soberly dressed in headscarves and coats.

Economically, Morocco is growing at a steady rate, and policies introduced by Mohammed VI as well as the boom in tourism have undoubtedly improved the standard of living for many Moroccans, as well as creating more job opportunities. However, many of these improvements have benefited only a small section of society (mainly the rapidly emerging middle class), and 15 percent of all Moroccans still live

although large sections of the population live on far less than this, especially in the countryside, where many families live below the poverty line. Morocco's illiteracy rate, again one of the highest in the Maghreb, hovers around 44 percent, a figure that rises sharply among girls in rural areas.

Education

In spite of these high illiteracy rates, the standard of education in Morocco, like almost everything else, is improving. School is free and compulsory until the age of 15, and increasing numbers of Moroccan children are now receiving at least a basic education – at the turn of the millennium only slightly over 50 percent of Moroccan girls and boys were completing primary school, a figure that has now risen to over 80 percent in just over a decade. There are over 300,000 students in higher education in Morocco, though opportunities for university graduates are still limited and it's not uncommon to meet a taxi driver or a waiter at McDonald's who has a PhD and speaks several languages.

Honouring tradition

The dazzling lure of the Western world with all its modern trappings has not, so far, destroyed Morocco's unique cultural traditions. Young kids may strut about in fake designer jeans and sunglasses with the latest mobile phones, mingling with friends of the opposite sex in internet cafés and debating world politics on Facebook; they may be fans of the latest American hip-hop band or British conceptual artist and may want to travel and see the world, but they all have one thing in common: an intense pride in and love for their country, and a deep respect for their national heritage. You may come across a young man in a hoodie and low-slung jeans painstakingly inscribing Arabic calligraphy or carving a stucco archway, or a fully

Proud children in Rabat.

ISLAM AND BARAKA

Islam is the dominant religion in Morocco – 99 percent of the population are followers. Moroccan Islam is largely of the Maliki school, within the Sunni branch of the faith. There are five 'pillars' of the Islamic faith: *Shahada* (the testament that there is no god but God), *Salat* (the observance of prayer five times a day), *Saum* (fasting at Ramadan), *Zakat* (giving alms to the poor) and *Hajj* (the pilgrimage to Mecca, which should be undertaken at least once in a lifetime). But the Qur'an and the Hadith (the sayings of the Prophet on Islamic conduct) make certain allowances (depending on how they are interpreted). The concept of *baraka* – grace, or a blessing supposedly bestowed by Allah – is, and has long been, an important aspect of faith in Morocco and remains a strong aspect of modern life. When the Berber tribes embraced Islam, they adapted it to include customs that were then absorbed into Moroccan culture as a whole. Morocco is littered with *koubbas*, the white-domed tombs of *marabouts* (holy men), to which the troubled and the sick make pilgrimages, hoping for some bestowal on them of the *marabout's baraka*. Although orthodox Islam forbids the worship of idols, most Moroccans see no harm in the faith they have in *marabouts*, in more liberal practices such as Sufism and in their acceptance of related sects, such as the Gnaoua.

Westernised girl singing a Berber folk song (perhaps with a rap laid over the top) or waxing lyrical about a Moroccan poet who lived 200 years ago. It is this ability to be effortlessly modern without losing touch with age-old tradition that sets Morocco apart from many developing – and Islamic – countries.

Family and community

Family is everything to a Moroccan. It binds everyone together and comes before anything else. As well as sharing all money earned (including sending a significant portion of

of Ramadan; and Aid el Kebir, commemorating Ibrahim's sacrifice of a sheep in place of his son, held 70 days after Ramadan), family events such as births, circumcisions, marriages, the return of the *Hajj* (the pilgrimage to Mecca that all able-bodied Muslims should do at least once in their lifetime if they can afford to) and burial are conducted according to cherished rituals. After the birth of a baby a lamb is slaughtered for a feast on the seventh day; if the family is poor, a chicken or even a rabbit will be used instead. For the circumcision of boys at the age of three or four – these days normally done

Out and about in Rabat.

earnings home for those who live abroad), most men continue to live with their families even after they are married, and even the smallest houses accommodate several generations of one family. In fact, they rather pity the tiny Western nuclear family, seeing it as lonely and without purpose. For a Moroccan, happiness is not about space or personal freedom; the most important thing is the health and wellbeing of your family. Even the most distantly related cousins are looked after and cherished as if they were a brother or sister.

Social and family traditions, and national and regional festivals, are fervently followed. As well as the big religious festivals (the birthday of the Prophet; Aid es Seghir, marking the end

under a local anaesthetic – another feast is held and the boy is dressed in traditional clothes and plied with money.

Arranged marriages (see page 69) are still fairly common, and lavish weddings lasting several days are still the norm. But an increasing number of brides and grooms are opting for a simple ceremony, and many couples are living together after the 'engagement' (a binding contract marked by an official ceremony and dissolved only by divorce or death), dispensing with the full-blown wedding traditionally held six months to a year later. Probably more than any other Islamic nation, Morocco is a country where traditionalists and modernists may comfortably coexist.

Ramadan

Ramadan is the most important event in the Moroccan calendar and a time of intense spiritual meaning for everyone, whether they are religious or not.

Ramadan, one of the five pillars of Islam, commemorating the revelation of the Qur'an to the Prophet Mohammed, is a deeply spiritual time for all Muslims, who must refrain from eating, drinking and smoking from dawn to dusk (the hour when a black thread cannot be distinguished from a white one). Sex is also prohibited, and Muslims are expected to spend more time in prayer and seeking forgiveness and humility. Some people are exempt, however: pregnant or menstruating women, travellers, the old or sick, and children.

While it is always the ninth month of the Islamic calendar, Ramadan is not a fixed date. The festival usually begins on the day of the new moon and moves backwards each year by roughly 11 days. Approximate dates for Ramadan over the coming years are 18 June to 16 July 2015, 6 June to 5 July 2016 and 27 May to 24 June 2017.

For travellers to Morocco, Ramadan does mean that a visit will be difficult: it is worth noting that tempers can be frayed, shops and restaurants, particularly in smaller towns or rural area, will often close down for the entire month and in the larger towns and cities will close for half an hour before sunset and for an hour after. Bank and office hours are also slightly shortened, but beyond this, Ramadan can be a fascinating time and lucky travellers might even be invited to a family *iftar* – the evening meal when the family break the fast – which is an experience not to be missed.

Breaking the fast

When the heat and quiet of a Ramadan day dwindle, the restlessness in the towns and listlessness in the villages metamorphose into a swelling sense of expectation. Just before sundown the streets empty and everyone hurries home. When the muezzin calls for the sunset (maghrib) prayer, Moroccans everywhere break the fast. The fast is first broken by a date and a glass of milk. Then, a bowl of *harira* – a thick broth of lamb, chickpeas, lentils and tomatoes. The *harira* is also eaten with

shebbakia, deep-fried pastries dipped in honey, which are either home-made or bought from the special *shebbakia* stalls that spring up during this time of year.

Cafés catch up on the business they have missed during the day, families parade along the main boulevards and clothes shops do a roaring trade as people prepare for the end of the month of fasting and prayer. Later in the evening, typically between 11pm and midnight, 'dinner' will be eaten before most people drift off to bed. This festive feast, at which families come together and celebrate, consists of tagines of meat or vegeta-

Honey-laden shebbakia, a Ramadan treat.

bles, couscous, endless plate-loads of patisserie and fruit and glasses of thick, milky drinks. Later, as the dawn prayer echoes from the mosques, drummers patrol the streets and alleyways rousing households for the *assohour*, a sleepy feast of thick pancakes spread with honey and served with mint tea or coffee.

The 26th day of Ramadan (Laylat el Quadr) commemorates the first revelation of the Qur'an to the Prophet and is the holiest night of the year, marked by a more elaborate feast and, for the devout, a night spent reciting the Qur'an. A few days later, on the 29th or 30th in the evening, the fast ends. The following day is Aid es Seghir, 'Little Feast', a public holiday when new clothes are worn and alms and food are distributed to the poor.

THE BERBER WAY OF LIFE

The Berbers make up more than half of Morocco's population, but only recently have their language and culture been recognised.

When the Arabs arrived in Morocco in the 7th century, they found a country inhabited by the fiercely tribal Berbers who have lived in Africa for 4,000 years. The Romans called these wild tribes the '*Barbari*', a name that has since been transformed into 'Berbers'.

Today the Imazighen, as they prefer to be called, represent a widespread group of tribes scattered from Morocco to Egypt, and south, to Mali and Niger.

Keeping language alive

The Berber language is split into three dialects: Tamazight ('language of the tree', from central Morocco / Middle Atlas), Taselhit / Shilha (High and Anti-Atlas) and Tarifit (or Riffian, from the Rif mountains). Following independence, the steady Arabisation of Morocco (encouraged as a way of asserting the country's identity after years of colonial rule) meant that Berber culture was systematically sidelined, and their language banned from being spoken and taught in schools.

Today, however, thanks to activism among Berber cultural associations the nation's Berber language is starting to revive. In 2011, Mohammed VI announced that Berber would be recognised as an official language of Morocco, and it is now broadcast on radio and television, and studied in the country's universities.

Tourism, too, is playing a significant role, given that it is the Berber way of life that many tourists come to Morocco to see, and meaning that responsible tourism can also encourage the revival and survival of this rich and ancient culture.

Musician at the Imilchil bride festival.

The wedding moussem of the Aït Haddidou tribe near Imilchil

In the mountains the Berbers' stone houses cling to the sides of rocky slopes, perched above intensely cultivated terraced fields

...erber camel guide taking a break.

...oat hair and sheep's wool are turned into textiles. Designs are ...spired by geometrical representations of the natural world.

Dancers and musicians perform in traditional Berber costume at the Imilchil festival.

THE BRIDES OF IMILCHIL

One of the most famous Berber festivals is the wedding *moussem* of the Aït Haddidou tribe near Imilchil in the High Atlas. Every September this tribe meets to celebrate the feast day of Sidi Mohammed el Maghani, the patron saint of the Aït Haddidou, and also to remember the sad Romeo and Juliet-esque legend that inspired the festival.

The story goes that lovers Tislit and Isli, unable to marry because of their feuding families and unable to live without each other, decided to drown themselves in nearby lakes. But even in death they remained apart as a mountain separated their lakes and thus prevented their souls from meeting in the afterlife.

Today, the Imilchil festival is held to enable the men and women of different local tribes to meet and later marry whom they choose. Dozens of potential brides, dressed in blue, white and red shawls, their cheeks rouged and their eyes lined with kohl, come to sing, dance, feast and flirt with their white-robed male counterparts. The festival is a time of great celebration and, though private in the past, is opening up more to tourism each year.

Woman dressed in Berber costume at Imilchil bride festival.

MOROCCAN WOMEN

Inequality between the sexes in Morocco is deep-rooted and goes back to the beginnings of Islam and before, but Mohammed VI's revolutionary social reforms have had far-reaching consequences.

At first glance – in urban Morocco – women appear to enjoy near-equality with men. They hold senior positions in the government and the private sector, the feminist press appears largely uncensored and foreign women's magazines fill the newsstands.

But scratch the surface and a very different picture often emerges, particularly in rural Morocco. The codes of Bedouin society, from which Moroccan Arab culture derives, stipulate that a woman is the vessel of her family's honour, and even to be the subject of groundless salacious gossip is a transgression on her part, deserving severe sanctions.

Since the 1950s, however, there has been a quiet war going on between Moroccan men and women, between the religious conservatives and the modernisers. Slowly at first and now with increasing speed, women have made headway in their battle, not least because they have found a very powerful champion.

Royal champion

In October 2003 Mohammed VI made a historic speech that called for a radical change to the legal position of women, and specifically reforming the Moroccan *mudawana*, or family law, which concerns marriage, divorce and the family, and was itself based upon Islamic *sharia* law.

In a sweeping reform, ratified by parliament in January 2004, women were granted equal rights to men in almost all aspects of law. By Islamic and Arab standards this was nothing less than a revolution, and it made Moroccan women among the most liberated in the Arab world.

The minimum marriageable age for women was raised from 15 to 18 years (equal to that of

Making argan oil in Essaouira.

men). Upon reaching 18 a woman could now marry whom she chose, without needing the permission of the male head of her family (her father or, in his absence, the oldest brother – even if he were her junior).

Women were given better rights in divorce settlements – including the right to apply for divorce and including an equal claim to the family home. Previously a woman could be divorced and thrown out of her home without even receiving notice (subsequently, in 2009, further new legislation gave women the right to divorce their husbands without the husband's consent).

Polygamy, though not common even before the new legislation, is now permitted only with the first wife's consent and with the permission of a judge. Men are no longer enshrined in law as the head of the family. Marriage is now viewed as a contract between equal partners and a woman is no longer obliged by law to obey her husband.

These changes to women's rights did not happen overnight. They came after many years of campaigning by women's rights groups and the feminist press, who walked a tightrope between incurring the wrath of the religious conservatives and falling foul of government censorship. The conservatives mounted huge public demonstrations against the campaigners and fielded parliamentary

Along with reforms aimed at the rights of women, Mohammed VI ensured that laws governing rights of children were also tightened.

and hold the key to political stability. Yet, though a growing minority are educated and ambitious, well over half of all rural women remain illiterate and even now only around 50 percent of all Moroccan girls go to school – presenting a major challenge for the government.

Group of friends in Casablanca.

candidates to try to block any moves to institute reform.

But with the succession of Mohammed VI a series of precedents in the royal household sent a bold message across the country that couldn't be ignored. When he married Princess Salima, not only was his engagement announced and the princess's photograph, name and family history made public, but the international press was even invited to the wedding. This was in complete contrast to the secrecy surrounding the domestic life of his father, who never revealed the number and names of his wives nor appeared with them in public.

Women today represent the future of the country's economic and social development

THE DAILY GRIND

Many urban Moroccan women today hold a job and run a home, in a country where a minimum of four children is the norm, washing machines are luxuries and lunch is a meal that working women rush home to prepare in their lunch break. Men do little to help with childcare or housework, although they may do the shopping, traditionally a male role in the Arab world. In rural communities, a woman's life is even harder due to negligible educational opportunities. Indeed, as inequitable as life in Morocco's cities is, most of Morocco's feminists turn their attention to fighting for the rights of the country's rural women.

Wild Weddings

A Moroccan wedding can be a long, drawn-out affair, but they are also unforgettable occasions where age-old traditions are still celebrated amidst a whirlwind of feasting and dancing.

In spite of the current strides being made in female emancipation, married is what most girls in Morocco want to be when they grow up. Arranged marriages are still common, though not the rule, and rarely happen against the wishes of the couple involved. In most cases, once a man is ready for marriage he will ask his close female relatives to help him choose a bride or ask them to approach the family of a girl he has already met. A meeting of the two families will then ensue to ascertain the man's prospects and respectability. It is imperative for the prospective bride to make a good match. Divorce, though not uncommon, still carries a stigma and can be disastrous for a young woman.

Once a couple decide to marry, preparations are made for the 'engagement', the legal part of the wedding (after the engagement there is no going back, short of divorce or death). Like the wedding itself, it is an elaborate affair, traditionally beginning with the groom proceeding to the bride's home laden with offerings – bolts of fabrics, cones of sugar, baskets of candles and spices – and a calf or sheep bringing up the rear. These days, such gifts have symbolic importance rather than material value and, sadly, the tradition is disappearing. The groom is responsible for providing the food for the engagement feast, and he will deliver this to the bride's home early in the day.

Marriage ceremony

The wedding itself is usually a two- or three-day event (though it can go on far longer) of elaborate feasts, regulated by strict protocol. For several days before the occasion, the bride is attended by a *negaffa*, who acts as her personal beautician – supervising depilation, coiffure and the application of henna to hands and feet – as well as instructing the bride in conjugal duties. During the celebrations, the *negaffa* flanks the bride at all times, announcing her when she enters a room and meeting her every need and supervising her changes of clothes (usually two or more traditional costumes, plus a white, Western-style dress). Until fairly recently, the *negaffa's* most important job was to witness the consummation of the marriage and confirm the bride's virginity, sometimes by brandishing the bloodstained sheets.

Segregated weddings

Traditionally, wedding feasts are sexually segregated and held at home or in a hired venue, though mixed-gender festivities in hotels are becoming fashionable. On the first night the emphasis is on

A wedding in Fez.

the groom, whose guests gather in the late afternoon for tea and *halwa* and are entertained by a small band; later on, a meal of two or three substantial courses will be served. The women will also attend, but will occupy a separate area or floor. At various points in the evening the bridal couple is 'presented', carried into the room on huge, gaudy ceremonial thrones.

The second evening focuses on the bride's female guests, who will be entertained by an all-female orchestra and possibly by drummers and Gnaoua musicians. More relaxed and more fun than the men's night, it is an occasion for women to put on their finery and let their hair down, dancing with one another and singing popular love songs.

Colourful mounds of spices.

MOROCCAN FOOD

Moroccan cuisine has influenced top chefs and restaurants all over the world, but you'll never find it as tasty or as subtle as the food served up in a Moroccan home.

Essentially, Moroccan cooking combines the desert nomads' diet of mutton, vegetables and dairy produce with more refined and exotically spiced specialities introduced in Morocco at the time of the Arab conquest. But over the centuries it has also incorporated other influences: southern European (olives, olive oil, fruit, tomatoes), sub-Saharan African, and French (particularly apparent in the country's Westernised restaurants).

Home cooking

The best Moroccan food is found in the home. The average Moroccan will rarely eat 'out' except perhaps at one of the many simple restaurants found in every town, where grilled *brochettes* (kebabs of marinated chicken or lamb), basic tagines, spicy *merguez* sausages and *kefta* (grilled minced lamb) are served.

There are, however, a growing number of high-end restaurants catering to tourists, particularly in cities like Marrakech, that reflect

Tagines, a great way to end a day's hiking.

A SWEET-TOOTHED NATION

Moroccans are addicted to sugar. Tea and fruit juices are served sweetened, and every home will have a supply of home-made sweets, the making of which is an art form. Classic sweet combinations include almonds, honey and breadcrumbs. During Ramadan, be sure to try *shebakkia*, deep-fried knots of pastry dipped in honey and sprinkled with sesame seeds. In the afternoon many Moroccans are in the habit of adjourning to a patisserie for coffee and cakes; in the home, the 'coffee hour', from around 7pm, is a special time when the day's news is exchanged over coffee, tea and sweetmeats.

the rich range of Moroccan cooking. Some are resolutely traditional, while others serve up more innovative and contemporary reworkings of typical Moroccan classics, influenced by the growing number of European (particularly French) and European-trained Moroccan chefs working in the country.

Couscous is regularly cooked at home, usually on a Friday, the Muslim holy day. A mound of steamed grain topped with chicken, lamb, beef or vegetables, it is traditionally served at the end of a meal, although these days it is more likely to be a meal in itself. A garnish of fried onions is often added, while almonds and raisins may also be scattered on top of it.

Bread is sacred in Morocco. Local people carrying their own bread to be cooked in the communal oven are a regular sight. Never wasted, bread is gathered up at the end of a meal to make breadcrumbs for sweets.

The famous Moroccan tagine comprises a stew of beef, chicken, lamb or just vegetables slowly cooked in the eponymous earthenware dish with a conical lid. More elaborate tagines add additional spices and ingredients, typically

The other popular everyday meat is chicken, or *djej*. Classic dishes include *matisha mesla* (chicken cooked in tomatoes, honey, ginger and cinnamon) and *djej bil loz* (chicken with spices and almonds), although you're more likely to encounter simple chicken brochettes roasted over an open charcoal fire or the ubiquitous servings of rotisserie chicken which can be seen slowly turning and browning in cafés across the country.

Another Moroccan classic is *pastilla* (or *bastilla*), a delicately flavoured sweet-and-salty pie combining slow-cooked meat wrapped in crisp dough combined with toasted almonds, sugar

Snack stall in Rabat.

fruit, such as *barrogog bis basela* (lamb tagine with prunes and almonds), *safardjaliyya* (beef tagine with quinces), or *sikbadj* (lamb with dates and apricots). Olives are also frequently added, while citrus-flavoured tagines cooked with lemon are also common. Tagines are typically made of solid clay (aficionados claim that unglazed and unpainted tagines impart the best flavour), although some of the elaborate examples you'll see in tourist souks are intended for decorative rather than practical use. Tagines are traditionally slow-cooked over a low, even charcoal fire. The tagine's conical lid traps steam, which then condenses and falls back into the pot, meaning that only small amounts of water are needed to create tender stews.

and cinnamom. *Pastilla* is traditionally filled with pigeon, although nowadays chicken is more commonly used.

Festive specialities

Special occasions in Morocco are celebrated with special foods. During Ramadan, Moroccans break their daily fast with fresh dates and a bowl of *harira* (see page 63).

Mechoui – although increasingly eaten at any time of the year – is traditionally the ceremonial dish marking Aid el Kebir, held 70 days after Ramadan. A whole sheep is roasted on a spit and brought to the table for everyone to carve off pieces and dip them into little dishes of cumin. After the feast you will see sheepskins pegged out on rooftop terraces, along with the intestines, which are sun-dried for flavouring winter stews.

Tanjia is another popular festive dish, closely associated with the city of Marrakech. Traditionally made by men for a party, it takes its name from the clay pot in which it is prepared. Lamb, spices, garlic and clarified butter are put into the *tanjia* pot, covered with pastry or a piece of cloth and then taken to the local hammam, where they are placed inside the embers of the hammam fire and left for at least four hours. The cost of this is usually a couple of dirhams and the result is a wonderfully warm and rich casserole that falls off the bone.

Favourite fish

Fish restaurants are found along the Mediterranean Coast, from Tangier to Ceuta, and the length of the Atlantic Coast. Oualidia on the Atlantic is famous for its oysters, as is Dakhla, in Western Sahara. Huge *araignée de mer* crab and *oursin* (sea urchins) are often found in season in Essaouira and Oualidia, and giant prawns caught off Agadir, octopus, squid, boned and stuffed sardines, skate and sole are available at the most modest quayside restaurant: in particular, check out the food stalls set up each morning on the harbours of Agadir and Essaouira.

Liquid refreshment

Islam's prohibition on alcohol means it is not used in cooking other than in French restaurants. Morocco does, however, brew beer and produce wine (see page 210), industries introduced under the French. Beer comes in several varieties, Flag Spéciale and Casablanca being the most common, along with foreign brands.

French influence means that European-style coffee is also universally popular. The country's traditional drink of choice, however, is mint tea – an infusion of mint leaves with either green or black tea, usually served incredibly sweet. Mint tea is prepared in silver teapots and served in painted glasses. When poured, the pot is held high above the glass in order to cool the liquid as it falls; a good, frothy 'head' or *ras* is considered a glass of tea well poured.

Mint tea, the Moroccan national drink.

SENSATIONAL SNACKS

The Moroccan pleasure in food is reflected in the amazing range of snacks sold by the country's army of street vendors. These range from cactus fruit (prickly pear) peeled to order (said to settle upset stomachs) to freshly roasted chickpeas, and snails in a cumin-flavoured liquor ladled out of giant vats. You will also find fluffy sugared *sfenj* (doughnuts), still warm from the oven, slices of tortilla (a Spanish-influenced speciality of the north) and freshly fried potato crisps sprinkled with sea salt. Bowls of *harira* soup, sometimes served with dates, are another popular starter or snack. One of the many culinary pleasures of Morocco is the variety of locally produced, fresh, seasonal and usually organic produce. In the Rif you can eat tangy white cheese (delicious with flat Moroccan bread) artfully displayed on a bed of leaves; in autumn in the south, freshly harvested dates are some of the best in the world. In the Atlas, depending on the season, you will find almonds, walnuts and pine nuts, and in the south, sweet honeydew melons costing just a few dirhams each are readily available, as is freshly caught fish. Lining nearly every roadside in populated areas are multitudes of grill restaurants, often doubling as butchers, that serve succulent lamb brochettes, kebabs or chicken – delicious with fresh bread and salad.

MAKING MUSIC

It is difficult to get away from music in Morocco, whether it's the muezzin's haunting call to prayer, hypnotic Gnaoua drumming, or the contemporary sounds of raï and rap.

The 1960s author and painter Brion Gysin thought hearing the music of Morocco was enough to make anyone become a Muslim. The Rolling Stones, friends of Gysin, didn't go quite that far, but they did dress in jellabas and team up with the Master Musicians of Jajouka: following guitarist Brian Jones's album *Brian Jones Presents the Pipes of Pan at Jajouka*, which was put together in 1968, the Stones recorded the track 'Continental Drift' with the Moroccan group for their 1989 album *Steel Wheels*.

Keith Richards summed up the extraordinary sounds of the Jajouka pipes and drums as follows: 'It sounds a bit like modern jazz, like John Coltrane or Ornette Coleman, although it's really pagan trance music.' Other groundbreaking artists inspired by the eclectic sounds of Morocco include Led Zeppelin, Jimi Hendrix, Ry Cooder and The Beatles.

Feel the beat

Wherever you go in Morocco, you are likely to be assailed by wonderful rhythms, whether it's the most common musical phenomenon – the voice of the muezzin calling the faithful to prayer – or the stereos of music shops pumping out the latest rap and pop. Possibly it will be the ululating calls of women celebrating a wedding or the beat of the *bendir* drum and the trance-like rhythms of the *guembri* that characterise Morocco's famed Gnaoua music, or haunting melodies of the Berber *ribab*. Moroccan music is characterised by its diverse influences: sub-Saharan African, Arab, Western and Berber, and increasingly today by its fascinating forays into, and adaptations of, modern Western music.

Street music.

Chabbi is a popular form of Moroccan music. Akin to the folk-music traditions of Europe and America, it started out as music performed by travelling entertainers. These days, *chabbi* has moved onto the radio and the television. Abdelwahhab Doukali and Hamid Zahir, two of the most popular singers of this type of music, began their careers, respectively, in Bab el Makina in Fez and in the Jemaa el Fna in Marrakech.

Inevitably, traditional Moroccan music and instruments have modernised and become electronic, and interesting fusions between the contemporary and the traditional – between Gnaoua and funk, *chabbi* and pop – are common. Much of this you will hear on the radio,

Morocco's big music festivals like Boulevard and Mawazine are attracting an increasingly stellar list of celebrities – Rihanna, David Guetta, Shakira, Kanye West and Kylie Minogue have all performed in recent years.

wafting from restaurants and as mobile phone ring tones. In contemporary raï music, too, which originated in the border towns of the Rif and western Algeria, style and lyrics have come a long way from their Bedouin roots –

Brazil and beyond. The festival that possibly best encapsulates the diversity of Moroccan music is the Gnaoua World Music Festival in Essaouira. It remains one of the most popular festivals and its Gnaoua music has inspired many Western artists and is increasingly becoming a major draw for travellers. This festival has undoubtedly helped to spawn the next generation of gatherings, such as the Transahara festival held in the dunes near Merzouga, that has been going since 2003, and the slightly older Tanjazz jazz festival in Tangier (see page 319).

Musicians in Marrakech.

raï's preoccupations these days tend to be sex, drugs and cars.

Festival fever

There are around 300 music festivals in Morocco every year. Immensely popular, the larger festivals such as Boulevard in Casablanca and Rabat's Mawazine – the country's biggest – tend to feature a mixture of contemporary Moroccan artists alongside major international stars.

The annual Fez Festival of World Sacred Music, established in 1994, is also an internationally acclaimed event that has featured, in past years, Ben Harper, Youssou Ndour and artists and orchestras from India to

THE GNAOUA

The Gnaoua brotherhood is descended from black slaves brought to Morocco from Mali, Mauritania, Guinea and Ghana in the 1600s and originally, so the story goes, from Bilal, an Ethiopian who was the Prophet's first muezzin. They dress distinctively in blue robes and caps trimmed with cowrie shells, and their music, inducing a healing trance-like state, is fundamental to their rituals intended to placate spirits *(djinn)*, whether good or evil. Today their music has evolved into a form of expression that, outside of wedding celebrations, is likely to be heard all over Morocco, but especially in Marrakech.

MOROCCAN MUSE

Over the years, a multitude of Western writers, artists and musicians have been drawn to the legendary 'interzone' of Tangier, where they produced some of their most iconic works.

Tangier, more than any other Moroccan city (and many European cities), has captured the imagination and acted as muse to generations of artists, writers, playwrights and musicians. The exotic image of Tangier that endures today was largely created by Eugène Delacroix, the leading exponent of Romantic painting in France. In 1832, he accompanied the Comte de Mornay, sent by Louis-Philippe as French ambassador to the Sultan of Morocco. He filled sketchbooks with pen-and-ink drawings, and watercolours of everyday life in Tangier – the bustle of the marketplace and the mysterious streets of the kasbah – later using these details in the great series of paintings on oriental subjects for which he is best known. 'I am like a man dreaming and who sees things he is afraid will escape him,' he wrote. 'The picturesque is plentiful here. At every step, one meets ready-made paintings that would bring 20 generations of painters wealth and glory.' Matisse was also stimulated by Tangier, painting at a window in the Grand Hotel Villa de France overlooking the Grand Socco (see page 122).

Anything goes

The artist's romantic vision of Tangier persisted, and the town's 'anything goes' atmosphere, engendered by its unique status as an international zone, attracted some of the 20th century's most celebrated writers and artists, wanderers and bohemians. Truman Capote summed up the attractions of the city when he first visited at the age of 26 in 1949: 'Virtually every Tangerine is ensconced there for at least one, if not all, of four reasons: the easy availability of drugs, lustful adolescent prostitutes, tax loopholes, or because he is so undesirable no place north of

Barbara Hutton, who used to hold legendary parties.

Port Said would let him out of the airport or off the ship.' The city's edgy, alternative atmosphere was an instant attraction for William Burroughs, who moved to Tangier after reading *The Sheltering Sky* by Beat father and long-time Tangerine, Paul Bowles. The easy availability of drugs and easy, louche living, seemingly unconstrained by rules and conventions, lured hippies in the 1960s and '70s, when Tangier was a key stop on the so-called 'hash trail.'

Several eccentric characters dominated the scene in the post-war years, Tangier's golden age. The hub around which all artistic and intellectual activity revolved was Paul Bowles, Tangier's most famous adopted son, who lived there for 52 years until his death in 1999.

Bowles first arrived in Tangier in August 1931 from France. He was travelling with the American composer Aaron Copland and together they took a house on the Old Mountain for a couple of months. 'In the late afternoon sunlight I walked slowly through complex and tunnelled streets. As I reviewed it, lying there, sorry to have left the place behind, I realised with a jolt that the magic city really existed. It was Tangier... the place I wanted to be more than anywhere else.'

In 1938 Bowles married the now iconic novelist Jane Auer, in what most of their friends

> Although now known as a writer, in the 1930s and 1940s Bowles was busy composing music, including scores for Tennessee Williams's early plays, and for ballet and film.

Massachusetts called Cory, and installed herself in the Hotel Rembrandt (still open today). Paul and Jane, though best friends, kept separate households, often occupying two apartments in the same building. Paul spent much of his time with the young

The painter Brion Gysin.

regarded as a marriage of convenience between two good friends. It was Jane's success with *Two Serious Ladies* in 1943 that inspired Paul to write short stories. With an advance for a novel and his dream still fresh in his head, he made plans to go to Tangier, where the idea for his celebrated novel about a couple adrift in the burning desert of Morocco, *The Sheltering Sky*, was already gathering momentum in his imagination. In 1947, Bowles took up permanent residence in Tangier.

Friends and lovers

Jane Bowles arrived in January 1948, in the company of her latest lover, a hard-drinking, middle-aged tea shop proprietor from

Moroccan painter Ahmed Yacoubi. Together they travelled to Ceylon, Italy, Spain and New York, though their friendship was interrupted in 1957 when Yacoubi found himself in court in Tangier for seducing a 15-year-old German boy and began naming names to the authorities interested in the gay community. Paul and Jane discreetly left the country for a while; their chauffeur sold the car and used the money to go to Germany. Yacoubi was eventually acquitted and life returned to normal, but from then on Bowles saw more of the painter and writer Mohammed Mrabet, whom Yacoubi detested.

Paul Bowles was engaged in a stream of projects, from recording traditional Moroccan folk music under the sponsorship of the Rockefeller Foundation and the Library of Congress to a series of translations from the Maghrebi dialect. Now he tape-recorded stories told to him by Moroccans, and translated them into English. These included a dozen books by Mohammed Mrabet, who still lives in Tangier, as well as stories and autobiographies by Driss Ben Hamed Charhadi and Mohammed Choukri, author of the wrenching *For Bread Alone*, all translated by Paul Bowles.

Jane's Moroccan lover Cherifa was famous for her magic, and was said to exercise tremendous power over her, to the concern of Jane's new lover, the Princess Marthe Ruspoli, whom she was with from the early 1960s onwards. When Jane collapsed from a stroke, rumours abounded that Cherifa had poisoned her.

Tennessee Williams visited Tangier in 1956 and he and Jane would spend long, lazy days on the beach and in a bar called The Sun Beach, where he drafted his *Cat on a Hot Tin Roof*.

In 1962, Paul Bowles wrote the music for Tennessee's *The Milk Train Doesn't Stop Here Any More*. Tennessee returned to Tangier in 1973, a visit that became the subject of a little book by Mohammed Choukri and translated by Paul Bowles, *Tennessee Williams in Tangier*, an account of the friendships that the two struck up in the cafés, bars and streets of Tangier.

In later years, Jane Bowles's depression finally caught up with her, and in 1967, Paul Bowles took her to a psychiatric hospital in Málaga. She died in 1973 after a stroke.

> Arguably the most famous piece of literature to come out of Tangier is William Burroughs's cult classic, The Naked Lunch, in which he coined the name 'Interzone' for Tangier. The book was written in Villa Muniria, now a hotel and largely unchanged since Burroughs's day.

Francis Bacon

Though Matisse delighted in Tangier, the painter Francis Bacon found the light 'too bright' for painting but enjoyed the city's other attractions, as Cecil Beaton tactfully commented in his *Diaries*: 'Francis's Tangier, a close intimacy with the Arab world, with the brothel life, and the freedom that can be found only in certain Mediterranean countries where access to women is difficult.'

Bacon first arrived in Tangier in 1955, driven there by his friend, Peter Pollock, in his white Rolls-Royce. He liked it so much that he returned the next year, this time with Peter Lacey. They stayed first at the Hotel Cecil, then the Rembrandt, before settling in a flat next door to the Villa Muniria (see page 80). Bacon spent most of the next three years there, returning to London periodically to paint, leaving Peter Lacey to play piano at Dean's Bar, hangout of choice for the literary and expat crowd.

Jane Bowles and her lover Cherifa walking the streets of Tangier.

Forbidden fruits

Bacon was a good friend of William Burroughs, who moved to Tangier in 1954. Burroughs said of his early days there: 'I lived in Tony Dutch's male brothel on the rue d'Arcos for quite a while. There wasn't much noise. I liked it in Tangier obviously, I stayed on. I wouldn't say I was in heaven, but I had every drug I wanted. Very soon I found a connection for junk, an opiate called Eukodol, and they could sell it across the counter.'

The English novelist Allan Sillitoe wrote one of his most acclaimed books in Tangier: *The Loneliness of the Long Distance Runner* was published in 1958 and made into a successful film by Tony Richardson in 1962. Sillitoe wrote it in the Villa Gazebo, on the Old Mountain, a red-tiled, blue-shuttered whitewashed house with wide verandas and sweeping views across the Strait to Spain, later occupied by American novelist John Hopkins, author of *Tangier Buzzless Flies*.

This same villa was the location of an experimental film by Antony Balch called *William Buys a Parrot*, in which we see Burroughs enter the house and admire the view from the garden while standing next to a bamboo cage containing Coco, the white parrot of Joe

Tennessee Williams.

McPhillips, Hopkins's friend and larger-than-life headmaster of the American School of Tangier.

Less celebrated writers, such as Rupert Croft-Cook and Peter Mayne, lived in Tangier in the 1950s. As William Burroughs remembered, 'Peter Mayne was very much an old Tangier hand. He wrote *The Alleys of Marrakech*. I remember a line in *The Narrow Smile*, 'There's a boy across the river with an ass like a peach, alas I cannot swim.' I suppose a lot of inland Arabs can't swim.'

Brion Gysin, the sound poet, painter, writer and performance artist, who rediscovered the Dadaist 'cut-up' technique used by his friend Burroughs, arrived in Tangier in the 1930s, and lived there, on and off, until his death in 1986. Though best known as a painter, his quasi-autobiographical novel, *The Process*, is a retelling of his solitary journey across the Sahara. The writer and poet Edouard Roditi, who had known Paul Bowles since the 1930s, arrived from Paris to see them and Jean Genet visited in 1969 and 1970, but he was more interested in meeting Moroccan writers than mixing with anyone other than Paul and Brion Gysin. Mohammed Choukri published a journal of his visit, *Jean Genet in Tangier*, translated into English, of course, by Paul Bowles.

Queen of Tangier

Woolworth heiress Barbara Hutton threw some of Tangier's most renowned parties, which are still remembered nostalgically today. Hutton's palace in the kasbah was the glittering venue for her soirees, and she had several walls in the medina knocked down to allow her Rolls-Royce, and the cars of her guests, to drive up to her front door. Hutton would receive her guests – from diplomats to cabaret artists, hairdressers and Tangier's expat and literary elite – seated on a gilded throne, dripping with diamonds and swathed in couture. Her parties would last until the early hours and were enjoyed by her Moroccan neighbours as much as by her guests. For one especially lavish party, she hired hundreds of camels to line the entrance to her house as a welcome for her guests. Even now, guides will enthusiastically point out her house to anyone passing by, the palace of the 'Queen of Tangier'.

THE SUMMER OF '61

The beautiful Villa Muniria was the setting for the so-called 'psychedelic summer' of 1961, when Allen Ginsberg, his boyfriend Peter Orlovsky, Beat poet Gregory Corso and psychedelic voyager Timothy Leary descended upon writer William Burroughs. Ginsberg had been there before, in 1957, when he managed to offend the painter Francis Bacon by offering him alcohol in an empty tin can taken from the garbage. Later Bacon forgave him and offered to do a 'big pornographic painting' of Allen and Peter together, although the distractions of the heady city meant that he did very little actual work during his stay.

MADE IN MOROCCO – ARTS AND CRAFTS

The medinas of Morocco are hives of traditional industry overflowing with exquisite examples of the country's flourishing arts and crafts.

Exploring the souks of Fez and Marrakech is like taking a long walk back down the corridors of time. More is revealed the more you delve, for it is in the hidden *fondouks* and courtyards off the main streets that traditional crafts and industries thrive in ways that have barely changed since Andalusian refugees introduced them over 1,000 years ago.

Crafts are grouped according to type, with the most valuable crafts located closest to the Great Mosque. Each craft is organised into a guild, with apprentices working under master craftsmen for several years. Only when an apprentice is deemed to have the necessary skills and mental application will the master craftsman declare him fit to work alone.

Urban inspiration

While the rural tradition is inspired by nature and animistic beliefs, the urban craft tradition takes inspiration from the Qur'an. Qur'an verses in highly stylised script are engraved, sculpted, carved, painted and embroidered on metals, plaster, wood and textiles. Allied to this abstract art is the use of complex patterns, often in the form of *zellige* (mosaics of tiny hand-cut glazed tiles), repeated again and again to produce a meditative effect on the beholder.

Traditional crafts are being revived in artisan schools throughout the country, like this one in Tetouan in the Rif.

The Berber silver jewellery of Tiznit, near Agadir, and traditional Moroccan ceramics on sale.

Copper, brass and silver are turned into trays, lamps, pots and tableware, often incised or damascened.

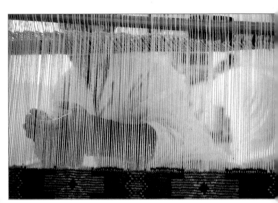

Weaving a carpet.

MOROCCO'S MAGIC CARPETS

Weaving is one of Morocco's oldest and most esteemed craft traditions, and carpets vary in colours and styles from region to region. Carpets are almost exclusively woven by women, and each one will tell the story of a particular tribe or family. The flat-woven *mergoums* of the Berbers are particularly dazzling for their striking geometric designs.

Carpets have many purposes. In the home they are laid over floors, hung on walls and slipped over couches. But they may also be used to wrap up a Berber bride on the way to her new home or to cover a funeral bier. Their symbols (snakes, crosses, tattoos, lozenges and 'eyes') are believed to have magical and protective powers.

Carpets sold in the big tourist souks are likely to have been resold several times over by various middlemen before they reach Western buyers, meaning that the original weavers might make as little as £15/US$25 for a rug which may eventually sell for £150/US$250. Buying from local associations and cooperatives means that both you and the person who actually made the carpet benefit. The Middle Atlas region is a particularly good source of quality carpets.

A man prepares pieces of stone to make zellige, ceramic tiles placed in geometrical patterns.

Potter at work near Casablanca.

Moroccan carpet salesman.

Metalwork in Fez.

THE CRAFTS OF MOROCCO

Morocco's ancient craft traditions – from lanterns and kaftans to carpets and ceramics – are thriving in the 21st century, and are being increasingly used by Western designers too.

Moroccan carpets can roughly be grouped into rural or urban. City carpets – usually Rabati – are influenced by the fine, oriental designs of classical Persian carpets and are intricately detailed. Rural Berber carpets – traditionally made for domestic use – are hand-woven from sheep's wool into patterns and symbols that tell the stories of a tribe. Carpets from the Middle Atlas – *zanafi* – have a deep, woollen pile to keep out the cold and are usually long and narrow. The creamy white *shedwi* carpets of the Beni Ouarain and Beni Mguild tribes are decorated with simple black or dark brown patterns. The carpets of eastern Morocco are coloured in indigo or green and covered with Berber designs of diamonds, crosses and triangles, and the *haouz* carpets of the west, between the Atlas and the Atlantic, have free-floating shapes and bright colours. *Kilims*, or *hanbels*, centred on Chichaoua, are flat-woven rugs with detailed geometric designs and usually coloured in black, white and yellow on a red background. All Moroccan carpets are made by women.

Classic pottery in Fez.

Ceramics

Tagines, soup bowls, ashtrays, vases, egg cups, plates – Moroccan pottery is rich and varied and encompasses both the traditional and the modern. As with carpets, it is the colours and designs of Moroccan ceramics that identify where they were created. The main ceramics centres are Fez, Safi and Meknes. The refined blue-and-white floral and abstract designs of Fez are much admired, while Safi is famous for its leafy-green glazes and for the tiles found edging traditional riads. The pottery of more remote rural regions is nearly always unglazed. Today, you can find increasingly modern designs and colours – often plain blocks of colour in crimson red, turquoise, pale pink or metallic black.

Clothing

Studded with sequins, roughly woollen, electrically nylon, elegantly linen – Moroccan garb has many guises. Classic items of clothing include the iconic kaftan, worn by Moroccan women at weddings and other special occasions: belted, angel-sleeved ankle-length gowns, in silk, satin or nylon and embroidered to varying degrees; the *jellaba*, a long, hooded over-garment for both men and women, and the *burnous*, a short variant for men only; the *hendira*, a handwoven woollen cape for women, traditionally a marriage cloak; and the *gandura*, usually sleeveless, worn by men over other layers.

Leather

For many visitors, a pair of supple *babouches*, leather slippers, stacked in irresistible multicoloured piles, are a must-have; the classic yellow *babouches* are still worn by Moroccan men of all ages, while white is the preferred colour when visiting the mosque. The traditional skill of crafting leather, mainly camel or goatskin, and dyeing it into a multitude of shades also

The woodwork of Morocco is just as beautifully made. Cedar and pine, lemon and orangewood are aromatically fashioned by *maalems*, master craftsmen, into carved doors, arched entranceways, wedding chests, musical instruments and soup spoons. The fragrant thuya wood of the south – prevalent in the souks of Essaouira – is greatly sought after and made into inlaid chess sets, polished animal sculptures and jewellery boxes.

Jewellery

Glittering jewellers shops exhibiting a glitzy

Dyeing leather at the Chouaras Tanneries, Fez.

Berber man making silver jewellery in Tiznit.

produces ottomans, handbags and suitcases and delicately tooled belts. Antique saddlebags, tasselled and in faded colours, also make attractive items to take home.

Metal and woodwork

Moroccan lanterns – intricately pierced and laced with coloured glass or edged in nickel – are icons of Moroccan design. But the craft of metalwork extends beyond lanterns, to tiny silver teapots, hammered and engraved copper or brass trays, antique silver perfume holders, brass door knockers rendered as 'hands of Fatima' and the finely wrought iron windows and balconies of traditional Moroccan homes.

array of golden necklaces, bracelets and earrings are found in medinas across the country, often in the old Jewish quarters, or *mellahs*. Out of the cities, the real draw is tribal Berber silver jewellery, decorated with turquoise, agate, jade, ivory, wood and amber. Berber women love jewellery – from brooches to fasten veils and heavy silver cuffs studded with turquoise and coral, to many-layered, beaded necklaces – some, for ceremonial purposes, being as large as a small child – and earrings depicting traditional Berber symbols. Tiznit, south of Agadir, is the main centre for silver jewellery in Morocco, and it is here that you are more likely to find the genuine Berber jewellery at affordable prices.

Zaouia of Moulay Ismail, Meknes.

THE ESSENCE OF ARCHITECTURE

Islamic principles, a challenging climate, tribal warfare and foreign visitors have all influenced the style of Morocco's architecture.

Moroccan architecture is heavily influenced by Islam, although factors specific to the country – natural resources and climate, a tribal history and European imperialism – have all modified the original Eastern pattern. Early Islamic influences had weakened by the time they reached the extreme west of North Africa, which meant many indigenous practices were left intact. And, as a staging post on the African, Saharan and Mediterranean trade routes, Morocco experienced a long and steady influx of various foreign styles. Regional differences also played a major role. In the high mountains, abundant supplies of oak, pine and cedar were used lavishly in the internal ornamentation of larger houses and palaces. In the south, tribal warfare and the struggle of emerging dynasties led to the creation of a solidly defensive architecture of tall, crenellated *ksars* and kasbahs.

Islamic influence

Nonetheless, the building of towns and villages presented an opportunity to express the ideals of the Islamic state. Islam touches every aspect of a Muslim's life, and Moroccan architecture reflects more than just a series of rules and customs laid down for religious buildings. Its emphasis on the community is reflected in the interlocked nature of domestic architecture.

Islam's asceticism finds expression in simplicity of form and respect for space. The Arabs of the 7th century, who had little architectural heritage, were never far from the desert and its incredible vastness. Spaciousness and lack of distraction are well suited to the observation of rituals and prayer.

Because Islam forbids animate representation, all ornamentation was abstract. While this

Inside the Zaouia of Moulay Ismail.

DEFINING A SPACE

For the Arabs, the aesthetic role of buildings has traditionally taken second place to the practical function of defining a space, a purpose emphasised by huge, dramatic gateways, enclosed courtyards and enormous defensive walls. A small gate in the blank wall of a medina street will lead into a beautiful riad courtyard, possibly containing a fountain, where one may sit for contemplation or rest – an oasis away from heat, dust and noise. Often paved or tiled in mosaics, with walls and pillars supporting a gallery in carved stucco or wood, the courtyard is open to the sky and all the rooms look onto it.

rule was never completely observed and plant and flower forms may often be identified, fine calligraphy is more usual. Kufic script is highly stylised – to the extent that, practically in cipher, it can be very difficult to read, even for a classical Arabist.

Gold and silver were similarly frowned upon, so less lavish materials were used. Stucco, worked into delicate lace-like patterns, arrived in the 13th century, while mosaic *(zellige)* of green, blue, black and red tiling became popular in the 14th century. Both were Eastern techniques perfected in Andalusia and imported to Morocco

entrance door and a minaret are the most notable external features, and the roof is usually of simple, often green (the colour of Islam), glazed tile work.

Early mosques did not include minarets; in fact, the earliest mosques were not even formally enclosed. Originally, the faithful would be called

'Believer is to believer', said the Prophet Mohammed, 'as the mutually upholding sections of a building.'

Medersa el Attarine, Fez.

Mausoleum of Mohammed V and Hassan II, Rabat.

by the Muslims of Spain. Similarly in the Andalusian fashion, intricate ironwork, which lends itself to abstract design, was employed for window and door grilles and for lanterns.

Mosques and medersas

The mosque, the most important religious building and the principal – although not the only – meeting place for prayer formed a loose prototype for all Islamic architecture. Modelled on the Great Mosques of Cordoba and Kairouan of 8th-century Spain and Tunisia (at that time, the most important cities of Western Islam), which, in turn, were based on Damascene models, most Moroccan mosques are rather plain on the outside. A highly decorated

to prayer from nearby rooftops. The square-shaped minarets of the Maghreb, unlike the circular minarets of the Middle East, correspond to the bell-tower of a church and were copied from early Christian towers in Damascus.

The interior of the mosque comprises a courtyard, known as a *sahn*, with a fountain or basin for preliminary ritual washing, and a hall for prayer, divided into aisles segregating the sexes situated alongside. The *mihrab* (a niche in the wall, often decorated) indicates the direction of Mecca. To the right of the *mihrab* is a pulpit called the *minbar*, often of carved cedarwood with intricate inlay: it is from here that the imam (prayer leader) reads the Qur'an.

Almost all mosques in Morocco are out of bounds to non-Muslims. You may, though, catch tantalising glimpses of the interiors through their doors.

Religious buildings open to non-Muslims include the country's historic medersas (madrassas), Islamic schools, some dating back as far as the 12th century, for the teaching of theology and Muslim law. While the medersas were often attached to mosques, they developed from domestic buildings – sometimes the homes of the principal teachers. As with mosques, a central courtyard with a fountain, often cloistered on the ground floor, was flanked by a hall for prayer, as well as classrooms and a library. The pupils' living quarters were situated above, on the first floor.

Many of the medersas were founded by the learned Merinids in the 14th century. The buildings are elaborately decorated with detailed carving, mosaic tiles and glasswork, Kufic script and stucco. The most outstanding are Medersa Bou Inania in Fez, commissioned by Sultan Abou Inan in 1350 , and the Medersa Ben Youssef in Marrakech , rebuilt in 1565 by the Saadian Sultan Abdullah el Ghallib.

Solid defence

As recently as the late 1930s, travel in Morocco could be a dangerous business. Larger towns were typically defended by strong walls and fortifications enclosing stables, barracks, food stores, granaries, arsenals, and water cisterns.

Such structures are usually notable for their size rather than their architectural finesse, although the design of the principal gateway (*bab*) into a city often provides an exception to this rule. Generally built of stone blocks and crenellated, two towers flank a central bay in which the gate is set. Above, the arch might be deeply carved in coloured stones, like the Oudaya Gate in the kasbah of Rabat, Bab Agnaou in Marrakech and the imposing Bab Mansour in Meknes.

Every dynasty left its stamp on the defences of the cities, often demolishing much of the

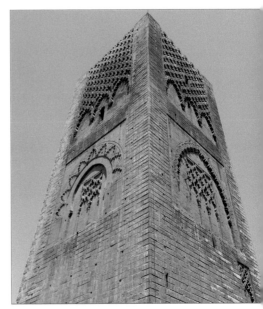

Rabat's Tour Hassan.

MEDINA LIVING

All Arab cities with some history have their medina. The Prophet Mohammed founded the first Islamic community in a city named Medina, second only to Mecca in importance, and it quickly became the prototype for other towns in the Arab world. To a follower of Islam, the pursuit of the ideal of a just and ordered city was obligatory. It is believed that on the Day of Judgement men and women will be assessed not only on their own merits but also on their performance in society. The design of the medinas, therefore, reflected communal values. Each quarter contributed to the benefit of the whole. Even during the French and Spanish protectorates, the integrity of the medinas was respected. Marshal Lyautey, the first French Resident-General, decreed that new developments serving the European administrators should be set apart from the medinas in order to preserve the old towns' way of life. However, though many of the medinas are intact, they have generally lost their administrative and political importance to the new towns. After independence, the richest families often moved to the more modern quarters vacated by the Europeans, leaving the medinas to the poor. Increasingly, however, Europeans are restoring riads either as private homes or to turn into hotels, preserving these historic towns.

work of its predecessors. The Almohads in Rabat (12th century) and the Merinids in Fez and Chellah (13th and 14th centuries) were particularly industrious in this respect. But it was not only the towns and cities that were in need of fortification. Even the poor, flat-roofed stone farms built on terraces in the Middle Atlas, homes of the Berber Chleuhs, were – and still are – well defended. .

In the south, these farms give way to the *ksar*, effectively fortified villages comprising a central square, a granary, a well, a mosque and a tangle of warren-like streets, all protected by

of towns possess one, although it is in the south that they are most evident. Square and built of crude brick, they show few openings on the outside. Yet their simplicity is often offset by geometric decorations carved into the mud-bricks. Close to the desert, the influence of Saharan Africa is clear.

Magnificent palaces

Unlikely though it may seem, such blank exteriors have contained some of Morocco's richest palaces. The sheer luxury, colour and decoration, as well as the quality of life within,

Royal Palace, Fez.

high walls punctuated by watchtowers. Made of pisé (a combination of pressed mud brick mixed with rubble), these *ksars* are extremely vulnerable to water and easily damaged by rain. The south of Morocco is littered with ruined *ksars*, often only a few decades old, abandoned by their former inhabitants who now prefer the more modern amenities and comforts of a breeze block concrete house with electricity and modern plumbing.

Strictly speaking, the difference between a kasbah and a *ksar* is that the former house individual families, while the latter enclose a whole community. That said, throughout most of Morocco the word 'kasbah' refers to the defensive stronghold of a town. The majority

FABULOUS PALACES

The El Badi Palace in Marrakech was built for fabulous receptions given by Ahmed el Mansour in the 16th century. Its courtyard had five elaborate pools lined with coloured tiles, the waters of which irrigated a series of gardens. Its marble came from Italy and its furnishings from as far away as China. Its magnificent kiosks, pavilions, towers and galleries made it legendary. Today it is merely an elegant ruin. The Dar el Makhzen Palace, built in Fez in the 13th century, is probably the finest in Morocco, but is now closed to the public. Several acres in size, its courtyard even contains a medersa and a mosque.

surpassed even the comforts of Europe for many centuries. Once again, the central feature was the courtyard, around which were grouped suites of rooms in a symmetrical pattern. Servant quarters and storage areas would often be built off the sides, and areas for cooking and the housing of animals would be located on the ground floor, often with their own central courtyard, as wealth and necessity dictated.

While the original structure of a palace was usually symmetrical, radiating from the central courtyard, later additions were often haphazardly planned. Nonetheless, certain

The interest in Moroccan architecture and style is now a global phenomenon. In 2010, for example, around 97 million people worldwide tuned in to an episode of House Hunters International devoted to the renovation of Riad Laksiba in Marrakech.

essential features had to be incorporated. There was always a judgement hall and a *mechouar*, an open space to hold large audiences, dominated by a balcony, or *iwan*, where the sultan could receive homage from his tribesmen. The harem (women's quarter), a restricted area, was entirely separate.

The decoration within these palaces was executed by top Moroccan artists and craftsmen, and while it is true that development and quality of style had degenerated into showy exuberance by the 18th century, there are plenty of examples of good work still preserved.

Nowadays, many former small palaces have been turned into museums and hotels (the Palais Jamai in Fez, the museum in the Kasbah of the Oudaias in Rabat, the Dar el Makhzen museum in Tangier and the Dar Si Said Museum in Marrakech), providing a chance for visitors to view them at close hand. Royal palaces (there is at least one in each major city) are generally recent in date but traditional in style, enclosed by extensive gardens and strictly out of bounds. Some sense of their scale may be glimpsed from their perimeters or when approaching a city by air.

Dynastic contributions

Compared with other architectural styles, Islamic design has remained relatively

unchanged over the centuries. Following the fall of Rome, urban development in Morocco did not begin again until after the Arab conquest. The Idrissid dynasty of the 8th to 10th centuries resumed building, establishing Fez as its capital.

During the Almoravid dynasty of the 11th and 12th centuries, when many Muslims were expelled from Spain, the brilliant civilisation of Andalusia took root in Morocco. It is thought that Abou Bakr founded Marrakech and his son, Ali Ben Youssef, built enormous fortifications at Taza, a city which, situated on the eastern approach to Fez (the Taza Gap),

Aït-Benhaddou.

was an important line of defence. Mosques were rebuilt, and domes, pillars and semicircular arches, together with plaster sculpture, were introduced.

The Almohads of the 12th and 13th centuries were prolific builders. Additions were made to Marrakech, most notably the walls. The power of masonry was the symbol of the period, and the Koutoubia Mosque in Marrakech and the Hassan Mosque in Rabat were both commissioned at this time.

The Merinid dynasty of the 13th to 15th centuries ushered in increasingly sophisticated work rather than particularly imposing buildings. The Merinids were responsible for most of the country's medersas.

Under the Saadians of the 16th and 17th centuries, Morocco became increasingly open to foreign influences. The Portuguese took control of coastal towns and built fortifications at Asilah, Safi and El Jadida. Art and architecture tended to repeat the styles of the past rather than innovate, although increasingly grandiose building schemes were commissioned by Ahmed el Mansour, who embellished Marrakech to a degree that impressed even a decadent Europe, and, particularly, by the great Alaouite Sultan Moulay Ismail at his new imperial capital of Meknes. Some 25km

Art Deco architecture in Tangier.

(15 miles) of wall were constructed around the city at Ismail's behest, along with a grandiose sequence of palaces and public works built using the forced labours of slaves and Christian captives.

Modern architecture

There was little further development in architecture until the French and Spanish protectorates, when European styles dominated the northern and coastal cities. Marshal Lyautey, the first French Resident-General, decreed that the European development of towns, to house the influx of European administrators, should be separate from the medinas so as to preserve the traditional civilisation. The new architecture,

combining French civic pomposity and Moorish motifs, was called 'Mauresque'. The 1920s even brought a smattering of Art Deco to Casablanca, Tangier and Marrakech. Sadly, most of the colonial villas of the Ville Nouvelle in Marrakech have been demolished to make space for large residential blocks, but good examples of Art Deco buildings can still be seen in Casablanca and Tangier.

Nowadays, the newest civic architecture is once again looking towards traditional Moroccan design for inspiration, but it is the Hassan II Mosque in Casablanca (open to non-Muslims; see page 166) that shows exactly what modern Moroccan craftsmen can achieve given enough funding.

Inaugurated in 1993 and costing more than US$750 million, the mosque is the largest in Morocco (and the third largest in the world). Though designed by a French architect, Michel Pinseau, the mosque was almost entirely the product of Moroccan craftsmen using (with

> *In Morocco, the tradition is for low buildings, so that the minaret of the mosque may easily dominate the skyline.*

the exception of Murano glass) Moroccan raw materials including granite from Tafraoute, marble from Agadir and cedar from the Middle Atlas. With some 10,000 craftsmen and apprentices labouring on the building, this single project boosted a huge revival of traditional Moroccan crafts.

RIADS

The traditional riad is designed to provide a haven for the senses, and a refuge from the crowded city streets outside. The name comes from *ryad*, the Arabic word for garden, referring to the leafy courtyard which typically forms the centrepiece of all riads, providing space and fresh air whilst also protecting the privacy of the building's inhabitants. Traditionally, these courtyards were planted with four orange or lemon trees, provided with a fountain, and their walls adorned with tile work lined with Qu'ranic inscriptions – a miniature oasis at the heart of an urban mansion.

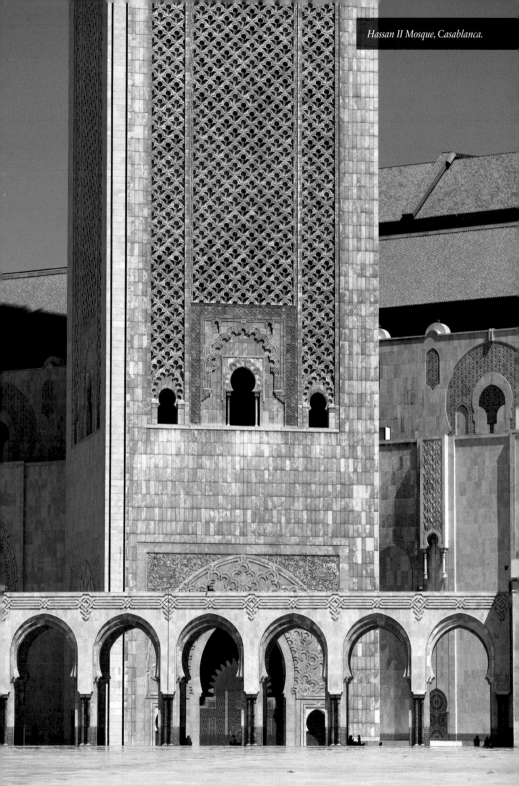

MOROCCAN INTERIORS

Saturated colour, gorgeously patterned tile work, rich rugs and textiles – Moroccan design has taken the world of interiors by storm.

Moroccan interior design is now firmly established across the globe thanks to a number of talented designers and architects and the thirst for new ideas. Today it is a synthesis of traditional crafts filtered and adapted by designers who started off decorating their own homes and quickly found there was an export market for their Mauresque lamps, cushions or *tadelakt* (polished plaster) fireplaces.

The concept of Moroccan design is relatively recent and is not so much Moroccan as a fusion of influences, ranging from the art of Matisse and Delacroix to Indian, Spanish and New Mexican traditions. Morocco is as much the crossroads as it is the foundation for this now internationally recognised design style.

Copyright? What's that?

The success of Moroccan style hinges on the adaptability and accessibility of its craftsmen. Sketch an idea and you can easily have someone make you a prototype. There is no such thing as copyright in Morocco, and with thousands of expatriates and creative individuals commissioning items to their own design, the Moroccan craft industry has one of the best and cheapest research and development facilities in the world. The rich exchange of ideas has ensured that thousands of craftsmen are still actively employed, and their craft is constantly adapting and developing to new markets. Design is a living activity; once it stagnates and ceases to adopt new ideas, it will die.

High ceilings, arched entrances, water features and simple, stylish decor are all classic features of riads – traditional Moroccan homes built around a central courtyard.

Keyhole arch leading from bathroom to bedroom in the Royal Mansour, Marrakech.

Arched doorways, clean lines, simple decor and splashes of colour are typical of Moroccan style.

Riad el Fenn's courtyard.

COURTYARD LIVING

Traditional riad design consists of rooms built around a square courtyard open to the sky, with a fountain in the centre and four trees – or 'gardens' – in each corner. Walls are thick, providing insulation against the heat of the sun and the cold of winter, and ceilings are high. Arranged around the courtyard are simple tiled or whitewashed rectangular salons, one on each side. Additional floors follow much the same pattern, with or without a surrounding veranda supported on arches.

Few riads extend beyond two floors; kitchens and bathrooms are usually tucked into corners. Windows look only into the courtyard, locking out the bustle of the medina and ensuring privacy. In order to provide additional light, large mirrors often cover the back walls of salons, reflecting light into the darker corners of the rooms. The furnishings are simple: carpets, wall-to-wall padded benches (banquettes) and low tables.

he Repose hotel, Rabat.

iad el Fenn, Marrakech.

Courtyard fountains provide the cooling sound of trickling water. Larger houses contain formal gardens with towering palms, banana and fig trees, alive with bird song.

TREKKING, BIKING AND SKIING

With a quarter of its land surface covered by spectacular mountains, Morocco offers endless possibilities for trekking and other adventurous pursuits.

Many of the most scenically beautiful and culturally interesting places in Morocco are inaccessible by car, meaning that trekking, walking and mountain biking often provide the most rewarding and revealing ways to see what many feel is the true Morocco. These remote regions reward visitors with their unhurried pace of life and a time-warped culture untouched by the modern world. They also offer the chance to spend time with local people, to eat traditional regional food and to see some of the most spectacular scenery that Morocco has to offer.

Many thousands of tourists visit Morocco each year specifically to explore the country's extensive mountain regions. Upland Morocco offers exceptional beauty and intriguing cultural encounters in equal measure, while an ever-growing list of local and foreign tour operators now offer well-organised adventure tours, making trips into the mountains easier to arrange than ever before.

Mountain trekking, characterised by multi-day hiking circuits, often incorporating one or

Mountain biking near Marrakech.

> Aït Bouguemez is referred to by locals as 'Happy Valley', as the people are always smiling and the idyllic landscapes are gentler than the rugged peaks and wild plains of other regions.

more summit climbs, attracts the lion's share of visitors, although other activities like **mountain biking**, **rock climbing** and **canyoning** are all growing in popularity. The Toubkal National Park in the High Atlas is by far the most visited region thanks to its proximity to Marrakech, while Jebel Sarhro, between the Dadès and Drâa valleys, Aït Bouguemez and the M'Goun massif,

north of the Dadès, and the Rif Mountains are also established trekking areas well worth exploring. Morocco's trekking main season runs roughly from May to October, when the snows have melted and high mountain passes and peaks are accessible, although there are also other winter trekking possibilities in more southerly locations such as Jebel Sarhro.

Trekking practicalities

Times have changed considerably since the first European expedition conquered Jebel Toubkal in 1923. Back then the notion of climbing a mountain for pleasure would have been an alien concept for High Atlas villagers, although nowadays there are plenty of mountain guides, mules to carry bags, and cooks available near all the major trailheads. As well as decent accommodation, some of the main trekking villages such as Imlil, Setti Fatma, Azilal and El Kelâa M'Gouna have an official *bureau des guides* or guide office. A number of excellent guides to trekking in Morocco are also available including *The Atlas Mountains* by Karl Smith, *Mountaineering in the Moroccan High Atlas* by Des Clark, and *Trekking in the Moroccan Atlas* by Richard Knight.

In all but the very busiest season you should be able to find a *guide de montagne* available for departure the following day. It is important to assess the need for a cook, and mule(s) to carry your bags, and ensure that you are clear on the accommodation and catering situation en route.

In the absence of other options, most trekking circuits require you to camp, although certain villages in the High Atlas offer basic lodgings. The Club Alpin Français (CAF) (www.caf-maroc.com) operates four refuges in the Toubkal National Park and has a list of recommended guides. The Kasbah du Toubkal (www.kasbahdutoubkal.com) is also an excellent resource; it has its own guide office in Imlil, provides a beautiful base at the foot of Jebel Toubkal and

Trekking through the M'Goun Gorge in the southern Atlas.

check that your guide is bona fide, however. Guides complete an extensive training course at Africa's only mountain guide training college at Tabant in the Aït Bouguemez Valley and carry a photo permit that you should insist on seeing (and checking that it hasn't expired – permits need to be renewed every three years). Discuss in detail your plans and objectives, agree on a price,

> *Most trekking centres have bureaux des guides, but good guesthouses in these areas are also a brilliant source of both information on hiking and assistance in terms of finding a guide.*

arranges treks into the surrounding region as well as ascents of Toubkal. Some regions have *gîtes d'étape*, village houses that serve hot meals and provide a bed for the night. Such houses are important to the rural economy; studies undertaken in areas of the High Atlas suggest that the revenue generated from lodging 20 hikers on a half-board basis is equivalent to a year's revenue from agriculture – a good enough reason in itself for staying in a *gîte* when possible.

Trekking without a guide is possible but not really advised even for experienced hikers, since guides serve not only as route finders but also as a vital means of communication with (and insight into) the mountain communities you'll be hiking through, (literally) opening doors in

It is recommended to bring your own basic first aid kit with you as the nearest decent hospital or clinic is likely to be as far away as Marrakech, or Tangier if you are in the Rif.

remote Berber villages and providing translation services and cultural interpretation en route. They also provide a potentially life-saving resource in the event of the sort of emergency that can befall even seasoned walkers in the event of adverse weather or an accidental fall.

Skiers at Oukaimeden.

As with all mountainous regions, the weather can be violently unpredictable – hot and sunny one minute, with blizzards and sub-zero temperatures the next – so ensure you pack with all eventualities in mind.

Reliable maps can be hard to find. There's a walking map of the Toubkal massif (available on Amazon), and it's also worth checking the tourist offices and bookshops of Marrakech and Chefchaouen to see if any local maps can be found.

The impact of trekking

With increasing numbers of trekkers, it is more important than ever to ensure that the local environment and people are affected only in positive ways by the influx. Many trekking centres

now have village associations, which use money earned from tourism to fund 4x4 ambulances, schools, health clinics and professional training for local men so that they can become licensed guides themselves. But trekkers must also play their part acting in a responsible manner. Cooking should be done on kerosene stoves rather than using precious wood, and, to prevent erosion and landslides, always follow existing tracks rather than creating new trails. All rubbish should be carried out (never simply buried or burned) and avoid buying plastic water bottles (bring a water purifier). If there is no toilet available, human waste should be buried well away from any watercourses, and avoid using any soap, detergent or even toothpaste close to natural water sources.

Where to go

The most visited of Morocco's hiking regions is the **Toubkal National Park** in the High Atlas, home to the country's highest peak, Jebel Toubkal (4,167 metres/13,671ft). Between late spring and early autumn, Toubkal, which is accessible from the village of Imlil, can be scaled in two days, although many walkers prefer to save the peak for the climax of a week's trekking – the 'Toubkal Circuit', starting from Imlil, which includes Tacheddirt, Azib Likemt, Lac d'Ifni, an ascent of Toubkal itself and a return to Imlil via the Toubkal refuge and Azib Tamsoult. Throughout much of the High Atlas Valley walks (as opposed to peaks) offer the best snapshot of rural life, which in many communities has hardly changed in centuries. The legendary hospitality of the Berber people and the sublime beauty of these villages leave a lasting imprint on all who visit.

Further to the east, the **M'Goun** (4,071 metres/13,356ft), Morocco's third-highest peak, sits in one of the most beautiful parts of the Central High Atlas, and the M'Goun massif circuit, of about six to seven days, is considered to be one of the toughest treks, with high peaks and wide rivers. It is also one of Morocco's most beautiful and least discovered. The stunning trailhead valley of Aït Bouguemez – the so-called 'Happy Valley' – is home to some of the country's best-preserved vernacular Berber architecture and is a hassle-free starting point for five- to 10-day circuits that scale M'Goun and explore the surrounding area. The highest point of the valley is around 4,000 metres (13,000ft) and it stretches for about 14km (9 miles). Head for this region during the summer months: temperatures rarely exceed 28°C (82°F), making it a welcome break from the heat of Marrakech, which lies some four hours (200km/124 miles) by road to the west.

One of the few valleys whose beauty compares to Aït Bouguemez is the **Vallée de la Tassaout**, accessed by the Tizi-n-Rogault pass from the M'Goun region. Villages in this valley are regarded as some of the finest in Morocco and offer interesting possibilities for hikers, whether they are camping or taking advantage of *gîte d'étape* accommodation in some of the hamlets along the Tessaout River. The Bouguemez and Tessaout valleys form two stages of a mammoth three-week High Atlas traverse that links this spectacular region with the Toubkal area, a programme offered by more and more foreign adventure tour operators.

Heading south

More peripheral, but no less striking, are the **Jebel Sarhro** and the **Jebel Siroua**, two mountain ranges, on the south side of the High Atlas. Both are accessible by tarmac road from Ouarzazate and offer adequate infrastructure in their respective trailhead towns of Nkob and Taliouine.

The Sarhro, which lies to the southeast of Ourazazate between the Drâa Valley and the Sahara is an isolated and savagely beautiful range of angular peaks and tabletop mesas and is also a fascinating area, particularly for nature-lovers, thanks to its vultures, Barbary falcons and other native species. Navigation difficulties and a profound shortage of water in the range make hiking here a challenge, so always engage a qualified local guide – *bureaux des guides* are found in the

Air charter is a growing business in Marrakech and Beni-Mellal, and the demands of skiers have made a considerable contribution.

main trekking bases of Kelâa M'Gouna, Boumalne de Dadès and N'Kob. The range offers the full gamut of possibilities, from multi-day circuits to hikes that head north to join the tarmac route around the town of El Kelâa M'Gouna, on the Ouarzazate–Er Rachidia road. Gite and refuge accommodation is practically non-existent here, so nights in the Sarhro are normally spent under canvas. Mules are also essential, as a large

amount of water and supplies usually need to be carried. Trekking in the Sarhro is best in winter, as in summer temperatures can be unbearable.

The Siroua region forms a volcanic bridge between the High Atlas and Anti-Atlas Mountains, and most treks in the region tackle the non-technical summit of Jebel Siroua (3,304 metres/10,839ft) to the north of the trailhead town of Taliouine. On a clear day this nublike summit offers some of the best views in Morocco, encompassing the High Atlas, the Anti-Atlas, the Jebel Bani and even the dunes of the Sahara. It is possible to stay in Berber houses,

Imlil is a popular centre for trekking.

and limited guide and mule services are available in Taliouine. The best place to enquire about guides and trekking routes is at the Auberge Souktana and the associated Yallahtrek agency. The best time to trek here is in the spring.

The Rif

Trekking in the Rif Mountains is fast becoming a popular alternative to the High Atlas. In addition to easier trails, the Rif has its own distinct and compelling culture, the Riffian people are some of the most fascinating in Morocco and trekking can be done virtually year-round – although it can get uncomfortably hot in summer. Most treks begin in the stunning blue-washed town of Chefchaouen, where guides and mules can be hired and routes planned. The local Association des Guides du Tourism de Chefchaouen is a good source of information, as is the Eco-Museum at the entrance to the Talassemtane National Park, and there are several tour operators outside Morocco that arrange trekking holidays (see page 323). The best trek takes four to five days. It begins in Chefchaouen and follows a wide loop at the base of Jebel Tissouka to the head of the Oued Farda, on to Akchour on the Oued Kelâa and 'God's Bridge'; from there an ascent of Jebel Azra and on through the Talassemtane National Park, ending in Bab Taza. If trekking alone and

On one of Oukaimeden's peaks.

without a guide in this region, it is essential to stick to well-used trails. Bear in mind that this is kif (cannabis) country and that unwitting hikers who accidentally walk through kif plantations – which are likely to be heavily guarded – will receive a very cold welcome.

Other mountain activities

Morocco's extensive network of *pistes* (unmetalled roads) makes the country ideally suited to **mountain biking**. Harsh gradients and poor surfaces in the Central High Atlas make off-road biking accessible only to experienced riders, but the Jebel Siroua, the Anti-Atlas Mountains and the Drâa Valley offer gentler possibilities. With the increasing popularity of mountain biking, a

few tour operators have been established, mainly based out of Marrakech, that rent good-quality bikes and arrange guided tours (see page 322). Local guides are highly recommended for all biking trips, for all the same reasons as they are for hiking and trekking. Abroad, the Cyclists' Touring Club (www.ctc.org.uk) in the UK and the International Bicycle Fund (www.ibike.org) in the US are useful sources of information.

Rock climbing is popular, particularly in the Todra Gorge and the Anti-Atlas Mountains around Tafraoute. Equipment hire and guide services may not be easy to come by, so organising a trip with a tour operator makes sense.

The Central Atlas Mountains around Aït Bouguemez are ideal for **canyoning**, but a shortage of skilled guides and good-quality equipment has left this in the hands of a few specialist (foreign) operators. Trips should be organised before you arrive in Morocco.

Skiing is not perhaps a sport you would normally associate with Morocco, but it is quite feasible in the High Atlas and Middle Atlas Mountains from December to April. Snow is by no means guaranteed, but the northern orientation of the one ski slope at Oukaimeden, about 75km (47 miles) south of Marrakech, the best-equipped resort, gives skiers the best chance of some downhill action. Services are rudimentary – there is one chair lift and a few drag lifts – and *piste* options are limited. The resort of Mischliffen in Ifrane also has decent skiing whenever there is snow. Off-*piste* skiing is possible in the Central High Atlas but can be life-threateningly dangerous without a qualified guide. The best routes are in the Aït Bougomez.

SAFE SKIING
Although it may be a nice idea to decide on the spur of the moment to ski in Morocco, with the intention of hiring equipment *in situ*, it is crucial to be properly equipped. In particular, personal, portable rescue beacons are absolutely essential. Small battery-operated radio transmitter/receiver devices of the type worn by cross-country and touring skiers in Europe cannot function in the Atlas, where rescue services are far away and, in any case, have no compatible electronic receiving equipment. You must also have adequate rescue and air repatriation insurance for skiing in the Atlas.

Sporting Passions

Morocco has surprisingly rich sporting traditions, being one of the traditional powerhouses of African football, as well as producing two of the world's greatest-ever Olympic runners.

Football is the nation's greatest passion. The Moroccan national football team, the Atlas Lions, was the first African team to reach the knockout stages of a World Cup in 1961 and the first African team to win a group in the 1986 World Cup before narrowly being beaten 1–0 by eventual runners-up West Germany. They also qualified for the World Cup finals in 1998 as well as winning the African Nations Cup in 1976 and the Arab Nations Cup in 2012. Leading Moroccan footballers have included Larbi Benbarek (The Black Pearl), Ahmed Faras, Mohammed Timoumi, Baddou Zaki and Mustapha Hadji. More recent exports include Marouane Chamakh, currently playing in the English Premier League with Crystal Palace after a spell at Arsenal. In rugby, Abdelatif Benazzi represented both Morocco and France, winning 78 caps for the French team and playing in three World Cups, including being a member of the French team that reached the 1999 World Cup Final.

Athletic prowess

It has been on the track, however, that Morocco has really excelled. Trailblazer for Moroccan athletics was the legendary Saïd Aouita, one of the greatest middle- and long-distance runners of all time, who won Olympic gold in the 5,000m in 1994 and at various times held world records in all distances between 1,500m and 5,000m. More recently, Aouita's exploits were rivalled by the great Hicham el Guerrouj – the so-called 'King of the Mile' – who won double Olympic gold in 2004 (in the 1,500m and 5,000m) as well as four world championship golds, whilst setting a string of world records throughout his career.

Women athletes have also made their mark. The hurdler Nawal el Moutawakel was not only the first Moroccan woman to win an Olympic gold (in 1984), but also the first African-born Muslim to do so. Hasna Benhassi won a silver medal at the 2004 Athens Olympics and silvers again at the World Athletics Championships of 2005 and 2007, and bronze at the Beijing Olympics in 2008.

Other leading Moroccan runners include Brahim Boutayeb and Khalid Skah, both of whom won Olympic gold in the men's 10,000m (in 1988 and 1992 respectively).

Morocco annually hosts what is described as the world's toughest foot race, the Marathon des Sables (www.marathondessables.co.uk). Founded in 1986, it is a gruelling seven-day, six-stage race covering between 200 and 250km (130–150 miles) across the desert and mountainous terrain of southern Morocco.

Tennis is also a sport that has captured the country's collective imagination since Younnes el

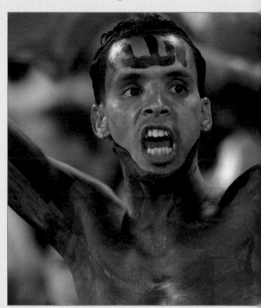

Moroccan football fan.

Aynaoui and Hicham Arazi both reached the quarterfinals of the Australian Open in 2000 – although no other Moroccan players have yet succeeded in matching their exploits. The Grand Prix Hassan II tournament, held in Casablanca, attracts top players from around the world.

In Morocco, golf is the game of kings, and the country has at least 12 royal golf courses as well as dozens of private golf clubs – there are over 10 courses in Marrakech alone. The country's major annual golf tournament is the King Hassan II Trophy, held in Agadir in March and attracting leading players from around the world, while in 2012 young golfing sensation Maha Haddioui became the first female Muslim to play on the professional golf circuit.

The Ziz Valley.

Medersa Bou Inania, Meknes.

The Anti-Atlas.

INTRODUCTION

A detailed guide to the entire country, with principal
sites cross-referenced by number to the maps.

Marrakech's Spice Square.

Travel in Morocco has come a long way since the days when Europeans needed to disguise themselves in *jellabas* and veils in order to penetrate anywhere beyond Tangier. Dusty old tomes on Morocco all contain photographs of their authors in native dress – though the writer Wyndham Lewis seemed to think this had more to do with a desire to dress up as Arabs than any real fear of attack.

In fact the naturally resourceful Berbers have proved the very opposite of their famously fierce image. Most have welcomed tourism and, particularly in the Atlas region, have also been quick to profit from it, often undermining at a local level the government's broader attempts to capitalise on big spending by foreign visitors.

Detail of Fez's Royal Palace.

Hotel development has increased on the Northwest Coast as well as in Essaouira and Agadir in the south, but, amazingly for a country with sandy beaches and reliable sunshine so close to Europe, Morocco has escaped the type of intensive development that has mushroomed elsewhere in the Mediterranean. The Moroccan government, reputedly seeking a better class of holidaymaker, has focused on Marrakech and pockets along the coast for up-market tourist development, with well-hidden, traditionally designed luxury hotels proliferating yearly.

But, despite long, blond, blue-skied beaches, fortified Portuguese fishing ports, lush oases in desert plains, and mountains offering trekking and skiing, the big draws remain the imperial cities of Fez, Meknes and Marrakech. Founded in the Middle Ages and expanded by succeeding dynasties, they contain superb examples of Islamic architecture and ways of living that have barely changed since medieval times.

Morocco's capital, Rabat, has a similar historic heritage but seems half-European by comparison, with Mauresque architecture and a conservative image. Here, more than anywhere, is a reminder that a large part of Morocco was governed by the French. Yet just 320km (200 miles) away lie the rolling dunes and palm oases of the south – landscapes that helped win acclaim for David Lean's classic film *Lawrence of Arabia*.

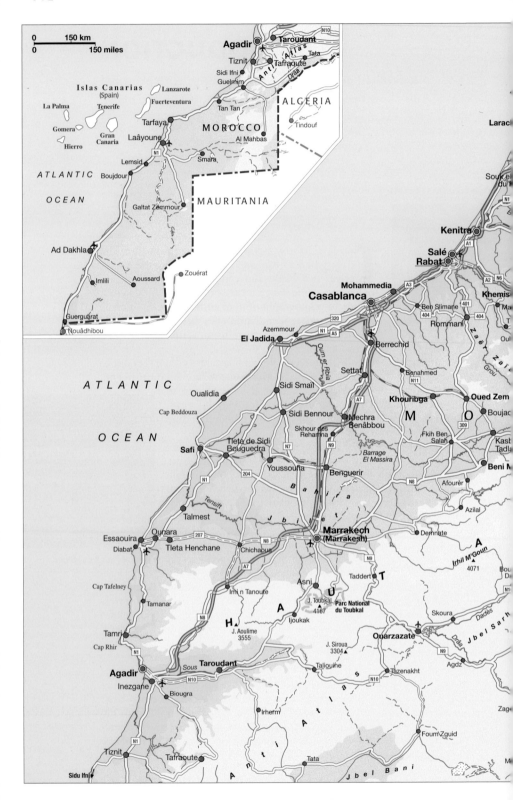

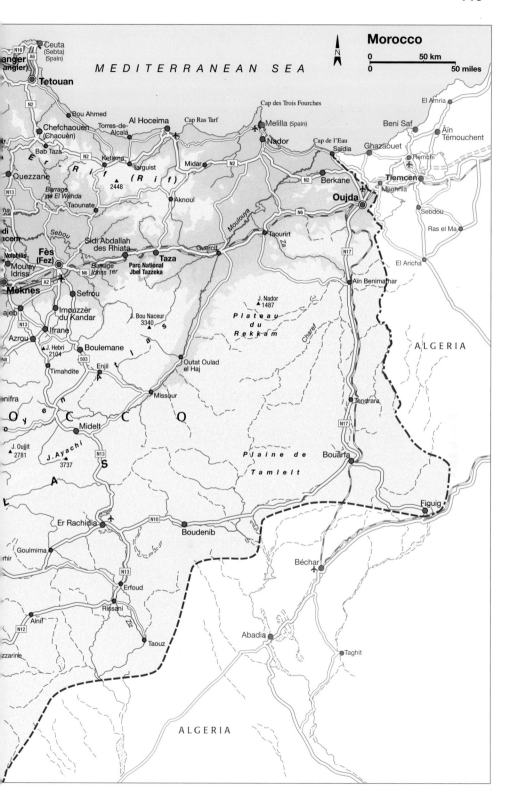

MEDITERRANEAN SEA

0   50 km
0   50 miles

N16 Ceuta
(Sebta)
(Spain)
anger
angier)
A6
Tetouan

El Amria

N2

Bou Ahmed
Cap des Trois Fourches
Al Hoceima
Cap Ras Tarf
Melilla (Spain)
Beni Saf
Chefchaouen
(Chaouèn)
Torres-de-
Alcalá
Nador
Âïn
Témouchent
Bab Taza
N2
Ketama
Cap de l'Eau
Saïdia
Ghazâouet
Remchi
Quezzane
Targuist
Midar
N2
Berkane
Tlemcen
Barrage
de El Wahda
2448
Er   Rif   (Rif)
N2
Maghnia
Oujda
Taounate
Aknoul
N6
Sebdou
Sebou
Taourirt
Ras el Ma
Sidi Abdallah
des Rhiata
Guercif
N13
El Aricha
Volubilis
Fès
(Fez)
Taza
Parc National
Jbel Tazzeka
N6
Barrage
Idriss 1er
N17
Aïn Benimathar
Moulay
Idriss
A2
Meknes
Sefrou
J. Nador
1487
Imouzzèr
du Kandar
J. Bou Naceur
3340
Plateau
du
Rekkam
N13
Ifrane
Azrou
J. Hebri
2104
Boulemane
N8
503
Enjil
Timahdite
Outat Oulad
el Haj
ALGERIA
Missour
nifra
Tendrara
Midelt
O   y   e   n   C   C   O
J. Oujjit
2781
J. Ayachi
3737
N13
Plaine de
Tamlelt
Bouârfa
N17
A
Figuig
Er Rachidia
N10
Boudenib
Goulmima
Béchar
N13
Erfoud
Rissani
Alnif
N12
Abadia
Taouz
Taghit
ALGERIA

Looking out over Tangier.

TANGIER

Located where Africa meets Europe, Tangier – legendary 'interzone', favourite hang-out for artists, writers and rock stars, compelling refuge for eccentric expats and international spies – is still one of the most vibrant cities in Morocco.

A rriving in **Tangier** , whether approaching from Spain and the sea, or over the hills from the south of Morocco, always sparks a frisson of anticipation. With its whitewashed houses tumbling over seven hills into the bright blue Mediterranean and the Straits of Gibraltar, and with Spain only 14km (9 miles) away, Tangier rests at the most northwestern tip of Morocco, and Africa. It has for millennia been a vital crossroads – between East and West, Africa and Europe, the Atlantic and the Mediterranean – and has adopted an eclectic and unique set of influences and styles.

Tangier's golden age

In its heyday, it was one of the most glamorous and exciting play-grounds for the international jet set and a mecca for artists, writers and musicians (see page 77). It was frequented by Matisse, Delacroix, Tennessee Williams, Cecil Beaton, William Burroughs, Allen Ginsberg, Truman Capote, Jack Kerouac, the Rolling Stones and Tallulah Bank-head. Brion Gysin, Paul Bowles and the British aristocrat David Herbert made the town their home, and Bar-bara Hutton, the Woolworth heiress, bought a house in the kasbah, where she held legendarily extravagant par-ties. Tangier's tax-free status also

attracted bankers and profiteers, and its 'international status' ensured it also became a haven for spies, arms dealers and exiles. Perhaps due to its unusual position and the influences of Europe that seep into the city on the breeze from Spain, Tangier has always been much more relaxed and liberal than the rest of Morocco, and this has attracted a raft of colourful and eccentric characters who discovered that they could reinvent themselves and revel in life lived on the decadent fringe, where anything went.

Main Attractions
Boulevard Pasteur
Place de France
Rue de la Liberté
Grand Socco
Church of St Andrew
Old American Legation
Petit Socco
Sidi Hosni
Kasbah Museum
Palais Mendoub

Walking through Tangier's medina.

When Tangier's international status was revoked six months after Moroccan independence in 1956, the removal of the city's free-port status – the basis of its prosperity – caused a sharp decline from which Tangier is only now recovering.

Vestiges of its former character still survive, however, and Tangier continues to exert a strong fascination on anyone with a literary or artistic bent. The famous bars it used to boast have nearly all closed, but others have now opened in their place, and Tangier retains a relaxed, faintly louche sort of air, always liveliest after dark when the lights come on and the city's night owls come out to play.

Tangier today

Tangier has long had a reputation for being slightly seedy, dangerous in parts, and rife with persistent touts and scam artists. This may have been true in the past, but Tangier has undergone a phoenix-like revival in recent years and is once again becoming a hip and vibrant destination. Soon after becoming king, Mohammed VI

kick-started a significant redevelopment of the city – notably to the Old Port, whose industrial shipping (and all the problems associated with it) has now been moved several kilometres outside the city, now replaced with a marina used solely for ferry passengers, sleek yachts and cruise ships.

Tangier's beautiful corniche (also known as Avenue Mohammed VI), left to fade over the years, has also had an attractive facelift, as has the central square, the Grand Socco; a new railway opened in 2003; and boutique hotels, riads and restaurants are cropping up across the city. All of this has improved Tangier's image considerably, but amazingly, its decadent, edgy and artistic allure remains.

Europeans have long been drawn to Tangier for its weather. In summer it rarely becomes unbearably hot, and it stays warm well into October. Even when it is cold and wet there are always some hours of sunshine during the day (be warned, though, midwinter nights can be very cold and damp).

A draw for Spanish and British tourists and expats, including day-trippers

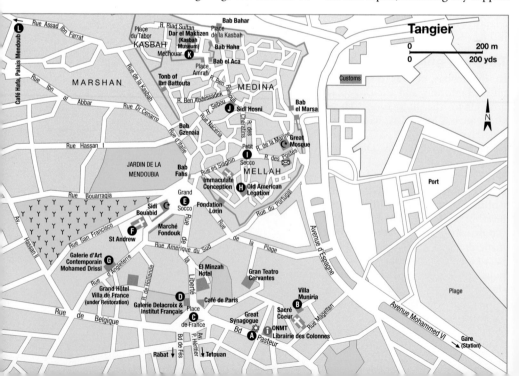

from Tarifa or Algerciras in Spain, Tangier is primarily a summer resort for Moroccans, including migrant workers travelling to and from Europe. On summer evenings the corniche and the streets between Boulevard Pasteur and the Grand Socco are thronged with families, young couples and groups of kids '*faisant le boulevard*' – a scene that could be anywhere in southern Europe.

Orientation

Like most Moroccan cities, Tangier is divided into the a medina and a ville nouvelle (new town). Tangier's medina, particularly its kasbah, is home to riad *maisons d'hôte*, some famous houses, the Petit Socco and the Kasbah Museum. The Grand Socco, just outside the medina walls, stands at the divide between old and new towns, with the Palais Mendoub on its northern side. To the west, just outside the medina, lies the beautiful Quartier Marshan and along the winding coastal road west is the Old Mountain, where many of Tangier's most famous expats used to live in atmospheric colonial villas. Still further out are Cap Spartel and the Caves of Hercules. The port and town beach lie to the east of the medina.

Boulevard Pasteur

Tangier's Ville Nouvelle has many places of interest, unlike most other villes nouvelles in Morocco. Heart of the district is the **Boulevard Pasteur** Ⓐ (also known as Avenue Pasteur), which starts at the southern end of the area, running up from Boulevard Mohammed V and the central post office. To its east, on the ocean side, streets containing small hotels wind steeply down to the sea, corniche, beach bars and the port; on the other side, inland, are shops, restaurants, nightclubs and bars. The new railway station is on the outskirts of town, at the end of Avenue de Tantan.

The main banks and the **tourist office** (No. 29) are on the boulevard, and the building at No. 27 houses the **Great Synagogue**, and at No. 54 you'll find the wonderfully restored **Librairie des Colonnes** bookshop, long a literary and intellectual focal point

The Grand Socco.

for the likes of Peter Bowles, Jean Genet and Mohammed Choukri. Further along is the perfumier **Madani**, where as well as finding popular Arab scents such as musk and amber you can have your own perfume specially tailor-made.

Just off Boulevard Pasteur, on the Rue de Salah Eddine et Ayoubi, is the wonderful Art Deco **Gran Teatro Cervantes**, once an important theatre and now sadly in a state of near-ruin; proposed renovations having been repeatedly stalled due to the failure of Moroccan and Spanish states to agree on how best to proceed with restoration. Also off Boulevard Pasteur, heading towards the sea on the Rue Magellan, is the **Villa Muniria** . The quaint Tanger Inn, attached to the Villa Muniria – setting for the 'Psychedelic Summer' of 1961 (see page 80), and where William Burroughs wrote *The Naked Lunch* – is still going. Burroughs wrote his novel in Room 9 of the hotel and David Cronenberg's film of the book was shot in a studio mock-up of it. The room concerned, which has barely changed since

The Teatro Cervantes, in need of renovation.

Burroughs's time here, was recreated in painstaking detail.

Continuing west, Boulevard Pasteur joins Avenue Mexique, the main shopping street, at the **Place de France** ●, an animated circus containing the 1920s **Café de Paris**, patronised by Jean Genet, Tennesse Williams, the Bowleses and a smattering of diplomats and spies.

Along Rue de la Liberté

On the northern side of the Place de France, at the beginning of Rue de la Liberté is the **Galerie Delacroix** ● (free), a small venue containing works by Eugène Delacroix, the French painter who toured North Africa in 1832, as well as interesting temporary exhibitions. The gallery forms part of the lively **Institut Français**, which hosts numerous exhibitions, literary events and films-screenings films, (check http://if-maroc.org/tanger for latest events). It is also home to the **Salle Beckett**, a venue for good French theatre and international films.

A few steps further north, on the other side of Rue de la Liberté, is El Minzah (see page 299), one of Tangier's grand old hotels, originally built by the fourth Marquis of Bute. Constructed in a Hispano-Moorish style, the Minzah was once the heart and soul of expat Tangier. Today, its former glamour has faded, but it is still a good place to go for a drink or a swim. A discreet entrance off the street precedes an elegant lobby leading to a tiled open courtyard, terrace, pool and spa.

Around the Grand Socco

Some 200 metres/yards further north, at the top of Rue de la Liberté, is the **Grand Socco (Place du 9 Avril)** ●, a large circular-shaped sloping square ringed by palm trees and cafés. It used to be the main market square and is still a bustling gathering point, where women come to sell bread and men sell second-hand clothes and other bits and pieces. In the evenings it forms the centrepiece of Tangier's convivial paseo, where people stroll and mingle, and a multitude of goods for sale are laid out on the ground.

Overlooking the Grand Socco is the recently restored Art Deco Cinema Rif, which screens old and new movies, and the colourfully tiled minaret of the **Sidi Bouabid mosque**, the first mosque (1917) to be built outside Tangier's old walls. On the north side of the socco is Bab Fahs, the main, horseshoe-shaped gate into the medina.

Spreading away to the northwest of the square are the extensive **Mendoubia Gardens**, always busy towards dusk with strolling couples, families and children, while immediately south of the square is one of Tangier's main market areas, the **Marché Fondouk**. Small shops, not much larger than cupboards, sell everyday items such as *babouches*, cooking pots and clothing. Halfway along, through a gap lined by women crouched over bunches of mint, coriander and fattened hens for sale, is one of Tangier's three food markets,

selling spices, vegetables, cheeses, olives, meat and eggs.

North towards the Kasbah

Running north off the socco, **Rue d'Italie** – steep with broad steps on either side – leads directly up to the **kasbah**, passing on the way the old **British telegraph office**. During the international era all the European powers had their own communications systems, and it was through the telegraph and post offices that Moroccan nationalists gleaned news of events in the French and Spanish zones in the early 20th century.

A turning into the medina off Rue d'Italie leads to the **Tomb of Ibn Battouta** (turn right at first junction and look for the green doors), the 14th-century Arab geographer and traveller who was born in Tangier (*see box*). The modest tomb, dimly lit and draped in a green cloth, is visited by pilgrims.

British legacy

Running off the southwest corner of the Grand Socco, **Rue d'Angleterre**, as its name suggests, is where you'll

Kasbah Museum.

IBN BATTOUTA

Tangier's most famous son is probably the 14th-century Arab geographer and traveller Ibn Battouta. He is commemorated, appropriately, in the name of one of the main ferries between Morocco and Spain. He was born in Tangier in 1304, and at the age of 21 set off on a pilgrimage to Mecca. But his intended trip of around six months became a 29-year journey, in which he vowed never to travel the same route twice. He ventured east to India and China, down the coast of East Africa to Somalia and what is now Tanzania, and through the Sahara Desert to Niger and Mali. On the way, he stayed in religious colleges or with local rulers and holy men.

Upon his return to Morocco, in 1354, he related his adventures to the Sultan of Morocco and was asked to dictate an account of his journeys to a young scribe called Ibn Juzayy. The account, which weaves observations, chunks of history told to him by scholars and kings, anecdotes and personal opinions, plus lines of poetry added by the scribe, evolved into the book known as El Rihla (The Travels). Partly a work of devotion, Battouta's Rihla was also a fascinating account of geography, customs and natural history as well as his own adventures. In the 19th century it was translated into French, German and English, and became a travel classic.

Walter Harris's tombstone in St Andrew's cemetery.

Walking down one of Tangier's hills.

find the main mementoes of British history in Tangier. Close to the square, the Anglican church of **St Andrew** , completed in 1894, was built to serve British expatriates. Inside, Islamic features – delicate stucco tracery, thin pencil pillars, Kufic script and keyhole arches – combine with English village-church trappings – pews and hassocks, copies of the Book of Common Prayer and, on the wall, an order of hymns and a flower-arranging rota.

In the graveyard the church's Muslim caretaker will point out the grave of Walter Harris, a famous correspondent for the London *Times* and devoted Moroccophile, who wrote many books on the country, including the classic *Morocco That Was*. His tombstone reads: 'He loved the Moorish people and was their friend.' Other notable tombs include those of 'Caid' Harry McLean, an Englishman appointed to train the Sultan's army, and Emily, 'Cherifa' of Ouezzane, a 19th—century English governess who met the Chereef of Ouezzane in Tangier. Their romance led to marriage, though they divorced after 14 years and she went

on to write a book about her life. One of the latest of the colourful expatriates to be buried in the cemetery was David Herbert (see page 115), who presided over expatriate life in Tangier until his death in 1995.

Further down the road, at No. 52, the old British Consulate building has been turned into the **Galerie d'Art Contemporain Mohamed Drissi** G (Tue–Sat 9am–1pm, 2–6pm; free), displaying works by Moroccan and foreign artists.

Close to the gallery, on Rue de Hollande, is the **Grand Hôtel Villa de France**, where Henri Matisse stayed and painted on two fruitful visits to Tangier in 1912 and 1913 (see page 122). Sadly, the dilapidated but still elegant hotel was closed in 1992 for restorations, which continue to this day.

Into the medina

Rue es Siaghin (Silversmiths' Street), to the right as you pass through the Fahs Gate (Bab Fahs), leads deep into the medina, passing the Spanish **Church of the Immaculate Conception** and the old *mellah* (Jewish)

HISTORY OF TANGIER

Tangier has a long history of foreign interest due to its strategic geographical location. The Carthaginians established it as a trading port in the 5th century BC. Next came the Romans in the 1st century BC, followed by the Vandals, Byzantines and Visigoths. By 705 the Arabs had invaded. Tangier prospered under the Arab dynasties until the 14th century, when Morocco's North and Northwest Coast became infested with pirates, which prompted the Portuguese to intervene. Having already captured Ceuta, they went on to seize Tangier. But resistance was strong, and in 1661, after two centuries, the Portuguese finally handed Tangier over to Britain.

Britain realised that Tangier was a covetable asset. Even Samuel Pepys, who unkindly described it as an 'excrescence of the earth', reckoned it would be 'the King's most important outpost in the world'. But they were also unable to repel native opposition and withdrew in 1684. From then on, Britain's prime objective in Tangier was to uphold the authority of the Sultan and prevent other European powers from colonising it. But Europe was equally keen to control the city, and by the 19th century it was overrun by diplomats.

The Treaty of Algeciras made Tangier officially an international zone, and in 1923 another statute handed it to France, Spain, Britain, Portugal, Sweden, Holland, Belgium and Italy.

quarter – the Jews being the city's traditional dealers in silver.

Housed in an old synagogue on nearby Rue Touahine, the **Fondation Lorin** (Sun–Fri 11am–1pm, 3–7pm; donation) has a fascinating collection of old photographs, prints, newspapers and posters from Tangier's past. It also holds temporary art exhibitions.

Old American Legation

The wonderful **Old American Legation** Ⓗ (museum Mon–Fri 10am–1pm, 3–5pm; by appointment at weekends; donation), also off the beginning of Rue es Siaghin, in Rue d'Amerique, is less easy to find (turn right just past No. 77 on Rue es Siaghin); an easier approach is from Rue du Portugal, outside the medina's walls. Although the building had served Britain's New World colonies since 1684, the Sultan gave the legation to the US in 1821. Morocco was the first country to recognise US sovereignty, and this legation was the first American government property outside the United States.

Today the elaborately decorated 17th- and 18th-century interior is used for concerts and exhibitions. Its permanent collection contains fine paintings, lithographs and photographs of Morocco, including work by the French painter Eugène Delacroix and contemporary Moroccan painters such as R'bati and Hamri, one by Yves St Laurent, and various attractive Naive and Impressionist works. There are also exhibits of letters written between George Washington and Sultan Moulay Ben Abdallah, a room dedicated to Paul Bowles, and exhibitions of paintings by American artists resident in Morocco. French- and English-speaking tours are conducted.

Petit Socco

The **Petit Socco** Ⓘ, now called Souk Dakhil, at the end of Rue es Siaghine used to be the site on which the forum of Roman Tingis once stood. Much later, it became one of the most infamous meeting places in the city, and the square still retains some of the low-life glamour that drew the likes of William Burroughs and Brion Gysin. It was here, on the terrace of the Café Central, that Burroughs supposedly gained inspiration for *The Naked Lunch*, although the cafés are now full of men watching television, playing cards and drinking coffee, rather than the writers or shady characters of the past.

North to the Kasbah

From the Petit Socco, **Rue des Cheratins** and **Rue Ben Raisouli**, festooned with souvenirs, meander up to through the northern medina towards the Kasbah. The area here is home to some of the most sought-after properties in Tangier. Barbara Hutton had a house here, **Sidi Hosni** Ⓙ, as did Richard Hughes, author of *A High Wind in Jamaica*. To see where Hutton held her famous parties, climb the stairs of Café Ali Baba (it has a psychedelic mural on the outside wall), overlooking Sidi Hosni's terraces. Before Hutton, Sidi Hosni (named after a

TIP

For one of the best views over Tangier, visit the salon de thé, Le Relais de Paris (see page 310), on the first floor of Dawliz, opposite the Grand Hôtel Villa de France. Its terrace overlooks the medina, port and bay – a scene that would have been enjoyed by Matisse from his room in the nearby hotel opposite.

In the medina.

Matisse in Tangier

Perhaps more than any other artist, Matisse is most closely associated with Tangier, managing to capture its true essence of light and mystery.

In 1941 Matisse told Pierre Courthion: 'The chief goal of my work is the clarity of light.' And it was the special quality of light that Matisse was seeking when he arrived in Tangier with his wife Amélie on 29 January 1912 on the packet ship SS Ridjani from Marseilles. He was also inspired by the legendary Orientalist painter of Morocco, Eugène Delacroix, who lit the flame of artistic passion for the unique light, colours and cultural landscapes of Morocco. Matisse excitedly stated that he had 'found landscapes in Morocco exactly as they are described in Delacroix's paintings.' Unfortunately when they got there it had been raining continuously for 15 days, and to Matisse's consternation continued to do so for most of February. They were installed in the Grand Hôtel Villa de France. Their room looked over the Grand Socco, St Andrew's church, the medina and the beaches along the bay, all of which Matisse

Matisse's Window at Tangier.

drew and painted. Because of the rain, his first painting in Tangier was of a vase of irises.

Shortly after his arrival, Matisse's old friend the Canadian painter James Wilson Morrice landed from Montreal and checked into the same hotel. They had not known of each other's travel plans but they renewed their friendship and, once the rain stopped, explored the city together, setting up their easels in the medina.

Amélie returned to Paris in March; Matisse followed two weeks later after he had finished a painting. The rains produced luxuriant foliage, and Matisse gained access to a private garden attached to the Villa Brooks, where he worked for over a month on Park In Tangier. He loved the intensity of colour in the lush vegetation, and when his friends back in Paris exclaimed delightedly over his painting he demurred, 'That's not how it is, it's better than that!'

He did three paintings of a Jewish girl called Zorah whom he found in the medina. He had to obtain permission from the hotel, which let him use a studio where the guests would not see her entering; it was easy to find male models and he did a number of studies of Sudanese mercenary soldiers as well as Riff tribesmen.

The second visit

Inspired by the work he achieved in Tangier, Matisse returned on 8 October and stayed once again at the Hôtel Villa de France. He only intended to stay a short while, but his work went so well that he changed his mind. Amélie joined him in November, travelling there with their mutual friend, the painter Charles Camoin; together the artists painted and sketched in the streets and cafés.

Morocco was a turning point for Matisse. Coming at the end of his Fauvist period, it ushered in the glorious decorative canvases that are his best-known work. He wrote: 'The trips to Morocco helped me to accomplish the necessary transition and enabled me to renew closer contact with nature than the application of a living but somewhat limited theory such as Fauvism had turned into made possible.'

Though he never returned to Tangier, its influence stayed with him. The wooden screens and embroidered wall hangings he collected became key motifs in many of his subsequent paintings. Elements of the work he did in Morocco are present even in his last great work, the 1951 chapel at Vence where the robes of his figures echo those of Zorah, all those years before.

local holy man buried on the site) had belonged to Walter Harris, correspondent of the London *Times* (see page 120), and then to the American diplomat Maxwell Blake. Hutton's bid for the property beat that of Generalissimo Franco.

Set within a further circle of walls, the Kasbah comprises the former sultan's palace and administrative quarter. The old palace, the **Dar el Makhzen** , was occupied as recently as 1912 by the abdicate Sultan Moulay Hafid, though by all accounts his stay was uncomfortable. It now provides a home for the Kasbah Museum (Wed–Mon 9am–noon, 1.30–4pm), on the west side of the *mechouar* (courtyard), worth visiting for the rich decoration alone, including original arabesques and *zellige*.

Exhibits, arranged in rooms lining the sides of two courtyards, include carpets, ceramics from Fez and Meknes, costumes, musical instruments, household implements and jewellery. The kitchen quarters contain an archaeological collection, including a mosaic from Volubilis.

Opposite the Kasbah Museum is a charming little café, Le Salon Bleu.

Outside the palace is the traditional *mechouar* (parade ground). From here (accessed via the palace's Andalusian Gardens), **Rue Riad Sultan** curls left around the ocean side of the kasbah to pass a door leading to an upstairs café, **Le Détroit**, once the most exclusive restaurant in Tangier, where owner and writer Brion Gysin entertained an elite circle of friends. The exclusivity may have gone, but the fine views remain, with a clear sight of **York House**, the machicolated residence of the English governors in the 17th century and now a dilapidated private house.

The Palais Mendoub and Quartier Marshan

From Place du Tabor, Rue de la Kasbah (outside the medina) leads down to Rue d'Italie (see page 119), while a five-minute walk west along **Rue Assad ibn Farrat** and **Rue Haj Mohammed Tazi** (also reached by taking a No. 1 or No. 11 bus) is the **Palais Mendoub**  (closed to the

Turn left as you leave the Palais Mendoub and left again after the hospital to reach Café Hafa, a secluded cliff-top café with far-reaching views over the Straits to Spain.

Tangier at night.

TIP

If you are travelling back to Tangier after exploring the coast east of the city, stop for a fish supper at the Café Lachiri, overlooking the river at Ksar es Seghir. Its superb fish and shellfish platter is excellent value.

public), the former Tangier home of the late American billionaire, publisher and Arabist, Malcolm Forbes.

This large white villa was for many years devoted to a museum of military miniatures, a passion of Forbes. It was here that Forbes held his much-publicised and unbelievably lavish 70th birthday in 1989. The event cost US$2 million and the entertainment included 600 drummers, acrobats and belly dancers and 300 Berber horsemen. Guests included Henry Kissinger, a Getty or two, and Elizabeth Taylor, who also honeymooned here with her eighth husband, Larry Fortensky.

Neighbouring the Mendoubia Gardens is the exclusive **Quartier Marshan**, where the iconic, though unassuming, Café Hafa can be found. Perched on a leafy hillside with steep and narrow terraces descending to the coastal road, the poignant allure of Café Hafa is its extraordinary view of Spain; on a clear day the European neighbour seems close enough to touch. At rickety blue tables old and young men sit, listening to music,

drinking coffee and gazing wistfully at Europe. In the late afternoon, this is a magical spot.

Town beach

Tangier's town beach is a vibrant place, particularly in the summer when it is thronged with Moroccans escaping the heat of Marrakech and Fez. It is lined with breezy beach bars and has wonderful historical and literary connections too, with legendary venues like **The Windmill**, where Joe Orton used to hang out, and **The Sun Beach**, where it is said that Tennessee Williams drafted *Cat on a Hot Tin Roof*.

West of Tangier

To the west of Tangier, the lovely headland of **Cap Spartel** ❷ offers alternative beaches to Tangier's well-populated sands and, if the wind is blowing from the east, more sheltered conditions for sunbathing (but be warned that the strong currents are dangerous for children).

The most interesting route to the cape is via the S701 Mountain Road,

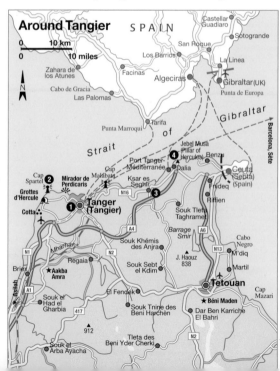

Around Tangier

passing exclusive properties belonging to Morocco's royal family and a residence of the king of Saudi Arabia. The Old Mountain itself is, in the words of Joe Orton, 'a replica of a Surrey backwater: twisty lanes, foxgloves, large pink rambling roses, tennis courts and gardens watered by sprinklers.'

The road loops the headland, passing the turn for the Cap Spartel lighthouse, erected by foreign diplomats in the 1870s, and a series of sandy bays, some with makeshift cafés. A little further along are the **Caves** (**Grottes**) **of Hercules** (9am–sunset), rock chambers inhabited in prehistoric times, and in the international era used for parties – including one hosted by Cecil Beaton, who served hashish and sea-cooled champagne. Beyond the caves, on a headland with incredible views, is the up-market **Hotel Mirage**, another Tangier institution.

Further on, the road passes the Roman site of Cotta, with the sparse remains of a small temple and a bathhouse dating from the 2nd and 3rd centuries. Also here is the surface terminal for a pipeline taking

natural gas from Algeria to Cordoba in Spain. Continuing down the coast, a magnificent beach stretches for 45km (28 miles) to the fortified town of **Asilah** (see page 142). A left turn before the main road to Rabat leads back to Tangier via the town's prison, home to a fair number of Western drug smugglers.

Taxi in the medina.

East of Tangier

East of Tangier lies another landmark headland, **Cap Malabata** (also with a lighthouse and a pleasant café), and, further east along the road to Ceuta, a string of good beaches, beginning with **Oued Dalian** and **Plage des Amiraux** (signposted), just a few kilometres from Tangier, and then, about 28km (17 miles) from the city, **Ksar es Seghir** ❸ with its pretty fort overlooking the mouth of a small river. A few kilometres beyond Ksar es Seghir is the new commercial shipping and ferry port, moved from Tangier in 2010. Beyond, the beautiful winding coastal road continues, past the 'Pillar of Hercules', **Jebel Musa** ❹, to the Spanish enclave of Ceuta.

Vast sandy beach at Cap Spartel.

LIFE AFTER DARK

Perhaps more than any other Moroccan town or city, Tangier has the most concentrated nightlife, and it certainly keeps the latest hours; many restaurants and clubs don't open until 9pm and close as late as 4am. It was once famous for its bars, in particular the Safari, Les Liaisons and The Parade, though none of these remain, and the nightlife scene of modern Tangier is nowhere near as characterful as that of yesteryear.

A bar's success depended upon the personality of its owners, and in the late 1940s and early '50s Tangier attracted its fair share of charismatic hosts and hostesses. Dean's Bar, then more like a fashionable club than a bar, is still running on Rue Amerique du Sud, but the eponymous Dean, who began his career as the lover of a rich and titled English gentleman, has long gone and it is now pretty much a dive.

Another iconic watering hole is Caid's Bar in El Minzah Hotel, named after Caid Harry McLean, which became the heart of Tangier's nightlife during both world wars. It is said to be the original inspiration for Rick's Café in Casablanca and definitely exudes a certain class, reminiscent of a bygone era. Other atmospheric bars, usually selling good cheap beer and tapas, are Chico's and Rubi's, both in the Ville Nouvelle.

THE RIF

Morocco's Mediterranean coast is backed by the rugged Rif Mountains, a neglected but beautiful region with stunning coastal drives and historic towns.

The Rif, known as the *bled es siba* (land of lawlessness), stretches from Cap Spartel to the border with Algeria and is one of Morocco's most strikingly beautiful regions. The Rif has for centuries been influenced by Spain, as an Andalusian style of architecture in the towns, a common fluency in Spanish and foods such as paella, tortilla and tapas all testify. Many of the Andalusian Muslims who fled Spain in the 15th and 16th centuries settled here, and from 1912 until 1956 the Rif, plus the short stretch of Atlantic coast south to Larache excluding Tangier, formed the bulk of the Spanish zone. Until this time the Riffians had existed outside the authority of the Sultan. Indeed, it is from the Rif that opposition towards the nation's rulers has traditionally stemmed, meaning that the region has long been ignored while the rest of the country has benefited from reform and development.

Following an assassination attempt that originated in the Rif, Hassan II was hostile to the region for his entire reign, and it was left to King Mohammed VI to overcome years of tension by making a tour of the north within months of his succession.

After decades of neglect, the region is finally receiving long overdue infrastructre investment. Motorways have now been built between the airport just south of Tangier and Jebel Musa and also between Ceuta and Tetouan. Another motorway connecting Fez with Oujda also opened in 2011, significantly improving access to the far east of the region.

The king's 'Plan Azur' is also intended to create a huge development near Saidia that will stretch along 6km (4 miles) of coast. For now, however, the entire coastline remains a magical place to explore and soak up a mixture of laid-back Mediterranean life and intriguing regional traditions.

Main Attractions

Ceuta
Cabo Negro
Tetouan
Chefchaouen
Al Hoceima National Park
Melilla
Zegzel Gorge

Tetouan.

Routes through the Rif

There are three main passages through the Rif. The N13 from Chefchaouen via Ouezzane (see page 135) skirts the range, offering the easiest driving for those wanting only an impression of the Rif en route to Fez, but offering plenty of impressive scenery along the way. A more spectacular route, however, is the R509 running over the mountains south from Ketama. Known as the Route de l'Unité, this was begun in 1957 just after independence in order to link Morocco's former French and Spanish zones, It was also the first road to be built from north to south across the Rif, following the old caravan route to Fez and constructed by voluntary national effort initiated by Mehdi Ben Barka, a prominent figure in the nationalist left. The other main thoroughfare through the mountains is the equally beautiful R505 which branches south off the N2 at **Kassita**, eventually arriving at Taza on the edge of the Middle Atlas (see page 223) after a drive though naked white hills.

Red mountains

The Rif Mountains rise sharply from the Mediterranean to the east of Tangier. Their foothills lie close to Tetouan, where, contrasting strongly with the low hills and gentle colours of the Tangier hinterland, the landscape is impressively rugged.

To the immediate east, trees cloak the limestone peaks as you climb towards the central Mount Tidiquin, the highest in the Rif range at 2,448 metres (8,031ft). Squat holm- and cork oaks give way to high cedar forests and the kif plantations of Ketama. The further east you travel, the redder the hue of the mountain range, a change that strikes the traveller on the road to Al Hoceima where the terrain becomes denuded and barren. From Al Hoceima to Oujda on the Algerian border, south of a fertile coastal plain the land is desolate, crossed by cracked river beds.

On the more inviting coast directly below the range are some of the finest sandy beaches to be found in Morocco. An increasing number of large hotels and holiday villages are

Pottery for sale in Chefchaouen.

fed by the international airport at Tangier and by well-off Moroccans from Fez and elsewhere, who flock to the area, but it is still possible to find gorgeous, unspoilt, secluded beaches between the pockets of development. Some of the country's best fish restaurants are also found along this stretch of shoreline. The resorts include M'diq, Cabo Negro (which also has an impressive golf course) and Martil.

Despite the recent development and investment, however, the area remains poor, and its inhabitants still complain of economic deprivation and neglect by central government. This helps to explain why the illegal cultivation of kif continues to be a major issue for the authorities (see box). A suitable climate, remoteness from Rabat and proximity to Spain and Gibraltar (the latter a key base in the trans-Mediterranean drugs trade) all conspire to make the region a perfect base for the cultivation of this illegal crop.

Heading east

There are now two routes east from Tangier. The N2 loops inland through a series of small villages and is a busy thoroughfare for locals. *Jibala* women dressed in typical pom-pom sombreros, red-and-white striped *ftouh* and coloured shawls, often rigged into a papoose to contain a baby, hold covered dishes of crumbling white cheese (either salted or unsalted) or honey. Men tout amethysts and pottery, and small boys offer strawberries, pine nuts, walnuts or whatever else can be harvested for sale.

Alternatively, the A4 motorway takes you from just south of Tangier to Jebel Musa, which on clear days affords views to the other 'pillar' of Hercules on the Spanish coast. It is at Jebel Musa that the Mediterranean officially meets the Atlantic. From here, the route grades down to a secondary road for a brief drive into Ceuta where you can again pick up the A6 motorway all the way to Tetouan, or take the N13 along the coast, which is more scenic.

Ceuta

If nothing else, **Ceuta ❶** would be worth a visit just for the surreal

TIP

In the Rif, you should expect to be stopped by customs officers and police looking for hashish, especially east of Tetouan and Chefchaouen, towards the kif-growing areas around Ketama. Roadblocks can be tiresome, as are the antics of the roadside drug sellers, who try to force cars to stop by leaping into their path.

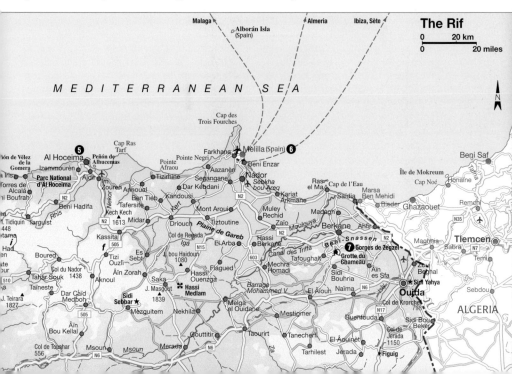

A tiled facade characteristic of Tetouan.

feeling of having arrived unexpectedly in Spain – and you could not be anywhere else, with its Iberian banks, restaurants, supermarkets and inhabitants.

There's more to Ceuta that mere curiosity value, however. This is one of the region's more appealing towns, perched on a tiny peninsula, with every inch of space crammed with grand Spanish buildings and florid houses. The town is also of considerable historical significance, not least for being the Moors' point of embarkation for their conquest of Spain.

Plaza de Africa and the walls

Ceuta's central square, the Plaza de Africa, is beautifully laid out, with mature palms, commanding architecture and cafés. On the south side of the square rise the two orange-and-white towers of the 17th-century **Cathedral Santa Maria de la Asunción** (where you'll also find a small museum), while on the opposite side of the square is the **Santuario de Nuestra Señora de Africa**, containing the 15th-century wooden effigy of Ceuta's patron saint who is also, oddly, its mayoress – an office granted in perpetuity by a unanimous vote of the municipality.

Immediately west of the plaza the Avenida Gonzales Tablas are the impressive **Los Muralles Reales** (Royal Walls), a complex tangle of fortifications dating all the way back to the 8th century. Inside the walls, the attractive **Museo de los Muralles Reales** (daily 10am–2pm, 5–9pm) hosts regularly changing art exhibitions.

East of the Plaza

East of the Plaza, off Avenida Alcaide Sánchez Prados, the **Museo de la Basílica Tardorromana** (Mon–Sat 10am–1pm, 5–7.30pm, Sun 11am–3pm; free) features a striking subterranean archaeological museum inserted into the remains of a 4th-century Roman-era basillica. Further southeast, down Paseo de Colón, the **Museo de la Legión** (Mon–Sat 10am–1.30pm; closed Sunday1st Sat of the month; free) offers an interesting look at the history of the Spanish Legion,

THE HASHISH INDUSTRY

The Rif is the largest area of cannabis cultivation and hashish production in the world, covering an area of roughly 120,500 hectares (300,000 acres), though the area of land given over to the production of cannabis and hashish is said to double every three to five years. The region's remote and traditionally lawless mountains provide a natural haven for cannabis production, as well as a more-or-less perfect climate, with cannabis best grown at an altitude of around 1,200 metres (3,900ft).

It is a huge business that was initially licensed in the 1940s, along with cigarettes. Cultivation was eradicated from the south of Morocco in 1954, while the country was still a French protectorate, but the Spanish refused to criminalise kif (the Arabic word for cannabis, meaning 'perfect bliss') in their northern enclaves. Hashish production was eventually made illegal throughout Morocco in 1961, although little progress has been made in curbing the industry in the north, and today Ketama is the focal point for this very lucrative industry which is, unofficially, the biggest foreign-currency earner for Morocco. As in most drug-growing areas around the world, the major obstacle is the poverty of the cultivators and lack of any viable alternative economic activity. Initiatives in partnership with the United Nations and the European Community were launched promoting alternative agricultural schemes, but punitively high EU levies (to protect European farmers) meant that most local farmers soon turned back to the cultivation of cannabis, despite punitive slash-and-burn raids by government authorities that reduced planted areas from 137,000 hectares to 47,000 hectares in 2003. Despite such measure, the Rif is still currently estimated to produce 80 percent of all hashish sold every year in Europe, with some 800,000 Riffians depending on kif production for a living, generating $10 billion annually in sales – a tenth of the national economy. The social and economic difficulties associated with kif production are of such national significance that in 2013 the Islamist-led government even floated the idea of legalising kif production within three years – although whether such unprecedented new legislation will ever come to pass in the face of presumably fierce Western opposition remains to be seen.

complete with uniforms, weapons and other bric-a-brac.

Further east, next to the Plaza de los Reyes, look out for the flamboyant **House of the Dragons** (**Casa de los Dragones**), a memorable architectural curiosity somewhere between a small French chateau and a Moorish pleasure palace, with a quartet of black dragons poised on its roof.

On the northeastern edge of town stand the remains of the town's vaulted **Arab Baths** (Plaza de la Paz; daily 11.30am–1.30pm, 6–8pm; free), built in the 12th and 13th centuries, though no longer in use and much diminished in appearance since they were built.

Mediterranean beach life

The beautiful headland of **Cabo Negro ❷**, the location of **M'diq** – what was once a fishing village and is now an up-market resort nestled on a breathtaking sweep of white-sand beach to the south – is fast becoming *the* place to go on the country's Mediterranean Coast, like a kind of Moroccan Marbella. Restaurants and cafés line the beach front and there is also a yacht club and an 18-hole golf course.

Set back from the beach are some grand villas, where Morocco's rich and famous retreat in summer. Once a year in July the yacht club hosts an annual Sailing Week. Accommodation is mostly at the higher end of the scale (see page 299). About 8km (5 miles) along is the beach town of **Martil**, which becomes very busy with Moroccan tourists in the summer months.

Tetouan

Tetouan ❸, flanked on all sides by forest-clad limestone mountains, is arguably the jewel of Morocco's Mediterranean Coast – It isn't until you arrive that you appreciate the town's location and realise how high the road has climbed. A striking, Hispano-Moorish whitewashed town sitting in the foothills of the Rif, it has variously been called 'the sister of Fez', 'little Jerusalem' and the 'daughter of Granada'. The town's past importance as the capital of the Spanish zone, where the Spanish High Commissioner lived, is apparent in its imposing civic architecture. Lovely wrought-iron balconies beneath tall windows and curlicued grille-work are reminiscent of those in Seville.

Tetouan was a busy trading centre even before the Spanish Protectorate (1912–56) added to its importance. At the beginning of the 16th century, the Jews and Muslims who arrived here from Spain practised piracy, making slaves of passengers and crews, then extracting fabulous ransoms. Ships of all nationalities were attacked, but Spanish vessels suffered particularly badly. Philip II blockaded Tetouan's port on the River Martil, leading to a decline in the city's fortunes. Later, under Moulay Ismail the town's economy prospered again.

Nowadays, Tetouan is a bustling town, its energetic character stemming perhaps from its history as

Spanish Ceuta.

Weaver in Tetouan.

the focus of political resistance in the Rif. It was here, in 1954, that a rally of 30,000 tribesmen protested against the deposition of Sultan Mohammed V.

Like most Moroccan towns, Tetouan is divided into a *ville nouvelle* –known as 'El Ensanche', with wide boulevards and flamboyant Hispanic–Moorish buildings– and the town's enjoyable medina.

El Ensanche

Marking the boundary between El Ensanche and the medina, the cavernous **Place Hassan II** is bounded on its northeast corner by the grandiose royal palace, built on the site of the old Caliphate palace. Elsewhere around the square stretch a sweep of distinctly Andalusian-looking whitewashed buildings, complete with green-shuttered windows, elaborate wrought-iron balconies and crenellated rooflines.

South of the square, in the old mellah quarter at the foot of Rue Luneta stand further large old Andalusian-style mansions. Many are in a state of

dilapidation, but even so the intricate enamelled tiling and fancy wrought ironwork decorating their exteriors demonstrate the difference between Spanish and Moroccan domestic architecture; on Moroccan houses adornment is all internal.

A short walk west of Place Hassan II on the Place el Jala is the rewarding **Archaeological Museum** (Mon–Sat 10am–6pm), displaying Moroccan artefacts from the Roman and Phoenician periods. Nearby, off the Place Moulay el Mehdi, is the pretty Spanish **Iglesia de Bacturia**, built in the 1920s and still holding Roman Catholic masses every Sunday.

The Medina

Inscribed as a UNESCO World Heritage Site in 1997, Tetouan's historic medina is one of the most enjoyable in the north, with a sprawl of whitewashed buildings dotted with innumerable mosques, a notable absence of traffic and hassle, and many shops and workshops in which crafts and trades continue to be practised in the traditional manner.

THE SPANISH ENCLAVES

Ceuta and Melilla, the two surreal Spanish towns clinging to the coast of Africa, are rewarding destinations for visitors, though the anomaly of their situations has given both places a political dimension far beyond the merely historical or picturesque. A Spanish possession long before Morocco ever became a nation, Ceuta continues to embarrass both Morocco, which wants it back, and Spain, which doesn't want to give it but realises that its own continued presence there – and in Melilla, its second enclave further along the coast – rather erodes the argument for wresting Gibraltar from the British.

Such friction has meant that crossing into Ceuta can be an exercise in frustration, with long queues of traffic and pedestrians (remember you will need your passport to get into both Ceuta and Melilla). When, after World War II, it belonged to the International Zone, it was not uncommon for passengers to be stripped and their cars taken apart. Things are not much better these days. As a tiny piece of Spain in Africa, Ceuta serves as a beacon of hope for many economic migrants keen to make a new life in Europe. Many of these travel here from deep inside

Africa, sometimes on foot. Once inside Ceuta, they can apply for asylum or, if they have the money, they may risk their lives on dangerous journeys across the Straits in vessels supplied by local mafias (people-smuggling attracts a less severe punishment than drug-smuggling). But currents in the Straits are unpredictable and the boats are invariably of poor quality: the bodies of drowned immigrants frequently wash up on beaches on both sides of the Med. An anti-immigrant fence between Ceuta and Morocco, equipped with security cameras and fibre-optic sensors, is the latest attempt to deter people from getting into 'Fortress Europe'. Its cost of £22 million was paid for by the European Union.

In addition to the autonomous cities of Ceuta and Melilla, Spain has three other sovereign territories in Morocco; the Islas Chafarinas, 45km (28 miles) from Melilla (comprising three islets, one housing a Spanish garrison); Peñón de Alhucemas (see page 137); and Peñón de Vélez de Gomera, an isthmus 200km (124 miles) southeast of Ceuta, whose population is again made up of military personnel.

The medina is entered through the **Bab el Rouah** on Place Hassan II, from where the attractive, trellis-covered Rue Terrafin heads into the labyrinth. The souks around Rue Terrafin are more geared towards tourists, although the **Souk el Houts** fish market, just north of Rue Terrafin about 100 metres/yds beyond Bab el Rouah, remains determinedly local in character.

Continue along Rue Terrafin and its continuation (first Rue Ahmed Torres, then Rue Sidi el Yousti) to reach the pretty eastern gate into the medina, Bab el Okla. Here you'll find the excellent **Ethnographic Museum** (Mon–Sat 9am–4pm), containing examples of Riffian and *Jibala* traditional crafts, along with the Artesanal School (Sat–Thu 9am–2.30pm, Fri 9–11am), home to numerous craftsmen and their apprentices at work.

East of Tetouan, the rough N16 coastal road between offers a beautifully scenic drive as it switchbacks along the rocky coastline before reaching, after about 25km (15 miles), the town of **Oued Laou**, which has a large souk every Saturday where handmade pottery and other regional goods are sold.

Chefchaouen

Tucked into the hills south of Tetouan, **Chefchaouen** ❹ (or just Chaouen, as it is sometimes known), ranks among Morocco's most charming places. It is an essential stop on any visit to the Rif region, a vibrant arts and crafts centre and generally a relaxed place to wind down for a few days and soak up the atmosphere. The town is famous for its achingly pretty blue-washed medina, with narrow winding cobbled streets punctuated by artisanal shops, miniature cafés, little pensions and festooned with trailing clematis and bougainvillea. Women wear the white, rather than black, *haik* (unless they are in mourning, when the reverse is true). In the summer Chefchaouen is cool

and in winter it can be blanketed with snow.

Chefchaouen was founded in 1471 by a Moorish exile from Spain, Moulay el Ben Rashid el Alami. It was built as a fortress from which to repel Portuguese invaders, while the kasbah was built in the 17th century by Moulay Ismail. The town served as the main refuge for Moriscos and Jews escaping from the Spanish Inquisition but was otherwise closed and insular, off limits to Christians until 1920, when the Spanish finally managed to conquer it. They discovered a community of Jews descended from the first refugee settlers speaking 10th-century Castilian, a language extinct in Spain for over 400 years, and leather craftsmen working in tanned and decorated leather, just as their ancestors had done in 12th-century Cordoba. It was the Jews who first painted the town blue, in the 1930s (see page 134).

Exploring the town

The N2 highway from Tetouan arrives just below the old walls. By climbing up through the marketplace you reach

Chefchaouen is well watered by springs in the surrounding hills, and fountains abound in the town.

Preparing fish in Tetouan.

Chefchaouen, set in the foothills of the Rif.

the Bab el Ain gateway, overhung by a wrought-iron lantern. This leads to the main square, the cobbled **Plaza Uta el Hamman,** shaded by trees, strung with lights and lined by bowed cafés, which is an excellent place to sit, appreciate the light and inhale the mountain air (not to be confused with the scent of kif drifting from the cafés' upper storeys).

Built of glowing sandstone on the opposite side of the square, in vivid contrast to the tiled-roofed, sugar-cube housing, is the ruined walled Kasbah, home to an art gallery and a small **Ethnographic Museum** (daily 9am– 1pm, 3–6pm), with exhibits illustrating the culture of the region. To the right of this are the cells where Abd el Krim, leader of a major Riffian tribal revolt against French and Spanish rule, was imprisoned in 1926. Next door is the 15th-century **Grand Mosque**, with its distinctive octagonal minaret.

From **Plaza Uta el Hamman**, the main thoroughfare leads through the centre of the diminutive medina, past the succession of tiny shops opening directly on to the steep, cobbled street.

The shops here are a good place to look for the leather goods for which the town is known.

On the far side of the medina is the town's second main square, **Place du Makhzen,** home to a cluster of pottery and gemstone stalls. Past here, it's possible to follow the river around the outside of the town walls to reach the waterfalls of the Ras el Maa, with its traditional mills and a ruined mosque. You'll probably also see local women washing clothes and sheep's wool, which they will then card and spin into yarn for home-weaving.

A superb view of the town can be had from the swimming pool/bar terrace of the 1970s-style Hotel Asma, above the town, next to the municipal campsite.

As well as being a major destination in its own right, Chefchaouen is also a major trekking centre, and the starting point for most hikes into the surrounding region, including the nearby peak of Jebel el Kelâa, the Talassemtane National Park and the Bab Taza circuit (see page 102). Ask at your hotel for a guide or directions, or try

Guides du Tourism de Chefchaouen or the Eco-Museum at the entrance to the Talassemtane National Park. If trekking independently, be sure to stick to well-used trails.

Ouezzane

The Riffian Berbers are renowned for their reverence for holy men *(marabouts)*, and it is an area with many religious associations. Chefchaouen is considered a holy city thanks to its associations with the marabout Sidi Abdallah Habti, as is **Ouezzane**, reached by taking the N13 southwest of Chefchaouen. One of the holiest places in Morocco, Ouezzane was chosen by Moulay Abdullah, a descendant of Idriss II, as the place in which to found the Taibia brotherhood in 1727. The resultant *zaouia* (shrine) prospered, as did its cherif, who lived in a sanctuary separated from the town. Historically the cherif of Ouezzane held more sway over the region's tribes than the Sultan; pilgrims from all over Morocco would come for his blessing, and criminals sought immunity from their crimes here.

The sanctuary, surrounded by gardens, was supposed to represent the Islamic paradise. In reality, wine, spirits and kif were sold along its approach and the cherifian family had its share of mortal troubles. The cherif of Ouezzane is still a person of moral influence today, considered one of the holiest men in the country after the king, and consulted on various matters of religious philosophy. Pilgrims are particularly noticeable in the spring, when they arrive for the annual *moussem* (religious festival-cum-fair).

Today the town is an important market for the surrounding olive-growing region and is famous for its woven wool textiles used for making *jellabas*. In character, Ouezzane is rather like Chefchaouen, though rather more sprawling, its white houses climbing up Bou Hellol mountain. Again, there is a strong Andalusian flavour, partly due to Ouezzane's once important Jewish population, whose large houses, faced with decorative tiling and fronted by wrought-iron balconies, are still much in evidence.

Party time in Chefchaouen.

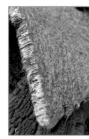

Cork-oaks grow abundantly in the Rif and are often seen stripped of their bark. The cork is harvested every 10 years or so for use in domestic and industrial products.

Goods for sale in Chefchaouen.

Scenic road to Ketama

Below Ouezzane stretches a fertile plain and the heavily populated triangle of Souk el Arba, Rabat and Meknes – part of the French zone during the protectorates, and one of the places where French troops rallied to help Spain defeat the Rif Rebellion. The Rif proper continues along the N2 to the town of Ketama. This is one of the most scenic roads in the region, twisting through mountains and agricultural land.

This journey along the spine of the range passes through some of the most spectacular scenery in the region. Each switchback reveals a new panorama or unexpected scene. Driving is slow, but the road is wide and, apart from in winter, the route is safe enough.

Vegetation is a mix of holm oak, cork oak, pine, gorse and cacti. **Ketama** is heralded by cedar and kif plantations and a large number of men attempting to persuade drivers to stop and buy chunks of hashish. The town remains virtually lawless and it is inadvisable to stay the night.

This is the heart of kif-growing country, and no place for tourists.

To Al Hoceima

East beyond Ketama, trees become fewer, and the red sandstone of the mountain a more violent colour. **Targuist**, the last stronghold of Abd el Krim and from where the Riffians' ammunition was distributed on muleback, is a gritty, workaday place situated on a small plain, its streets laid out in a militaristic grid fashion.

Al Hoceima ❺ to the north, on the other hand, reached by taking the N2 from Aït Yussef ou Ali (birthplace of Riffian revolutionary Abd el Krim), is a very different matter. Once an ancient trading port, the modern town was founded by the Spanish only in 1925. Following Morocco's independence the town found itself at the epicentre of the small-scale Rif Rebellion of 1958–9, during which Hassan II, then the crown prince, landed with 15,000 troops in a rented British-owned ferry and managed to defeat the insurgents. His repression of the uprising was characteristically ruthless, employing napalm and flame-throwers to raze Al Hoceima and many surrounding villages to the ground. It was the last time Hassan ever ventured into the north of the country.

Despite this early reverse, Al Hoceima has subsequently flourished, and is now the second-largest port in the Rif, after Nador, as well as being an increasingly popular destination with Moroccan tourists – thanks to the town's unexpectedly laid-back and cosmopolitan atmosphere, and the large sums of money being ploughed into tourist infrastructure hereabouts. The town is prettily situated, atop cliffs above a large crescent-shaped beach and bay. Further to the west of the town is the attractive port, with an active fishing fleet. It is possible to visit the fishing harbour, but be careful where you

point your camera as the port is also used by the Moroccan Navy, and the police are particularly sensitive.

Some 300 metres/yds off the shore of Al Hoceima is the diminutive fortress of **Peñón de Alhucemas** or 'Lavender Rock'. One of the last *plazas de soberanía* (sovereign territories) in North Africa belonging to Spain, this striking rock citadel it is just 1.5 hectares (3.5 acres) in size and has only a couple of houses, a fort and a church clinging to its rocky sides. The fortress cannot be visited, although you can get a good view of it by heading east of Al Hoceima along the N2 and then taking the narrow tarmac road, signposted Asfiha Plage, which leads down a very steep descent to a grey-sand beach with a good view of this vestigial reminder of Spanish sovereignty.

National park

The Al Hoceima National Park covers an area of 470 sq km (181 sq miles). Several endangered species are protected here, as well as plants and marine life. The park has several

rough tracks threading through it and offers good hikes and biking opportunities, as well as several empty and isolated beaches that you can hike to. At one of these beaches is the Peñón de Vélez de la Gomera, another *plaza de soberanía*. RODPAL (the Rif Association for the Development of Rural Tourism; 19 Calle Ajdir; tel: 0539-98 18 33) is a good source of information on the park and can provide trail maps and itineraries as well as arrange home-stays in local villages.

The Peñón de Vélez de la Gomera can also be reached along the coast by car from **Cala Iris**, west of Al Hoceima, at the end of the tarmac S610 road. Cala Iris is a tiny fishing port, with a few cafés. The cobblestoned port was rebuilt in 1998 with Japanese help as a sign of friendship. Nearby is a tiny beach and pleasant campsite.

Melilla

Towards Nador, the landscape changes from the fertile Nekor River plain to virtual desert just south of the Spanish enclave of **Melilla ❻**.

Modernist house in Melilla.

Al Hoceima.

*Holy Week procession
in Melilla.*

Melilla's waterfront.

Nador, below Melilla, is an industrial town of no great interest except as the entry point to the Spanish enclave.

Melilla, like Ceuta, is worth a visit (you'll need your passport) both for curiosity value and as a worthwhile destination in its own right. It's particularly interesting for students of Modernisme, the Catalan version of Art Nouveau, thanks to numerous buildings designed by former city architect and Melilla resident Enrique Nieto (a disciple of Gaudí), which dot the streets.

Modernisme aside, the top sight here is the ancient walled citadel known variously as **Melilla La Vieja** (Old Melilla) or **Medina Sidonia**, set on a little promontory overlooking the sea on the east side of the centre. Here you'll find the interesting little **Museo de Arqueologia e Historia** (Tue–Sat 10am–1.30pm, 4–8.30pm, Sun 10am–2pm; free), the still-functioning cisterns of **Aljibes de la Peñuelas**, the 17th-century church of **La Purísima Concepción** and a Museo Militar (Tue–Sun 10am–2pm;

free) at the top of the fort, which has fantastic views.

Twenty-nine kilometres (18 miles) from Melilla is the **Cap des Trois Fourches**, which offers panoramic views of Melilla and the coastline. Beyond is a cultivated plain, watered by the River Moulouya. This river once marked the boundary between the French and Spanish protectorates, and historically helped form a barrier against Algeria, although it was also through here that the Beni Merin tribe, the founders of the Merinid dynasty, entered Morocco before capturing Fez in 1248.

The Zegzel Gorge and Beni Snassen Mountains

The N2 road from Nador to Oujda skirts the forest-clad **Beni Snassen Mountains**, where an agreeable detour from Berkane is possible. The road to Zegzel is a bit rough at first, but soon improves and launches into the **Zegzel Gorge** ❼ (Gorges de Zegzel) after passing through a few modern villages. The road meanders along the bottom of the gorge until it climbs up to give superb views of craggy, forest-covered, flat-topped hills. Parts of the route are flanked by orchards growing an amazing array of fruits, including tangerines, apples, quince, pomegranates, almonds and apricots. Beehives fill in the spaces between the trees, and viewpoints look down over brown stone villages with cool white courtyards.

The drive through the peaceful farms of the Beni Snassen Berbers continues to the S403 junction, where a left turn leads to **Tafoughalt** (pronounced 'Taforalt'), which is worth a visit on a Wednesday for its weekly market. Turn right to get back to the N2. From Tafoughalt it is possible to visit the **Grotte du Chameau**, a large limestone cave system that derives its name from a camel-shaped stalagmite situated near the entrance. The drive down to the main road from the junction soon

opens out into a spectacular view back to the Beni Snassen Mountains and northwards over the Moulouya plain towards the sea.

Borderlands

Borders in the Maghreb are determined by politics rather than cultural differences, and an Algerian influence is felt instantly in **Oujda,** Morocco's easternmost city. The language is similar to Algerian Arabic and many women have adopted an Algerian style of dress (the veils of Algerian women are relatively short, covering only the nose and mouth). The music of Oujda, too, is more in tune with Algeria. Modern *raï* music, now fashionable in Europe as well as the Maghreb, developed in the brothels of the border towns of Oujda and Algeria's Oran.

Owing to its strategic importance, Oujda has always been prized. Since its founding in 994, it has passed through many hands: the Almoravids, the Almohads, the Merinids, the Saadians, the Alaouites and the Turks, whose vast empire did not penetrate

much further west than this. It was also the first town to be threatened by the French, who were hovering on the Algerian border long before their protectorate was agreed in 1912.

Sidi Yahya, 6km (4 miles) off a built-up suburban road leading southeast of Oujda, is a popular excursion for Moroccans and Algerians. The body of Sidi Yahya, reputed to have been John the Baptist, is said to be buried here, and Jewish, Muslim and Christian pilgrims all converge here. At weekends, and particularly at the August and September *moussems*, it is packed with visitors. Water or oil is placed in the domed tombs to receive the saint's blessing, after which it is administered to the sick, and female petitioners wash in the streams and knot strips of fabric to the trees in order to bind their contract with the saint.

Sadly, the border to Algeria is closed, and travelling across it is out of the question, while travelling the road south to the border town of Figuig – a long and dusty drive of over 360km (224 miles) – is also inadvisable.

Oleander, with its deep root system, flourishes in the driest terrain, including the eastern Rif.

Oujda.

CHERIF OF OUEZZANE

Sidi el Hajj Abd As Salaam Bin el Arbi, the cherif of Ouezzane in the middle of the 19th century, was an alcoholic, kif addict and eccentric. Admiring all things European, he married an English governess, Emily Keene, who became the cherifa of Ouezzane in 1873. That the cherif of Ouezzane, a respected Muslim spiritual leader, had not only married a Christian, but had also given up his three Muslim wives to do so, caused great consternation among his people. The marriage was not a success, though Emily Keene remained in Morocco until her death and is buried in the St Andrew church in Tangier. Rumours abounded during the cherif's lifetime that he had made a deal with the French to take Sultan Moulay Hassan's place should he be overthrown.

The ruins of the ancient city of Lixus.

THE NORTHWEST COAST

From Cap Spartel, 40km (25 miles) of golden sand run all the way to the fortified town of Asilah, famous for its vibrant summer arts festival. A little further along the coast is laid-back Larache.

Rabat

The triangle of land bounded by the main roads connecting Larache, Fez and Casablanca is Morocco's most densely populated. The spine of the region, the N1 highway, is one of the busiest in the country, linking Morocco, and indeed Africa, to Tangier, the point closest to Europe. In July it is packed with migrant workers returning home from Europe for their annual holiday. Parallel to the N1, and rather quieter because it is a toll road, is the A1 motorway between Tangier and Rabat.

Moroccans are frequent stoppers and constant eaters on any journey, and so road-side stalls, selling anything from melons to pottery, are many, as are *grillade* cafés, their smoking braziers casting a fragrant cloud over the road. Don't be nervous about eating at these cafés; the meat is usually of good quality and very fresh.

Turbulent past

The coast along this Atlantic stretch has been heavily influenced by Spain and Portugal. In the 15th and 16th centuries the Moroccan ports were regularly besieged, and one by one they fell to either Spanish or Portuguese forces. In the 17th century, the area – along with Tangier, Ceuta, Tetouan and Rabat – formed part of

the Barbary Coast and was plagued by pirates. The Iberian influence is strongest in Asilah and Larache, towns colonised intermittently by Spain and Portugal until 1691 and 1689 respectively. These early influences were compounded by the Treaty of Fez in 1912, when both towns fell under the Spanish Protectorate. They contain large populations of Spanish origin, and Spanish rather than French is the second language, while architecture and food also reflect a Spanish heritage.

Main Attractions
Asilah
Larache
Lixus
Moulay Bousselham
Ksar el Kebir
Kasbah de Mehdiya

Football on the beach in Asilah.

From the outskirts of Tangier, the N1 highway and railway south cross a breezy agricultural plain, keeping the sea within sight for most of the way, sometimes across small lagoons. After **Gzanaia** it passes the so-called Diplomatic Forest, a favourite spot for picnics at weekends and during holidays, beyond which is a stunning sweep of wild beach dotted with a couple of very good beach cafés, and, on the inland side, an American base, with its forest of transmitters and aerials.

Alluring Asilah

Asilah ❶, 46km (30 miles) south of Tangier and a favourite excursion from the city as well as a relaxed destination in its own right, is an enchantingly pretty town, with citrus trees, windblown palms and excellent, informal fish restaurants with outdoor tables lining the corniche. The beautiful medina, sheltered by sea-facing ramparts, has been completely restored and increasingly gentrified, and is now one of the most picturesque places in Morocco, home to

Shades of blue in Asilah.

hundreds of sparklingly clean white-washed houses with shutters and doors in a thousand shades of blue. A short string of low-key hotels and holiday complexes lie north of the town along with the railway station, 2km (1 mile) from the centre.

Asilah has been in existence since 1500 BC, when the Phoenicians used it as a trading base. In 1471, the Portuguese conquered the town and built its ramparts, but abandoned it 68 years later. Moulay Ismail took Asilah in 1692 and it became the centre of all pirate activities in the country during the 19th and 20th centuries. Like most of northern Morocco, it came under Spanish control during the years of the Protectorate.

Modern Asilah, like Essaouira, is a magnet for artists, and many of the white houses of its medina are enlivened by brightly painted murals left behind after the annual and increasingly popular arts festival, the Asilah Cultural Festival. This takes place in late June/July and attracts not just artists but also writers, musicians and performers, who stage exhibitions and

events throughout the month, turning the town into a huge open-air art gallery, with the walls of the medina becoming an enormous blank canvas for artists.

The Medina and Palais de Raisuli

Asilah has lots of charming little shops, mainly in the medina and just outside it, selling the usual Moroccan souk wares, as well as paintings and sculptures and the red coral jewellery that the town is famous for. Accommodation is mostly basic and in the new town, though an increasing number of riads and holiday homes are beginning to open in the medina. The best restaurants line the corniche, and the nicest beach (busy in the summer) is Paradise Beach, just south of town.

The main entrance to the medina, **Bab el Kasaba**, is off Place Zellaca, around the corner from the seafront, where there is also a small marina. Around halfway down the ramparts overlooking the sea is the imposing Palais **de Raisuli** (also known as the

Palais de Culture) was built in 1909 by the legendary Mulai Ahmed er Raisuni (or Raisuli), the 'last of the Barbary pirates', who achieved fame through a series of kidnappings, most notably of the London *Times* journalist Walter Harris (Harris, despite being imprisoned with a headless corpse, nevertheless succeeded in befriending his captor).The peasants who were forced to build Raisuli's palace called it 'the House of Tears', alluding to the hardship of their labours. Today, it can be visited only during the arts festival, when it serves as one of the main venues.

At the southern end of the ramparts, the **Shrine** (**Koubba**) **of Sidi Mamsur** and an old Islamic graveyard can be seen, though neither is accessible to non-Muslims. This is a popular place from which to view the town, particularly at sunset.

Larache

Some 87km (54 miles) south of Tangier, **Larache** ❷ (or El Araich in Arabic), on the mouth of the Oued Loukos, is even more Spanish in

Fishing boat.

Moulay Bousselham.

The ruins of ancient Lixus, above Oued Loukos near Larache.

character than Asilah. Overlooking the bay, the fortifications of the **Kasbah de la Cigogne (Stork's Castle)** were built by the Spanish rulers during the 17th-century, but are not currently open to the public. The circular **Place de la Libération** (previously Plaza de España), the main square, was built during the time of the Protectorate, when Larache served as the chief port for the Spanish zone. Hotels, bars and restaurants – many serving excellent fish – all reflect the Spanish influence, though the blue and white paintwork is badly peeling and the stucco embellishments are a little knocked about. Larache's decayed elegance enhances its laid-back charm, reinforced by the relative lack of tourists compared with Asilah down the coast.

The beach is on the other side of the River (Oued) Loukos and approached by a circuitous route following the turn-off to Lixus, just north of the town (buses ply the

Near the Place de la Libération in Larache.

route), or by crossing the estuary by ferry. From here, there is a pretty view of the town, with moored fishing vessels in the foreground against a backdrop of the Kasbah de la Cigogne and medina rising in a higgledy-piggledy heap. The estuary is a good site for spotting birds, including crested coot, red-crested pochard, moustached warbler and Spanish sparrow, though the lagoon at Moulay Bousselham (see below) is the most important birdwatching area along this stretch of coast.

Ancient Lixus

Scattered over a hill on the right-hand side of the road leading to the beach are the ruins of the town of **Lixus** ❸ (open site; free), founded by the Phoenicians in about 1100 BC, possibly as their first trading post in North Africa. As a Carthaginian and later Roman town, it was employed in the production of *garum*, an anchovy paste popular in Roman cooking. It is one of several claimants to the site of the mythical Garden of the Hesperides, home of the golden apples sought by Hercules in his penultimate labour.

Apart from some megalithic stones, built into the acropolis and oriented towards the sun, most of the surviving remains date from the Roman period. At the top of the hill there are foundations of temples, a theatre and amphitheatre, ramparts and houses and, near the bottom, the remains of the salt and *garum* factories. Most of the floor mosaics have been removed to the museum in Tetouan (see page 132), though one (rather battered) of Oceanus can still be seen in situ in the baths by the theatre.

South of Larache

From Larache there is a choice of three routes south: the coast road, the motorway and the N1 striking inland. Lying on the coastal route across a large lagoon is the fishing village and religious destination of

Moulay Bousselham ❹. A *moussem* is held here every summer when pilgrims visit a cave containing a sacred stalactite, while the shrine (*koubba*) of 10th-century Egyptian divine Moulay Bousselham, after whom the settlement is named, occupies a prominent position near the village. The lagoon and surrounding marshlands, now protected as the **Merja Zerga** (blue lagoon) **National Park**, are a magnet for birds, most noticeably ducks and waders, including the greater flamingo. Winter is the best time to birdwatch.

If you are planning to travel on to Fez from Larache, take the N1 inland to **Ksar el Kebir** ❺, once an important power base coveted by the Spanish and Portuguese in Larache and Asilah. It was near here that the Portuguese fought the battle of the Three Kings in 1578 (see page 32), resulting in the death of the Portuguese King Sebastian and the eventual rise of Ahmed el Mansour, the star of Morocco's Saadian dynasty.

Beyond Ksar el Kebir, outside the town of **Arbaoua**, is the old Protectorate border, where the former checkpoint is gathering weeds. During the French and Spanish protectorates, passports had to be shown in order to pass. After independence, Mohammed V made a ceremonial visit to the spot to declare the checkpoint formally closed.

Beyond is the turning for the rewarding detour to Ouezzane (see page 135). Continuing along the N1, the surrounding hills level out onto a rich, well-populated plain whose focus is **Souk el Arba du Rharb** (*arba* meaning Wednesday, the day of its souk, and *rharb* meaning west). Thanks to the rich alluvial soil and the use of modern technology, this one of the richest agricultural regions of Morocco, specialising in cereals, sugar cane, early vegetables and fruit for export, as well as livestock.

Southeast of here is **Sidi Kacem**, an industrial centre and rail junction, through which most people pass on their way to Meknes or Fez.

Back on the coast, heading south of **Moulay Bousselham, the** A1 autoroute passes through the remains of the ancient **Mamora Forest** (Forêt de la Mamora) of cork oaks, acacias and eucalyptus to reach **Kenitra**, the administrative centre of the region. Founded by the French in 1913 on a bend in the River Sebou, one of the most important rivers in Morocco, Kenitra is industrial in character and not particularly interesting for visitors, but the **Kasbah de Mehdiya** ❻, 11km (7 miles) to its south on the mouth of the river, is impressive. The Spanish, who captured the point in 1614, built the fortress upon a prototype conceived by Louis XIV's military engineer. Moulay Ismail, however, drove the Spanish out and established his own man there, the Caid Ali er Rif, the governor responsible for the Moroccan gateway and palace.

South of Kenitra, routes cross the edge of the Mamora Forest before hitting the suburbs of the city of **Rabat** (see page 147).

FACT

The vast Mamora Forest is fast diminishing. Constantly plundered for firewood and cleared for agricultural use, it has almost halved in size over the past 50 years.

Fortifications at Asilah.

RABAT AND SALÉ

Morocco's capital is conservative in character, with grand architecture, verdant boulevards and pleasant cafés. Just across the river lies its twin – the former pirate base of Salé.

The youngest of the four imperial capitals, Rabat has less in the way of historic medersas and mosques than Fez, Meknes or Marrakech, but is nonetheless an appealing city, with plenty to see. Symbol of the city is the landmark (albeit unfinished) Tour Hassan, one of a trio of minarets built by the Almohads (the others being the Giralda in Seville and the Koutoubia in Marrakech), while the picture-perfect Kasbah of the Oudaias, set scenically above the River Bou Regreg, is another highlight. There's also an attractive medina, and Ville Nouvelle, an excellent Archaeological Museum (possibly the best in the country), and a memorable Merinid necropolis, the Chellah, just outside the city walls – not to mention the twin city of Salé just over the river .

If you are arriving in Rabat by train, be sure to get off at Rabat Ville and not Rabat Agdal, a leafy suburb west of the centre. Rabat Ville railway station is conveniently situated next to the parliament building at the top of Avenue Mohammed V, the city's main commercial spine, which has some interesting examples of Mauresque architecture. From here it is an easy walk to a number of small hotels or a short taxi ride to some more upmarket options (see page 301). The medina lies at the other end of Avenue Mohammed V, in the shadow of the Kasbah of the

Oudaias overlooking the sea and the mouth of the river.

Rabat's history

Rabat was founded in the 10th century near the ruins of the Phoenician, later Roman, port of Sala Colonia at the mouth of the River Bou Regreg. This first *ribat* (Islamic military community) later became capital of the 12th-century Almohad conqueror Yacoub el Mansour, who ruled an area extending from Tunisia to northern Spain. Under El Mansour, Rabat

Main Attractions

Hassan Tower
Mausoleum of Mohammed V
Kasbah of the Oudaias
Souk es Sebat
Archaeological Museum
Royal Palace
Chellah Necropolis
Medersa Abu el Hassan
Zaouia of Sidi Abdellah Ben
  Hassoun

The zaouia of Abou el Hassan.

enjoyed its first – and perhaps most stellar – period, symbolised by the vast Almohad walls which still survive largely intact today, enclosing a vast area now containing the medina, Ville Nouvelle and Mechouar (royal palace complex).

With the death of Yacoub el Mansour, Rabat lost much of its importance and was not to recover its status as capital until the French occupation in 1912. The largely abandoned city was partially resettled by Andalusian refugees in the 17th century, who occupied the northern end of the original city, fortifying their new home by constructing the line of walls that now mark the southern side of the medina. At the same time, the local fleets of the so-called Salé Rovers, based in the Kasbah of the Oudaias, began embarking on a spree of international piracy, terrorizing shipping from Europe to West Africa and establishing their own autonomous mini-state, the Bou Regreg Republic, until being finally brought to heel at the turn of the 19th century.

Modern centre

Now all is engulfed in the Rabat-Salé conurbation of over 1.7 million inhabitants. Modern **Rabat** has a reputation, not entirely justified, for respectability going on dullness. Casaouis (inhabitants of Casablanca) are fond of dismissing it as provincial, but by Moroccan standards Rabat is a tolerant and Westernised city, with an attractive Ville Nouvelle which wouldn't look out of place in the south of France, and a decent selection of restaurants and bars to keep you busy after dark.

The Ville Nouvelle is still bounded on its southern and western sides by the great Almohad Walls. From the great gate of **Bab er Rouah**, the finest of the five city gates, they run down past lawns and orange trees to the El Had Gate (Bab el Had) at the corner of the medina, where the Central Market stands. It was at Bab el Had that the last pre-Protectorate sultan exhibited the heads of defeated rebels. Now for most of the year, swifts and martins flock to the spot at dusk, nesting in the regular holes in the masonry (designed to support the crossbeams of small mobile platforms for repair work to the walls).

On the other side of town another well-preserved section of Almohad wall encloses the palace area and, beyond the palace, the Chellah Necropolis overlooks the valley.

Almohad legacy

Following the road round above the valley, one comes to the principal Almohad site in Rabat, and the city's iconic symbol, the **Hassan Tower (Tour Hassan) ❶**. Magnificently situated on the crest of a hill commanding both Salé and Rabat, this is the unfinished minaret of the great Hassan Mosque, begun by Yacoub el Mansour in 1196.

Upon his death in 1199 work on the mosque seems to have ceased, but the main structure of the building was well advanced. The design was

The Ville Nouvelle.

monumental: 21 east-to-west aisles in the prayer hall, with space for 40,000 worshippers (double the capacity of the Kairaouine in Fez) would have made it the second-largest mosque in the world after Samarra in Iraq.

The shell of the mosque was destroyed at the same time as the city of Lisbon in the earthquake of 1755. Many of the 400 columns have now been re-erected upon a foundation of modern flagstones. Parts of the mosque's outer wall survive, and a large sunken water tank near the tower, which was to have fed the fountains in the ablutions court, has been converted into a monument to the victims of the independence struggle. But the site of the mosque is now no more than a great white open space between the modern mausoleum of Mohammed V and Hassan II on one side and the Hassan Tower on the other.

The tower, designed by the same architect as the Giralda in Seville and the Koutoubia in Marrakech, rises to only 44 metres (144ft) out of its projected 80 metres (262ft). Within the tower's 2.4-metre (8ft) thick walls is an internal ramp up which mules carried building materials and which is usually open to visitors (although it is currently closed for restoration works). The climb itself and the splendid view from the top are convincing proof of the real height of the truncated structure, despite its stocky look.

With a 16-sq-metre (172-sq-ft) cross-section (as against the Koutoubia's 12 sq metres/39 sq ft), the Hassan Tower would, if completed with its upper ranges of tile work and its lantern, have appeared more slender than either of its sister towers. But the harmony of its decorative carving (different on each face at the lower level, the same on three faces at the upper), the magnificence of the site and the rich ochre of its stone make it one of the most memorable pieces of architecture in the country.

Mausoleum of Mohammed V

On the other side of the rows of columns stands the flamboyant **Mausoleum of Mohammed V** ❷ (daily 8.30am–6pm; free), an uninspired

Family time in the Ville Nouvelle.

Rabat and Salé

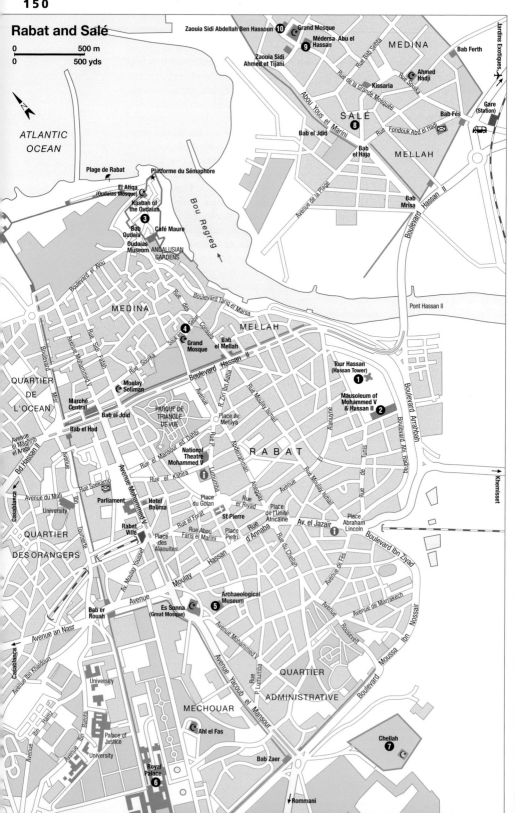

0   500 m
0   500 yds

N

ATLANTIC
OCEAN

Zaouia Sidi Abdellah Ben Hassoun **10**
Grand Mosque
Médersa Abu el **9** Hassan
Zaouia Sidi
Ahmed et Tijani
MEDINA
Rue Bab Sebta
Rue de la Grande Mosquée
Kissaria
Rue Souika
Ahmed Hadji
Bab Ferth
Abou Yous el Marini
SALÉ
Bab el Jdid
Bab Fés
Gare (Station)
Bab el Haja
Rue Fondouk Abd el Hadj
MELLAH
Jardins Exotiques
Khemisset

Plage de Rabat
Platforme du Sémaphore
El Atiqa (Oudaias Mosque)
Kasbah of the Oudaias **3**
Bab Oudaia
Café Maure
Oudaias Museum
ANDALUSIAN GARDENS
Bou Regreg
Boulevard Tariq el Marsa
Pont Hassan II
Bab Mrisa
Avenue de la Plage
Boulevard Hassan II

MEDINA
Souk es Sebat
Rue des Consuls
4
Grand Mosque
Bab el Mellah
Moulay Soliman
Rue Souika
MELLAH
R Zin bin Attia
Boulevard Hassan II
Tour Hassan (Hassan Tower) **1**
Mausoleum of Mohammed V & Hassan II **2**
Boulevard Arrahah
Boulevard Abi Radraq

QUARTIER DE L'OCEAN
Marché Central
Bab el Jdid
Bab el Had
Avenue Mohammed V
Avenue el Maghrib el Arabi
Bd Hassan II
PARQUE DE TRIANGLE DE VUE
Place de Melliya
Rue Moulay Ismaïl
Rue Patrice Lumumba
National Theatre Mohammed V
Rue el Kahira
R A B A T
Alaouyine
Rue Moulay Ismaïl

Avenue du Mall
University
QUARTIER
DES ORANGERS
Tournerie
Casablanca
Parliament
Hotel Balima
Rabat Ville
Place des Alaouites
Avenue Mohammed V
Rue el Mansour ed Dahbi
Rue el Foral
St Pierre
Rue Abou Faris el Marini
Place du Golan
Place Pietri
Rue d'Annaba
Rue Piétri
Rue er Riyad
Place de l'Unité Africaine
Av. el Jazair
Place Abraham Lincoln
Rue du Chellah
Boulevard Ibn Ziyad
Avenue de Fés

Avenue an Nasr
Casablanca
Bab er Rouah
Avenue Ibn Khaldoun
University
Avenue Ibn Batota
Avenue Ibn Hani
Palace of Justice
University
Av. Moulay Youssef
Moulay
Avenue
Es Sunna (Great Mosque) **5**
Archaeological Museum
Hassan
Avenue Mohammed V
Avenue Yacoub el Mansour
Rue Lumumba
QUARTIER
ADMINISTRATIVE
Avenue Roosevelt
Avenue de Marrakech
Boulevard Ibn Ziyad
Ibn Nossair
Moussa

MECHOUAR
Ahl el Fas
Chellah **7**
Bab Zaer
Royal Palace **6**
Rommani

product of architectural styles that haven't changed in 400 years. It's redeemed, however, by the genuine popular piety of the many Moroccan visitors who come here to pay their respects to Mohammed V – and perhaps also his son and successor, Hassan II, who is also buried in the complex. Constructed out of white Italian marble, the mausoleum was designed, oddly enough, by a Vietnamese architect, Vo Toan, but is entirely traditional in style. Four gilded doors, guarded by elaborately costumed guards, lead into the richly tiled and decorated central chamber, encircled by narrow balconies from which visitors look down at the tomb of Mohammed below, set beneath a golden dome. A similarly sunken mosque stands to the rear of the mausoleum, hidden behind a green-tiled roof.

Kasbah of the Oudaias

From the Hassan Tower, roads lead down to the pretty riverside corniche, dotted with fishing boats and yachts, and with the walled **Kasbah of the Oudaias** ❸ rising imposingly

ahead from a rocky bluff overlooking the Atlantic. Built by Yacoub el Mansour on the site of the original *ribat*, the kasbah also contained the Sultan's residence in Rabat. In the 17th century, the period of the corsair state known as the Republic of Bou Regreg, the kasbah's inhabitants lived off the piratical exploits of the so-called Salé Rovers. Their captives used to be sold in the **Old Wool Market**, a triangular space still used by the wool trade, across the road from the kasbah's entrance. Moulay Ismail (see page 33), whose reign spanned and paralleled that of Louis XIV, put an end to the vicious little republic, took over the corsair business himself and constructed a new palace within the kasbah, which is now the Oudaias Museum (see page 152). He also installed in the kasbah the warlike Oudaias tribe, whom he charged with the tasks of subjugating the equally fractious Zaer tribe south of Rabat and keeping the corsairs in line.

The 12th-century **Oudaia Gate (Bab Oudaia)** is beautifully decorated with geometric motifs on a

Kasbah of the Oudaias.

The Hassan Tower.

superposition of arch around arch, working outwards from the central keyhole to the massive square block of the whole gate. From here, the main street runs straight into the kasbah. Pass through the angled entrance in the side tower and you find yourself next to the interior face of the gate and in the main street of the kasbah.

Halfway along this street on the left is the **Oudaias Mosque** (**Mosque el Atiqa**), built in the 12th century and restored in the 18th century by an English architect, 'Ahmed el Ingles'. At the end of this street is the **Platforme du Sémaphore**, which has stunning windswept views out to sea and across to Salé.

Turning right off the main street and follow any of the twisting alleys downhill to reach (eventually – depending on how many dead-ends you run into) the **Café Maure** on the ramparts overlooking the river. Alternatively, the café and Andalusian Gardens can more easily be reached by taking the small gateway on your right as you walk up to the Bab

Signposted from the Andalusian gardens, Café Maure, with its cool breezes and shady, rush-covered benches, is a delightful place to adjourn for sticky Moroccan pastries and a glass of mint tea.

Mausoleum of Mohammed V.

Oudaias, which takes you directly into the gardens.

Next to the café are the **Andalusian Gardens** – a peaceful oasis, created by the French during the Protectorate – and the **Oudaias Museum** (Wed–Mon 9am–4.30pm). The museum not only contains a fine display of jewellery, costumes and carpets, but is of interest in itself as a handsomely decorated royal residence, with elegant reception rooms opening onto a central courtyard.

The medina

The Kasbah of the Oudaias stands at the northeast corner of Rabat **medina**, the four sides of which run first along the river, then past the cemetery on the coast, down the Almohad walls running from the lighthouse in to El Had Gate, and finally along the Andalusian-era walls on Boulevard Hassan II. When, in the 17th century, the last wave of Muslim refugees were expelled from Spain, many of them settled in Salé and Rabat. They found the latter in ruins and almost deserted, and the area within the

old Almohad defences far too large for their needs. So they put up the Andalusian walls to contain the part they settled, rebuilding the area – the present medina – in the architectural style of their Spanish homeland.

When, in 1912, the French made Rabat the protectorate capital, Marshal Lyautey forbade the development of the medina by European builders and ordered the creation of a new town outside its walls, which would be a colonial showcase. The initial consequence of this policy was urban segregation, which was much criticised by Moroccans, but in the long run it has preserved the traditional Moroccan towns better than any others in North Africa.

Exploring the medina

The entrance to the medina is a little downhill from the **Bab Oudaia** by the **Rue des Consuls**, the only street in which foreign consuls could formerly set up shop, and today largely given over to touristy handicraft shops. The first section is occupied by carpet, rug and wool merchants. Popular types of carpet include the urban-style Ribati, characterised by strong reds and blues in geometrical patterns, and the generally smaller Taznacht with their softer-hued vegetable dyes and cruder patterns often including animal and plant motifs (never as strictly taboo in the Maghreb as elsewhere in the Muslim world). Most of the big carpets are now produced by sweated labour in carpet factories, but private carpetmakers sell in the souk held in this street every Thursday morning.

Halfway up the Rue des Consuls, side by side on the left, are two old *fondouks* (inns for travelling merchants and their pack animals), which now house leather workers' workshops. A few yards further up on the left, a more modern *fondouk* has become a cloth-sellers' *kissaria* (shopping arcade), arranged round a small garden. The street continues with leather and clothes shops until you come to a small crossroads. Ahead and on the left is the former Jewish quarter, or *mellah*, while to the right the road leads through a covered market – the **Souk es Sebat ④**, which is

Storks nesting at Chellah Necropolis.

Kasbah of the Oudaias overlooks the Atlantic.

TIP

Early evening activity in the capital centres on and around Avenue Mohammed V. The landmark Hotel Balima has a nice terrace from which to watch the promenade, while near the hotel are several good places to eat including Le Grand Comptoir (see page 311) and Le Bistrot du Pietri.

Shopping in the medina.

lined with jewellery shops, shoemakers and fabric merchants, and past the medina's **Grand Mosque**. On the corner of the side street beside the mosque is a 14th-century Merinid fountain, a survival of pre-Andalusian Rabat, which has been incorporated into the facade of the Librairie al Maarif bookshop.

This leads straight into the **Rue Souika**, the medina's main shopping street. The goods on sale hereabouts are fairly workaday, and the entire area is frequently jam-packed with dense crowds of local shoppers. Work your way slowly through the throngs to emerge at the **Marché Central** (Central Market).

The area behind the Central Market is veined with *derbs* – narrow cul-de-sacs between windowless walls leading off the main thoroughfares. Within the *derb*, massive iron-studded doors open, through the traditional blind entrance-way with a right-angled bend, into the courtyards of private houses. These old-style, inward-turned houses were described by Leonara Peets in 1932 as 'lidless clay boxes in which the Moroccan man hides his women and his home life… a rectangular well of two storeys, with all the windows directed onto the internal patio'. It was on the roof terraces of such houses that the womenfolk, who otherwise never went out except to visit the baths, were allowed to emerge in the late afternoon, when men were banished from the rooftops.

Behind the Central Market, to the left as one faces the medina, there is a small **flea market** in which interesting oddities are sometimes found.

To the Archaeological Museum

The Central Market faces **Avenue Mohammed V**, which runs through the centre of the Ville Nouvelle shopping area before broadening out into a rather elegant palm-lined promenade, the scene of the evening walkabout, past the superb Mauresque **main post office** and **Bank al Maghrib** to the modern **parliament building** and straight on up to the 18th-century Great Mosque es Sunna of Rabat at the top of the hill, whose huge minaret rivals (and echoes) that of the Tour Hassan itself.

Those disappointed by the ruins of **Sala Colonia in the Chellah** (see page 156) should visit the **Archaeological Museum ❺** (Wed–Mon 8.30–11.30am, 2.30–5.30pm), one of the finest collections in Morocco, with highlights including notable artefacts from Lixus, the Chellah and elsewhere.

It is the artworks recovered from Volubilis (see page 212), displayed in the **Salle des Bronzes**, however, which are the real highlight of the museum. When Rome ordered the evacuation of Volubilis in the 3rd century, the citizens, expecting to return shortly, quickly buried their works of art outside the city, where they were to remain undisturbed for 17 centuries.

In addition to many charming small Graeco-Roman statuettes, there

are three or four pieces of particular interest: the Guard Dog (centrepiece of a fountain), the ivy-crowned *Youth* (the *Ephebus*, copied from Praxiteles), the *Rider*, and, above all, the busts presumed to be those of Cato the Younger and the young King Juba II of Mauretania Tingitana (see page 24). The head of Cato, austere and fastidious, is entirely convincing as the enemy of Julius Caesar who killed himself as the latter's autocratic power became inevitable.

The head of Juba, however, is the pièce de résistance of the collection – the product of *'pays berbère, occupant romain, esthétique grecque'* (Berber country, Roman occupant, Greek aesthetic). Undoubtedly a Berber youth, it could easily have been a bust of their king.

Royal Palace

A short distance west of the museum, on the busy intersection joining Avenue an Nasr and Avenue Moulay Hassan, stands **Bab er Rouah** (Gate of the Winds), the most impressive of the surviving Almohad gates, which now doubles as an art gallery with changing exhibitions.

The main entrance to the **Royal Palace ❻ (Mechouar)** complex, lies roughly halfway between the Great Mosque and the Bab er Rouah. Visitors are allowed to walk or drive through the archway here into the palace area, a virtual town within a town, containing the modern palace, the House of Government (Dar el Makhzen), the Prime Minister's office and the Ministry of Religious Affairs. The resident population of 2,000 includes extended branches of the Alaouite ruling family (others are distributed among the palaces in other towns) as well as retainers (serving and retired), a guards regiment and cavalry, who can sometimes be seen being drilled in the area's considerable open spaces. The complex also contains a mosque, at which the king, when in Rabat, leads the midday Friday prayer on feast days.

Chellah Necropolis

The central road through the *Mechouar* brings you out through the Almohad

Young lad in Rabat.

The shopping street of rue des Consuls, Rabat.

FACT

The eels in the pool of the Chellah Necropolis hammam are thought to confer fertility. They are supposedly ruled over by a giant eel with long hair and golden rings, and draw their magic from the saintly Shems, as does the small spring rising in the gardens below the ruins.

Bab er Rouah, a 12th century Almohad gate.

walls on the far side, just 10 minutes' walk from the **Chellah Necropolis ❼** (daily 8.30am–6.30pm) towards the left. The walled Chellah citadel, stretching down the hillside almost to the level of the valley, was for 1,500 years the site of the port – Phoenician, Roman, Berber and Arab – of Sala, until, in the 13th century, its inhabitants took themselves and the name of their town across the estuary. Rabat remained the assembly point for armies bound for the Spanish wars, however, and the first three Merinid sultans in the 13th and 14th centuries used Chellah as a burial place for their dynasty. (The other Merinid necropolis is outside the walls of Fez, their main capital.)

The Chellah remains an arresting sight to this day, just a few hundred metres from the new city but seemingly marooned in a different age. From the outside, its high crenellated walls give it the appearance a medieval European castle rather than an Islamic necropolis, set in isolated, picture-perfect splendour amidst a pocket of open countryside dotted with thorny trees and scrub.

Entrance is through the imposing main gate (formerly decorated in a blaze of colourful but now vanished tile work), with the characteristic keyhole arch embellished with stalactite corbels.

Inside, paths lead down through half-wild gardens and scented trees (notably the huge white trumpets of the hallucinogenic *Dattura* or bella-donna tree, also known as the 'jealous tree' for its power to send people mad). Ahead is the main sanctuary, home to a cluster of domed saints' tombs and a ruined Merinid mosque and *zaouia*. To your left, in front of the sanctuary, are the slight remains of the Romano-Berber town of **Sala Colonia** – or what was left of it after the Merinids had quarried it for their own buildings – with the bases of a few columns and other rather enigmatic stone fragments of a former temple, forum and various residential buildings.

It's the sanctuary itself, however, which is the main attraction. Entering the sanctuary you find yourself immediately in the courtyard of a small mosque built by Abou Youssef Yacoub, the 'King of the *djinns*', who

is believed to have buried his gold nearby and set the *djinns* to guard it. The columns and mihrab of the mosque's ruined prayer hall stand beyond the courtyard, while to your left rise the picturesque remains of a former minaret, topped with an enormous stork's nest.

Various royal tombs can be seen scattered around the sanctuary. The two most prominent lie immediately behind the mosque. Walking anticlockwise around the mosque you reach first the tomb of Abou el Hassan, known as the Black Sultan, with part of a richly decorated wall still standing behind it. Further around (the sexes being segregated in death as in life) lies the tomb of his wife, the former Christian slave Shems Ed Duna (Morning Sun), whose saintliness is commemorated in local legend.

To the left of the mosque stand the ruins of the *zaouia* of Abou el Hassan, a place of religious retreat and study. Small cubicles surround a courtyard with a central pool, beyond which a small prayer hall culminates in a *mihrab* (niche pointing towards Mecca) encircled untypically by a narrow passageway, now blocked with thorn branches and rubble. Legend has it that walking seven times around this *mihrab* is as good as a pilgrimage to Mecca – perhaps the reason why it is now blocked up. At the other end of the central court, down some steps beside the minaret, are the old latrines with accommodation for eight (remarkably generous provision for the occupants of only 16 study cells). The inmates would have slept in dormitories above the cubicles. Emerging again from the mosque on the side opposite the Roman remains, you find the ground slopes down to the ruins of a hammam (steam bath), in which a sunken pool houses a colony of eels.

Twin city

The main **Hassan II** Bridge over the **River Bou Regreg** (Father of Reflection) leads directly to the centre of **Rabat's** twin city **Salé ⑧**. Salé is notably more traditional than cosmopolitan Rabat, and although massive ongoing development is gradually transforming its staunchly Islamic character and dragging the city into the 21st century, the old medina at least retains its resolutely time-warped atmosphere.

The town of Salé acquired its present name in 1260 when, following the sack of the former town on this site by Alfonso X of Castile and the enslavement of most of its inhabitants, the population of the Chellah (Sala Colonia) crossed the river to settle here and rebuild the town. For the next six centuries Salé's economic importance was greater than that of Rabat.

From the 13th to the 16th centuries it was Morocco's principal trading port, and when, after the last wave of Andalusian resettlement in the early 17th century, Rabat and Salé formed the short-lived corsair state of Bou Regreg, Salé was predominant. The hero of Daniel Defoe's story *Robinson Crusoe* was captured and sold into slavery by the Salé Rovers.

Salé medina walls.

The Chellah Necropolis.

TIP

The easiest way to reach Salé from Rabat is to ride the swift modern tram, which now connects the two cities. There are two lines with numerous stops in Rabat (including one right next to the station) that will take you to various points just south of the Salé medina.

From the Salé end of the Hassan II Bridge, the first town gate you see is the unusually tall **Bab Mrisa** (Port Gate), built by the Merinid sultans to admit seagoing boats by means of a now vanished canal which allowed them to dock within the town walls. Turn left here and follow the outer walls to reach a second gate, the Bab el Haja. Turn right here through the walls and then head around the left-hand side of the square ahead of you.

Straight ahead (still bearing left), you enter the main trading streets of the **medina**. Here craftsmen and shopkeepers flock together by trades, grouped guild-like in their own narrow streets. This is very much a traditional Moroccan town, visited by few tourists and entirely free of hustlers. The long straight road up to the left (Rue de la Grande Mosquée) takes you to the area of merchants' mansions and religious centres (*zaouias*) around the Grand Mosque. Behind the mosque to the right is the **Medersa Abu el Hassan** ❾ (daily 8.30am–5.30pm) – a lovely little Merinid religious college, just as

finely wrought and well preserved as the great Bou Inania medersas in Fez and Meknes, but much smaller. There is the same prolific decoration – first zellige (faïence mosaic), then incised stucco, and finally carved cedar-wood. Steps lead up to the dormitories on the upper storey and the roof, with views across the river to Rabat.

Immediately beyond the Grand Mosque lies the **Zaouia of Sidi Abdellah Ben Hassoun** ❿, the 16th-century patron saint of Salé, revered by the corsairs. His cult survives in an annual procession on the eve of Mouloud (the Prophet's birthday), during which men in period costume carry large lanterns, intricately made of coloured wax, from Bab Mrisa up to the saint's shrine, where they dance and sing. Souks Ghezel (wool) and Merzouk (textiles and jewellery), just beyond the covered Kissaria market, are worth exploring.

Pottery complex and exotic gardens

Some 3km (2 miles) southeast of Salé lies a thriving cooperative of **potteries**, the **Complexe des Potiers**, located beside the airport road out of Rabat. Salé pottery is marked by delicate economical designs in white and pastel shades, often including the Roman *fibula*, or brooch fastener – a traditional motif in Berber decoration. Unfortunately this faïence work chips easily, unlike the hotter-fired Fez stoneware, with its characteristic scrollwork and resonant blues and whites.

About 10km (6 miles) north of Salé on the Kenitra road, recognisable by the sunhats for sale on racks outside the gate, are the **Jardins Exotiques** (www.jardinsexotiques.com; daily winter 9am–5pm, summer 9am–7pm), a botanical adventureland with liana bridges and winding jungle paths. Designed by a French conservationist to illustrate a variety of ecosystems, the gardens are a bit run-down, but the obstacle course is still fun.

The zaouia of Abou el Hassan.

A further 6km (4 miles) north there is a turning off to the five-star Hôtel Firdaous and the attractive sandy swathes of the **Plage des Nations** (but beware: swimming here is dangerous due to the currents).

Rabat to Casablanca

Anyone travelling without their own transport can get to Casablanca easily by train. Drivers have a choice of three clearly indicated roads, the toll motorway, the N1 or the coast road, which can be busy at weekends when it becomes ensnarled with beach-bound city dwellers.

Many of the Atlantic beaches are subject to currents that make swimming dangerous, but a number of small sandy bays between Rabat and Casablanca are both attractive and safe. About 10km (6 miles) south of Rabat on the coast road brings you to **Temara beach**, actually a series of beaches – Contrebandiers, Sables d'Or (Sidi el Abed) and Sehb ed Dahab. Around Sables d'Or there are several restaurants, discos and sports facilities, and Sehb ed Dahab has a marina. All get very crowded in summer.

Also in Temara is the **Jardin Zoologique de Rabat** (www.rabatzoo. ma). Upgraded in 2012, the zoo comprises five zones, each representing one of Morocco's ecosystems, from the Atlas Mountains to the Sahara, with wildlife including Atlas lions, mouflons, oryx, elephants and giraffes.

At **Skhirat**, 30km (19 miles) south of Rabat, the king's seaside palace – the scene of a bloody attempted coup against Hassan II in 1971 – is flanked by excellent beaches, the up-market L'Amphitrite Palace hotel (www. lamphitrite-palace.com) and smart villas.

Some 70km (40 miles) from Rabat and 30km (19 miles) before Casablanca lies the long, thin coastal strip of **Mohammedia** – a town with a split personality: on the Casa side, there are an oil port, factories and poor districts; on the Rabat side (described as East Mohammedia), a playground for rich Casablancans, with hotels, good beaches and sports facilities that include an 18-hole golf-course, a marina, water sports, riding, a casino, a racecourse and some good fish restaurants.

TIP

The Robert Trent Jones-designed Royal Dar es Salam Golf Club, on the outskirts of Rabat off the Rommani Road, comprises two 18-hole courses and one 9-hole course. Visitors can gain access to the club as temporary members.

Salé ferry boat.

JUBA II

Juba II, born in North Africa around 50 BC, was a Berber prince who was taken under Julius Caesar's wing in Rome and became a famous scholar of his time and a benefactor of the arts and sciences. Brought up by Caesar and his nephew Octavian, Juba later married Cleopatra Selene, the daughter of Antony and Cleopatra, and became king of Numidia (part of present-day Algeria and Tunisia) and Mauretania.

He reigned for 45 years, and was one the Rome's most loyal client kings and also one of the most 'gifted rulers of his time' according to Plutarch. Juba's son with Cleopatra Selene, Ptolemy, who succeeded Juba as king, was murdered by Caligula, allegedly for wearing a more brilliant purple toga than that of the emperor himself.

Hassan II Mosque.

CASABLANCA

Though nothing like its Sin City image in the classic Hollywood movie that appropriated its name, Casablanca is an exciting and fast-changing metropolis.

Morocco's economic capital, Casablanca, is quite unlike anywhere else in the country. A genuine modern metropolis, the city is developing at an astonishing rate, with a burgeoning business sector, a westernised middle class and a cosmopolitan outlook reminiscent of southern France rather than the Maghreb. This is the beating heart of modern Morocco – brash, borderline manic and a little rough around the edges, but with a sense of dynamism and big-city pizzazz you won't find anywhere else in the country, from the raucous late-night bars and overflowing cafés of downtown through to the upwardly mobile modern suburbs of Maarif, Anfa and Aïn Diab.

Casablanca – 'Casa' as the locals refer to it – may lack the historic monuments and mazy souks of older cities (although the city's small but interesting original medina survives surprisingly intact) but compensates with other attractions. These include the remains of the fine old colonial-era city centre, dotted with examples of the distinctive Art Nouveau-style Mauresque architecture which flourished here during the French period, and, especially, the magnificent Hassan II Mosque, one of the finest such buildings on the planet. Most of all, however, it's the sheer energy and

exuberance of the place that's likely to linger longest in the memory – offering a salutory corrective to the picture-perfect medinas and mountains which dominate popular perceptions of the country.

History

The original Berber town of Anfa was destroyed by an earthquake in 1755. Rebuilt as Dar el Beida (the White House, or 'Casa Blanca'), its population had barely reached 20,000 by the turn of the 20th century, not a 10th

Main Attractions
Place du 16 Novembre
Place Mohammed V
The Medina
Villa des Arts
Jewish Museum
Quartier Habbous
Hassan II Mosque
Aïn Diab

Café culture.

Coffee in Casablanca.

In the medina.

of that of Fez at the same time. Since then, however, it has risen to be the main port and industrial capital of Morocco, with an ever-expanding population of around 4 million, making it the third-largest city in North Africa after Alexandria and Cairo.

Development has come at a price, however, and the city is now ringed with extensive bidonvilles (shanty towns), the breeding ground for suicide bombers who attacked foreign and Jewish targets in the city in May 2003. The bombings sent a shockwave through Morocco, whose people have always prided themselves on their tolerance. Subsequent press coverage exposed the appalling conditions of life in Casablanca's slums. If combating poverty was King Mohammed's stated priority before 2003, it has now become essential if he is to prevent the poor from falling into fundamentalism and extremism.

Ironically, Casablanca has never had any real link with the film of the same name that made the city famous. Not one scene was shot within a thousand kilometres of Casablanca and the film bears even less resemblance to today's city than it did when it was made. The nearest hint of the film that a visitor will find is at the popular 'Rick's Café' (see page 312), a chic movie-tribute restaurant near the port.

Colonial Casablanca

Downtown Casablanca is one of the liveliest places in Morocco, always busy, especially after dark, when the district's innumerable pavement cafés, down-at-heel bars and fast-food joints stalls fill up with crowds of locals, remaining lively until the small hours. Physically, the centre remains very much a French period piece (despite ad hoc development and prolonged neglect which still threatens many historic buildings),

ART DECO STYLE

Casablanca's Art Deco buildings are some of the best preserved in the country, and it is the city's unusual blend of Parisian Art Deco with local Moroccan craftsmanship that is especially interesting. This 'Mauresque' style, introduced into the villes nouvelles of Morocco during the French Protectorate, combined traditional Moroccan elements such as *zellige* tile work with European architectural styles of the 1930s such as ornate wrought-iron decorative elements and carved facades. Casablanca's buildings serve as a visual reminder of the Protectorate era and are best seen in the area around Boulevard Mohammed V and Place Mohammed V, in buildings such as the Rialto cinema, Hotel Volubilis, and the Main Post Office.

encapsulating the distinctive Mauresque style – a blend of local Moorish elements and European Art Nouveau and Art Deco motifs – which is the city's architectural trademark.

At the heart of the district, the triangular **Place du 16 Novembre ❶** is lined with several striking Mauresque buildings, as is **Boulevard Mohammed V**, running east off the square, lined with various flamboyantly decorated apartment blocks as well as the ornate Chambre de Commerce and the Le Matin/Maroc Soir buildings, both with intricately decorated facades, and Le Petit Poucet bar, once frequented by Antoine de Saint-Exupéry (Edith Piaf and Albert Camus also visited). Just off the Boulevard Mohammed V on Rue Mohammed Al Qory is the landmark Art Deco Rialto Cinema, while just south of here **Rue Ibn Batouta** is home to a further clutch of Mauresque landmarks, including the beautiful Hotel Volubilis. Also on Boulevard Mohammed V near the Rialto you'll find Casablanca's ramshackle but picturesque **Central Market**, with a tightly packed collection of shops and stalls, mainly selling food, in a quasi-souk-like building also dating from the French period.

Southwest of here, **Place Mohammed V ❷** is the centrepiece of colonial Casablanca, a spacious square surrounded by a trio of local landmarks: the huge, Moorish-looking Palais de Justice; the Préfecture, or Wilaya (the former police headquarters); and the extravagant Mauresque-style Post Office.

On the northern side of the square, look out, too, for the eye-catching Banque al Maghrib, with its elaborately sculpted facade.

The port and medina

Return to Place du 16 Novembre and then walk a few metres northwest to reach the **Place des Nations Unies**, dominated by the vast Hyatt Regency Casablanca. Northeast from here stretches the broad **Boulevard Houphouet-Boigny**, one of the most attractive roads in the city, studded with palm trees and lined

Villa des Arts.

with handicrafts shops under a long, Moorish arcade.

At the end of the boulevard you reach the entrance to Casa's workaday port area, home to a couple of good seafood restaurants.

Alternatively, from the Place des Nations Unies, dive through the walls bounding the north side of the square to enter Casablanca's small but entertaining **medina** ❸, which survives, untouched and thoroughly incongruous, at the heart of the modern city. The southern end of the medina next to the Place des Nations Unies is all hustle and bustle, with a tightly packed cluster of spice, jewellery, clothing and other souks, along with dense crowds and many amiable but persistent faux-guides offering their services. Heading north, the medina becomes quieter and more village-like in character, dotted with a couple of attractive old mosques and a small surviving section of the original town ramparts now occupied by the attractive La Sqala café-restaurant (see page 312).

A short walk further north brings you to the popular Rick's Café, with the majestic Hassan II Mosque (see page 312) rising a 10-minute walk further on.

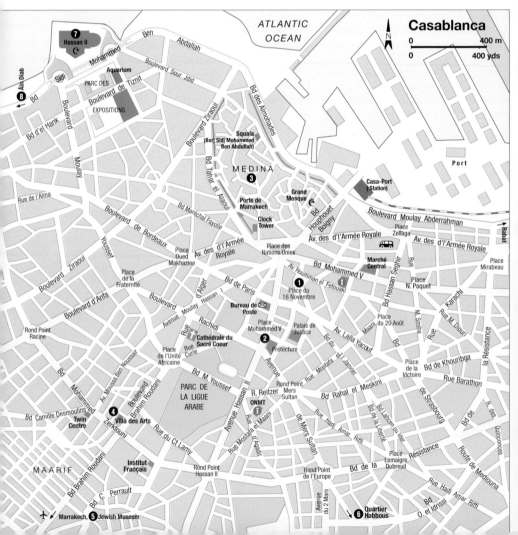

Modern Casablanca

West of Place Mohammed V and Place des Nations Unies stretch the Casablanca's up-market modern suburbs. Walking west from Place Mohammed V through a series of park-like squares brings you to the landmark Cathédrale du Sacré Coeur (1930), a striking white building in quasi Cubist-Gothic style, with elaborately ribbed windows.

A short walk beyond lies the **Villa des Arts ❹** (30 Boulevard Brahim Roudani; Tue–Sat 9.30am–7pm; tel: 0522-29 50 87, www.fondationona.ma/vdacasa.htm; free), in beautifully restored French-era colonial villa, showcasing regularly changing exhibitions of contemporary Moroccan art, as well as hosting other musical and cultural events.

Further south, **Boulevard Mohammed Zerktouni** is home to numerous up-market cafés, government buildings and the heavily fortified US embassy. Walking up the boulevard to the junction with the Boulevard d'Anfa brings you to Anfa district and the heart of modern Casa, with wide avenues and streets, busy with traffic, and lined with office blocks housing banks, advertising agencies, computer companies and architectural practices, as well as the landmark **Twin Centre**, a huge high-rise office and commercial development visible for miles in every direction.

Art Deco architecture.

Aïn Diab's beach.

Cultural destinations

The **Jewish Museum** ❺ (81 Rue Chasseur Jules Gros; tel: 0522-99 49 40, www.casajewishmuseum.com; Mon–Fri 11am–5pm) in the suburb of Oasis (take a *petit taxi*) is the only Jewish museum in the Arab world. It is a small but fascinating museum of Jewish Moroccan culture located in a superb modern building exhibiting ancient Jewish Moroccan texts, traditional costumes, jewellery and devotional objects as well as photographs of Jewish sites in the country.

The **Institut Français** (121 Boulevard Mohammed Zerktouni; tel: 0522-77 98 70, http://if-maroc.org/casablanca) in the centre of town also puts on cultural events, and there are a few art galleries worth visiting in town. **Les Transculturelles des Abattoirs** (Rue Jaafar el Barmaki, Aïn-Sebaa Hay Mohammedi; tel: 0526-51 58 29, www.flickr.com/groups/abattoirs09) has modern exhibits in what used to be a slaughterhouse. **Matisse Art Gallery** (2 Rue 6 Octobre; tel: 0522-94 49 99; Mon–Sat 10am–7pm; free), **Galerie d'Art L'Atelier** 21 (21 Rue Abou Mahassine Arrouyani; tel: 0522-98 17 85; www.atelier21.ma; Mon 3–8pm; Tue–Sat 10am–1pm, 3–8pm; free) and the **Loft Art Gallery** (13 Rue el Kaissi; tel: 0522-94 47 65; free) all have exhibitions by both international and Moroccan artists.

Quartier Habbous

A 10-minute drive from the centre (take a *petit taxi*) takes you to the **Quartier Habbous** ❻, a faux-medina built in the 1930s in the neo-Mauresque style by the French. This attractive complex is now a shopping district specialising in Arabic bookshops and traditional utilitarian objects. It is easy to walk around and hassle-free. Especially worth visiting here is the famous **Pâtisserie Bennis** in the Rue Fkih el Gabbas. Nearby is the Royal Palace in Casablanca, with its high walls and hidden gardens.

Hassan II Mosque

West along the corniche is the **Hassan II Mosque** ❼ (open to

Place Mohammed V.

non-Muslims Sat–Thur for guided tours only at 9am, 10am, 11am and 2pm), built for Hassan II on his 60th birthday in 1989 and inaugurated in 1993. This magnificent building – the largest mosque in Morocco and the fifth-largest in the world – complete with library, museum, steam baths, Qur'anic school and conference facilities, was designed by French architect Michel Pinseau and financed by voluntary subscriptions. Built on the sea bed with water on three sides, it incorporates Moroccan materials – cedar-wood from the Middle Atlas and marble from Agadir and Tafraoute.

The cost, in all more than US$750 million, was met by various means. Special officials collected contributions from every home in the land, and some employers deducted a percentage from their workers' wages.

The prayer hall, with a retractable sunroof over the central court and a glass floor over the sea, has space for 25,000 worshippers, while another 80,000 can pray on the surrounding esplanade. The marble minaret is 210 metres (689ft) high, making it the tallest religious building in the world, beating the Great Pyramid of Cheops and St Peter's in Rome. It took 35,000 workers 50 million man-hours to complete. Visible for hundreds of kilometres out to sea, this is the largest mosque outside Medina and Mecca. A 32km (20-mile) Star Wars-style visible laser beam, points, like a giant finger, from the top of the minaret towards Mecca.

Along the corniche

Casablanca's playground is the corniche of **Aïn Diab** ❽, a rich residential area along the coast, west of the mosque, with restaurants and nightclubs. Billed as one of the best restaurants in Africa, **A Ma Bretagne** (see page 312) lies at the western limit of the corniche, not far from the *Marabout* **of Sidi Abderahmen**, a picturesque cluster of white tombs rising on a rocky outcrop.

The beach along the front of the corniche, lined with beach bars, is popular and crowded in the summer.

Rick's Café.

El Jadida's Cité Portugaise.

SOUTH OF CASABLANCA

This stretch of coast is little visited by foreigners, but it is worth exploring for the old Portuguese port of El Jadida, the oyster beds of Oualidia and the pottery of Safi.

The coast south of Casablanca is served by several roads. The A3 autoroute connects Casablanca to El Jadida, opening up speedy access to the coastal strip, but if time is not a priority the more scenic R320 coastal road is still the best way to see the landscape. To the west, the Atlantic breakers are intermittently hidden by sand dunes or placid lagoons. To the east is a tussocky plain grazed by sheep and punctuated by scattered farm buildings. Occasionally the melancholy character of the region is relieved when the road sweeps within feet of an unexpected and inviting sandy cove.

Portuguese legacies

About 80km (50 miles) south of Casablanca at the mouth of the River Oum er Rbia (Mother of Spring), the main road passes the little town of **Azemmour** ❶. The view of the town from across the river is one of the most memorable in this country of set piece, almost painterly views. Indeed, Azemmour has long been a magnet for artists; many of the medina houses and walls are covered with murals, while more recently the beach is becoming increasingly popular among kite- and windsurfers.

Azemmour is the first of a string of former Portuguese ports you reach

travelling along this stretch of coast. The town was occupied by the Portuguese from 1513 until 1541 – their old fort is now the kasbah. From within, the medina is unspectacular but pleasant. The old *mellah* is now abandoned, but the synagogue is still there and can be visited, assuming you can locate the guardian.

El Jadida

About 16km (10 miles) further south, 100km (63 miles) from Casablanca, is the fast-changing town of

Map on page 171

Main Attractions
Azemmour
El Jadida
Kasbah de Boulâouane
Oualidia
Safi
Sidi Bouzid

The Portuguese Cistern at El Jadida, a Unesco World Heritage site.

Fish supper.

El Jadida.

El Jadida ❷, offering an interesting mix of cultural and hedonistic attractions.

The Portuguese held El Jadida, which they called Mazagan, for 250 years, and the fortified and moated medina (adjoining the harbour), which they constructed survives largely intact. Now protected as a Unesco World Heritage Site, this area – known as the **Cité Portugaise** – retains its original cobbled streets and a distinctively Portuguese architecture not found anywhere else in Morocco. The most remarkable relic is the **Portuguese Cistern** (daily 9am–1pm, 3–6.30pm), pillared and vaulted like a church crypt, and unexpectedly lovely, particularly around midday, with oblique shafts of sunlight reflected in the shallow water. Orson Welles filmed part of his *Othello* here. The cistern was once the armoury and fencing school for the Portuguese garrison. Round the corner the old Church of the Assumption, now restored, stands in a quiet square in the centre of the Portuguese Town. The minaret of the

nearby mosque was once the Portuguese Lighthouse.

The citadel's ramparts are well preserved, including the old Porte de la Mer, the original sea gate at which ships unloaded their cargoes. A walk around the fortifications offers superb views, particularly at the Bastion d'Ange, although for the best panorama you'll need to hike out at high tide to the end of one of the city's two breakwaters. These reach out on either side of the port, giving beautiful views back towards the citadel, with its monumental walls lifting out of the sea, the foreground framed by colourful fishing boats.

On the other side of the spacious Avenue Mohammed V, the old medina comprises a busy commercial network of shops and souks. In a small square to the south of the main thoroughfare is the interesting wool market and auction place. El Jadida is justly famous for its woven *jellabas* and *haiks*, and the square is full of tailors and shops full of colourful slippers and silk. During the afternoons auctioneers tour the square selling

individual lengths of textiles to the highest bidder.

To the north of the citadel along the coast there is a covered fish market, which is also an excellent place to eat, as is the licensed **Restaurant du Port** (right in the port, past the police barrier), with privileged views of the citadel walls.

El Jadida is currently in the throes of rapid change. Many properties in the Cité Portugaise have already been bought up and restored by foreigners and wealthy Moroccans, while massive investment is also pouring into the five-star mega-resort of **Mazagan**, just north of El Jadida, where a beautiful stretch of beach has now been equipped with its own a glitzy modern hotel complex, complete with casino and world-class golf course.

A few kilometres south of El Jadida, on the picturesque coast road, is the site of the annual *moussem* of Moulay Abdallah, usually held in the third week of September. The festival centres on the whitewashed and green-tiled *zaouia*

of the same name, situated within the 12th-century walls of Tit. The *moussem* has one of Morocco's most famous displays of *fantasia* (Moroccan horsemanship).

The Kasbah de Boulâouane

Inland from the coast stretches the Rehamna plain, a vast rolling agricultural area settled by the descendants of Arabian Bedouin, who migrated west as early as the 11th century, laying waste to the land as they went. Today the coastal plains are known for huge phosphate mines.

Of most interest in the area is the rarely visited **Kasbah de Boulâouane ③** (best seen en route from El Jadida), a huge fortress set within a tight bend of the Oum er Rbia River that rises among the cedars of the Middle Atlas and drains into the sea at Azemmour.

The Kasbah was built by the great Alaouite Sultan Moulay Ismail in 1710 as one of a series of forts designed to contain areas controlled by the Portuguese. The walls are still

TIP

El Jadida's corniche on the northern side of town is the place for cafés. A whole string of them line the pavement, each with its own character.

Women in El Jadida.

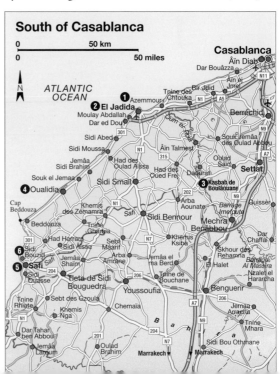

South of Casablanca

TIP

Fishermen in Oualidia sell and grill fish fresh from their boats on the beach, but the gourmet's choice for the best seafood in town is undoubtedly L'Ostréa II (see page 312), on the northern edge of town amongst its own oyster beds.

in good condition, and it is possible to walk along the ramparts. Much of the interior is now rubble, except for the elegant arched inland gatehouse, a few interior walls, some underground chambers, the mosque (still sometimes used by local villagers) and a small adjacent *marabout*. The short, stubby minaret can be climbed via a narrow staircase, but the view is disappointing for all except the very tall, as its parapet is just too high for most people to see over.

Elsewhere in the kasbah, the guardian will point out, among the ruins, remains of *zellige* tiles, carved plasterwork and columns of pure white Carrara marble, which Moulay Ismail acquired from Italy in exchange for an equal weight of sugar. Outside the walls, on the northern side, a walled corridor leads down the slope to a tower, which was presumably designed to give the kasbah access to water from the river.

Near the kasbah are the famous Boulâouane vineyards, which produce a delicious rosé, Gris de Boulâouane.

South to Oualidia

About 90km (56 miles) further south of El Jadida, past a series of coastal salt-marshes, you come to the pretty little bay and lagoon of **Oualidia ❹**.

Oualidia has become a hugely popular resort – both for foreigners and Moroccans – who are drawn to the calm waters of its lagoon, relaxed beach atmosphere and famed oysters and seafood.

There are two sections to Oualidia: the new town, above the beach, which has a few cafés, food stalls and banks; and the beach resort, down by the lagoon, where most of the town's tourist development is concentrated. There are a few good hotels (see page 302), most with excellent fish restaurants, as well as the deluxe **La Sultana** hotel, situated at the northern end of the lagoon.

Ouladia is now the most popular beach resort south of Casablanca amongst locals and is often crowded in summer, especially at weekends. Boats can be hired to cross the lagoon and access less crowded beaches on the other side of the bay. Most of the best

Safi medina.

restaurants – all simple and informal – are lined along the beach. The oyster farms *(parc à huîtres)*, such as Oyster Farm No. 7, at the northern edge of the lagoon just outside town, can also be visited. Several secluded sandy coves can be reached by driving north out of town and then crossing over a little sandy track through marshy land to the long spit of land that separates the lagoon from the open sea. A windswept *marabout* (shrine) is situated at the end of this section of land and is a beautiful, peaceful spot.

The final 66km (40 miles) of the R301 to Safi is a stunning drive along dramatic cliffs, including **Cap Beddouza**, with enticing views down onto sandy but difficult-to-access beaches.

Safi

About 150km (94 miles) south of El Jadida is **Safi ❺**. In the 17th century Safi was Morocco's chief port of trade with the Christian world, until overshadowed by Essaouira; it is now an important phosphate and fishing port, and also one of the main centres of ceramic-making in Morocco.

The town's two main monuments were left behind by the Portuguese, who occupied it briefly in the early 16th century. The **Dar el Bahr** (Château de la Mer), on the shore below the medina, is well preserved, with cannons from various parts of Europe on its ramparts, reflecting European competition for commercial influence in the town after the Portuguese were driven out. In the middle of the medina, **St Catherine's Chapel**, part of an unfinished Portuguese cathedral, is an attractive blend of Gothic and Renaissance elements, adorned with the arms of King Manuel I.

Up on the hill behind the medina, another Portuguese stronghold, called the Kechla, was enlarged and beautified by a son of Moulay Ismail. Today the building is the **Musée National de Céramique** (**National Ceramic Museum**: Wed–Mon 8.30am–noon, 2.30–6pm) and contains a worthy

collection of pottery from all over the country; it is worth a visit both for the ceramics and the delightful green-tiled courtyard.

North of the medina, on the so-called **Colline des Potiers** (Potters' Hill) are the massed kilms, chimneys and workshops of the Safi potteries, which turn out brightly coloured earthenware plates and vases with distinctive geometrical patterns, as well as more contemporary designs originally commissioned by European importers which have become popular in Morocco. Safi pottery is found all over the country, but rarely as cheaply as at the numerous roadside stalls along this stretch of coast.

The road up to the clifftop to the north of the town brings you to the village of **Sidi Bouzid ❻** with its *zaouia* (the Mahgreb term for a religious school or medersa), a good restaurant (Le Requin Bleu) and a magnificent view of town and port. One can watch the long procession of sardine boats returning to port while sampling the spiced sardines that are the local speciality.

Boats in Oualidia.

Safi is the place to buy good quality pottery.

ESSAOUIRA AND THE SOUTHWEST COAST

Crashing Atlantic waves, fierce winds, idyllic countryside and darkly brooding battlements lend drama and romance to the coast between Essaouira and Agadir.

Rabat

Main Attractions
Essaouira
Iles de Mogador
Diabet
Sidi Kaouki

The southwest Coast between Essaouira and Agadir has developed greatly in the last few years. Once a forgotten strip of land with minimal rainfall where local people fought to cultivate barren-looking fields in a constant struggle against poverty, it now has new roads which have opened up much more of the coast, particularly Essaouira (one of the focuses of the king's Vision 2010 Plan Azur), which is now linked to Marrakech by a recently upgraded road. Its stunning sandy beaches, wild winds and huge surf have made it a world centre for wind- and kitesurfers. The area is also a popular trekking destination, with several agencies offering camel and horse treks along the coast (in some cases the only way to visit some of the most magnificent beaches). Argan oil, a local product, is also achieving international recognition as a healthy component in everything from salad dressings to cosmetics.

Essaouira: star attraction

Essaouira ❶ is the region's major draw, and there is a great deal more to it than wind and beach. It first attracted international attention when Orson Welles chose it as a location for his 1952 film *Othello*, but has long been a magnet for artists, travellers and those seeking an escape from the hurried pace of other towns in Morocco.

Winston Churchill stayed here, at the Hôtel des Iles, as did Jimi Hendrix, who spent a few weeks in Essaouira in July 1969, and Bob Marley a year or so later, when the town provided a countercultural haven for hippies. Today it is also the location for the popular Gnaoua Festival of World Music, the Moroccan equivalent of Woodstock (www.festival-gnaoua.net, see page 319), which attracts tens of thousands of music-lovers in the early summer, as well as the Printemps Musical des Alizés d'Essaouira (see page 319)

Fishing boats lined up in Essaouira's harbour.

One of the European-made cannons poised for action on the ramparts.

The fresh seafood in Essaouira is hard to beat.

classical music festival in spring (www. printempsmusicaldesalizes.com).

The town lies beneath low, rolling hills, dotted with olive and argan and carved up into small stony fields that are blanketed in wild flowers in spring. Houses are painted a fresh white and blue, gulls swoop on the sea breezes, the medina is one of the prettiest in Morocco and there is a thriving fishing harbour.

Yet the Atlantic beats against Essaouira with vigour, and the town's fortifications, rooted in a ragged outbreak of rocks above a sandy bay, and a crop of rocky islands opposite, also give the town a rugged, windswept aspect when seen from beyond the walls.

Despite it being popular for so many years, Essaouira remains amazingly unaffected. The peaceful medina – a Unesco World Heritage Site – is entirely pedestrianised and the souks are a joy to explore. There are beautiful arts and crafts to be found, especially the paintings of Essaouira's local artists, and everything from chess sets to elephants carved out of thuya wood. The beaches stretching to the south of town are a mecca for surfers, windsurfers and kitesurfers while vast quantities of investment continue to pour into the medina, with derelict houses being steadily bought up and restored by both foreigners and wealthy locals, and transformed into private homes or boutique guesthouses and restaurants.

Currently there are direct flights to Essaouira from Casablanca and Paris, although most visitors approach from Marrakech, a three-hour journey along the new road.

Pirate enclave

Essaouira has been inhabited since Phoenician times. In the 1st century BC, King Juba II made it a centre of the famous Tyrean purple dye (used to edge the robes of Roman senators), which was created from the murex and purpura shells found on the Iles Purpuraires just off the coast. In the 15th century, the Portuguese established it as a trading post and free port for Europeans and their Jewish agents engaged in trans-Saharan gold, ivory and slave trading. They called Essaouira 'Mogador', though the town itself wasn't built

until the mid-18th century, by Alaouite Sultan Sidi Mohammed Ben Abdallah, who used it as a base from which his corsairs could carry out their raids. The ramparts, the town and the harbour were built by a French architect working for Ben Abdallah.

In the 19th century it quickly became a thriving town, and many of Morocco's Jews migrated here, occupying important positions in the town. In 1860 a traveller and writer called James Richards recorded in his *Travels in Morocco* that 'the population is between thirteen and fifteen thousand souls, including four thousand Jews, and fifty Christians.'

Orientation

The rather empty and windswept **Place Moulay Hassan** Ⓐ, dividing the harbour from the medina, is the town's main square, overlooked by the pretty **Casa Vera** building in whose shadow you'll find the **Gelateria Dolce Freddo**, serving up delicious Italian ice cream. The pretty magnolia-lined street running off the northeast corner of the square is lined with restaurants including the popular rooftop **Taros Café**

(see page 313) – one of the liveliest corners of town after dark.

High walls line the southern side of the square. Duck through the archway to reach **Avenue Oqba**, lined with palm trees and with a string of florid Moorish mansions (including Galerie Damgaard; see page 179) on one side and whitewashed houses perched high on the walls on the other – one of Essaouira's prettiest and most peaceful corners.

Between Place Moulay Hassan and the port is one of Essaouira's main eating attractions – the grilled fish stalls (grillades) lined up under blue-and-white awnings. Delicious freshly caught fish and seafood, from shark and swordfish to giant crabs and sea urchins, are laid out every lunchtime and evening and cooked for you on the spot – the best cheap meal in town.

Past the *grillades* is the port, a vibrant place to wander around, particularly in the afternoons when the fishing boats bring in their catch. The port is enclosed in one of Essaouira's two surviving sections of ramparts, the **Skala du Port** Ⓑ, dating from the 1770s, with a pair of squat rectangular towers at either

FACT

Thuya trees grow in the flat sandy conditions around Essaouira. Short, like scrub-oaks, they seem an unlikely source of the beautifully grained and coloured wood characteristic of the region.

Looking down over the medina.

Essaouira's broad sandy beach.

end and a delicate neoclassical gateway in the middle. An Arabic inscription above the gateway records the fact that the ramparts were designed, incongruously, by an English renegade known locally as Ahmed el Inglizi (also known as Ahmed el Alj). El Inglizi appears to have originally been a member of the infamous Salé Rovers pirate clan, and is also thought to have worked as an architect and engineer in Rabat, although his original identity remains unknown. For a small fee you can walk along the ramparts (daily 9am–5.30pm) and climb one of the towers for sweeping views of town and coast.

A short distance out to sea, directly opposite the harbour, lies a cluster of islands, formerly known as the Iles Purpuraires, now christened the **Iles de Mogador**. At the end of the 19th century, the islands were used as a quarantine station for pilgrims returning from Mecca who might be importing plague, and more recently as a prison. Various operators such as Essa Evasion (tel: 0254-79 21 39, www. essa-evasion.com) run daily boat trips around the islands, offering a close-up view of the decaying prison complex and the islands' abundant birdlife.

Into the medina

Essaouira's main souk streets – **Avenue de l'Istiqual** and **Avenue Sidi Mohammed ben Abdallah** – lie within the medina beyond Place Moulay Hassan, with endless shops piled high with colourful souvenirs. Small archways and sections of wall subdivide the various sections of the medina, while walking southeast down Rue Mohammed el Qory brings you to the outer medina walls and the impressive **Bab Marrakech**, complete with huge circular bastion, the most impressive of the town's various gateways.

Turn left up Rue Laalouj from Avenue Sidi Mohammed to reach the town's second section of **ramparts**, the **Skala de la Ville** ❻ (also known as the Skala de la Kasbah), an imposing stretch of fortifications topped with dozens of European cannons, several of British manufacture, offered as gifts from merchants to the Sultan Mohammed Ben Abdallah.

Directly beneath the ramparts lies

the small but fragrant **carpenters' souk**, crammed with little workshops in which craftsmen can be seen carving everything from boxes, bracelets, picture frames and chess sets through to tables and cabinets out of thuya and cedar-wood. One of the finest woodworkers' souks in Morocco, it supplies shops and bazaars all over the country and abroad. To bring out the rich patina of thuya wood, the handicrafts are rubbed with cotton balls soaked in vegetable oil.

Art, activities and food

Other than wandering around the medina and soaking up the atmos-phere, there isn't much in the way of cultural attractions, but the **Museum of Sidi Mohammed Ben Abdallah**  (Wed–Mon 9am–6pm), in Rue Laalouj, is well worth a visit for its collection of jewellery, musical instruments and costumes. There are dozens of other lit-tle galleries dotted about town, which are hard to miss on any wanderings through the medina (see box).

Along the Boulevard Mohammed V, running from the medina to the end of the beach, there are several lovely beach restaurants, the most popular of which is the **Chalet de la Plage** – as well as the very well organised **Club Mistral**, (page 324) where surfboards, kites and windsurfs can be rented. The **Ranch de Diabet** (page 324) arranges rides (horse and camel) on the beach, into the surrounding countryside and to historic sites and *marabouts*. For those wanting more of a thrill, quad bikes can be hired from Quad Pro Isfaoun (tel: 0524-47 49 06), Sahara Quad (tel: 0673-44 95 41; www.saharaquad.net) and Palma Quad (tel: 0666-70 99 99; www.palmaquad.com).

At the farthest end of Essaouira's beach lies **Diabat** ❷, a sleepy jumble of whitewashed houses made famous by a visit from Jimi Hendrix and now edged by a huge Sofitel golf and spa resort. The **Auberge Tangaro** (see page 302) is still a wonderful place to stay, despite the resort having been built being right in front of it.

Beaches south of Essaouira

Further along the coast, off the N1 roll-ing its way over the foothills of the High Atlas to Agadir, minor roads and tracks

Art for sale.

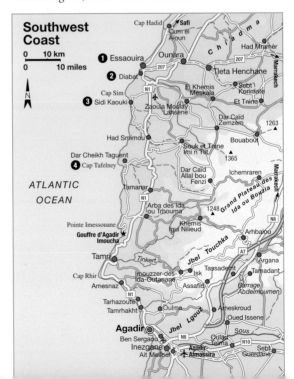

Southwest Coast

0   10 km
0   10 miles

N

Café Jimi Hendrix, Diabat.

Surfers at Sidi Kaouki.

lead to what the Moroccans call *plages sauvages* (wild beaches), long stretches of white sand-duned beaches thickly fringed by prickly gorse and argan trees and disappearing into thin mists in the distance. Surfers, who have been coming to Essaouira for years, frequent **Cap Sim** and Diabat.

Sidi Kaouki 3, a beach just south of Essaouira, and dominated at its northern end by a spectacularly sited *marabout*, offers an excellent and very accessible alternative to staying in Essaouira itself. It has become the focus for the more experienced surfing and windsurfing brigade, with a few places to stay, including the excellent Hotel Villa Soleil (see page 302), with rooms overlooking the sea, and Windy Kaouki (www.windy-kaouki.com), where you can arrange water sports and horse riding trips. Sidi Kaouki's superb sandy beach goes on for miles but it is prone to being very windy. The small tarmac road continues behind the beach along the coast, giving access to yet more stupendous beaches, some with rocky headlands offering reasonable windbreaks.

Cap Tafelney 4, surrounded by hills and sheltering a small community of picturesque fishing huts (some of which sell a frugal selection of sea-damp provisions), offers one of the coastline's longest undisturbed beaches for anyone willing to get away from the tiny tarmac access point on its northern end.

The road from Essaouira to Agadir is long, winding, remote, and frequently doused in sea mists, even in midsummer. The region is thinly populated, although there are several argan oil cooperatives along the way where you are welcome to stop and discover the secrets of this unique oil derived from the thorny argan tree (see page 283). There are very few petrol stations along this stretch, so fill up before you start. Most of the coast, remote and parched, is the preserve of camel drivers and shepherds. It is accessible at Imessouane, but most of the coast's secret beaches can only be discovered only on foot.

As the road descends to Agadir, it meets sand-heaped shorelines, blasted by crashing waves, their profiles broken by natural sculptures of sea-battered rocks, offering a tempting escape from Agadir's commercialised attractions.

Fez el Bali, with the Kairaouine Mosque in the centre.

FEZ

The old city of Fez is one of the world's last pockets of medieval civilisation, peppered with mosques, medersas and palaces, and home to a vibrant array of crafts and trades that have barely changed in 1,000 years.

Nowhere is quite like Fez. One of the oldest and most historic cities in North Africa, Fez was for many years Morocco's capital and one of the world's greatest centres of Islamic learning – the 'Athens of Africa', as it was reverentially christened, home to possibly the world's oldest university (established 859) and the largest mosque outside Mecca and Medina. It was also one of the Maghreb's great trading centres and cross-cultural melting pots, its original Arab and Berber population significantly bolstered by refugees from Andalusia and migrants from Tunisia.

Wrapped up within its imposing circuit of crenellated walls, the old medina city of Fez el Bali remains the world's most perfectly preserved medieval city, said to be the planet's largest car-free urban area – with mules still more common than motorbikes, and with tanners, metalworkers, potters, carpenters and shoemakers continuing to practice their crafts as they have done for hundreds of years. Physically the medina remains the most baffling in the country (possibly the world), a vast maze of narrow streets honeycombed with innumerable alleyways, courtyards, dead-ends and blind turnings opening up here and there to reveal a sudden glimpse of a minaret soaring above the rooftops or the splash of colourful tiles decorating a

Fez women.

roadside fountain. Foreign money and increasing numbers of tourists have poured into the city in recent years but have done little to change the medina's essential character, and despite the handicrafts shops and hawkers lining the major streets, the medina remains absorbingly untouched, mysterious and fundamentally secretive.

Imperial city

The first French Resident-General, Marshal Lyautey, declared Fez el Bali and Fez el Jdid a historic monument

Main Attractions

Medersa Bou Inania
Souk el Attarine
Place el Nejjarine
Zaouia of Moulay Idriss II
Kairaouine Mosque
Place Seffarine
Chouaras Tanneries
El Andalous Quarter
Merinid Tombs
Ibn Danan Synagogue &
 Jewish Cemetery

and slapped a preservation order on it, which preserved the city's remarkable medieval culture but without providing for its future economic health (whose subsequent decline was exacerbated by the construction of the Ville Nouvelle and the transfer of many economic and administrative functions to the new capital of Rabat). For many years, the future of the medina hung in the balance – the once-great palaces crumbled and fell and the medina became tattered and worn. In 1981 Unesco named it a World Heritage Site, and in recent years both money and tourists have come flooding in. Much as in Marrakech, there has been a boom in foreigners buying old riads and restoring them to their former glory. Fez is enjoying a huge surge in popularity, with boutique riad hotels and restaurants opening. But, as the soul of spiritual, intellectual and cultural Morocco for over 1,000 years, it also is more serious and aloof than Marrakech.

An overview of Fez

Fez (also spelt Fes, or Fès) is now served by motorway from Rabat, and even if you are coming from Marrakech it is faster to take the long way around via Casablanca rather than the seemingly more direct road via Beni Mellal and the Middle Atlas (though the latter is more attractive).

Fez itself divides into three main parts: the original medina-city, now known as **Fez el Bali**; the misleadingly named 13th-century district of **Fez el Jdid** (New Fez); and the **Ville Nouvelle**, built by the French in the 19th century. The three areas are quite widely spread out, and it's the best part of a 30-minute walk from the Ville Nouvelle to Fez el Bali – a pleasant enough stroll via Fez el Jdid, although you might prefer to catch a *petit taxi* (around 20 to 30dh) between the two, especially if you've been hiking around the medina all day. Various buses also connect the two districts, although working out routes can be tricky, and it's generally a lot less bother to catch a cab.

In high summer, the heat can be stifling. Indeed, Fassis (local residents) who can afford it escape to the North Coast during July and August. Air

Fez at night.

conditioning is practically essential, and hotels with pools are at a premium.

The first city

The original medina-city, **Fez el Bali**, stretches out on both sides of the small Oued Fez river. The area divides into two parts, facing one another across the Oued Fez. The **Kairaouine Quarter** on the west bank of the river dates from about 825, when over 2,000 Arab families from Kairouan in Tunisia came here as refugees. The **Andalous Quarter** on the east bank was established a few years earlier, when 8,000 Arab families settled here, expelled from Andalusia by the Christians and bringing with them the skills and learning that made Fez an outstanding centre of culture and craftsmanship.

As Arab rule in Spain drew to its end, further influxes of refugees from Cordoba, Seville and Granada arrived. They introduced the mosques, stucco, mosaics and other decorative arts, and a variety of trades that are still central to the medina's economic survival. The strategic division between the two quarters was used by warring factions through the centuries until Youssef Ben Tashfine of the Almoravide dynasty took control in the 11th century. Although Marrakech was his capital, he did great things for Fez, demolishing the wall dividing the two quarters and building a bridge across the river. This helped, but even today you are aware of the distinction between the two.

Kairaouine Mosque detail.

Mosques were built in each quarter and, seen from above, the quarters appear to form a kind of amphitheatre around the **Kairaouine Mosque** (Fez's most important building), the green tiles marking out its total area. To the right of the Kairaouine as you look down on the city, a thin minaret marks the other great religious monument of Fez, the Zaouia of Moulay Idriss II. The Andalous Mosque, a similar focal point, is on the east bank of the river.

Most visitors enter Fez el Bali via the landmark Bab Boujeloud, set back behind a large open square. Approaching from Fez el Jdid, you

Rooftops of the Kairaouine Mosque.

don't immediately see Bab Boujeloud, which is hidden behind buildings, although you will see a large gateway away to the left which is easily mistaken for Bab Boujeloud itself, although it leads only into the self-contained Kasbah des Filalas rather than the main medina itself.

Batha Museum

Before plunging into the medina proper, it's worth a visit to the **Batha Museum ❶** (Wed–Mon 8.30am–noon, 2.30–6pm) in the Dar Batha Palace on Place de l'Istiqlal, just south of the main entrance to the medina at Bab Boujeloud. Inside, rooms open off a central garden, each one dedicated to a particular Moroccan craft and its application in everyday life. The guide (who expects a small tip) will shed light on the purpose of the various articles on display, from the measure for determining the optimum level of alms to the bristle necklace placed around the necks of male calves so that their mothers, painfully pricked when their young came to suckle, would kick them away, forcing them to graze on the herbs that made their meat particularly sweet.

Exploring Fez el Bali

One of the main entrances to the medina is through the **Bab Boujeloud ❷** to the east of the palace area. Cars are not allowed in the medina, but parking is available around the gates, which are also ringed by simple cafés and restaurants, including the popular **Medina Café** and **Le Kasbah**. Taxis can be picked up from Place Baghadi just by the gate, while all long-distance buses (apart from CTM services) leave from the main bus station nearby, just outside Bab Mabrouk.

The Boujeloud Gate, built in 1913, is one of Fez's more recent *babs* (gates) but is traditionally tiled and decorated: blue and gold outside, reputedly to represent the city of Fez, and green and gold inside to represent Islam. Just

inside the gate, the square splits into the two main streets: **Talaa Kebira** (Grand Talaa), the upper one on the left (inside the gate make a left turn followed immediately by a right), and the less interesting and quieter **Talaa Sghira** (Small Talaa), running parallel straight ahead.

Initial impressions of the medina may be chaotic, but in fact its various areas followed a carefully planned structure. Each quarter has its own mosque, *foundouk*, Qur'anic school, water fountain, hammam and bakery, where everyone in the quarter brings their own dough to be baked in the central ovens (marks of identification help avoid confusion). Daily prayers are attended in the mosque of the quarter, the Grand Mosques being used on Fridays, when people flock from all areas for this special prayer day.

Medersa Bou Inania

Just off the square, on the upper reaches of Talaa Kebira, is one of the most famous sights in Fez, the much-photographed **Medersa Bou**

Oranges with cinnamon, a favourite Moroccan dessert.

Kids playing in the mellah.

Sounds and smells stimulate and soothe in turn in Fez's medina. One of the nicest aromas is of fresh mint, large bundles of which are sold on every street corner.

Bab Boujeloud.

Inania ❸ (daily 9am–noon, 12.30–6pm), an exuberant example of Merinid architecture. Medersas, or Islamic schools, formerly played an important role in the cultural life of Morocco, supported by endowments from sultans and revenues from local inhabitants, and some of the most beautiful are in Fez. Medersas served as lodging houses for students who were strangers to the town, the idea being that segregation from the wider community would help them concentrate on their religious studies. For convenience, they were built close to the mosque where the students went for their lessons. Similar in structure to mosques and private houses, medersas are centred on a courtyard and elaborately decorated with *zellige*, lacy stucco and cedar-wood carvings. Students often spent more than 10 years at university, so places to live were at a premium.

Local lore

According to local sources – almost certainly unreliable in view of the Moroccans' love of cautionary tales – the origins of the Medersa Bou Inania are rooted in a rich subsoil of sex and scandal. The Sultan Abou Inan was renowned for his extravagant lifestyle and extensive harem, but there came a point in his dissolute life when, deeply in love with a concubine, he vowed to atone. He made his lover his wife and, as a public display of his new-found piety, commissioned the Medersa Bou Inania to be built on the site of public latrines inside Boujeloud Gate. But unfortunately the object of his love was a former prostitute-dancer, and his viziers – though impressed by the new medersa – were outraged that the Sultan should honour a whore in this way. The clever Sultan took them to the newly completed building. 'Did you not use to piss where now you pray?' he asked, inviting them to see the corollary. From then on the Sultan's new wife was considered a pillar of respectability.

Abou Inan wanted his medersa to rival the Kairaouine Mosque, and it did indeed become one of the most important religious buildings in the

A GUIDE TO GUIDES IN FEZ EL BALI

Finding your way around Fez el Bali is a challenge, and most strangers to the city find it worthwhile to hire a guide. Fix a price before you start, though at the end he (or she) may disarmingly suggest you pay what you think the tour was worth. Don't get drawn into this. There are fixed rates for official guides (posted in the tourist office) so work on that basis – though you'll most likely be asked for more. You can arrange an official guide through your hotel or the tourist office on Place Mohammed V. Despite the Tourist Police (Brigade Touristique), 'faux guides' can still be a problem, particularly around Boujeloud Gate.

Part of your tour will inevitably include an expensive visit to a carpet emporium or cooperative. If you have no desire to buy and are short of time, try to make this clear at the outset, although you won't be believed. If you do find yourself being sucked into the sales patter, retreat politely. If you are guideless and taking your chance alone in the medina, remember that any young lad will guide you out (for a few dirhams) should you get lost. Recently, too, the city has placed coloured signposts around the medina directing visitors on five different walks, themed by traditional Fassi culture – these also serve as pointers to the nearest major landmark in the likely event that you become lost.

city. He failed in his aim to have the call to prayer transferred here from the Kairaouine, but it was granted the status of Grand Mosque, unheard of for a medersa, and midday prayers are still heard here (during which the building is closed), making it is one of Morocco's few buildings in religious use that can be entered by non-Muslims.

The building follows the usual layout, but the quality and intricacy of the decoration are outstanding. The courtyard facade is decorated with carved stucco, above which majestic cedar-wood arches support a frieze and corbelled porch. The examples of cedar-wood carving, stucco work, Kufic script writing and *zellige* work are outstanding.

Opposite the Bou Inania there once stood a remarkable water clock, with thirteen wooden blocks balancing 13 brass bowls (only seven of the original bowls remain) protruding beneath 13 windows. Sultan Abou Inan erected it opposite the medersa to ring out the hour of prayer, hoping its originality would bring further fame to his beloved religious school. Unfortunately, its 14th-century mechanics have defeated modern horologists and the clock has been silent for over five centuries. According to legend, a curse was put on the clock when a passing Jewess was so alarmed by its chime that she miscarried her child.

In 1990, following the discovery of documents detailing the working of the clock, a programme of restoration was begun. However, the work is proving more complex than expected and the clock has yet to be repaired. Near the water clock is the **Café Clock** (see page 313), a wonderful place for a drink or lunch.

Talaa Kebira

Fez el Bali's main thoroughfare, **Talaa Kebira**, bisects the entire Kairaouine Quarter, running from just inside the Bab Boujeloud to the Kairaouine Mosque and on to the Zaouia of Moulay Idriss II (see page 191). Many of the medina's most interesting sights lie on or just of the road.

From Bab Boujeloud, Talaa Kebira runs steadily downhill for most of its length down into the valley of the Oued Fez and the Kairaouine Mosque. A few hundred metres past the Medersa Bou Inania, you pass a cluster of **fondouks** – just a few of the more than 200 *fondouks* that once dotted Fez el Bali. Now mainly used as warehouses, these were created at about the same time as the medersa as lodgings for traders and their mules: large two-storey buildings with rooms arranged on galleries around spacious centre courtyards.

Notable examples include the **Bousl Hame** at No. 49 Talaa Kebira (on the left), now occupied by an interesting drum workshop, and, about 50 metres/yds beyond, the **Qaât Smen** (signed on the right), home to a small butter and honey market (announced by the strong smell of *smen* – an aged and expensive butter used in the best couscous). Shortly past here (also on the right) is the ramshackle **Fondouk Tazi**, with a small cluster of pottery

TIP

As Talaa Kebira starts to go downhill a few hundred metres past Medersa Bou Inania, look out on the right for the one-time home (marked by a plaque) of Ibn Khaldoun, a famous 14th-century historian from Tunis who wrote a seminal history of the Arabs.

Medersa Bou Inania.

Fez's 14th-century water-clock.

Babouches for sale.

view, framed by the bulging upper storeys of the buildings.

The road now changes its name to **Rue es Chrabliyine** (Slipper-Makers' Street), lined with dozens of shops selling *babouches*, the traditional soft leather shoes still worn by many Moroccans. With their backs turned down so that they are easy to slip on and off on entering a home or mosque, *babouches* come in a wide range of colours, though, for men, yellow is the popular choice for everyday use and white for Fridays and other holy days. Women's *babouches*, in velvet, silk and nylon, as well as leather, come in a huge range of colours, often bejewelled or embroidered with gold thread.

Past the babouche shops, the street descends steeply again, narrowing and disappearing beneath a latticed wooden roof as it enters the **Souk el Attarine** ❹. This area is the commercial centre of the medina, honeycombed with the densest and most disorienting tangle of alleyways you'll find anywhere in Morocco and promising instant confusion the

stalls and workshops, and, a few metres beyond (on the left) the largely derelict and memorably smelly **Fondouk Lbbata**, piled high with sheepskins being stripped from carcasses prior to curing and tanning.

Past the *fondouks*, Talaa Kebira begins to descend more steeply, passing beneath a small archway beyond which the fine green and white minaret of the late 18th-century **Chrabliyine Mosque** comes suddenly into

WATER, WATER EVERYWHERE

Islam blossomed in dusty, dry lands where trees, flowers and water were (and are) especially treasured. Considerable thought was therefore expended in solving problems of irrigation, and in cities water was introduced wherever possible, in splashing fountains and pools, both to provide a convenient supply of drinking water, and also in order to help to cool the air within crowded medinas. The fact that Fez has so many fountains is thanks to the vision of the Almoravid Sultan Youssef Ben Tashfine, who rerouted the Oued Fez river and created an elaborate network of channels in order to carry water throughout the city. By the late 11th century every mosque, medersa and *fondouk*, as well as most of the richer households, had water, and there were numerous street fountains and public baths. The system included a successful method of flushing the drains.

The sound and sight of Fez's many drinking fountains refresh the senses, though many have now run dry, and it is best not to drink from those that still have water in them. The fountains are notable for elaborate *zellige* settings, exemplified by the magnificent Nejjarine Fountain. Wear, tear and pollution have dulled the brilliance of the stonework, and in some cases destroyed the pipes feeding the fountains, although restoration work (www.fez-riads.com/restoration) is slowly returning them to their former glory.

moment you step off the main drag. Souk el Attarine itself is the medina's traditional perfume and spice-sellers' souk, selling old-fashioned Arabian perfumes such as musk and amber, although many of the tightly packed shops are now filled with more workaday household items.

Continue through the souk, looking out for the Dar Saada restaurant on your left. Directly opposite this, a small alleyway leads straight into the picture-perfect little **Souk el Henna**, a tiny little square shaded by a pair of venerable plane trees. Huge piles of local pottery lie stacked up along one side of the square, while opposite are a line of traditional herbalists with baskets of green henna leaves, camomile, rose buds, antimony and olive soap – not to mention more outlandish items such as powdered chameleons to treat warts and charms to ward off the evil eye.

Place el Nejjarine

Exit the back of the Souk el Henna, then turn left and right to reach the intimate **Place el Nejjarine** ❺.

Dominating the corner of the square is the wonderful **Fondouk el Nejjarine** (daily 10am–5pm), dating from the late 17th century and heavy with the scent of worked cedar and thuya wood, which has been beautifully restored and now serves as a museum devoted to woodworking techniques and tools. Here craftsmen crouch over finely carved tables, bed heads, chairs and every kind of wooden creation.

The **Nejjarine Fountain**, the focal point of the square, is an outstanding example of *zellige* decoration and stands almost like a shrine to water. On your right, a large covered workshop is devoted to the making of extravagantly chintzy snow-white palanquins and thrones used on a variety of festive occasions – to carry boys undergoing circumcision, or to carry a bride or bridegroom to their wedding.

Zaouia of Moulay Idriss II

Exit Place Nejjarine the way you came in and continue directly ahead to enter the *horm*, the sacred area around

Medina stall.

The Future of the Medina

Fez is one of the most culturally important – and most fragile – cities in the world. But there is hope for its future.

Fez embodies all the problems facing medinas in the modern world. For centuries it was the political and cultural capital of Morocco and is still seen as the centre of intellectual endeavour. But its 1,200-year-old medina relies upon the interdependence of industries and social structures for its survival. Contrary to some visitors' impressions, it doesn't exist as a museum, and its souks do not stock merely tourist trinkets; the Fassis rely on their industries, and their leather goods, silverware and cedar work are sold throughout the country to Moroccans. Over 200,000 people live and work in the medina, and it's clear to anyone wandering through the packed souks that tourists are irrelevant to most of the inhabitants.

Old methods are still used by the tradesmen and artesans. There isn't room in the city to introduce new technology, open new factories and streamline

In the medina.

production, even if they were wanted. So far only some of the potteries have been moved out of the centre to hillsides close by, where new technology could be introduced. But such progress is beset by problems: break a part of the vast structure of the medina and it all might crumble.

Overcrowding is the main cause of Fez's ills. Over the past 50 years people have been moving into the town from the countryside to find work, putting Fez under severe strain. Certain public infrastructures, such as water supplies and 13th-century sewage systems, are at breaking point. There is no new housing available, and shanty towns have spawned on the nearby hillsides. The different quarters of the city are gradually losing their individual functions.

Preserving Morocco's heritage

But there is also cause for optimism. In 1980 Unesco launched an appeal and introduced an ambitious programme of restoration. In 2001 a development plan for the medina was adopted, which safeguards houses close to collapse and promotes regional tourism. Now working in partnership with the World Bank and the Italian government, Unesco has set up Ader-Fez (Agence Pour la Dédensification et la Réhabilitation de la Médina de Fès). Their task is enormous and would seem impossible, but work is under way. The objective is to keep the medina as a working structure – reinforcing its foundations both physically and administratively. The project has extended to include Fez el Jdid as well as Fez el Bali. One of the elements that contributed to Fez being declared a site of Outstanding Universal Value is the 'survival of architectural know-how' – the fact that the medieval craft traditions of the city remain a living, essential part of trade and commerce in the city – and the continued authenticity of the city. Unesco and all those involved in the restoration and preservation of the medina acknowledge that it is the survival of these trades that contributes to the survival of the medina itself, through the restoration of its palaces and houses.

In recent years, there has been a considerable surge in tourism, with expats and wealthy locals buying and renovating decaying riads into guesthouses and boutique hotels, and kick-starting the general gentrification of the medina as a whole. Increasing numbers of expats also now choose to live in the medina, making vital contributions towards rescuing some of the city's most historic buildings.

the **Zaouia (shrine) of Moulay Idriss II** ❻, the effective founder of Fez. The boundaries of the *horm* are marked by chest-high wooden bars set across all entrances to the area; until the French Protectorate this barred not only mules and donkeys but also Jews and Christians. It also marked a refuge for Muslims, who could not be arrested in this area.

The zaouia itself is announced by bright stalls selling candles, incense, padded baskets for gifts, and nougat, dates and nuts, the usual signs in Morocco that one is approaching a shrine – along with beggars accosting pilgrims on their way to devotions. The tomb was built by the Idrissids in the 9th century but was allowed to fall into decay until it was rebuilt in the 13th century by the Merinids. The Wattasids rediscovered the tomb and from this period it became the revered shrine it is now. Non-Muslims are not allowed inside, although you can look through for a glimpse of the richly tiled and carpeted interior, complete with a trio of chandeliers and a pair of grandfather clocks. In September the shrine is the focus of a huge *moussem*.

Continue past the shrine to reach the **Kissaria** ❼, a covered market arranged around a tight (and supremely disorienting) grid of narrow alleyways and selling the luxury items traditionally sold in the vicinity of the Kairaouine Mosque – embroidery, silks and brocades, as well as imported goods.

Medersa el Attarine

Find your way back to Souk el Attarine and then continue east to reach a major junction, with the vast Kairaouine Mosque stretching away to your right. Immediately in front of you is the **Medersa el Attarine** ❽, one of several medersas around the Kairaouine Mosque. The medersa was built by Sultan Abou Said between 1322 and 1325 and is similar in design to the later Bou Inania

(see page 187); no doubt many of the same master craftsmen worked on its interior. The medersa is no longer in religious use and can be visited (daily 9am–6pm), offering glimpses into the neighbouring Kairaouine Mosque from its rooftop.

The Great Mosque

All roads in the medina lead to the vast **Kairaouine Mosque** ❾ (closed to non-Muslims), which serves as the Great Mosque of Fez el Bali. Rivalled in size only by the Hassan II Mosque in Casablanca, it covers 16,000 sq metres (4 acres) and can accommodate more than 20,000 people. It was founded in 859 by Lalla Fatima el Fihrya, a pious woman from Kairouan, Tunisia, one in a wave of immigrants from Kairouan. The mosque, then merely a small prayer hall, was built in memory of her father.

Each of Morocco's sultans added to the mosque and changed it. The Merinids' alterations in the 13th century cast it in its present mould. Green tiled roofs cover 16 naves and the tiled courtyards have two end pavilions,

Facade of the Nejjarine Fountain, one of the finest in Fez.

Hides being left out to dry.

In a Fez souk.

added by the Saadians, and a beautiful 16th-century fountain reminiscent of the Court of Lions of the Alhambra in Granada. Despite its size, the mosque has been so thoroughly buried by surrounding buildings that it is surprisingly difficult to get any real sense of its extent or shape, and although tantalizing glimpses of the interior can be had through the various entrances when opened during prayer time –overall the mosque remains (for non-Muslims at least) a frustratingly mysterious presence at the heart of the medina. The best views of the complex are to be had from the rooftops of surrounding buildings – the lofty Borj Kairaouine, opposite the Medersa el Attarine, offers possibly the best.

The sanctuary interior is austere, with horseshoe arches over some 270 columns. It was most probably the first university in the world, and was considered a great seat of learning; its reputation attracted over 8,000 students in the 14th century, and it even boasted a future pope, Sylvester II (pope 999–1003), among its students, as well as Ibn Khaldoun, the great Arab polymath, and Averroes (Ibn Rushd). The university remains one of the most important centres of spiritual and intellectual Islam in the world.

The **Kairaouine Library**, on the far side of the mosque, is also thought to have been built in the 9th century. Closed to the public, it contains one of the largest collections of Islamic literature in the world.

Walk anti-clockwise around the mosque to reach the pretty little tree-shaded **Place Seffarine ❿**. The square is mainly occupied by piles of huge cauldrons are stacked in every available space and the workshops of various metalworkers, whose arrhythmic cacophony of hammering can be heard long before you reach the square itself. The same skills were used on the redecoration of the great doors to the Royal Palace, visible across Place des Alaouites as you approach Fez el Jdid from the Ville Nouvelle (see page 200). If you can gain access to the **Medersa Seffarine** close by, climb up to its roof for a view of the overall scene.

TRADITIONAL COSMETICS

Moroccan women take great pride in their appearance, often using cosmetics until well into old age. Though they may let their figures go, their faces remain unlined and their hair stays beautifully strong and shiny.

Nowadays, all Moroccan markets have numerous stalls selling international-brand toiletries and cosmetics, but tried-and-tested traditional beauty products, such as antimony for the eyes, crushed rose buds and cloves to scent the hair, olive-oil soap for the skin and red salve for the cheeks and lips remain popular. Henna is used by almost everyone. As well as adding lustre to hair, it is used to decorate women's hands and feet on special occasions such as festivals and weddings, when professional henna painters are hired to create the most intricate designs. The henna leaves are boiled to produce a green paste that is piped onto the hands in elaborate designs and fixed with lemon juice. When dry the crusty paste is removed, leaving lace-like orange patterns. As well as being decorative, the henna is said to protect its wearer from the evil eye.

In recent years an interest in Moroccan beauty products has spread through Europe. In particular, argan oil (see page 283) is gaining a reputation for its healing properties, especially for erasing skin blemishes.

Chouaras Tanneries

Take the north exit from Place Seffa-rine and follow the road around for a few minutes to reach the **Chouaras Tanneries** ⑪, on the River Fez – hustlers anxious to show you the tanneries (and extract a healthy tip in return) will most likely descend on you en masse as soon as you approach the area. These are the larg-est of the three tanneries in Fez – and announced by the pervasive and stomach-churning stench of fresh animal hides steeped in urine. Guides offer visitors sprigs of mint to block out the stench.

The area has hardly changed since medieval times. Hides are treated in a honeycomb of small open-air stone vats, each bright with a differently coloured dye and marvellously pho-togenic when the light falls on them in the mornings, like some enormous painter's palette, while surrounding roofs are hung with drying skins. The tanneries are run as a cooperative, with each foreman responsible for his own workforce and tools. Jobs, which are strenuous and smelly but well paid,

are practically hereditary. Visitors are trooped through the walkways and helped up small uneven steps to van-tage points for photographs.

Andalous Mosque.

The Andalous quarter

Back at Place Seffarine, take the southern exit (opposite the road to the tanneries) and cross the bridge over the Oued Fez – a remarkable, modest little river, given its signifi-cance in the city's history. Beyond here stretches the **El Andalous Quar-ter** ⑫, named after the Arab refugees from Spain who settled here in 818. This is the second of Fez el Bali's major quarters, although it sees few tourists, and has relatively few sights and a determinedly workaday atmos-phere compared with the touristy Kairaouine district.

The quarter's major landmark is the magnificent **Andalous Mosque** ⑬, founded shortly after the Kairaouine Mosque in the 9th century and embel-lished by the Almohads at the begin-ning of the 13th century (to reach the mosque, turn right immediately inside the Bab Recif gateway and follow the

Medersa el Attarine.

road as it winds uphill – overhead signs will point you in the right direction if you get lost). The great north gate is particularly impressive, towering over the surrounding streets and decorated with *zellige* tile work and a magnificent cedar porch.

A couple of medersas stand in the lee of the mosque. Follow the alleyways around the right-hand side of the mosque to reach the **Medersa es Sahrija**, an early 14th-century structure with an ablutions pool in the centre of the courtyard. Its *zellige* decorations are some of the oldest in the country and it has an impressive ancient wood *minbar* (pulpit), although it was closed to visitors at the time of writing.

Walking up the hill brings you out of the medina at the **Bab Ftouh** gate, from where buses and taxis leave for the Ville Nouvelle via the ring road.

Across from Ftouh Gate is the main cemetery, which on Fridays becomes as busy as a railway station, as families come to sprinkle water on the graves, to leave sprigs of olive and to picnic beside the tombs of their dead loved ones. Non-Muslims are not welcome.

Passing the time with a board game.

Round the city walls

Retrace your steps back down through the Andalous Quarter, across the river and back to Souk el Attarine, then take the road north (opposite the back of the Souk el Henna) to Bab Guissa – once again, helpful overhead signs point you in the right direction if you become lost. This area of the medina is determinedly local, with hardly any tourists in sight, offering an interesting alternative view of old Fez in the raw, away from the handicraft shops and tourist emporia of Talaa Kebira.

En route to Bab Guissa, a turning on the right leads past the elaborate stucco entrance of the **Zaouia of Sidi Ahmed Tijani**. The inspiration behind a major Sufi sect of North and West Africa. Ahmed Tijani (1737–81) began his journey to sainthood at the age of seven, by which time he had memorised the Qur'an.

Past here, the historic **Sofitel Palais Jamai Hotel** offers a good place for lunch or tea on the terrace by its pool. The hotel was built at the end of the 19th century as a palace by the Ulad Jamai brothers, viziers of

Sultan Moulay Hassan. The brothers eventually fell foul of the political machinations of the day, and when Moulay Abd el Aziz succeeded to the throne in 1894 they were sent in fetters to Tetouan. Walter Harris, correspondent of the London *Times*, related their fate in his book *Morocco That Was*: 'In the course of time – and how long those ten years must have been – Haj Amaati died. The Governor of Tetouan was afraid to bury the body, lest he should be accused of having allowed his prisoner to escape. He wrote to Court for instructions. It was summer, and even the dungeon was hot. The answer did not come for eleven days, and all that time Si Mohammed Soreir remained chained to his brother's corpse.'

Continuing north you exit the medina at the Bab Guissa and the ring-road around the medina city walls, the so-called **Tour de Fez**. High on a steep hillside opposite Bab Guissa are the remains of the **Merinid Tombs ⓮**, the mausoleums of the last Merinid sultans. Described in the chronicles as beautiful white marble with vividly coloured epitaphs, the tombs are now a no more than a cluster of crumbling ruins. The views are sensational, however, offering a bird's-eye panorama of the medina and the chance to appreciate the scale, complexity and sheer mind-boggling density of the medina from a privileged vantage point.

Behind the Merinid Tombs is the five-star Hôtel Les Mérinides, an ugly but brilliantly positioned hotel. The Borj Nord, a 16th-century military fortress dating from the Saadian era, is just below the hotel and is now a museum, the recently restored **Arms Museum ⓯** (Musée des Armes; Tue–Sun 9am–noon, 2–5pm), which houses a collection of weapons, including the huge cannon used during the battle of the Three Kings.

Looking across the medina from the Arms Museum you can make out the **Borj Sud**, standing sentinel on a hillside on the far side of the medina amid olive trees and gravestones. Many of the hillsides surrounding Fez are dotted with white tombstones, as there is no room for graves inside the city. On Friday, the Muslim holy day,

Metalwork in the Place Seffarine.

it is customary for families to visit the graves of loved ones.

Descending from the Arms Museum, the Tour de Fez brings you back to Bab Mabrouk and the large open square in front of Bab Boujeloud, where you began you tour of the medina.

Fez el Jdid

East of Fez el Bali stretches the confusingly named quarter of **Fez el Jdid** (New Fez), built by the Merinids in the 13th century and sprawling between the medina and Ville Nouvelle, with the old Jewish *mellah* on its southeastern side. Fez el Jdid was laid out by the Merinids during the 13th century to incorporate an impressive Royal Palace and gardens, and as the administrative centre of Fez; its regal grandeur and wide-open spaces still contrast strikingly with the nearby medina. The quarter's significance diminished greatly when the French moved the centre of government to Rabat.

West of Bab Boujeloud stretches the Avenue des Français, which borders the peaceful and attractive **Jardins du Boujeloud** (also known as the Jnane Sbil; daily 8am–6pm; free) on one side. The walls between Fez el Bali and Fez el Jdid were joined at the end of the 19th century and some of the buildings around this area date from that time.

The western end of Avenue des Français leads you into the small square of the **Petit Méchouar** at the back of the Royal Palace, ringed by high walls and a perplexing number of gateways. Heading due south from here leads you into the **Grande Rue de Fez Jdid**, a lively souk street crammed with clothes and textile shops – usually gridlocked with local shoppers from late afternoon onwards – from which you emerge at the impressive Bab Semarine at the western end of the old Jewish *mellah*.

Jewish Fez

The *mellah* – the first Jewish quarter in Morocco – was originally sited by the Bab Guissa gate. When Fez el Jdid was built, the Jews were ordered to move to their new quarter near the Sultan's palace. Many Jews with

Moroccan pottery.

interests in the medina preferred to become Muslims and thus stay in Fez el Bali. Those who did move were promised protection in consideration of supplementary taxes.

The name *mellah*, which means 'salt' in Arabic, alludes to the job of draining and salting the heads of decapitated rebels before they were impaled on the gates of the town, a task traditionally done by Jews. Morocco's Jews held an ambiguous position prior to the protectorates; although they were ostensibly under the Sultan's protection, their freedom was limited. No Jew was allowed to wear shoes or ride outside the *mellah*, for instance, and further restrictions were placed on their travel elsewhere.

Very few Jewish families are left. What remains are their tall, very un-Arabian buildings with distinctive wooden balconies which line the lively **Rue des Merinides**, the heart of the district. Just off this road lies the **Ibn Danan Synagogue** ⑯ (Sat–Thu, no set hours, a guardian will let you in; donations), which dates from the 17th century and is a reminder of the mixed cultural heritage of Morocco. After falling into disrepair, the synagogue was restored in collaboration with the World Monuments Funds and Morocco's Ministry of Culture and reopened in 1999.

The nearby **Jewish Cemetery** (Cimetière Israelite de Fes) is one of the oldest in Morocco, with rows of tightly packed, pristine white gravestones laid out on the slope of the hill stretching down towards the river. The adjacent **Habarim Synagogue** (daily 7am–7pm; donations) contains the remains of several eminent rabbis, as well as a woman who allegedly refused to convert to Islam and marry the Sultan and was killed as a result.

The west end of Rue des Merinides emerges into the spacious Place des Alaouites. Dominating the square is the flamboyant **Royal Palace** ⑰ (**Dar el Makhzen;** closed to the public) &, originally built by the Merenids but constantly reworked ever since, and most of what you can see today is largely modern. The entrance to the palace bounding Place is undoubtedly impressive,

Donkeys carry the load.

El Andalous Quarter.

in a slightly Hollywood sort of way, with huge brass doors surrounded by multi-coloured bands of plasterwork, *zellige* and calligraphy. The grounds, said to cover 40 hectares (100 acres), are enclosed by high walls.

Ville Nouvelle

West of Fez el Jdid stretches the **Ville Nouvelle**, built by the French after World War I on a grid system that is simplicity itself to navigate after the medina. Fez's Ville Nouvelle is less interesting than others in the country, lacking the Maurequse touches of Casablanca and Rabat, or the sheer glamour of Marrakech, although there's a decent if uninspiring selection of hotels and restaurants here if you prefer not to stay in Fez el Bali. The Ville Nouvelle is also usually livelier than the medina in the evenings, as this is where most Fassis choose to spend their time (as in all cities in Morocco, the medina is considered a backward and dull part of the city). The best cafés are found along Avenue Mohammed V, particularly on the crossroads with Avenue Mohammed es Slaoui,

Dyeing leather in the Chouaras Tanneries.

where every corner is occupied by a busy café terrace.

Beyond the city

Exit routes west of the Ville Nouvelle head through fertile landscapes to Sidi Kacem or Meknes (see pages 203). A few kilometres in the other direction are the hot springs and cool sources of **Sidi Harazem**, where the ubiquitous mineral water is bottled. Site of the shrine of Sidi Harazem, a Sufi mystic, this is a popular pilgrimage site, and can get very crowded at weekends. Unfortunately much of what was once an attractive spot has been concreted over, making it a disappointing escape from the harsh summer heat in Fez.

Much further afield, but more rewarding, is the N8, the main route south of Fez to Marrakech. This promises a long but glorious journey through the Middle Atlas Mountains via the delightful Immouzzer du Kandar or the pretty little town of Sefrou, where Moulay Idriss lived whilst building Fez, and on to the cedar forests of Azrou and Ifrane.

One of Fez's old fondouks.

One of Meknes's gates.

THE MEKNES REGION

The smallest of Morocco's four imperial cities, Meknes offers a fascinating snapshot of the megalomaniac rule of Sultan Moulay Ismail and a perfect base for day trips to the superb Roman remains of Volubilis and the holy town of Moulay Idriss.

Rabat ● ● Meknes

Main Attractions
Meknes
Volubilis
Moulay Idriss

The smallest of Morocco's four great imperial cities (and the seventh-largest city in the country), Meknes is rather eclipsed both by Fez and Marrakech, but it does see its fair share of foreign visitors and is well worth visiting as a destination in its own right. Its proximity to **Fez ❶** (see page 183) means that it is often treated as a day's excursion from there rather than as a base in its own right, even though it has several further places of interest on its own doorstep, including the fascinating remains of the Roman city of **Volubilis** and the pilgrimage town of **Moulay Idriss**, where the tomb of Idriss I, founder of the Idrissid dynasty, is located.

Meknes ❷ nestles in attractive countryside peppered with shrines and springs and is renowned for the quality of its olives, as well as lying at the heart of the country's premier wine-producing region – if you drink a glass of Moroccan red or white, chances are it came from somewhere near here.

Visiting Meknes

Many people come to Meknes as a day-trip from Fez, sometimes combined with a trip to Volubilis, although this makes from rather a rushed visit and really allow you to do justice to either place. Staying a night or two in Meknes makes for more leisurely and rewarding experience, as well as giving

you time to take in the holy town of Moulay Idriss en route.

Meknes can be reached directly from Fez along the N6, while the short drive to Volubilis from Meknes is very straightforward, heading north on the 413, with Moulay Idriss first (about 25km/16 miles, from Meknes) and Volubilis less than a mile further on. The road between Volubilis and Meknes runs through fertile hills planted with vines and dotted with the white domed tombs of *marabouts*.

Fresh bread is bought daily.

Moulay Ismail

Meknes was the imperial capital of Moulay Ismail, an effective but ruthless sultan who ruled for 55 years (1672–1727) over a more or less united Morocco. During that period Morocco became a significant power in the Mediterranean world – the sultan considered Louis XIV, the Sun King, his contemporary in France, a close friend.

Moulay Ismail was also renowned for his ruthless tyranny, however. As a celebratory gesture to mark the beginning of his long rule in the mid-17th century he displayed 700 heads on the walls of Fez, impressing his new subjects with a sense of their own vulnerability and setting the tone for the long reign of terror which followed.

The British diplomat John Windus, who visited Ismail's palace in 1725 and recorded his impressions in *A Journey to Mequinez*, observed how 'about eight or nine [in the morning] his trembling court assemble, which consists of his great officers, and alcaydes, blacks, whites, tawnies

Father and son at the mosque, Meknes.

and his favourite Jews, all barefooted; and there is bowing and whispering to this and the other eunuch, to know if the Emperor has been abroad (for if he keeps within doors there is no seeing him unless sent for), if he is in a good humour, which is well known by his very looks and motions and sometimes by the colour of the habit he wears, yellow being observed to be his killing colour; from all of which they calculate whether they may hope to live twenty-four hours longer.'

Before Moulay Ismail took control, Meknes was a relatively minor city in the grand scheme of Morocco – always in the shadow of Fez, despite the fact that it was well placed between the Middle and High Atlas mountains and the coast and the interior. Founded in the 10th century by a Berber tribe known as Meknassass, it passed through the hands of all the major dynasties, from the 11th-century Almoravids and the 12th-century Almohads to the Merinids, who built a medersas here, and the Saadians. It was customary for the viziers of the Fez-based Merinid sultans to keep

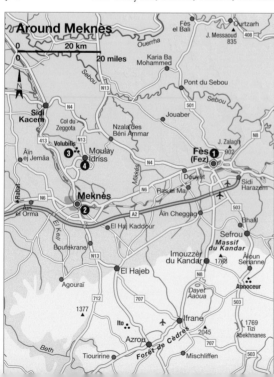

second residences in Meknes, but beyond that, it was considered of no great importance.

Before becoming sultan and moving the court from Fez to Meknes, from where he ruled with an iron grip for 55 years, Moulay Ismail had been the governor of Meknes on behalf of his father, the Alaouite Sultan er Rashid, whom he succeeded in 1672. Both as governor and sultan, Ismail's excesses were notorious. Reports vary wildly, but some say that he had a harem of 500 wives and concubines, and of the hundreds of children he fathered he had the girls strangled at birth and was not averse to slicing off the limbs of sons who displeased him. To enforce his rule as sultan, he formed an army of 30,000 Sudanese soldiers – the feared 'Black Guard' – who roamed the country, keeping the tribes in check.

Grand designs

Meknes's location, surrounded by fertile land and well connected to local trade routes, made it a good choice for a new imperial capital, while Moulay Ismail immediately set about defending the city itself by building a complex defensive system comprising vast fortifications – including some 25km (15 miles) of walls – a granary and reservoir. Stone was plundered from Volubilis and from El Badi, the grand Saadian palace in Marrakech. 1

More than 25,000 unfortunate captives were brought in to carry out Moulay Ismail's grandiose building works, labouring relentlessly by day and then being herded into subterranean prisons by night. Describing Ismail's brutal treatment of his slaves – which included white slaves kidnapped from the coasts of England and Europe – the British writer Scott O'Connor, in *Vision of Morocco*, adds: 'When the slaves died they were used as building material and immured in the rising walls, their blood mixed with the cement that still holds them together in its grip.'

Ismail's megalomaniac vision left Meknes a graveyard of huge palaces and fortifications, and the imperial city now presents an impressive but

Bab Mansour.

Cherries grow in abundance around Meknes in the summer.

sombre sight, built (literally) out of the blood and bones of those who once laboured upon it. The remains of some 30 royal palaces and 20 gateways, plus mosques, barracks and ornamental gardens can still be seen, magnificent and lunatic in scale.

Meknes remained capital until Moulay Ismail's death in 1727, when his grandson and heir, Mohammed III, removed the court to Marrakech. Mohammed III destroyed a number of buildings as a parting shot, while the great earthquake of 1755 (which also flattened Lisbon) contributed to the slow ruin and decline of this once-great city.

Place el Hedim and around

Begin a tour of Meknes on **Place el Hedim Ⓐ** (whose name translates as the rather sinister, but apt, 'Destruction Square'), from where the medina spreads northwest and the Imperial City and Moulay Ismail's tomb extend southeast. The square was formerly part of the medina but was razed to the ground by Moulay Ismail to create an approach to the main entrance of his palace via the Bab Mansour. Food stalls cling to the eastern side of the spacious space, large and rather empty by day, although it fills up towards dusk with miscellaneous musicians, snake charmers, story-tellers and other

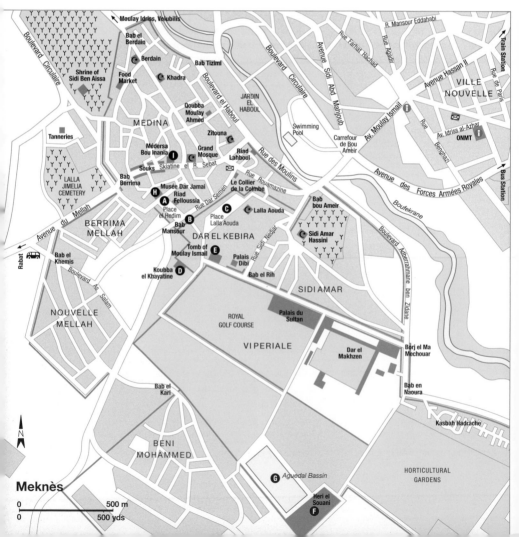

Meknès

0 — 500 m
0 — 500 yds

street performers, while the food stalls fire into life, shooting great clouds of smoke into the night air – like a miniature version of Marrakech's celebrated Jemaa el Fna. The **Dar Jamai Museum** (see page 210) stands on the northwest side of the square.

The area is dominated by the imposing **Bab Mansour gateway** Ⓑ flanked by two square bastions supported in part by incongruous white marble columns plundered from Volubilis, the squatness of the overall design relieved by the intricate swirl of blue and green tile work, which covers virtually every surface. A smaller but similar gateway, the **Bab Djemaa en Nouar**, stands a short distance further along to the right.

According to legend, the gate was designed by (and named after) a Christian renegade named El Mansour. Asked by the sultan whether he could ever improve the finished gateway's architecture, the unwary El Mansour is said to have answered yes, whereupon he was promptly executed for his pains – although whether because the sultan feared he would

take some new and enhanced design to a rival patron, or simply because El Mansour had failed to produce his best work in the service of the sultan, remains unclear. The story may well be apocryphal in any case, since the gateway wasn't completed until after Sultan Moulay Ismail's death in 1732, although it gives a nice impression of the Moulay Ismail's ruthless personality, whatever its veracity.

Tours of the imperial city start here. Although a guide – picked up in Place el Hedim or around Mansour Gate – can be useful, the layout of the city is easy to grasp and it is possible to manage without one.

Turn left in front of Bab Mansour, then right through a smaller gateway about 50 metres/yds further along the walls, to reach the tranquil and spacious **Place Lalla Aouda** Ⓒ. Turn right and walk across to the back of the square to reach the **Koubba el Khayatine** Ⓓ (Ambassadors' Hall; daily 9.30am–6pm), a simple pavilion thought to have been used as a place for receiving visiting ambassadors and for bargaining over the ransoms

Meknes Royal Golf Club.

Place el Hedim.

The Royal Stables.

The Tomb of Moulay Ismail.

demanded for Christian victims of Barbary Coast piracy, in which Moulay Ismail had a controlling interest. More recently, the pavilion was used by tailors (*khayatine*) making military clothing.

Adjacent to the pavilion is a stairway leading into subterranean chambers that were once used as grain stores, though the macabre story goes that they were also a prison for thousands of white slaves captured by the Barbary pirates and brought to Meknes to help Moulay Ismail build the city. The chambers, which were blocked off by the French, who also added the skylights, once extended 7km (4 miles) in each direction.

Moulay Ismail's tomb

Head through the brightly tiled gateway opposite, on the far side of the road, to reach Meknes's chief attraction, the **Tomb of Moulay Ismail E** (Sat–Thu 9am–noon, 2–6pm; donation). Restored by fellow Alaouite Mohammed V in the 1950s, it is one of the few shrines in Morocco that can be visited by non-Muslims. The others are the mausoleums of Mohammed V and Hassan II in Rabat and the shrine of Sidi Yahiya (see page 139) near Oujda. Entrance is via a sequence of high-walled courtyards – lavishly tiled and decorated, although despite the grandeur of the overall conception the detail is rather underwhelming compared with many other shrines and palaces in the country. Beyond these lies the inner sanctuary in which the tomb is situated – you're not allowed into the sanctuary itself, although you can peek through the door for a glimpse of Moulay Ismail's last resting place.

Moulay Ismail's reputation for violence and cruelty does not seem to have diminished the reverence paid to him. It is perhaps odd that such a bloodthirsty ruler should have a shrine of such magnificence, and one that still attracts pilgrims from all over Morocco. People believe that his tomb has *baraka* (luck or magic), which will rub off on believers. A doorway off the mausoleum opens on to a private cemetery (no entry) containing the tombs of people who wished to be buried alongside this famous ruler.

The royal palaces

Continuing along the road past the mausoleum of Moulay Ismail brings you to the heart of royal Meknes. Past the small Bab el Rih gateway the road is hemmed in on either side by high, virtually unbroken walls, riddled with nesting birds, making it look like some gigantic open-air corridor. According to legend Moulay Ismail was fond of having himself conveyed along this well-concealed driveway in a carriage pulled by his eunuchs or concubines.

The walls on the left-hand side of the road conceal the **Dar el Kebira**, Moulay Ismail's main palace complex. The palace was destroyed by his son, and its various gateways and the shells of its palace walls subsequently incorporated into a labyrinthine residential quarter, which you can explore by entering via the Bab el Rih. Beyond the walls on the right-hand side lies the **Dar el Makhzen**, a more modern palace, completed at the end of the 18th century. This has been restored and is used by the present royal family as an occasional residence, while its gardens and walls have been turned into an exclusive royal golf course. Entry is forbidden.

Heri el Souani

At the far end of the corridor road, behind the Dar el Makhzen, are the **Heri el Souani** ❶ (daily 9am–noon, 3–6pm), the vast granaries and store rooms of the royal complex and one of the most remarkable sights in the Imperial City. It's a good 25 minutes' walk to the granaries from the Tomb of Moulay Ismail and you may prefer to catch a *petit taxi* or (more picturesquely) to hire one of *calèches* (horse-drawn carriages) that hang out around the tomb.

The Heri el Souani comprise a sequence of immense high-vaulted chambers divided into 23 aisles, which were used as storerooms and granaries – the size of the complex designed to protect against the possibility of siege or drought. For a good overview of the complex, climb the stairs to the remaining part of the roof. Olive trees provide shade. The **Aguedal Basin** ❶, round the corner from the Heri el Souani (and visible from its roof), covers 4 hectares (10 acres) but, as with all the sights within the Imperial City, its abandoned grandeur creates a mournful and gloomy atmosphere. Moulay Ismail's vision was mighty but the spaces he created were never filled – the scale was too huge.

The **Royal Stables** (not open to visitors), 3km (2 miles) further along the route in the quarter of Heri el Mansour, are the most extreme example of Moulay Ismail's excess, They were built for more than 12,000 horses, each with its own groom and slave. The grain – sufficient for a siege lasting years – was stored below in the granaries, at a temperature kept constant by the thick walls. Ismail also constructed a channel providing fresh water for the horses without them having to move from their stalls. The crumbling remains still give an indication of the extent of decoration that once existed; tiles and *zelliges* are visible on pieces of partially overgrown wall. By and large, though, the place now belongs to goats.

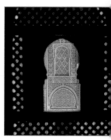

Medersa Bou Inania.

Aguedal Basin.

Not far from here is the modern-day **Haras Régional**, a stud farm and training centre for Arabian horses. Experienced horsemen or women can take out temporary membership and help exercise the horses, but anyone can pay a visit. Some of the horses are pure Arabian, some Berber and others mixed.

More compact and delicate-looking than the thoroughbred, the Arabian is famed for its power as well as its beauty, but its most valuable asset historically was its endurance, a quality prized by the Bedouin, its human counterpart in weathering the hardships of the desert. A tribe's horses were its chief pride, its partners in raiding and war. Years of working and living together (horses often bedded down in the family tent) forged a deep bond of affection between man and horse that transcended the usual human/animal relationships and inspired legends and poetry.

The cylindrical minaret of the Medersa Moulay Idriss.

The medina and souks

Returning to the Mansour Gate, enter the **medina**, at the west end of the Place el Hedim. The **Dar Jamai**

Museum  (Wed–Mon 9am–5pm), housed in the Dar Jamai, is discreetly positioned at the corner of the square beside the entrance to the medina. It is worth a visit to see the fine examples of Berber rugs, and also has an interesting collection of local artefacts and pottery. The building itself was built for Mohammed Ben Larbi Jamai, grand vizier at the court of Moulay Hassan (sultan 1873–94) by the same architect who built the Jamai Palace in Fez, though it is on a less grand scale. Some of the upper rooms are decorated and furnished to give an idea of domestic life in the 19th century. Like all the other grand palaces, it has an inviting garden filled with flowering shrubs and birdsong.

The main entrance to the medina and its central souk area street is right next to the museum. Follow the road into the souks for about 100 metres/yds (veering around to the right en route) to reach a T-junction. The main souk area lies off on your left from here, a dense and confusing area of tiny shops packed around even tinier

THE WINE INDUSTRY

The low hills around Meknes are the main centre of Morocco's wine industry, though the vine-growing area stretches from Rabat/Casablanca to Fez. The industry was set up by the French, who did the same in Tunisia and Algeria, both of which also continue to produce wine, in spite of the Qur'an's admonishments against alcohol.

Over the last few years the variety and quality of Moroccan wines has greatly improved. Of the reds, Les Coteaux de l'Atlas, from Les Celliers de Meknès, is the most prestigious. Other good-quality Meknes reds are the Beni M'Tir Larroque Cabernet Sauvignon and Merlot blend and the Comtesse de Lacourtabalise. Medaillon Cabernet, from the Domain des Ouled Thaleb vineyard near Benislimane, is also among the best of the reds. Beauvallon Chardonnay, from the Beni M'Tir vineyard, and the Medaillon Cabernet Blanc, from Benislimane, are among the best whites.

Of the less expensive wines, the Meknes Vins de Cépage Cabernet Sauvignon, Merlot and Syrah are all quite drinkable, as are the Meknes Gerrouane Rosé and Gris, and the Benislimane Semillon Blanc and Cuvée du Président Cabernet Rosé. To buy wine in Morocco you need to go to a specialist shop in the *ville nouvelle* of a city or to one of the supermarket chains such as Marjane or Acima.

alleyways, frequently reduced to pedestrianised gridlock by the sheer weight of local shoppers during busier hours. Much of the merchandise on display is relatively humdrum, although if you hunt around you may stumble upon more traditional areas devoted to carpets, textiles and slippers, as well as a small **carpenters' souk**, permeated by the sweet smell of cedar and thuya wood. Continuing through the souk, you eventually emerge at the west end, site of most of the artisan markets. It is quite a scruffy area but has some interesting workshops, including basket-makers and saddlers, fabric sellers, metalworkers, cobblers and coppersmiths.

Return to the T-junction and head in the opposite direction – the streets here are calmer and emptier, and are also where you'll find most of the medina's tourist-oriented riads, shops and restaurants. A short walk brings you to the Great Mosque. Turn left here to immediately reach the **Medersa Bou Inania ❶** (daily 9am–5pm), started by the Merinid Sultan Abou Hassan, who built the Chellah in Rabat and the Medersa el Hassan in Salé, but finished by Sultan Abou Inan (1350–58), builder of the Medersa Bou Inania in Fez. It is similar to other Merinid medersas, with a central ablutions fountain in a tiled courtyard, quarters on two levels for around 50 students and a prayer hall on one side. As usual, every inch of wall is painstakingly covered in stucco, *zellige* work and woodcarvings in abstract patterns and arabesques, which creates a mesmerising intensity designed to reflect and reiterate the greatness and oneness of God. Go up to the roof for good views of the surrounding area, including the green-tiled roof of the Great Mosque next door.

Beyond the medina

Outside the medina, beside the vast Bab el Berdain (Gate of the Saddlers) spreads a huge cemetery containing the shrine of **Sidi Ben Aissa** built in the 18th century (closed to non-Muslims), which is the focus of a *moussem* on the eve of Mouloud (the Prophet's birthday) that changes every year. The

Fruit and vegetable stall.

THE AISSAWA BROTHERHOOD

One of the best-known Sufi fraternities in Morocco is the Aissawa Brotherhood, which was founded in the 15th century by Sidi Ben Aissa and quickly spread throughout North Africa. Like other Sufi sects, it advocates music-induced trance as a means of drawing closer to God. One of the ways in which Sidi Ben Aissa revealed his mystical powers was through his immunity to scorpion and snake bites. He was said to confer the same magical powers on his followers. Once in a state of trance, they could eat anything, however grim, without ill effect. At one time, on the eve of Mouloud (the Prophet's birthday), the date of their annual *moussem*, over 50,000 devotees would convene. Once in a state of trance, they would devour live animals and pierce their tongues and cheeks. Their rituals were similar to those of the Hammaadcha of Moulay Idriss, whose *moussem* is described in Paul Bowles's *The Spider's House*.

The Moroccan government has outlawed the most extreme practices of these cults, but their annual *moussem* – the largest in Morocco – still takes place, usually in April, in Meknes at the shrine of Sidi Ben Aissa, and they are very much involved in the everyday lives and rituals of their followers and of Moroccans in general. They perform healing ceremonies and attend circumcisions and are paid to capture snakes that have invaded houses.

Great Mosque.

event is one of the biggest *moussems* in Morocco, attracting members of the Sufi-inspired Aissawa Brotherhood from all over North Africa (see box).

The new and old *mellahs* (Jewish quarters) to the west of the medina and Place el Hedim have markets and souks of their own. This is one of the poorest parts of town, busy but run-down, with ramshackle buildings incorporated into the crumbling walls.

The Ville Nouvelle

Clearly separated from the imperial city of Moulay Idriss by the valley of the Oued Boufekrane, which runs through the valley between the city's two halves, is the French-era **Ville Nouvelle,** built in the early in the 20th century. There is little of interest here, but it does have a good selection of hotels, restaurants and cafés. Although it is fairly lively by day, Meknes, both the Ville Nouvelle and the old, has relatively little going on in the evening compared with other larger Moroccan cities, including nearby Fez.

Volubilis

Set on a plateau around 30km (18 miles) north of Meknes, and visible for miles around, is the ruined city of **Volubilis** ❸ (daily 8am–sunset), formerly the most remote outpost of the Roman Empire in Africa, at the furthest reaches of that great empire. Moulay Ismail stripped the ruins of their marble for use in his own city at Meknes, while most of the important finds have been removed to the Archaeological Museum in Rabat. Even so, it remains one of the most impressive monuments of the Classical age anywhere in North Africa, particularly thanks to its superb mosaics, which remain safely in place,

It is frequently possible to have Volubilis to yourself: the best times to visit are late afternoon and early morning, when temperatures are cooler and coach parties have either gone or are yet to arrive.

A tour of the ruins

Volubilis is small and easy to cover; the most important remains are clearly labelled and the arrows describe

Dar Jamai Museum.

a roughly clockwise tour. Some of the main buildings have been half restored or reconstructed. The most remarkable finds include bronze statues (now in the Salle des Bronzes in the Archaeological Museum in Rabat; see page 154) and the amazingly well-preserved mosaics, many of which remain in situ. For purposes of identification, the houses are named after the subject of the mosaic they contain. All the houses follow the same basic structure: each had its public and private rooms. The mosaics usually decorated the public rooms and internal courtyards, the baths and kitchens being the private areas of the house.

Following a well-worn path through olive groves and across the small **Fertassa River**, clamber leftwards up the hill to the start of the site, where an arrow will direct you around to the left. The first house you come to on the clockwise tour of the site is the **House of Orpheus** ❹, the largest house in its quarter, identified by a clump of cypresses to the left of the main paved street. It has three mosaics: a circular mosaic of Orpheus

charming the animals with his lyre, remarkable for its detail and colours, another of nine dolphins, believed by the Romans to bring good luck, and a third portraying Amphitrite in a chariot drawn by a seahorse.

From here, cut up to the modern square building containing a reconstructed olive press, one of several that have been found on the site. Next to it are the 3rd-century **Baths of Gallienus** ❸, originally the most lavish public baths in the city, as their proximity to Volubilis's main civic buildings – the Capitol, Basilica and Forum – required. The grand houses in Volubilis had their own elaborate heating systems, providing hot water and steam for baths, but the public baths also provided a meeting place to chat, gossip, do business, exercise, and eat and drink.

From here, the street leads to the **Forum** (public square), Capitol and Basilica – an impressive collection of administrative buildings, which

Men in Moulay Idriss.

Roman columns at Volubilis.

THE HISTORY OF VOLUBILIS

Volubilis was built on the site of a Neolithic settlement and an important Berber village, thought to have been the capital of the kingdom of Mauretania. From AD 45 Volubilis was subject to Roman rule, making it the empire's most remote base. During this time, olive oil production and copper were the city's main assets. The profusion of oil presses on the site confirms this. It benefited from local springs as well as the Fertassa stream running through the site. Most of the buildings date from the beginning of the 3rd century, when the number of inhabitants was probably around 20,000. By the end of the 3rd century the Romans had gone. After this, Volubilis maintained its Latinised structure, but when the Arabs arrived in the 7th century the culture and teachings of Islam took over. By 786, when Moulay Idriss I arrived, most of the inhabitants were already converted. He built a new town (Moulay Idriss) nearby, and Volubilis began to decline. Much later, in the 18th century, Moulay Ismail removed most of its marble to adorn his palaces in Meknes. Volubilis didn't come to the attention of the outside world again until two foreign diplomats stumbled upon it on a tour of the area at the end of the 19th century. Excavations were begun during the French protectorate in 1915 and continue today, funded by the Moroccan government. In 1997, Unesco declared Volubilis a World Heritage Site.

Roman ruins at Volubilis.

comprised the centre of the city. The **Capitol** is distinguished by a crop of freestanding Corinthian pillars and a flight of 13 steps on its north side. Originally the central area would have contained a temple fronted by four columns surrounded by porticoes. An inscription dates the temple to AD 217 and dedicates it to the cult of Capitoline Jove and Minerva.

The **Basilica** is a larger building beside the Capitol. It isn't easy to see its structure now, but it would have been divided into five aisles (note the stumpy columns) with an apse at both ends. It doubled as the law courts and commercial exchange. The **Forum**, which completes the administrative centre, is an open space that was used for public and political meetings. It is of modest proportions and nothing remains of the statues of dignitaries that would have adorned the surrounding buildings.

Between the Forum and the Triumphal Arch is the **Acrobat's House**, containing two well-preserved mosaics. The main one depicts an acrobat riding his mount back-to-front and

holding up his prize. Another house nearby contained the famous bronze *Guard Dog* that is exhibited in the Archaeological Museum in Rabat.

The **Triumphal Arch** is the centre point of Volubilis –an impressive ceremonial monument, albeit serving absolutely no practical purpose. Contemporary with the Capitol, it was built by Marcus Aurelius Sebastenus to celebrate the power of the Emperor Caracalla and his mother Julia Domna. It is supported on marble columns and decorated only on the east side, while records and the inscription suggest it was formerly surmounted by a huge bronze chariot and horses.

The main paved street, **Decumanus Maximus**, stretches up to the **Tangier Gate**, the only gate out of the city's original eight which remains standing. Off the street are the ruins of many fine houses, the fronts of which were rented to shopkeepers, who would have sold their wares from shaded porticoes on either side – not unlike the layout of a typical Moroccan souk today.

Further splendid mosaics can be found north of the Forum. The **House of Ephebus ①**, for example, boasts a Bacchus mosaic, depicting the god of wine in a chariot pulled by panthers. A wonderful bronze statue of an *ephebe* (young man) wearing a leafy diadem was found in this house and is now in the Salle des Bronzes in the Archaeological Museum in Rabat (see page 154). The **House of Columns ①**, recognisable by the remains of columns guarding the entrance to the courtyard, has an ornamental basin surrounded by brilliant red geraniums. The **Knight's House ①**, next to this, is in a poor state except for the stunning mosaic of Bacchus discovering the sleeping Ariadne, one of the loveliest sights of Volubilis.

Many of the larger houses off Decumanus Maximus contain well-preserved mosaics; in particular, don't miss the **House of Venus ①** (marked by a single cypress tree) and the **House of the Nereids ①**, a couple of streets in. The former contains stunning mosaics of mythological scenes, including the abduction of Hylas by nymphs and one of the bathing Diana being surprised by Actaeon. The House of the Nereids yielded the stunning bronze heads of Cato and Juba II – also in the museum in Rabat.

The well-worn path curls round behind the Basilica and Forum, leading back to the entrance, where one can adjourn for a mint tea in the café, and examine some of the statuary in the garden.

Moulay Idriss

Although hundreds of tourist buses visit Volubilis, only 1km (0.5 mile) away, only a few stop off in **Moulay Idriss ①**, the small, picturesque whitewashed town clustered on a hilltop around a shrine to Moulay Idriss I, whose tomb rests here. Moulay Idriss is considered a holy town – at one time Christians were forbidden to enter – though it is relaxed and friendly today. Its chief appeal for non-Muslim visitors is its picturesque setting, which can be enjoyed over a mint tea in the square, Place Mohammed VI (where you can also park your car if driving). There are a few cafés

FACT

The position, atmosphere and mosaics of Volubilis combine to make the site a worthwhile stop. Geckos running up and down crumbling walls, darting into invisible holes, occasional whiffs of highly scented flowers, the clear air and the silence on the plateau all enhance the magic.

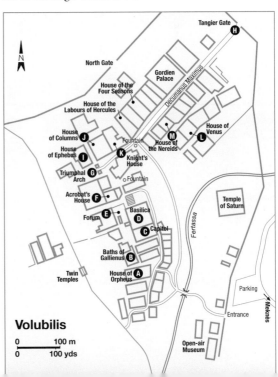

Mosaic at Volubilis.

Volubilis

0 — 100 m
0 — 100 yds

The Triumphal Arch at Volubilis, built in honour of the Emperor Caracalla in the 3rd century AD, remains in surprisingly good shape.

and places to eat here, and the mausoleum of Moulay Idriss is at the top of the square. Today there are also a few places, best of which is the charming Dar Zerhoune (see page 304).

Set in the spur of the hills just east of Volubilis, Moulay Idriss appears to be a compact, predominantly white whole, but it is really two villages; the Khiber and the Tasga quarters join together around the mosque and shrine. Although Meknes is only 25km (16 miles) away, the town is seemingly oblivious to the 21st century, with few concessions to Western visitors.

Town history

At the end of the 8th century, Moulay Idriss el Akhbar (the elder) arrived in the village of Zerhoun. A great-grandson of the Prophet Mohammed, he had fled to Morocco to escape persecution and death. He stopped first at Volubilis, later building his town nearby, and set about converting the Berbers to the Islamic faith. He was well received by the mountain people, who recognised him as their leader, and he became the founder of the

Moulay Idriss.

first Arab dynasty in Morocco. A year later he began founding Fez – a labour completed by Idriss II, the son of his Berber concubine, Kenza.

News of his popularity and success reached his eastern caliph, and an emissary was sent to poison him in 791. His dynasty lived on through his son, born two months after his death.

Exploring the town

The **main square** – more of a rectangle, in fact – opens out from the holy area. This is the busiest part of the town, especially around the tiled fountain, with several pleasant cafés. Opposite the entrance to the shrine makeshift stalls sell candles and padded baskets to present offerings. Nougat is a speciality of the town, as it is in many other places of pilgrimage in the Arab world.

The **mausoleum** itself was rebuilt by Moulay Ismail, who destroyed the original structure at the end of the 18th century in order to create a more beautiful building, which was then later embellished by Sultan Moulay Abderrahmen. Wooden bars (like those

around the zaouia of Moulay Idriss II in Fez) demarcate the area around the tomb, indicating the point beyond which non-Muslims must not pass.

For a view (albeit distant) of the shrine, you'll need to head up to one of the various viewpoints around town. The best views of the town are from the Terrace **Sidi Abdallah el Hajjam panoramic restaurant**, above the Khiber quarter (although it's tricky to find amidst the narrow streets hereabouts – you might want to take a guide). From here the structure of the town is clear: white and grey cubes cascade down to the point where the quarters merge beside the tomb and zaouia, the green-tiled roofs and arched courtyards of which are clearly visible. On the way up to the terrace, look out for the **Medersa Moulay Idriss**, embellished with what it said to be the only cylindrical minaret in Morocco, and very different from the usual square minarets of the Maghreb). Inspired by minarets seen in the Arabian Gulf, it was commissioned by a pilgrim returning from Mecca in the 1930s; its green ceramic tiles are inscribed with verses from the Qur'an.

Annual festival

As the location for the most important shrine in Morocco, Moulay Idriss is the focus for a huge annual *moussem* which takes place every August, attracting pilgrims from all over Morocco as well as several Sufi fraternities, such as the Aissawa, Hamaacha and Dghoughia, c-induced rituals (see page 211). The more extreme activities of these sects have been outlawed by the government, but it is rumoured that they continue in places unobserved.

The *moussem* is held after the harvest, usually beginning on the last Thursday in August. Originally a purely religious festival, it has come to include *fantasias*, singing, dancing and markets. The hillsides are covered with tents, and prayer and feasting continues throughout the festival. Tourists are tolerated, but it is a purely Muslim festival, and it's probably sensible to visit during the daytime rather than in the evening.

The only inhabitants left in Volubilis are the storks, which nest on top of the Roman columns.

View over Moulay Idriss.

A LAND OF SHRINES AND PILGRIMS

Pilgrimages play an important role in Islam. Though the *Hajj* to Mecca is the greatest pilgrimage of all, many smaller journeys are made to local shrines within Morocco.

Shrines are found everywhere in Morocco, ranging from simple *koubbas* and *marabouts* (small one-room shrines, usually domed) to large and elaborate *zaouias* that are centres for religious brotherhoods.

They are magnets for pilgrims, who come to pray, grieve and ask for cures. Women will petition their favourite saint for help in childbirth or for a cure for infertility. They may bring small offerings or knot strips of fabric to the grille of the tomb to bind their contract with a saint. Water or oil may be put into tombs to receive a saint's *baraka* (blessing), after which it will be administered to the sick.

All over the world high places are often also holy places, and this is frequently the case in Morocco. Here, white koubbas stand out against the barren landscape.

In place of Mecca

Completing the *Hajj* (pilgrimage to Mecca, the birthplace of the Prophet) is a life goal of most Muslims. The cost of the journey is saved for over many years, and families will club together to finance the trip for ageing parents. The return of a *hajji* (one who has complete the Hajj) is celebrated by the whole family. Presents from Mecca, such as prayer beads, watches, gilded tissue boxes or verses from the Qur'an embroidered in gold thread, are treasured, even though many will have been manufactured in the Far East.

Moroccans too poor to travel to Mecca will undertake a series of pilgrimages to local holy sites, such as the shrine of Moulay Idriss I, in the eponymous town of Moulay Idriss near Meknes, or the tomb of Moulay Idriss II in Fez.

Muslim burials generally take place on the day of death.

Elaborate entrance to the Zaouia of Moulay Idriss II, the patron saint of Fez; non-Muslims are not allowed to enter the shrine.

Berber woman at the Imilchil wedding festival.

GOING TO A MOUSSEM

Moussems are annual festivals, usually held to honour a local saint but sometimes also celebrating a more secular aspect of life, such as a change of season or a harvest. The famous wedding festival of Imilchil, the camel market at Tan Tan, the Date Festival in the south near Erfoud or the honey *moussem* near Agadir are all well-known examples.

Moussems can be huge affairs, attracting pilgrims from miles around, and in the case of the biggest festivals, from all over Morocco. Equal to their religious significance is the opportunity they present for trade. Huge tented encampments spring up overnight, livestock of all types is haggled over, and every conceivable commodity of rural life is bought and sold. The festivals are accompanied by music, dancing and *fantasias* (displays of horsemanship), and often the ritual slaughter of an animal in a ceremony that mixes pagan and Islamic elements.

Since the days of the French Protectorate, the government has used the opportunity presented by the *moussems* to keep tabs on the tribes, in particular to register marriages and collect taxes.

e Zaouai of Moulay Idriss II is a holy shrine dedicated to the onymous ruler, who governed Morocco in the 8th century.

Inspecting a camel at the camel market at Tan Tan.

lgrims visit the mausoleum of Moulay Idriss II in eknes in the hope that it will cure their ailments.

Sefrou street scene.

THE MIDDLE ATLAS

Unlike the High Atlas, this area is relatively
unexplored. But those who do visit will discover
outstanding mountain scenery filled with lakes and
waterfalls, the royal resort of Ifrane and fabulous
Berber carpets.

The Middle Atlas is a huge but relatively little-visited mountain region stretching between the High Atlas and the Rif, and from the Atlantic Coast up to Taza. It is a stunning area of forests, upland pastures, running rivers and lakes, high enough to be blanketed in snow in winter, but not as harsh as the High Atlas, rising to a peak of 3,356 metres (11,010ft) at Jebel Bou Naceur. The mountains are also home to the Beni Mguild Berbers, some of Morocco's most gifted nomadic weavers.

The mountains emerge in the west as the Zaër Zaïane highlands, inland of the Rabat/Casablanca coastline, and dip down towards the High Atlas at Kasba Talda. They then re-emerge from the High Atlas north of the great artificial lake, Bin el Ouidane, to become the Middle Atlas proper, crowned with stands of lofty cedars and running northeast between Midelt in the south and Azrou in the north. The range continues past the Fez and Sefrou, becoming the Jebel Tazzeka, then falters at the Taza Gap, guarded by Morocco's least touristic medina city.

The Zaër Zaïane highlands

The R401 southeast of Rabat winds through the cork oak trees and steep valleys of the Temara Forest, over rolling hills and through cleared rich agricultural land up to **Rommani** (Wednesday souk), where the R404 turns left to **Maaziz**.

Beyond Maaziz on the R407, Tiddas is set in a large agricultural valley dominated by neat rows of apple orchards. Past here, the road climbs steeply through forests of fir trees towards **Jebel Mouchchene** (1,086 metres/3,563ft), with scattered hamlets and fields offering views to the south of tree-covered hills.

After El Harcha, a dead-end road leads to **Tarmilate**, home of the

Main Attractions

Jebel Tazzeka National Park
Taza
Sefrou
Tafradous
Ifrane
Azrou
Kasba Tadla
Cascades d'Ouzoud

Sculpture in Ifrane commemorating the last wild Atlas lion.

Oulmes and Sidi Ali bottling plant. The town is set on a spur, surrounded by higher forested peaks. Accommodation is available in the once stylish 1930s **Hôtel des Thermes** (tel: 037-52 31 73). Company-owned, the hotel is rarely visited by tourists, but has clean rooms, hot baths, a licensed restaurant and a congenial atmosphere at a very reasonable price. From the hotel there is a pleasant walk down the deep valley to **Lalla Haya**, the source of Morocco's most famous mineral water. The spring emerges hot and slightly sulphurous, and gushes through an iron pipe into a large basin streaked with red iron deposits. It is a great place for a restorative bath.

The nearby town of **Oulmes** has very little to offer except its souk each Tuesday. The place has an air of rural poverty and, like Tarmilate, is surrounded by shanty town housing, the homes of peasants who work on the surrounding company-owned farms.

From here the R407 makes its way southwards through holm oak forest, past the shrine of Sidi Otmane to Khenifra.

Imouzzer du Kandar.

The Jebel Tazzeka

Most trips into the Middle Atlas begin in the region of Fez. The N6 from Fez, heading east, takes you past the enormous **Idriss I Dam** (Barrage Idriss I). An easily missed turnoff to the north at Sidi Abdallah des Rhiata quickly twists back on itself to go under the main road and climb immediately up into the spectacular rust-red-stained Zireg Gorge. This is the start of the **Jebel Tazzeka National Park**, perhaps the most beautiful upland landscape in northern Morocco. The loop road (which eventually comes out at Taza) climbs through cork, evergreen oak and pine trees with spectacular views over forest wilderness inhabited by reintroduced Barbary deer. Along the way are a couple of picnic sites with kiosks and display maps. To the north of the R507, the 1,980-metre (6,495ft) summit of **Jebel Tazzeka** itself is easily identifiable by its aerial mast and is accessible via a signposted track.

Taza

Taza ❶ lies midway between the Rif and the Middle Atlas in a mountain pass known as the Taza Gap. The town was founded in the 7th century by Berbers, and for centuries saw waves of invaders pass through the Taza Gap on their way down through the country. It later grew to importance when the Almohads occupied it in the 12th century, making it their second capital (Tin Mal being the first) after failing to capture Marrakech from the Almoravids.

The medina (also known as Taza Haute) is set on a hill above the Ville Nouvelle and is blissfully untouristy, if you've just come from Fez. There are few historic monuments to visit, though you may get glimpses of the **Andalous Mosque**, built in the 12th century. Near the **Gate of the Wind** (Bab el Rih) is the **Grand Mosque**, built by the Almohads also in the 12th century. In the heart of twisting pedestrian alleys of the

pale-ochre medina, near the **Sidi Azouz Mosque**, are the souks full of tapestries, jewellery, wickerwork and local Berber crafts. But the real draw here is the chance to buy the increasingly sought-after dark-brown and cream woollen carpets woven by the Beni Ourain tribe.

Cherry country

Two routes head south from Taza to Sefrou, in the heart of the Middle Atlas. The first route backtracks along the main N6 to Fez and then heads south down the R503 to Sefrou; the second also starts out on the N6, but turns off at Bir Tam Tam onto a single-track road, reaching Sefrou via a slightly longer but more scenic drive.

Sefrou ❷ is rarely disturbed by tourists despite being just 30km (19 miles) from Fez. It was once a major centre for Morocco's Jews, popularly known as 'Little Jerusalem' and with a sprawling *mellah* occupying half the entire medina – you can still see many distinctive Jewish houses with wooden balconies, similar to those found in the *mellah* at Fez. The whole medina

is dissected by the River Aggai, which enters the town via a small waterfall above a separate *ksar,* enclosed in its own set of walls.

Modern Sefrou, however, is most famous for its Cherry Festival. Held in June to mark the end of the cherry harvest, the festival offers several days of music and celebrating and culminates in the crowning of the Cherry Queen.

A detour to Boulemane

Immediately east and south of Sefrou there are a few roads open to normal road vehicles including a worthwhile detour along the P5033 to Tazouta and then the P5016/15 via Skoura and Tafradous to Boulemane. The last has no accommodation, although there is a café. The rewarding drive follows the Gigou Valley, with views of the towering cliffs of the Tichehoukt massif (2,796 metres/9,170ft) to the south. On one particularly tight twist in the river stands **Tafradous**, accessible only via a footbridge that leads up an enormous ramp to a village built like a

A cedar tree rises near Azrou.

Sefrou is a pleasant town unspoiled by tourists.

MIDDLE ATLAS HIKING

With ancient forests and a wealth of flora and fauna, the Middle Atlas is a paradise for hikers – the most popular hikes being the Jebel Tazzeka Circuit near Taza and various treks in the area around Azrou. The Jebel Tazzeka Circuit begins 10km (6 miles) from Taza at the Cascades de Ras el Oued (which only flow in spring) and the little village of Ras el Ma, from where the view of the Taza Gap can be admired. If you do not have a car, you can hire a grand taxi. Information and guides can be found in Taza.

Twenty-five kilometres (16 miles) further on from Taza are the Friouato Caves (Gouffre du Friouato), supposedly the largest and deepest in Africa. The route back from the caves to Taza takes in compact Bab Bou Idir, which is a good base for further hikes around the area. In summer, the Jebel Tazzeka National Park office can provide information on trails, which are also marked. A few kilometres on from Bab Bou Idir is Jebel Tazzeka itself, which has a rough trail leading to the summit that takes a few hours to ascend and descend for fit climbers. Azrou is also a popular base for short hikes into the surrounding cedar forests, with glimpses of the Barbary apes for which this region is known. Hikes can involve just a day or an afternoon from Azrou or longer four- to six-day treks starting from Ain Leuh. Guides can be found in Azrou.

crusaders' castle. This one site alone makes the whole drive worthwhile.

Touring the lakes

From Sefrou, head south again on the R503 and just after Aioun Senanne, take a smaller single-track road off to the right heading for **Imouzzer du Kandar 3**. Built by the French and characterised by tidy avenues lined with deciduous trees and a cheerful square, the town offers a plethora of cafés and a park with a couple of ponds, and is a good place to stop for lunch.

Just south of Imouzzer du Kandar, the P5016 heads off on the left, marking the start of the signposted 'Circuit Touristique des Lacs', which weaves around a series of pretty little lakes nestled amongst the mountains. Immediately beyond the turnoff you'll reach the **Dayet Aoua 4** lake, on whose shore you'll find the imposing Chalet du Lac. Despite its rather austere exterior, this has a good restaurant and the most enormous potbelly stove to ensure that the place stays warm even on the coldest nights.

The lake tour continues around a series of less-visited lakes, Dayets Afourgah, Iffer, Ifrah and Hachlaf, via a series of tiny tarmac roads, each reasonably signposted. The area is

particularly frequented by fishermen and it is said that Hassan II used to enjoy taking off from his palace in Ifrane for the day to fish in the waters here.

Ifrane

Ifrane ❺, south from Sefrou on the N8, is something of a shock. Cool and tranquil with manicured lawns, pristine red-roofed houses, oak and London plane trees and the outward appearance of a Swiss Alpine resort (it is often referred to as 'Little Switzerland'), it is a surreal place to come across in the heart of Morocco.

Ifrane was built as a summer retreat by the French in 1929 and today is where the king and rich Moroccans come in the summer to escape the heat of the plains and in the winter to ski. The population of Ifrane is very young and very chic. The celebrated El Akhawayn University (where courses are taught in English) is on the edge of town, as is the Hotel Mischliffen, a five-star hotel and ski lodge owned by the king. There is a tourist office on Avenue

Prince Moulay Abdallah and, in the centre of town, a rather depressing statue of a lion, commemorating the last Atlas lion, which was shot near here in 1922.

Azrou and beyond

Some 20km (12 miles) southwest from Ifrane, **Azrou** ❻ is an important market town known for its Berber carpets, beautifully situated in the heart of the Forest of Cedars (Forêt de Cèdres). The French-era Place Mohammed V is bordered one side by the Hôtel des Cèdres and the Relais Forestier restaurant. The other side of the square gives onto a small souk. Every Tuesday a large market, at which locals come to sell kilims, fruit and vegetables, is held about a kilometre north of the town.

There are a growing number of licensed mountain guides in the region – a good choice if you want to explore more of the area on foot or by 4x4. It is probably best to ask at your hotel for the best guides. Barbary apes (which are actually monkeys, not apes) are often seen

East of Sefrou is one of the main olive-growing areas of Morocco. There are some 50 varieties of olives altogether, and as many ways of preparing them.

Sefrou market.

Cascades d'Ouzoud.

Ifrane was built by the French.

on roadsides throughout the region. These macaques are yellow-brown or grey in colour, with pink faces. They live only in the forests of Morocco and Algeria and are now an endangered species, with only a few thousand left in the wild.

South from Azrou, a rough track off the N13 takes you to the huge and ancient Gouraud Cedar, a tree said to be over 800 years old.

More practical if you haven't got a four-wheel-drive vehicle is the route further south to the turnoff for the Mischliffen and Jebel Hebri ski resorts. Situated in the crater of an extinct volcano, **Mischliffen** is one of Morocco's major skiing centres, despite sometimes-erratic snowfall. Skis can be rented here during the season, which runs (if there is snow) from January to March. Out of season there's not much to see at either resort apart from a couple of stationary chair lifts, although **Mischliffen** does have a few hotels which make a good base for walks through the forest.

Further south again on the N13 is the isolated lake of **Aguelmame de Sidi Ali**, surrounded by 2,000-metre (6,560ft) peaks.

Cedar country

From Azrou the P7215 heads south through cedar forests with good views down into the valley below and on to **Ain Leuh** ❼, which has a thriving Wednesday market. Continuing south on this winding road, you reach the picturesque hollow containing the springs that form the **Oum er Rbia**. The main spring has a car park beside a pool, a pleasant spot for a summer dip and a walk towards the spring (in fact, four separate springs) that cascades in waterfalls from underneath the mountains to form the Oum er Rbia River, the longest in Morocco.

Between here and Khenifra is the small **Aguelmam Azigza Lake**, at the end of a highland sheep meadow, surrounded by a half-moon of cedar forest and limestone cliffs.

The road continues to wind through evergreen oak forest, which gives way to lofty stands of cedar, some of the trees reputedly measuring over 60 metres (195ft) tall, before reaching **Khenifra**

on the banks of the Oum er Rbia and built around a small, tightly packed medina. Houses are a dark brick red with the woodwork of windows and doors painted turquoise. The way out of town towards the mountains is via a busy street that offers tantalising glimpses up cobbled side alleys.

El Kbab, reached by turning off the N8 just after the town of El Herri, is a small pottery- and carpet-making centre and also hosts a market on Mondays.

Towards the High Atlas

From El Kbab, a winding mountain road that takes you through the mountainous uplands where the Middle Atlas and High Atlas merge.

Roughly 40km (25 miles) due south of El Kaba, **Arhbala** was once a French administrative centre but the red tile and stone houses that are so typical of towns in the Middle Atlas. A further 40km (25 miles) or so west of Arhbala at Tiz n' Isly, the road forks; the left-hand fork takes you south to the village of Imilchil in the High Atlas. Continuing ahead on the R317 instead brings you after a further 30km (19 miles) to the pretty village of **El Ksiba**, which has a busy souk on Sundays.

Five kilometres (3 miles) northwest of El Ksiba you rejoin the main N8. Turn left here and drive a further 20km (12 miles) to reach the former garrison town of **Kasba Tadla ❽**, with a kasbah built in the 17th century by Moulay Ismail. Two walls enclose the town, which has a couple of run-down mosques and a former governor's palace. Around Kasba Tadla and Khenifra there are acres of olive plantations and many mills.

Thirty kilometres (19 miles) south of Kasba Tadia on the N8, the large market town of **Beni Mellal** is one of the main cities of the Middle Atlas, although of little interest to visitors. Press on instead to **Bin el Ouidane ❾** a further 50km (31 miles) south. Situated on the shore of the Bin el Ouidane Lake, the town has become

a centre for water sports, and nowadays there are a few luxury holiday homes and hotels, with private jetties for Morocco's inland sailing enthusiasts.

From Bin el Ouidane, take the R304 via Azilal and then branch off onto the 980 to the **Cascades d'Ouzoud ❿**. The cascades are a popular spot and are especially beautiful in spring, when the waters crash into the El Abid River canyon 100 metres (328ft) below. There are a couple of camping spots lining the edge of the water at the foot of the falls and there is a little village at the top of the falls, which also has a restaurant and place to stay, Riad Cascades d'Ouzoud (page 304), with sweeping views across the surrounding countryside, good Moroccan food and guided tours into the surrounding region. From the village, a path heads down to the waterfalls, past rickety stalls selling trinkets and some rudimentary cafés. Little boats can be hired to paddle about in, and further downstream, away from the bustle of the falls, you can swim in some calm pools.

TIP

You may be hassled by 'guides' at the Cascades d'Ouzoud, but don't bother paying for their services as the walk down to the falls is clearly marked and much more peaceful alone.

Barbary ape.

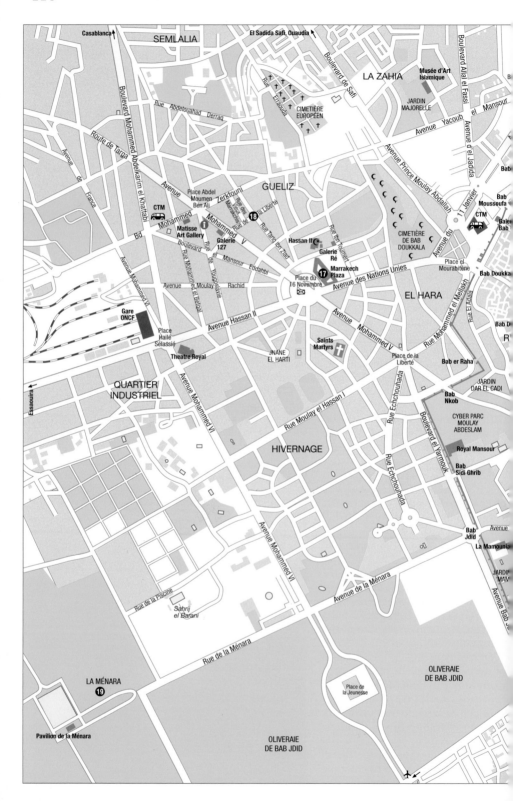

Marrakech

0   500 m
0   500 yds

MARRAKECH

Resting in the shadow of the Atlas Mountains, Marrakech is capital of the south and the country's most vibrant and popular tourist destination, with an eclectic character blending African and Arab, modern and traditional, oriental and European.

Rabat

●Marrakech

Marrakech, the 'Red City', is probably the most exotic in Morocco, and a meeting place of cultures and continents. It was the first capital of a united Morocco (back in the 11th century) and it is where tribesmen from the so-called Bled el Siba (land of lawlessness) meet those from the Bled el Makhzen (land of government). Situated at the geographical heart of the country, it is the first great city north of the Sahara and one of Morocco's four great Imperial Cities.

Over 1,000 years old, Marrakech has long enchanted writers, film stars, colonialists, fashion icons, hippies and rock stars. It is Morocco's most popular destination, receiving over 30 percent of all visitors to the country. From the exotic souks of the medina to the Westernised glamour of the Ville Nouvelle, Marrakech is a riot of contradictions and extremes – at once African and Arab, Eastern and Western, desert town and modern city, religious and secular, elegant and rough-edged. Marrakech can also seem daunting, but the best way to enjoy the city is to surrender to it; a visit here is all about getting lost, letting go and opening up to whatever experience or encounter comes your way.

The city is a vibrant centre of trade and increasingly the focus of all foreign investment in Morocco.

Jemaa el Fna, Marrakech's main square.

Marrakech today is expanding rapidly (the population stands at just over 1 million), with riads in the medina being bought and renovated, five-star hotels such as the Four Seasons and Mandarin Oriental opening and satellite suburbs under constant construction.

In winter, Marrakech is dominated by the towering Atlas Mountains. The majestic, snowcapped peaks loom over the city in the clear blue winter air, an unbroken wall filling the entire southern horizon. In summer, the city

Main Attractions
Koutoubia Mosque
Jemaa el Fna
Souks
Medersa Ben Youssef
Marrakech Museum
Saadian Tombs
El Badi Palace
Bahia Palace
Dar Si Said Museum
Majorelle Gardens

On the move.

roasts under the desert sun, which can push temperatures up to 50°C (134°F) in the shade. But winter or summer, the city has a perpetual party atmosphere. Marrakchis are charming, hospitable, full of humour and intensely proud of their city, which for the most part is one of the most tolerant and liberal in Morocco.

History

Marrakech was founded by the Almoravids, religious nomads who emerged from the south to build their capital on the Tensift River in 1062. Austere, veiled warriors – much like the Tuareg – they constructed a walled kasbah and mosque that eventually became the capital of an empire that not only united all of modern Morocco, but also most of Spain and much of Algeria. Under the leadership of Youssef Ben Tashfine, Marrakech became a cosmopolitan centre of culture and learning with Andalusian-style mosques and palaces. The legacy of the Almoravids remains most tangibly in the city's walls and system of underground irrigation

Women walking by the kasbah.

channels that fed the new city and its fabulous gardens.

Orientation

Marrakech is split into two distinct areas: the traditional Moroccan walled medina, and **Gueliz** and **Hivernage**, which together comprise the French-built Ville Nouvelle.

Of most interest to visitors – and where most stay – is the **medina,** with its winding alleyways, colourful souks and historical monuments enclosed within ancient pink walls of sun-baked mud brick, or pisé. The medina can be further divided into quarters, with the most obvious partition falling between north and south of Jemaa el Fna. North of the square are the densely packed souks, each specialising in a particular trade. Behind and on either side of the souks are residential quarters, with the Medersa Ben Youssef and the Marrakech Museum two of the key sights here.

South of Jemaa el Fna is the Jewish quarter *(mellah)*, the Kasbah and the Royal Palace, and the greatest concentration of historic monuments.

Three main arteries serve this quarter: Avenue el Mouahidine/Avenue Houmman el Fetouaki running from Avenue Mohammed V (Marrakech's main street) past the Koutoubia Mosque and *mellah* market and ending at the busy junction next to the Place des Ferblantiers, a pleasant pedestrian square which acts as a useful reference point in navigating the area; and the two streets Riad Zitoun el Kedim and El Jdid (old and new), direct routes from the Jemaa el Fna to Place des Ferblantiers.

Gueliz is dominated by the broad, tree-lined Avenue Mohammed V, the main artery linking the Ville Nouvelle with the medina. Running north from the medina, beginning at the Koutoubia Mosque (where a busy junction leads off right to the Club Med and the Jemaa el Fna), Mohammed V, as it is known, cuts through the walls at the Bab Nkob gateway and ends on the far side of Gueliz at a busy traffic circle marking the start of the Casablanca road.

Many of the city's more up-market bars, restaurants and shops lie on this main street or in side streets running off it. However, most visitors now stay in one of the many hotels in the medina, most of them located in the literally hundreds of restored and converted riads scattered across the area, many of them offering superlative levels of luxury and authentic Moroccan atmosphere. Similarly, restaurants and shops have opened across the medina, but Gueliz is still the place to go for variety and a more relaxed atmosphere, particularly at night, when the medina all but shuts down.

Café in Gueliz.

Hivernage, the residential quarter bordering the southern edge of Gueliz, is now where most of the large hotels and bars are found. To the northeast of the medina is the Palmeraie of Marrakech, where some of the most exclusive hotels and private villas (plus several golf courses) are located.

Historic sites

The tallest feature on the medina skyline is the **Koutoubia Mosque ❶** (Mosque of the Booksellers). Completed by the Almohad Sultan Yacoub el Mansour in the 12th century, it is

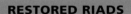
In the souks.

RESTORED RIADS

Over the past decade or so, increasing numbers of expats have been buying up dilapidated riads in Marrakech and renovating them into holiday homes and (increasingly) luxurious boutique hotels and maisons d'hôte (guesthouses). A riad is a traditional Arab medina house with a courtyard containing four trees or small 'gardens' and a fountain in the centre. Accommodation can also be found in a *dar* – a smaller, less grand version of a riad – with a courtyard but not a garden. The result is that visitors can now find an amazing array of accommodation, catering to all budgets and tastes (see page 298 for information on how to book).

At the latest count, there were over 500 riad hotels in the medina, and the craze has now spilled over into towns across the country. A riad may not have some of the amenities of a hotel (such as a television, a minibar or telephone), but it does offer the full medina experience, characterful accommodation, and often charming and knowledgeable hosts. Many will arrange day and longer trips: horse riding, trekking and desert excursions. Breakfast is always included, as well as lunch and dinner on request. These are particularly good ways of sampling the most delicious Moroccan home cooking, more authentic than in many restaurants.

the city's most important landmark and serves as a useful reference point if you become disoriented. The present-day mosque, like nearly all mosques in Morocco, is closed to non-Muslims.

A mosque was originally built here by the Almoravids; the Dar el Hajar (House of Stone) can still be traced in an excavation alongside the Koutoubia Mosque. The original mosque was destroyed by the Almoravids' successors, the Almohads, who descended from Tin Mal in the High Atlas and captured the city in 1147. The Almohads soon built their own mosque, but evidence suggests that this may have been wrongly aligned to Mecca, since a second mosque was completed in 1158 as an extension of the first, presumably to correct the original alignment of the prayer hall. Excavations undertaken in 1948 revealed the foundations of columns that would have supported the roof of the first Almohad mosque, and it is still possible to see, on the northern wall, the bricked-up arches that connected the two buildings. The same excavations also revealed evidence of a machine to raise and lower a screen (a *maqsurah*) to separate the ruler from the general populace.

It is the minaret that is the pride of the mosque today. It served as the model for the Hassan Tower in Rabat (see page 148) and the Giralda in Seville. The minaret is nearly 70 metres (230ft) high, and follows the Almohad proportions of 1:5, with the tower five times as high as it is wide. This proportion is found in nearly all Almohad mosques. The exterior of the tower is decorated with carved stone tracery, each side displaying different patterns. The rough stone of the tower would once have been covered with pink plaster and decorated. Remnants of this decoration can be seen in the lines of coloured tiles at the top of the restored tower.

Marrakech's famous calèches (horse-drawn carriages) can be hired from the Place du Foucauld, leading from the Koutoubia to Jemaa el Fna. The 'Tour des Ramparts' takes in all 16km (10 miles) of Marrakech's city walls. Fares are posted inside the calèche, but it is best to agree a price before setting off – the rate is officially 100dh per hour, although you may have to bargain hard to get this price.

Central square

The **Jemaa el Fna** ❷ is the heart of life in the medina and has been for 1,000 years. Its name means either 'Assembly of the Dead' or 'Mosque at the End of the World'. The great trans-Saharan caravans, laden with spices and slaves, salt and gold, used to arrive here and it has long been a focal point for all manner of spectacles. Its constant activity inspired Peter Mayne in *A Year in Marrakesh* to call it 'an inland, tideless sea'.

Today, Marrakchis and tourists alike come here to witness what many consider to be the world's greatest open-air show. On any given day, you will come across acrobats, magicians, fortune-tellers, dentists, snake charmers, Gnaoua musicians, orange-juice

Fruit bounty.

sellers and storytellers. Jemaa el Fna is the soul, the living legacy, of Morocco's oral tradition. Though busy in the day, Jemaa el Fna really comes alive at sunset. This is when the famous food stalls are set up. It is possible to eat anything from goats' heads to snails, *merguez*, tagines and couscous. Best value is the *harira* soup at just a few dirhams a bowl. The atmosphere is intoxicating: lamps glow amid swirling clouds of fragrant smoke from a hundred *grillades*, families and tourists wander from stall to stall, trade is hustled for and stories told. A less intimate way of enjoying the spectacle is from a terrace of one of the many ringside cafés, with the Café de France an old favourite, but now rivalled by the nearby Le Marrakechi and Les Terraces de l'Alhambra, not to mention a dozen or so other cafés around the square.

Souk Smarine and Souk el Kebir

Flowing northwards from Jemaa el Fna are the **souks** ❸ of the medina, a warren of shadowy tunnel-like streets punctuated by pools of sunlight. Inside these twisting alleys is a world brimming with sequined *babouches*, silken kaftans, multicoloured carpets, spices, antiques, wickerwork, lanterns, pottery and jewellery. Shouts of *'balek'* clear a path for over-laden handcarts, bicycles and mopeds. The souks of Marrakech are a sensory overload, but the best thing to do is take a breath and dive in.

Since the establishment of the Tourist Brigade (plain-clothes police dedicated to protecting tourists from 'faux guides' and other annoyances), visiting the souk has become an almost hassle-free experience. Though the souk appears to be a disorganised jumble of shops selling a head-spinning array of goods, the maze of twisting streets is really a network of individual markets, with each souk having its own name and specialising in its own craft. What the experts call rebound navigation, relating everything to a few easily recognisable landmarks, is the best method of finding your way around, although the authorities have helped make sense of the maze by erecting

TIP

Apart from a few banks just off Jemaa el Fna on Rue de Bab Agnaou, there are no banks or ATMs in the medina, so stock up here or in Gueliz before you head into the souks, as almost all places will only accept cash.

Food stalls on the Jemaa el Fna.

Souk signage.

On the Jemaa el Fna.

hundreds of little overhead signs pointing the way to the nearest major landmarks – and if you do get completely lost, any local will help set you back in the right direction in return for a few dirhams.

Entrance to the souks is via **Souk Smarine** (also known, French-style, as Rue Semmarine), hidden by a tangle of alleys selling olives, dried fruits, cheap shoes and ladies' clothing. Take the allleyway directly opposite the Café de France to reach the entrance to the souk, marked by a large arch tightly hemmed in by shops. Straight ahead, through the arch, is the broad, covered Souk Smarine itself, with a string of up-market shops aimed firmly at passing tourists.

The main road through the souk forks after about 200 metres/yds, with the left fork leading into Souk Attarine, and the right fork leading to Souk el Kebir and the Kissarias (see below). Just before the fork, turn right to reach the **Rahba Kedima ❹**, or Spice Market, in a small triangular square which once hosted the city's slave market, now ringed with the shops of dozens

of traditional *herbalistes* and apothecaries selling spices of all colours, animal skins, live chameleons and tortoises (for spells) and cures for every ailment imaginable. On the northern face of the square is the lovely **Café des Epices** (see page 315). An entrance on the square's north side leads to the surprisingly peaceful **Criée Berbère**, Marrakech's main carpet souk, home to dozens of rug shops in which it's easy to lose a couple of hours (or longer) sipping mint tea as shopkeepers unfurl endless carpets for your inspection.

Back on the main road through the souk, follow the right-hand fork into **Souk el Kebir**. A small jewellery souk is located off on the right, while just beyond, on the left, are the **Kissarias,** a sequence of self-contained covered alleyways running at right angles to the main souk. Traditionally, these were where up-market clothing, blankets and fabrics were sold, although many of the stalls have now been engulfed in replica football strips. Beyond here the main road through the souk disappears into the labyrinthine alleyways of the **Souk Cherratin**, the main leather-workers' souk, piled high with purses, bags and belts.

Medsersa Ben Youssef

Several small exits lead out of Souk Cherratin and the covered souk area into the open spaces of the Place de la Kissaria, a large open space surrounded by several of Marrakech's major landmarks. Continuing north brings you to the **Medersa Ben Youssef ❺** (daily 9am–6pm). When the original 14th-century Merinid medersa was rebuilt by Abdallah el Ghallib, the Saadian sultan made it the largest Qur'anic school in Morocco in a deliberate attempt to snub the imams of Fez, the religious centre of the country. The entrance is unremarkable, but succeeds in enhancing the visual impact on entering the main courtyard, where a rectangular marble pool reflects

the intricately carved cedar-wood and plaster of the walls and the sky above. The spacious courtyard leads to a prayer hall whose decoration balances detailed carving and *zellige* tile work in a classically Islamic display of rich but disciplined beauty.

Bounding the north side of the Place de la Kissaria, the sprawling **Ben Youssef Mosque** is more interesting for its history than for the building itself. Rebuilt several times, the current mosque dates back only to the 19th century and is thought to be merely half the size of the original. A mosque was first built by the Almoravids in the 12th century and would have been contemporary with the **Koubba el Baroudiyn ❻**, a diminutive two-storey pavilion once used as an ablutions chamber before entering the mosque and one of the very few surviving examples of Almoravid architecture in Marrakech. Embodied in the architecture of the *koubba* is the kernel of all Andalusian art that followed, including the distinctive zigzag battlements and pine-cone shaped arches.

Cultural centres

Just north of the medersa, on Rue Toulat Zaouiat Lahdar, is **Dar Bellarj** (daily 9am–6pm; tel: 0524-44 45 55, www.darbellarj.org), meaning House of Storks, a non-profit public arts centre, set up by a Swiss foundation, in one of the medina's most beautiful riads.

Nearby is the **Marrakech Museum ❼** (Place Ben Youssef; daily 9am–6pm), opened in 1997 and funded by the Omar Benjelloun Foundation, which also restored the medersa and the Koubba el Baroudiyin. Located in the restored 19th-century Dar Mnebhi Palace, the museum displays a wonderful collection of Islamic calligraphy and, in the former hammam, a collection of 18th- and 19th-century lithographs and watercolours of Moroccan seaports. However, its real purpose is to build up a collection of contemporary Moroccan art and to hold exhibitions and other cultural events.

On Rue Ahal Fès, just south of the museum, is the **Maison de la Photographie** (www.maisondelaphotographie.ma; daily 9.30am–7pm), a tiny whitewashed riad filled with exquisite black-and-white photographs of Marrakech and Morocco from 1870 to 1950 – the private collection of owners Patrick Manac'h and Hamid Mergani. There is a gorgeous little terrace at the top that serves lunch.

Souk Attarine and around

Return to the fork by the **Rahba Kedima** and head up into Souk Attarine to explore the western side of the souk district. **Souk Attarine** itself is the main perfume souk, beyond an alleyway on your right leads into the **Souk des Babouches**, crammed with traditional Moroccan-style leather slippers (*babouches*) in every conceivable colour and variety, from workaday yellow, red and white slippers through to brilliantly sequinned and bejewelled wedding slippers.

Alternatively, continuing along the main road brings you to the north from the Souk des Teinturiers is **Souk**

TIP

The Tribune de Marrakech, a free quarterly magazine available in many hotels and restaurants, is an excellent place to find out about the city's cultural events, new restaurants and bars.

Lavish interior of the Marrakech Museum.

Mounds of aromatic spices.

Ben Youssef Medersa.

Addadine, the blacksmiths' souk, a fairy tale little alleyway hung with innumerable metal lanterns gleaming magically in the low light. Close by, on the left (hustlers will probably leap upon you as you approach) is the **Souk des Teinturiers**, or dyers' souk, where multi-coloured skeins of green, yellow and red wools and silks are hung up to dry, with irresistibly photogenic results.

Mouassine quarter

South of the dyers' souk is the **Mouassine** quarter, pleasantly peaceful after the hustle-and-bustle of the crowded souks. Centrepiece of the district is the **Mouassine Mosque** ❽ dating from the Saadian dynasty and probably the most impressive in the medina, although little can be seen from the ground as it is surrounded by shops and houses. Several of the surrounding shops allow visitors up onto their roofs (for a small tip), revealing views of the mosque's green tiled roofs and tranquil open courtyards below. Next to the mosque stands an impressive sixteenth-century Saadian-era

drinking fountain, fronted with three arches and a discreet carved beam. Right next to the fountain, the small **Moro** boutique sells well-chosen things from across Morocco.

A short turn down Rue Mouassine is the **Café Arabe** (see page 315) – a haven of calm in the middle of the souks. It has a fabulous roof terrace which affords a stunning view of the whole medina, with the Koutoubia and Atlas Mountains in the distance.

Along Rue Dar el Barcha

Head north along Rue Mouassine to reach the junction with **Rue Dar el Barcha**. The area around here is dotted with the remains of dozens of atmospheric old *fondouks* (caravanserais) in which visiting traders would formerly have lodged during their trips to the city. All follow a similar plan, with rooms set over two storeys around a large central courtyard in which camels were formerly stabled, although the camels have long since gone, and many of the rooms have now been converted into small workshops and shops, with merchandise

set out in the courtyard. Two well-preserved examples (not signposted) can be found on either side of the road at the top of Rue Mouassine, along with another trio of places as you turn left into Rue Dar el Barcha. Continuing along touristy Rue Dar el Bacha, dotted with up-market handicrafts shops, and its continuation, Rue Bab Doukkala, brings you out to the edge of the medina at Bab Doukkala. En route you'll pass the old **Dar el Glaoui** ❾, formerly the palace of the Pasha Glaoui, although the large pink-walled complex is not currently open to the public. The Glaoui, a Berber clan from the region of Telouet, were tribal overlords in the most traditional sense who collaborated with the French to rule Morocco. Aided by their own army, they controlled the ancient medina, as they did the whole of the south, with a mixture of terror and generosity.

On the one hand, they ran hundreds of brothels catering for French Legionnaires and had a posse of informers and spies who blackmailed and murdered on their behalf. On the other,

they showered mistresses with riches, held lavish banquets and gave away fortunes to the poor. While the Pasha entertained Hollywood film stars, and even attended the Coronation of Queen Elizabeth II, his enemies where tortured and executed in dungeons straight from the pages of a medieval horror tale.

Zaouia Sidi Bel Abbes and the northern quarter

Heading to the northern tip of the medina along Rue Bab Taghzout, you pass through some of the most peaceful residential quarters (part of this northern quarter was outside the original medina walls and many of the houses here belonged to rich Fassis) before finally reaching **Zaouia Sidi Bel Abbes** ❿, the sanctuary of Sidi Bel Abbes (1130–1205), Marrakech's most revered holy man, and one of the city's seven saints. Inside the complex is a mosque, hammam, abattoir, market and cemetery, and non-Muslims can walk through its beautiful painted courtyard, with the huge and ornate mosque door at one

TIP

Many of the slightly larger riad hotels allow non-guests to have lunch and use their pools, for a fee. Les Jardins de la Koutoubia, Les Jardins de la Medina (see page 305) and Riad el Fenn (see page 305) are three in the medina that offer this service, as do Sofitel and Es Saadi in Hivernage. It's usually not necessary to book ahead, except at weekends and in peak periods.

Spice Market.

end. The sanctuary is also the focus of an annual pilgrimage begun by Moulay Ismail, and the shrine is frequented by those seeking cures, especially for blindness.

At the very northernmost point of the medina is one of Marrakech's best-kept secrets, **Souk el Khemis**, a fascinating flea market, with Western and Moroccan finds from much of the last century.

The brave can still visit the **tanneries** of Marrakech. Walk south along the eastern edge of the medina walls onto Rue de Bab Debbagh and follow your nose from there. Though smaller than the tanneries of Fez, the ones in Marrakech are nevertheless worth a visit, if you can bear the smell. They are a fascinating insight into a medieval trade that survives largely intact, and also into the process by which the bag or shoes you recently bought in the souk are made.

The Kasbah Mosque and the Saadian Tombs

The main entrance to the Kasbah from outside the medina is through the monumental, **Bab Agnaou gateway**, built by Yacoub el Mansour to mark the entrance to the Almohad Royal Palace. Just beyond this gate is the 12th-century **Kasbah Mosque ⓫**, topped by one of the city's largest minarets. This mosque is the second Almohad monument in Marrakech, although practically nothing of what you see today belongs to the original construction. Rebuilt for the first time about 30 years after the Koutoubia, but before Rabat's Hassan Tower, it is built from brick rather than stone and has been much restored.

Next door to the mosque (and clearly signposted 'Tombeaux Saadiens') are the **Saadian Tombs ⓬** (daily 9am–4.45pm), dating from the 16th century and built by Ahmed el Mansour, the second Saadian sultan, on the site of an older cemetery which was reserved for descendants of the Prophet. The Saadians emerged from Tamgroute in the Draa Valley during the 16th century, when Morocco was in turmoil after the collapse of the Merinids. They swept through the country on a wave of religious fervour

El Badi Palace.

and nationalist sentiment, capturing Marrakech in 1524. When the religious leaders of Fez rebuffed their claims of Sheriffian descent (from the Prophet), they made Marrakech their capital instead of Fez.

Abdallah el Ghalib succeeded to the Saadian throne after the murder of his rivals. A strong leader, he made a considerable impact on Marrakech, rebuilding the original Medersa Ben Youssef (founded by a Merinid Sultan in the 14th century) and the kasbah; he also built the Mouassine mosque and founded the *mellah*. His successor and half-brother, Ahmed el Dehbi (also called El Mansour, the Victorious) built the Palais el Badi and the Saadian Tombs.

After the collapse of the Saadian dynasty, the tombs were bricked up by Moulay Ismail in the late 17th century, and only rediscovered by a French aerial survey of the medina in 1917, unexpectedly revealing one of Marrakech's most intimate and magical monuments. A prayer hall embellished with a superb *mihrab* leads into the complex's pièce de la resistance, the central domed **mausoleum of Ahmed el Mansour**, built in the late Andalusian tradition, with every surface covered in lavish zellige tile work and carved stone decoration. El Mansour's tomb lies in the centre of the chamber, flanked by the slightly smaller tombs of other members of the Saadian dynasty, the whole lit by shafts of sunlight cast by the overhead lantern. Beyond here is the second and less impressive mausoleum of Mohammed ech Sheikh, the founder of the Saadian dynasty. The diminutive enclosure tends to get overrun with tour groups for much of the day – visit early in the morning, if possible, before the coach parties arrive.

El Badi Palace

The **El Badi Palace** ⑬, ('The Incomparable'; daily 9am–4.45pm), near the Place des Ferblantiers, is an elegant ruin between the *mellah* and the kasbah. Built by Ahmed el Mansour in the 16th century, it was once a palace of outstanding beauty, covered in white Italian marble. Little remains except an enormous open courtyard housing a rectangular pool and traces of the underground water system that once irrigated its gardens. The palace took 25 years to complete and, at the hands of Moulay Ismail less than a century later, only 12 years to destroy. Look out, too, for the spectacular *minbar* (a movable staircase from which a mosque's imam delivers his Friday sermon and leads prayers) from the Koutoubia Mosque. Inscriptions on the *minbar* show that it was made in Cordoba for the Koutoubia but was most likely commissioned by the Sultan ibn Tashfine around 1120, for the original Almoravid mosque. The workmanship involved in the marquetry decoration of the staircase – no two of the 1,000 panels are exactly the same – shows something of the splendour of Marrakech during the 12th century.

The view from the top of the ramparts of the palace is lovely, taking in

TIP

As a change from the cafés overlooking Jemaa el Fna, try some of those lining the Marrakech Plaza in Gueliz (see page 244). They are just as good for people-watching, and a little retail therapy can also be indulged in afterwards.

Souk el Khemis.

Kilims (flat-woven rugs).

Mountain view from La Mamounia hotel.

nesting storks and the rooftops of the medina.

Just outside the Badi is the busy Place des Ferblantiers, a square devoted to the crafting of lanterns, with a couple of simple restaurants situated around its edges. On the eastern side of the square is the popular **Kosybar**, which has a great terrace. On Avenue Houmman el Fetouaki is the *mellah* market, a dazzling display of fruit and vegetables, flower stalls and butchers' shops. East, into the *mellah* proper, is the **Bahia Palace** ⑭ (daily 9am–4.45pm), built in the 19th century by grand viziers to the Alaouite sultans.

The Bahia (which translates as 'The Brilliant') is a stunning display of the period's post-Alhambra decoration, using the very finest Moroccan craftsmen and superior workmanship. The beautiful series of gardens, courtyards and cool reception halls, with their intricate *zellige* floors, painted cedar ceilings, finely carved stucco and magnificent wooden doors, are impressive. During the French Protectorate it served as the governor's residence; today it is officially part of the Royal Palace and parts of it, including most of the upstairs rooms, are used for lodging guests; Jackie and Aristotle Onassis are among those who once stayed here. In total, the palace covers around 8 hectares (20 acres) and has a total of 150 rooms, only a fraction of which can be seen by the public.

Hidden museums

North of the Bahia Palace a couple of further rewarding museums lie hidden amongst the backstreets of the medina. Off the picturesque shopping street of Rue Riad Zitoun el Jdid a narrow alley (opposite the point at which the western side of the street opens up into a miniature square) is the beautiful **Maison Tiskiwin** ⑮ (daily 9am–12.30pm, 2.30–6pm). The home of Dutch anthropologist Bert Flint, the building doubles as a private museum containing a superb collection of Berber textiles and pottery.

Heading south from Maison Tiskiwin, take the first turning on your

Local icons

left (between the District Urban Jamaa Lafna building and the Hammam Ziani) to reach the excellent **Dar Si Said Museum** ⓖ (Fri–Wed 9am–5pm). The museum occupies a particularly impressive riad, built in the 19th century by the brother of the Grand Vizier Ba Hmad, who was responsible for Bahia Palace (see page 242). Exhibits scattered around the labyrinthine ground floor include an impressive selection of Moroccan artefacts – ornate wooden doors and painted windows salvaged from southern kasbahs; old Qu'rans and antique leather-work bags; brightly coloured traditional clothes and fabrics.

Exhibits aside, it's the building itself that really captures the imagination. Twisting corridors eventually lead to a central courtyard, with a beautifully tiled fountain set beneath a painted wooden gazebo and gorgeously painted and tiled doors to all four sides. From here, steps lead up to the spectacularly decorated chambers above, with intricately tiled and painted ceilings and a selection of wedding palanquins and assorted carpets.

Marking the line between the medina and Gueliz is **La Mamounia** (see page 305), Marrakech's most iconic hotel and once upon a time – before the riad boom – the only place worth staying in town. Extensively refurbished, the Mamounia is again one of the most desirable addresses in Marrakech. It may be beyond most people's budgets, but it is worth having tea in the spectacular gardens or a cocktail in the Art Deco Churchill Bar, named for the man who spent many a holiday painting here and who thought the Mamounia's gardens were the 'loveliest spot in the whole world.' Other famous guests have included Roosevelt, the Rolling Stones, Alfred Hitchcock, Nelson Mandela and Tom Cruise.

Heading north along the medina walls, you will hit the Mamounia's most recent competition, the dazzlingly beautiful **Royal Mansour**. Commissioned and owned by the king, it is indeed fit for a king and celebrates the very best craftsmanship that Morocco has to offer. Non-guests

Bahia Palace detail.

Bahia Palace tiles.

Majorelle Gardens and the distinctive blue pavilion.

are welcome for dinner or a drink, but reservations must be made in advance. Edging the Royal Mansour is the **Cyber Parc**, named for its Wi-fi terminals placed in parts of this beautifully laid-out garden – a blissfully cool and shady place to escape to on a hot afternoon.

Gueliz

Northwest of the medina stretches Marrakech's Ville Nouvelle, providing a cosmopolitan contrast to the old medina complete with art galleries, up-market boutiques where you don't have to haggle, swanky cafés and some of the city's best restaurants. From the Cyber Parc, follow Gueliz's main artery, **Avenue Mohammed V**, into the heart of the city. One of the first major landmarks you'll reach is the glitzy **Marrakech Plaza** ⑰, a fountain-filled space bordered with European shops and cafés. Ahead, just after the Place du 16 Novembre, is **Grand Café de la Poste**, a lovely French brasserie and one of the chicest places to eat, drink and hang out, set inside one of

the few remaining colonial buildings in the Ville Nouvelle. On the other side of the road is a giant Zara store and opposite that, **Café Elite**, one of numerous up-market coffee shops and patisseries in the area, usually full of glamorous Marrakchis.

Dozens of restaurants fill the streets leading off Place du 16 Novembre (see page 316), and there are also several great bars, notably the Bab Hotel (corner of Boulevard el Mansour Eddhabi and Rue Mohammed el Beqal), the Sky Bar of the Hotel la Renaissance (corner of Boulevard Mohammed V and Boulevard Mohammed Zerktouni), African Chic (Rue Oum Errabia), which has live music, and l'Apero, on Rue Abou Hayane Taouhidi.

Art and shopping

Art galleries exhibiting Moroccan and international artists are scattered around Gueliz, from the **Matisse Art Gallery** (www.matisseartgallery.com; Mon–Sat 10am–7pm; **free**), just off Rue de Yougoslavie, to **Galerie Ré** (www.galeriere.com; Mon–Sat 3–7pm or by prior appointment) on Rue

ibn Toumert and the lovely **Galerie 127** (tel: 0524 43 26 67; www.galerie nathalielocatelli.com; Tue–Sat 3–7pm or by prior appointment) on Avenue Mohammed V, which specialises in photography. Many of the city's travel agencies and car rental places can also be found on Mohammed V along the west side of the road north of Place du 16 Novembre.

Rue de la Liberté ⑱, and **Rue du Vieux Marrakchi** are the two best shopping streets in Gueliz, with some fantastic boutiques, including **Michelle Baconnier** on Rue du Vieux Marrakchi. Shops on Rue de Liberté include **Darkoum**, selling antique furniture, fabrics and artefacts from India and Morocco; **Atika**, a popular shoe shop; **L'Orientaliste**, which has everything from perfume to tea glasses and prints to lanterns; **Scènes de Lin**, selling hand-embroidered linens and fabrics; and chocolatier **Jeff de Bruges**. **Kechmara**, at the end of Rue de Liberté, is popular for lunch.

Bisecting Rue de la Liberté is Rue Tariq ibn Ziad, which has Marrakech's only restaurant-bookshop, the **Café du Livre**, which does a good breakfast and lunch and is a nice place for a drink.

Hivernage, the Menara and Agdal Gardens

Most of Marrakech's bars and nightclubs, such as Teatro, Jad Mahal, La Suite, So Bar and Le Comptoir Darna, are located in Hivernage. The **Menara Gardens and Pavilion** ⑲, (daily 8am–6pm; free) created in the 12th century by the Almohads, is a lovely place to visit, especially early in the morning, or just before sunset and between the months of December and April, when the snowcapped Atlas rise up in the distance, and are reflected in the rectangular pool that was created as a reservoir. The pavilion, used by sultans for romantic liaisons, was restored by Moulay Abderrahman in the 19th century.

The other great garden of Imperial Marrakech is the **Agdal Gardens** (Fri–Sat 8am–5pm; free), a large open space some 3km (2 miles) south of the Kasbah along Rue de la Kasbah. The shade of the innumerable olive, orange and fig trees make the park a popular retreat for Marrakchi families on summer weekends. The gardens date right back to the Almohad period and are crisscrossed with an extensive network of wells and subterranean channels that bring water to the gardens from as far away as the foothills of the Atlas Mountains.

Majorelle Gardens

The breathtaking **Majorelle Gardens** ⑳ (www.jardinmajorelle.com; daily Oct–Apr 8am–5.30pm, May–Sept 8am–6pm), just off avenue Yacoub el Mansour, are amongst Marrekech's most unforgettable sights. The gardens and Moorish villa were built by Jacques Majorelle, a French orientalist painter, in the 1920s, and the iconic bright-blue pavilion in the gardens was designed in the 1930s. The gardens opened to the public in 1955 and years later the house was bought by Yves Saint Laurent and Pierre Bergé.

Majorelle Gardens.

Avenue Mohammed V.

TIP

On the northern edge of Gueliz, the French Institute (Tue–Sat 8.30am–noon, 2.30–6.30pm) offers a library, exhibition space and occasional events and films. It also has a vibrant little café. Its programme is always posted at the main entrance to the Central Market in Gueliz.

The garden's Islamic Art Museum hosts regular exhibitions, and a stone memorial to Yves Saint Laurent rests in a bamboo-shaded corner of the garden. A lovely courtyard restaurant serves good lunches and teas. Just outside the Majorelle, a little cluster of stylish juice bars, cafés and shops is blossoming.

Great escapes

Outside the southern walls is a fortress called the **Squallet el Mrabit**, which once housed a squadron of cavalry to help defend the city. From the **Er Rob Gate**, taxis and buses travel to the Ourika Valley (about an hour's drive into the Atlas Mountains, see page 249) and Imlil in the High Atlas (see page 246).

The city's role as an oasis is brought home on a circuit around the **Palmeraie** (said to have sprung up from the discarded date stones of the Almohad army besieging the Almoravid city). The Palmeraie, sandwiched between the Casablanca and Fez roads (signposted 'Circuit des Palmeraies'), is also home to Marrakech's rich and famous, as well as a series of palatial villas and hotels set in luxuriant gardens. **Le Palmier d'Or** is a good place for lunch and arranges camel and quad rides through the palm groves. The Palmeraie also has several large hotel complexes, such as **Palmeraie Golf Palace** (www.pgpmarrakech. com), offering tennis, mountain biking and golf. **Le Royal Golf de Marrakech** (www.royalgolfmarrakech.com), on the route de Ouarzazate, is a fantastic old golf course with excellent views of the Atlas and a good club restaurant. A little further on is the **Amelkis Golf Club,** part of a more recent resort development.

About a 45-minute drive from Marrakech is the stunning lake of **Lalla Takerkoust**, offering a choice of restaurants (Le Flouka and the Relais du Lac are the best), picnic sites, plus swimming, pedalos, canoeing and jet-skiing. Elsewhere outside Marrakech you can rent quads, ride horses and take hot-air balloon or helicopter rides over the surrounding countryside.

One hour from Marrakech is the village of **Imlil**, at the foot of Jebel Toubkal (see page 251), and the same distance, but on a different road out of town, the ski resort of **Oukaimeden,** which can have snow from December to March (see page 250).

Royal favourite

Hassan II spent much of his time in Marrakech in the last months of his life, and it is said that this is also the favourite city of King Mohammed VI, who comes here often. As a result, old gardens have been cleaned up and new ones planted around the medina walls. The city is also the location for dozens of festivals and events, most notably the Marrakech International Film Festival (www.festivalmarrakech. info), the Marrakech Biennale (www. marrakechbiennale.org) and the Popular Arts Festival (www.marrakechfestival. com), as well as being the finishing point for the gruelling Marathon des Sables (see page 318).

Dates for sale in the medina.

A Garden City

Marrakech is an oasis city. Despite ferociously hot summers, its gardens flourish and offer blissfully cool and tranquil escapes from the hustle and bustle of city life.

Some 160km (100 miles) from the coast and far below the cooler altitudes of the Atlas Mountains, Marrakech is a furnace in summer. For Marrakchis, relief is found in dark interiors, private courtyards and, most pleasingly of all, in the city's gardens.

The gardens of Marrakech have always surprised and delighted visitors. The British writer Osbert Sitwell called Marrakech 'the ideal African city of water-lawns, cool, pillared palaces and orange groves'. It was the promise of gardens and flowers that drew Matisse to North Africa. He went in the footsteps of the writer Pierre Loti, who found 'nothing but carpets of flowers', and the painter Eugène Delacroix, who remarked on 'innumerable flowers of a thousand species forming carpets of the most varied colours'.

Gardens are also earthly intimations of Paradise, the Eden of the afterlife described in the Qur'an as 'gardens watered by running streams'. Entwined foliage, a motif of Islamic decorative art, runs riot over stucco carvings and faïence tiling in Moroccan mosques and medersas.

Garden variety

Marrakech's great gardens are 19th- or early 20th-century creations, though in most cases they replace earlier gardens – originally agricultural estates – which withered and died during tribal warfare.

The vast Agdal Gardens, 3km (2 miles) long and 1.3km (.75 mile) wide, were planted by the Almohads with olive, lemon, orange and apricot trees, and have two large irrigation pools that lend a cooling presence on hot days, when virtually all of Marrakech descends with picnics, music and much merriment.

A more modern addition to the city's gardens is the Cyber Parc, set just outside the medina walls. Cool and shaded by ancient palms and citrus trees and punctuated by bright-pink bougainvillea, pale-blue oleander and deep-green grasses, this is a wonderfully peaceful place to stroll around, and is popular with young couples, who sit demurely on stone benches dotted around the park.

On a smaller scale are the magical Majorelle Gardens, named after their creator, the French painter Jacques Majorelle. Lovingly restored by Yves Saint Laurent, the garden is a kaleidoscope of tropical colour. Walkways are painted a dusty pink, flowerpots bright yellow or turquoise, contrasting with the vibrant orange of the ornamental carp in the lily-padded pools.

Smaller gardens are also found in the old palaces that have been turned into museums. The garden in the Bahia Palace, for example, is a walled oasis, where the Grand Vizier's wives and concubines came to stroll and play to the accompaniment of birdsong. Pathways are laid out symmetrically, but this is no prissy arrangement of neat flowerbeds and clipped box hedge. Instead plants, flowers and trees intertwine and overarch in an explosion of perfume (roses, jacaranda, jasmine, orange blossom), juicy fruits (pomegranates, figs, carob, peaches, grapes), and the intoxicating pollen from the datura tree, known as the 'jealous tree' and said to drive people mad. It is no accident that the best-loved plants in Morocco are those that release their scent at night, when their heady perfume contributes to the voluptuous courtship of lovers.

A quiet spot in the Majorelle Gardens.

THE HIGH ATLAS

Climb the highest mountain in North Africa, swim under waterfalls in the Ourika Valley, visit the seat of the Almohad dynasty – the Atlas Mountains are packed with possibilities.

Tagines in the Ourika Valley.

Any mountain range 700km (450 miles) long and with summits over 4,000 metres (13,000ft) high must be counted as a major topographical incident on planet earth. Since the first attempts by Europeans in the early 19th century to follow Arab trade routes across this great barrier, the number of foreign travellers penetrating the Atlas up until World War II probably never exceeded a thousand. The slogan 'Death to the infidel!' applied to all unaccompanied strangers in this region.

The Atlas mystique lasted even after a prominent pass, Tagharat, and a distinct summit, Gourza (3,280 metres/ 10,700ft), had been reached by outsiders in 1871. The Hooker-Ball-Maw expedition observed, 'The climate is admirable, the natural obstacles of no account, but the traditional policy of the ruling race has passed into the very fibre of the inhabitants, and affords an obstacle but impassable to ordinary travellers.'

These days the Atlas is more accessible, and its inhabitants, having developed keen entrepreneurial instincts, are more hospitable towards visitors.

Lie of the land

Three main roads penetrate the High Atlas from **Marrakech** (see page 231): the spectacular Tizi N'Test pass (see page 264), the less interesting N8 through the western Atlas to Agadir (best in winter, when the high passes are often closed due to snow), and the well-maintained, though vertiginous, Tizi N'Tichka pass to Ouarzazate (see page 265). West of the Tizi N'Tichka, the High Atlas rises up to the jagged peaks of the Toubkal massif, before descending to the Tizi N'Test pass. From the Tizi N'Test, the Atlas Occidental continues westwards, north of the city of Taroudant, running down to meet the Atlantic Ocean between Agadir and Tamri. South of Toubkal the Jebel Siroua is a remote outlying plateau of extinct volcanic plugs filling the gap between the High Atlas proper and the Ouarzazate–Taroudant road.

Ourika Valley

If you are staying in Marrakech but not planning to travel very far afield, it would be a shame not to venture into the Atlas for at least a day or two. One of the easiest and most popular excursions is to the **Ourika Valley**, about an hour's drive south along the P2017 (the 'Route d'Ourika'), which passes through Marrakech's nursery flower gardens and winds up into the lush foothills of the Atlas. In spring the hills are carpeted with wild flowers and blossoming fruit trees, while in summer the cool and shady landscape attracts crowds of picnicking Marrakchis at weekends.

Just over 30km (18 miles) from Marakech, is the village of **Tnine Ourika**, which has some good tagine restaurants and a weekly souk on Mondays. A number of interesting local tourist initiatives can be found nearby. These include **Nectarome** (www.nectarome.com), a beautiful 'bio-aromatic' herb garden, producing organic essential oils and cosmetics, where you can also have lunch; **Safranerie** (www.safranourika.com), another beautiful herbal garden, specialising in saffron and various tisanes; and, most interestingly, the **Ecomusée Berbere de L'Ourika** (www.museeberbere.com), where local guides offer rewarding insights into local life and culture in the valley.

The easiest way to travel round the High Atlas is to hire a driver.

Houses built into the hillside in the Ourika Valley.

Charcoal-grilled lamb in Asni.

Continue up the road, following the river, to reach the village of **Setti Fatma ❶**, high in the cleft of the valley. A busy mule track cuts deeper south, but the main attraction is the series of seven waterfalls on the far side of the river, the first of which is reached after an easy climb through the rocks and trees. In the summer this is a popular spot for tourists and Marrakchis alike, with swimming in a deep, icy rock pool, while above, wild monkeys stalk the craggy heights and shower walnuts on the unwary.

Oukaimeden

Returning back down the Ourika Valley from Setti Fatma, and then turning left onto the P2030 brings you to the ski resort of **Oukaimeden ❷**, located at a breathless 2,650 metres (8,700ft) above sea level. The season, if there is sufficient snow, runs roughly from late December to the end of March, with pistes ranging from nursery to black level, although there is little in the way of piste-grooming, so conditions can be rough; rescue services are virtually non-existent and the nearest hospital is

in Marrakech – best not to go off-piste. Donkeys are available to carry you and your skis from the pistes to the car park, and ancient ski equipment can be rented at the bottom of the pistes.

There are six button lifts and one chair lift to the top of **Jebel Oukaimeden** – the highest ski lift in North Africa. A local viewpoint with an orientation table is set at the end of the chair lift, with wide vistas south to Toubkal and the Tazahart Plateau, and northwards over the Haouz plain and Marrakech. There are prehistoric rock engravings along the north side of the pasture plateau. Huge flocks of sheep and goats graze here in early summer, brought up by villagers from the lower valleys. While an asphalt road goes back to the city, a mule path winds westwards, over the Tizi N'Oukaimeden, down paths through stunted walnut forests and evergreen oak, back to the terraced fields of the Mizane and Asni, a good five-hour hike.

The Toubkal massif

Shimmering in the haze beyond the pink walls of Marrakech, long flecks

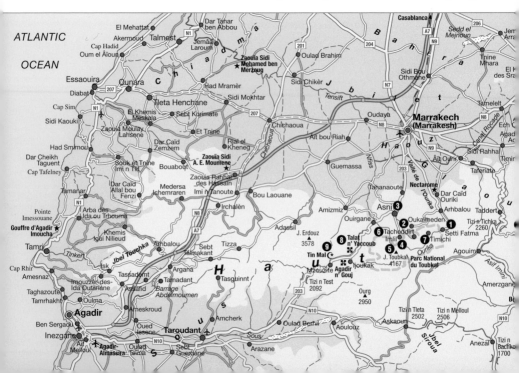

of snow barely 60km (38 miles) away brush the rugged profile of the southern horizon. This is the Toubkal massif, the craggy mass of rocky peaks and deep valleys that contains the highest summits of the Atlas chain. Roads teeming with people and domestic animals, scooters and lorries belching diesel fumes, cross the hot Haouz plain to **Asni** ❸. The town's bustling Saturday souk remains a mainly traditional affair, though you'll also now find people selling carpets, fossils and other local trinkets. There are a few basic hotels and restaurants in Asni, but most people choose to stay in Imlil. A turning to the right before the market leads up to Moulay Brahim and the Kik Plateau.

To the south of Asni, somewhere in the distance at the head of the Mizane Valley, towers Jebel Toubkal, at 4,167 metres (13,670ft) the highest mountain in North Africa. To reach the road-head at **Imlil** from which all treks in the surrounding area and ascents of Toubkal begin, take the signposted left turn after the post office. There is a good tarmac road running 17km (11 miles) up the valley, offering spectacular views towards the Toubkal massif. The road passes the superbly sited **Kasbah Tamadot** hotel (see page 307), owned by Richard Branson.

Imlil

Imlil ❹ is a charming mountain village, with several good cheap places to stay, a scattering of restaurants and lots of souvenir shops, selling carpets, fossils and jewellery. There is also a Bureau des Guides in the village (just opposite the car park, tel: 0524 48 56 26), and anyone travelling independently for the first time in the area is recommended to pay it a visit, even if they have no intention of hiring a guide. Trekking companies are another option and deal with all the logistical problems of organising porters, provisions and accommodation. The more self-reliant can always backpack and dispense with the local services, but it would be wise to seek advice on routes and weather conditions.

Thousands flock to Imlil in spring and early summer to climb **Jebel**

Imlil is a popular base for climbing Mount Toubkal or trekking in the surrounding mountains.

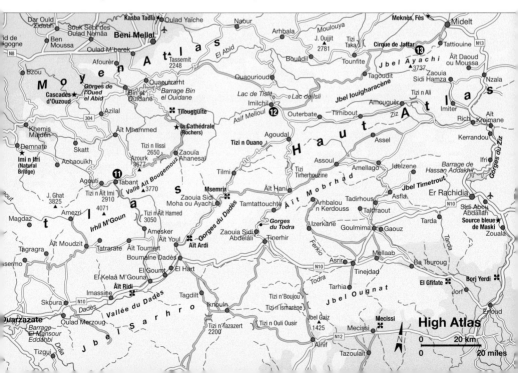

TIP

To find out about trekking facilities in advance of your stay in Morocco, see page 323. In Marrakech, most *maisons d'hôte* also now arrange tailored trips, with all the necessary elements (guide, transport, accommodation) included.

View from the terrace at Kasbah du Toubkal.

Toubkal **5** and/or trek in the surrounding foothills – two of the most popular attractions in Morocco. For a mountain of this height and accessibility to have had its first recorded ascent (by a French party under the Marquis de Segonzac) as late as 1923 testifies to the tribal fortress mentality maintained by local people well into the 20th century. There's also a well-developed hiking trail around the mountain – the 'Toubkal Circuit' (see page 100) – offering circular treks of between seven and 10 days, staying overnight in remote huts, Berber outposts and sometimes in open-air bivouacs.

One of the best places to use as a base, as well as to hire guides and arrange treks, is the stunning **Kasbah du Toubkal** (see page 253), a beautifully restored kasbah at the top of Imlil with 360° views of Toubkal and the mountains around. The kasbah was the location for Martin Scorsese's film about the Dalai Lama, *Kundun*. Most importantly, it is run by locals from the surrounding villages, and a 5 percent 'surcharge' on the price of the rooms goes to the local Village Association, which funds ambulances, clinics and schools. The kasbah also has a trekking lodge halfway up Jebel Toubkal.

Day hikes

From Imlil, for those shod in boots, there are a number of easy day hikes up to the **Tamatert pass** in the east (see page 254) or the **Mzic pass** in the west, both giving superb views back and beyond to the continuing chain of ridges and peaks overlooking the villages and green terraced fields of the Berbers.

Aremd (also known as Aroumd or Armed) is the last village in the Mizane Valley before the long hike up to the high mountains. It is an important trekking centre with a range of gites, a small hotel and a campsite. The valley here, more open than at Imlil, is a beautiful place to spend a day or two acclimatising before an arduous trek or recuperating before descending to Marrakech.

The religious shrine of **Sidi Chamharouch** (complete with associated

shops catering for pilgrims), lies two hours away by foot or on mule back along the trail in the upper Mizane. Like a beacon, its white roof draws many on a day's outing. Among this huddle of little houses squeezed into a niche at the foot of a rock slope, all Berber life is exposed to public view.

Ascending Toubkal

Jebel Toubkal can usually be climbed in two days – the first day reaching the CAF Toubkal Refuge at 3,207 metres (10,522ft), which is about seven hours from Imlil, and reaching the summit (five hours) and returning to Imlil (five hours) on the second day. A lot of people include the ascent as part of longer treks (see box). Note that the ascent can only be made when the snows have melted, between May and October, unless you have suitable equipment (crampons, ice axe) and experience of extreme winter mountain conditions.

The **CAF Toubkal Refuge** has good dormitory facilities and a large communal area for cooking and eating. A spring supplies the hut, via a buried pipe, although it is still recommended that you boil drinking water. Gully water in the stream below flushes the toilets. Refreshments and simple meals can be ordered from the warden. During the summer months it is sensible to book a place in the refuge via a message carried by the in-season shuttle of mules and porters from Imlil (do this a day before going up to the hut). Camping below the hut is becoming increasingly popular. You have to leave the refuge by 6.30am – not necessarily a bad thing, given the importance of making an early start.

If you climb Toubkal outside the summer trekking season you may need crampons and an ice axe for complete comfort as well as stout boots and proper clothing. Knowing the prevailing conditions, a guide will advise exactly.

The ascent is reasonably straightforward, a gradual walk up a stony slope, until one reaches the notoriously slippery upper scree, where care must be taken as one false move could well be dangerous. Moreover, the path has been ruined by the careless footwork

Imlil.

TREKKING GUIDES

Nationally qualified trekking guides are called *accompagnateurs,* and are registered with the Ministry of Tourism. They all speak French and sometimes English, Spanish or German. The guides will also take charge of the hiring of mules and the provision of supplies on longer expeditions. As a rule, one mule can carry the baggage of three trekkers equipped for three to four days. In places where mules cannot go, loads are carried by porters.

Prices for guides and mules/muleteers are regulated. If you expect extra duties, such as the guide also doing your cooking, or if you choose to take a muleteer and no guide, you may have to pay more than the usual rates. All prices are exclusive of the guide's food, which you are expected to provide.

of thousands of tired limbs. The summit is crowned by a pyramidal metal marker, and views stretch as far as the eye can see over the Atlas massif.

The route is graded by Atlas mountaineer Michael Peyron as *type boulevard* and, indeed, after about three hours, the summit appears like a big open corral. You'll find people – usually the T-shirt and flip-flop brigade – stamping their feet and trotting round to keep warm. The major danger in climbing Toubkal is from altitude sickness – if you start vomiting or develop a severe headache, head back down immediately – although highly changeable weather conditions may also prove a threat if you're not properly equipped.

Other treks around Imlil

A popular trek, which can be lengthened or shortened according to taste, takes the path from Imlil over the **Tamatert pass** to the crossroads village of **Tacheddirt** ❻, in a relaxing three and a half hours. Tacheddirt itself is an appealing Berber settlement, epitomising the traditional mountain way of life. There is accommodation in a mountain hut or in a couple of gites in nearby villages.

The major climb to the **N'Addi pass** (2,900 metres/9,600ft) that looms behind the village is rewarded by views of ravines and peaks zebra-striped with long streaks of snow. Riding a mule will be allowed only on the easy down slope (where there is a Jeep road) to the broad pastures of Oukaimeden below. At the head of the Tacchedirt Valley lies the Tacchedirt pass, leading to the large village of **Timichi** ❼, from where paths lead over the **Tizi N'Ouattar**, again to Oukaimeden, or continue to Setti Fatma at the head of the Ourika Valley (see page 249).

For the really adventurous, the towering **Likemt pass** offers routes over to the southern side of the Atlas, descending eventually to Ammzouzerte in the Tifnout Valley, at the head of which lies the remote **Lac d'Ifni**. Seen from the height of the moraine that blocks its southern end, the lake is like a blue-green jewel set in a bowl made by towering naked

Road through the Tizi N'Tichka pass.

peaks. From its northern shore a path sets off across rocky ground to a tortuous gully that leads up to the mountain's highest and most spectacular pass, the **Tizi Ouanouns**, to regain the head of the Mizane Valley, which descends first to the Toubkal Refuge and finally back to Imlil. The entire round trip is a one-week trek, without rest days or excursions to explore or climb nearby peaks.

All this merely scratches the surface of an area rich in opportunities for trekking, with many more routes heading off west of Imlil for almost as many days as you have the energy to walk.

To Ouirgane and Tin Mal

Back on the **Tizi N'Test** road, continuing south of Asni (see page 251), the route continues to **Ouirgane**, a sleepy village nestled in gentle foothills near a lake reservoir. There are several lovely places to stay – or just to have lunch – here (see page 316), and the village offers an especially welcome escape from the heat of Marrakech during the summer months.

A little further on is **Ijoukak** where a piste leads into the less visited, but beautiful, **Agoundis Valley**. Close by stands the ancient kasbah of **Talat N'Yaccoub 8**, surrounded by olive groves, with the foaming River Nfiss lapping at the foot of its ramparts. Dominating an adjacent knoll, with the snows of the western Igdet as a backdrop, is the **Agadir N'Gouj**, a former stronghold of the Goundafi tribe that was notorious in the 19th century for its dungeons. The entire area is now regarded as one of the outstanding beauty spots of the Great Atlas chain.

Higher up on the other side of the stream is the striking 12th-century mosque at **Tin Mal 9**, a fortified holy town that was the birthplace of the Almohad movement, which eventually gave rise to the famous Berber dynasty of the Middle Ages. The mosque was built in 1156 by Abd el Moumen, who was the successor to Ibn Toumert, the theologian founder of Tin Mal. Although the town was ransacked by Merinids in 1276, the mosque remained the only thing

FACT

The mountain range was named the Atlas by Europeans inspired by the Greek myth. According to the story, the Titan Atlas was turned to stone by Perseus, supporting the heavens. Bowed by the weight, Atlas genuflected towards the setting sun in northwest Africa.

Mountain restaurant.

Fossils for sale.

Atlas rocks.

as it reaches the very top of the vertiginous **Tizi N'Test Pass**, at 2,092 metres (6,867ft) the second-highest mountain road in Morocco. Despite its wild beauty, the area is actually an environmental disaster, as vast forests have been chopped down for building materials and firewood. Here, and similarly along the eastern boundary of the Toubkal massif, plainly marked by the Tichka pass commercial road, the watershed divides the lush from the barren. A quilt of green fields stitched round a few oases occasionally brightens the monotony.

The Western High Atlas

West of the Tizi N'Test road rises the Occidental or Western High Atlas, remote to most tourists, but surprisingly densely populated and supporting a thriving agricultural economy. The **Seksawa Valley**, its boxy dwellings planted on mountain sides prickling with television aerials, is the principal road for lorries travelling to and from Marrakech. Adventurous tourists bent on exploration away from the crowds will find many

standing. In the early 1990s it underwent a complete restoration and was declared a Unesco World Heritage Site in 1995. It is one of the few in Morocco that non-Muslims can visit (outside prayer times).

The mountain behind the mosque is **Gourza**, first climbed by the Hooker botanical expedition in 1871. Past here, the road narrows

GEMS AND FOSSILS

In the High Atlas and Middle Atlas, makeshift stalls selling rocks packed with crystals and semi-precious stones, such as amethysts and quartz, can prove irresistible. The usual advice is, be cautious, as some of the items being hawked are not genuine. That said, many are, and you will sometimes see European gem traders examining stones under a magnifying glass. At one such stall, in 1996, a British geologist discovered an intensely blue pyramid-shaped rock, which the stallholder told her was lapis lazuli. Realising that it wasn't but still intrigued by the rock, she bought it for a few dirhams and on her return home took it to London's Natural History Museum. Tests revealed it to be an entirely new mineral containing silicon, aluminium, calcium, magnesium, iron and oxygen.

Fossils, too, are found on these stalls, including some impressive examples of ammonites. Morocco is one of the world's best sources of this fossil, though check carefully, as sometimes the ridges have been enhanced by a chisel. And it was in Morocco, again in 1996, that the bones of a meat-eating African dinosaur as large as Tyrannosaurus rex were found. Though scientists had known of Carcharodontosaurus saharicus prior to the find, only one other skeleton of the dinosaur had hitherto been found and that had been lost.

diverting sights in this region, including the picturesque Tichka Plateau.

One rewarding way of visiting the area is by mountain bike (they can be hired in Marrakech and Agadir). The mountains are not as rugged as the Toubkal, and the area is more densely covered by piste. As a base for such expeditions, one could do much worse than **Imouzzer des Ida Outanane** (see page 280), with its good hotel and nearby waterfalls.

East of the Toubkal massif

On the eastern side of the Toubkal massif, the Yagour Plateau (dotted with pre-historic rock engravings) and the Zat Gorge lead down to the **Tizi N'Tichka Pass**, meeting the main N9 road between Marrakech and Ouarzazate just above **Taddert**. This is a one-street town, lined with grill shops and the last truck stop before a dizzy series of heart-stopping hairpin bends takes you up and over the 2,260-metre (7,412ft) Tizi N'Tichka Pass.

The Tizi N'Tichka is a superb drive, but it is mainly a transport artery and is little used as a starting point for trekking. About 20km (12 miles) east of the Tichka and deliberately sidetracked by the main road built in 1936 lies **Telouet** ❿ the old Glaoui seat of power situated on the ancient caravan route. Telouet is famous for its kasbah, deserted after the fall from grace of the self-styled Sultans of the South. First visited by a European in 1889 and once host to Wilfred Thesiger on his treks through the Atlas, the crumbling ruin is sufficiently intact to give an impression of past splendour. A guardian can unlock its gate and give a small tour, pointing out the once-magnificent reception rooms and the bower from which the privileged guests of the Glaoui could watch *fantasias* staged in the arena below.

Further up the **Animter Valley,** the path leads through a fertile valley up to the isolated Tamda Lake, full of trout and surrounded by stones, tightly packed with tiny fossils. The surrounding mountains are bare and lonely and largely uninhabited. Eastwards the path meanders across the Tizi N'Fedhrat to the picturesque village of **Magdaz** (see page 259)

QUOTE

'I became lost in the castle, and found my torch shining upon white but manacled bones in a dungeon. With the turbulent history of Telouet they could have been either a hundred or less than five years old.'

Gavin Maxwell, Lords of the Atlas, 1966

The kasbah at Telouet.

Road-side stalls selling crystallised rocks and minerals are scattered throughout the High Atlas.

The High Atlas roads are not for the faint-hearted.

and the start of the mountains of the M'Goun Massif (in the Central High Atlas; see page 258) with its fertile valleys and canyons.

The Central High Atlas

Rolling away east of the Tizi N'Tichka Pass (and northeast of Ouarzazate) are the mountains of the Central High Atlas. The main trekking base on the north side of this range is the beautiful **Aït Bouguemez Valley**. Known as the 'Happy Valley', this broad expanse of greensward sprinkled with small villages stretches roughly from Agouti to Jebel Aroudane; Agouti and Tabant are the main trekking and tourist centres. Once a remote Shangri-La, the valley has only recently opened up to the modern world following the construction of a new tarmac road in the early 2000s from the market town of **Aït Mhammed**.

Trekking is normally problem-free from early May to Oct, but can be difficult at other times. Mules and porter assistance are essential.

An outdoor centre and guides school has been opened at **Tabant** ⓫

by the CFAMM (Centre de Formation aux Métiers de la Montagne), while between Tabant and Agouti, the **Dar Itranean** eco-tourism lodge (tel: 023-45 93 12) also organises treks and cultural tours. Out in the mountains, accommodation is provided in gites, some of which offer facilities such as hammams, hot showers and electricity powered by generators or solar panels.

The main focus for trekking here is the mighty **M'Goun Massif**, south of Agouti and Tabant. The stunning landscapes, rich culture, rare wildlife and relative lack of tourists compared with the Toubkal massif are all conspiring to attract increasing numbers of intrepid trekkers and nature-lovers.

Dominating the area is the tremendous barrier ridge of **Irhil M'Goun**, 20km (12 miles) long and the second-highest peak in the High Atlas at 4,071 metres (3,356ft). Ascents of the mountain remain a formidable test of endurance until sleeping quarters are established. Easy summits to climb include the mammoth whalebacks of **Azurki** (3,677 metres/12,100ft) and **Ouaoulzat** (Wawgoulzat) (3,736

metres/12,340ft), which take four or five hours each.

Here are fine expeditions to be made to big limestone synclines such as **Tignousti** and **Rat**, and cross-country and river bed journeys of several days to remote Berber villages such as **Magdaz**. The spectacular sheer-sided gorges of **Tessaout** and **Arous**, draining southwest and northwest respectively from M'Goun, invite wetsuited wanderers and rock climbers.

M'Goun Gorge

Striking through the heart of the M'Goun Massif, a dramatic canyon trek leads through the **M'Goun (Achabou) Gorge** as it winds south from the Central Atlas massif to the Dadès Valley at El Kelaa M'Gouna on the N10. Treks through the gorge take two days, supported by mules and porters and walking from Tabant over the Aït Imi pass to El Mrabtin. The best time to tackle it is June to late July, when assorted plunges and wading shallows are appropriate for bathing suits and gym shoes. There are no technical difficulties, but pack animals unable to follow through the narrower sections are obliged to detour along a dizzy man-made staircase on the canyon wall.

Berbers use the river bottom as a conventional thoroughfare, and you will stumble upon family groups crouching among the boulders, brewing mint tea. The trek is subject to the varying water level and to weather conditions (it can be dangerous in thunderstorms).

To quote the Berber specialist Michael Peyron: 'Not all of it is hard work; there are moments when the magic of the canyon plays on the mind inducing serenity and reverie.'

Demnate and other approaches

Another way into the High Atlas region is from **Demnate** (100km/62 miles due east from Marrakech). Tourism here is still in its infancy, although the town's crumbling mud-brick kasbah and craggy fortifications are impressive, while just outside town is the curious **Imi N'Ifri**, an impressive natural bridge-cum-archway.

Mountaineers in the High Atlas.

TIP

In addition to the many carpet shops in Midelt, the closest town to Jebel Ayyachi, take a look inside Kasbah Myrien, a carpet workshop run by Franciscan nuns that produces good-quality kilims and Berber blankets.

Coming from the south, the valleys off the N10 Dadès road from Ouarzazate to Skoura, El Kelaa and Boumalne du Dadès are harder still, and the preserve of seasoned climbers and walkers accustomed to treeless and waterless wastes. Guiding services can be found at El Kelaa M'Gouna. Getting a lift to Boutaghrar on the River M'Goun cuts out the worst of the walk there.

Imilchil

Wreathed in romantic legend, **Imilchil** ⓬ village is home to the Aït Haddidou, a tribe of semi-nomadic shepherds originating from Boumalne du Dadès in the 11th century. The village is best known for its famous Marriage Festival (see box), held a few kilometres south of the town. At other times it provides a good, quiet base for exploring the surrounding mountains, with gentle river walks beside turreted buildings or longer strolls on piste tracks across kilometres of pasture between the lakes.

Imilchil is technically in the High Atlas, although it's easiest to reach from Kasba Tadla in the Middle Atlas

Berber women looking through clothes for sale at the Imilchil Marriage Fair.

(see page 227), driving past the twin lakes of **Tislit** and **Isli**.

Recommended vantage points near Imilchil are **Amalou N'Tiffirt** (2,470 metres/8,100ft), which takes one hour to climb, and **Bab N'Ouayyad** (2,804 metres/9,200ft), which takes three hours. Summits here tend to be merely long hikes rather than more challenging ascents. **Msedrid** (3,077 metres/10,100ft) is probably the most frequented, and takes two days without a four-wheel-drive vehicle.

Those touring on wheels can leave Imilchil by the scenic road south to **Agoudal**, one of the highest inhabited villages in Morocco. After some spectacular scenery over the Tizi Tirherouzine pass, the road eventually arrives in **Aït Hani**, where it continues to Todra. Alternatively there is the more difficult but thrilling road from Agoudal to Msemrir and the Dadès Gorge, crossing the Tizi N'Ouano.

For those wishing to continue eastwards from the site of Imilchil's *moussem* there is the faster road to **Amouguer** and **Rich** where it joins the N13 between Er Rachidia and **Midelt**.

The latter, spectacularly perched on the edge of a high plain, has hotels and restaurants and is a good stop-off en route to the Tafilalt Valley in the south. It is also an important market for carpets, fossils and minerals (azurite, malachite and aragonite).

Secret canyons

Northwest of Agoudal, towards **Anergui**, over the vast undulating tableland called Kousser, the terrain is cracked by several precipitous canyons. The spectacular Tiflout is the principal gorge, fed by snaking tributaries of considerable complexity. These gorges and their branches have been used for centuries by the Haddidou Berbers during their migrations. Some of the main branches include the Melloul, a stretch of 20km (12 miles) between Anergui and Imilchil populated by cliff dwellers, along with the Tiflout (35km/ 22 miles), Wensa (15km/9 miles) and Sloul (15km/9 miles). Approaches and exits add to these distances.

Potholing, caving and rock climbing techniques, sometimes calling for bold swims in 'squeezes' (tunnelled rocks), require special equipment and experience. Wood and rock bridges (*passerelles*) should be treated with caution.

Jebel Ayyachi

The eastern ranges of the High Atlas culminate with a flourish at the dramatic **Jebel Ayyachi** (3,750 metres/ 12,300ft), The **Cirque de Jaffar** ⑱, named after a local saint, provides a rough but driveable dirt track along the base of the *jebel* and also serves as the best departure point for an ascent of the mighty **Ayachi** (3,737 metres/ 12,300ft) itself. Picturesque rock cataracts, the ravines of the Ijimi Valley and clumps of dwarf conifers combine to make the area a popular picnic spot.

Snow cover on the mountain is normal until at least June. Most attempts to reach the summit start at dawn from a bivouac at 2,200 metres (7,200ft), about 30 minutes above the road, and a fit party can attain the summit in five to six hours. Seen from the north in full winter robe, 40km (25 miles) long and with a dozen named summits, the mountain is one of the most arresting spectacles in Morocco.

Tasty High Atlas lamb.

WEDDING FESTIVAL

Imilchil is best known for its annual Marriage Fair, held every September. The *moussem* celebrates the Romeo and Juliet-esque legend of two star-crossed lovers from rival tribes who were forbidden to meet, let alone marry. Heartbroken, they drowned themselves in the nearby lakes of Tislit (the woman) and Isli (the man), which were formed from their tears. The families of both tribes later decided to establish a day every year on which men and women of different tribes could marry each other. Today, the festival draws hundreds of visitors from the area. Men and women dressed in traditional finery go courting from tent to tent while families negotiate dowries. Engagements are made, though actual marriages – contrary to belief – do not happen during the *moussem*.

THE SOUTH

Beyond the High Atlas spread the spectacular landscapes of the south – sandcastle architecture, vast palm oases and the great river valleys of the Drâa and the Ziz that edge the Sahara.

Nothing north of the Atlas prepares one for 'Le Grand Sud', a vast expanse of desert and semi-arid mountains stretching to the Algerian border. There is hardly a road in the region that cannot be described as spectacular. It is a film-maker's dream: wide valleys studded with palm-packed oases, mud-built castles rearing out of the ground, jagged blue mountains stretching across almost every vista. Ridley Scott's *Kingdom of Heaven* and countless other films were shot here, glorying in the wide desert landscapes hung with backdrops of the snow-covered Atlas Mountains.

Southern Morocco runs westwards from Figuig, on the Algerian border, to Goulimime in the southwest (the gateway to the Western Sahara; see page 284), a distance of almost 1,000km (600 miles). It is bounded by the Atlas Mountains to the north and by the Algerian border to the south, where it is lapped by the sands of the Sahara.

Central valleys

Of particular interest are the central valleys, the Drâa, the Dadès, Ziz and Tafilalt, and the Saharan dunes further south. The geography of the region is shaped by the Anti-Atlas, a range of outlying rust-red, semi-arid mountains that break up the south. In the east, the Sarhro wedges the Drâa up against

the Jebel Aklim massif; in the north the Dadès drains between the Sarhro and the Atlas proper; and eastwards the Tafilalt peters out on the edges of the Grand Erg Occidental.

The Drâa is Morocco's longest river, a huge wadi that finds its source in rivers flowing south from the Atlas and is augmented by streams from the Anti-Atlas. It survives the increasing aridity of its southward journey, turns west to form the border with Algeria, and eventually emerges exhausted at Tan Tan on the Atlantic Coast.

Main Attractions
Kasbah Aït Benhaddou
Ouarzazate
Zagora
M'Hamid
Erg Chigagga
Skoura
Boumalne Dadès
Dadès Gorge
Todra Gorge
Taroudant

Dadès Gorge.

Early morning traffic of mules, donkeys and people is a sign that there is a souk close by: watch out for a large encampment of tents.

Travelling around the south is best by car; there are numerous hotels and guesthouses, although these are often difficult to reach for visitors limited to public transport.

Routes to the south

From Marrakech, three passes cross the Atlas Mountains to the south. The most spectacular is the tortuous **Tizi N'Test** (2,093 metres/6,866ft), which leads to Taroudant via a winding 306km (190-mile) road. The second route south from Marrakech is over the Tizi N'Tichka (2,260 metres/7,415ft) to Ouarzazate (190km/118 miles), along a wider, better-maintained road.

Buses and *grands* taxis serve both routes, but they stop at many small villages along the way and progress is slow: buses to Taroudant via the Tizi N'Test take seven or eight hours, and via the Tizi N'Tichka to Ouarzazate around six hours (four in a *grand taxi*). In winter both passes are often closed (though never for any great length of time), in which case the only accessible route south is via the less

interesting route from Imi N'Tanoute to Agadir.

Kasbah Aït Benhaddou

If your main aim of travelling south is to see the Drâa Valley, the Tizi N'Tichka to Ouarzazate, the gateway to the Drâa, offers the best route, but 18km (12 miles) before Ouarzazate, there is a short side road to the Unesco World Heritage listed **Kasbah Aït Benhaddou ❶**, probably the most celebrated, filmed and photographed kasbah in Morocco. Featured in numerous films (including *Lawrence of Arabia*, *The Sheltering Sky* and *Gladiator*), it is the best-preserved kasbah in Morocco, still inhabited by a few families who are happy to show you around their homes and recount stories of their filming experiences.

Access to the kasbah from the road is through the small modern town of shops, restaurants and *auberges* that have sprung up to service the stream of visitors; from here a small wooden bridge leads over the Mellah River to the kasbah. The kasbah is really a town of many smaller kasbahs, all

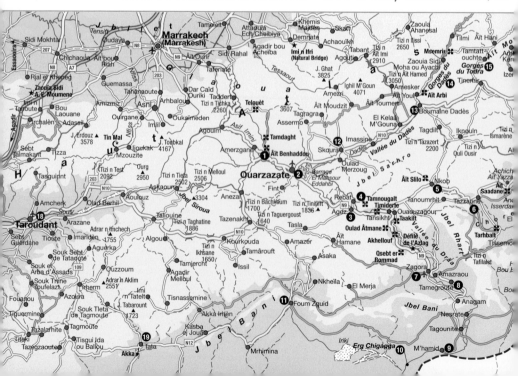

built from the same deep-red earth and often with intricate details carved into their walls. The huge gate is not part of the original design, but a film fantasy built for *Romancing the Stone* so that Michael Douglas could drive a plane through it.

A few kilometres north of the kasbah, across a broken-down bridge, is the much smaller **Kasbah Tamdaght**, now abandoned to a family of storks, but once another Glaoui seat of power and still showing traces of its beautiful original decoration. From here a rough but spectacular piste continues north along the old trade route to Telouet (see page 257).

Springboard for the Drâa

Ouarzazate ❷, the capital of the south, sits astride the Drâa, at the end of the Tichka road, dominated by the Atlas range, which fills its northern horizon. Served by a plethora of hotels and an international airport, the town was originally a base of the French Foreign Legion and is now increasingly important to Morocco's film location industry. The huge Atlas Film

Studios are just outside town and can be visited. Ouarzazate itself is modern and of little character or interest, but has some hidden features that bring its short history to life.

The Legionnaires have left their mark in the church, which is still maintained by Catholic nuns, and on **Chez Dimitri** restaurant, on Avenue Mohammed V. Once a wild drinking hole, Dimitri's is now famous as one of the best restaurants south of the Atlas, thanks to its colourful founder. Dimitri was an energetic Greek, who jumped ship in Casablanca as a 14-year-old in 1928 on his way to the United States. He eventually made his way to the Legionnaire post of Ouarzazate, where he set up his restaurant. His son, who now runs the place, grew up rubbing shoulders with the likes of Orson Welles, and had his own moment of film fame playing the son of Anthony Quinn in the 1962 film, *Lawrence of Arabia*.

At the end of Avenue Mohammed V is the **Kasbah Taourirt** (daily 8am–6pm), a huge complex, the size of a small town, originally built by

Aït Benhaddou.

The South

0   20 km
0   20 miles

Chicken brochette.

the Glaoui dynasty for their local chiefs, retainers and myriad servants. Much of the kasbah has fallen into ruin, although small sections have now been patched up with Unesco assistance including the original residence of the Glaoui rulers, complete with traces of its lavish decoration, surrounded by a beautiful little labyrinth of mud-brick houses and twisting alleyways, hemmed in behind high walls.

Around 10km (6 miles) west of town is the **Kasbah Tiffoultoute**, another fine, if crumbling, old Glaoui complex which was briefly turned into a hotel and restaurant for the cast of *Lawrence of Arabia.*

Further along the road from Tiffoultoute, a piste heads off west, passing a small lake to reach the peaceful green oasis of **Fint,** hidden deep in a small river valley surrounded by barren hills.

Along the Drâa Valley

The Drâa Valley is an extraordinary natural wonder. Two hundred kilometres (124 miles) long and ranging from 10 metres (33ft) to 10km

Ouarzazate.

(6 miles) wide, it stretches from just south of Ouarzazate to Zagora. The history of the Drâa stretches back to prehistoric times and it was known to the kings of Carthage and the ancient Romans. It is also the route that the great trans-Saharan caravans from Timbuktu formerly followed into central Morocco.

South of Ouarzazate, the road winds through arid hills, cut by an impressive gorge with a black patina, eventually descending into the oasis of Agdz. Before the descent, a dirt track signposted **Cascades du Tizgui** offers a rewarding side trip down a terrifyingly steep piste into an unexpectedly Arcadian gorge, with waterfalls and pools in which you can swim.

Back on the N9 is **Agdz ❸**, an old caravan town with a busy market square full of carpet and pottery shops, surrounded by a sea of palm trees and standing in the shadow of Jebel Kissane. Nearby are the remains of yet another rambling old Glaoui kasbah, also used as a secret detention centre by Hassan II in more recent years.

Agdz is where the Drâa oasis really begins. Stretching southeast as far as the eye can see is a rich, deep-green swathe of lush palm trees lapping at the edges of the craggy rust-coloured cliffs that border it on either side. While Agdz itself may not be all that interesting, the magnificent 16th-century *ksar* (fortified village and kasbah) of **Tamnougalt** ❹, on the other side of the oasis, is another matter. Guides charge a small fee to show you around; their fee goes towards restoring the village, the oldest pisé *ksar* in Morocco. The obligatory guides are generally very knowledgeable, and usually make for a rewarding visit. Though most of the families have moved into breeze-block houses outside the kasbah, a few remain and are happy to show you around their houses. Just outside the kasbah is **Chez Yacob** (tel: 0524-84 33 94, www.lavalleedudraa.com), which does a decent lunch on its terrace and has eight simple rooms.

A detour to Tazzarine

Most visitors continue on the N9 straight to Zagora, but for a side trip, a turnoff at **Tansikht**, around 30km (19 miles) east of Agdz, marks the start of the R108 road to **Tazzarine** and **Alnif**, the latter linking up with the road between Erfoud and Rissani in the Tafilalt. Once an arduous two-day drive across a bone-crunching piste, it is now surfaced and easily passable in a normal car. This is also a rewarding drive along the southern slopes of the Jebel Sarhro, containing some of Morocco's most dramatic desert mountain scenery.

Driving east from Tansikht, the road runs first through the large village of **Nkob** ❺, a southern outpost of the Aït Atta Berbers of the Jebel Sarhro, dotted with almost 50 mud-brick kasbahs and with a lively souk on Sunday.

Nkob is also the southern starting point for the spectacular piste crossing the Tizi N'Tazazert and for treks into the remote **Jebel Sarhro**, a rugged wilderness whose extraordinary geology has given it a reputation as the 'Monument Valley' of Morocco; the Bureau des Guides on the main road can organize treks, as

The Drâa Valley.

well as tours of local kasbahs and the surrounding countryside.

Further along the road is **Tazzarine** , famous for its henna. Although the town is less attractive than Nkob, it is situated in a spectacular valley and has some places to stay.

On to Zagora

Back on the main N9 highway south of Agdz, the valley widens considerably. Here the banks are clothed in tall reeds and often strewn with freshly washed clothes. Across the valley stands the **Kasbah Timiderte;** isolated like a medieval fortress, and one of the classic images of the southern Drâa.

As the towering metropolises of mud multiply on either side of the road, the Sahara begins to make its presence felt, costumes change, and the colourfully clad women of the mountains are replaced by black-swathed and much darker-skinned people, originating from Mali and Mauritania. As the road approaches Zagora the changes are increasingly noticeable, the enclosed villages more densely packed, and reed-built

Proud vendor.

palisades check the increasing quantities of drifting sand.

Zagora ❼ is the main market town of the south, a disappointingly dull outpost of featureless modern streets and government buildings – although the remains of an 11th-century Almoravid, fortress clinging to the side of Jebel Zagora, offers a reminder of the town's antiquity. Zagora once sat at a major confluence of trade routes, with trans-Saharan caravans from the south breaking their journey here before continuing east and north – as a much-photographed signpost pointing towards Timbuktu (a mere 52 days' march by camel) suggests.

Tamegroute

About 12km (7 miles) south of Zagora is **Tamegroute** ❽, a dusty little town with a tiny Saturday souk. Tamegroute is dominated by a *zaouia* of the Sufi Naciri brotherhood that has been a centre of religious learning since the 11th century. It was also the cradle of the Saadian dynasty (see page 32). The *zaouia* (daily 9am–noon, 2–6pm; donation) incorporates a 17th-century medersa and adjacent library, home to treasured Islamic commentaries written on gazelle skin dating from before the 13th century.

Desert dunes

South of Tamegroute the first sand dune appears around **Tinfou**, approximately 10km (6 miles) south of Zagora although these pale in comparison to the much grander sand-seas further south at the small town of **M'hamid** ❾. M'hamid marks the end of the road south, literally – a wild place, swept by sandstorms and edged by dunes.

For centuries, Arabs, nomad Berbers, Jews, Draoui (inhabitants of the Drâa Valley), Tuareg and Sahrawi people have co-existed peacefully in this region,. More recently, the town was garrisoned by the camel corps of the French Legion, and was later targetted by Polisario guerrillas (see page 48), although is now entering the tourist mainstream thanks to the stunning desert scenery surrounding it on all sides.

M'hamid itself has a few shops and lots of 'guides'; it is now the main centre for local camel-treks and a pit stop for four-wheel-drive excursions into the desert.

It is also the starting point for trips to **Erg Chigagga** ❿, a spectacular array of Saharan sand dunes stretching 40km (25 miles) across the desert.

Reaching the dunes takes two to three hours and a 4x4 or camel is the only way to get there. These extraordinary dunes are what most visitors to this region have come to see, and a night in a tented camp under a vast blanket of stars, with no electricity, light pollution or noise, is unquestionably the experience of a lifetime. Boutique tented camps have become very popular and range from the basic to the super deluxe (see page 298).

The area around the dunes, in the **Iriki Basin** (once a huge lake) is a wide mirage-haunted region,

occasionally inundated by freak rains in the surrounding hills. It is inhabited by ancient Arabic-speaking nomads, descendants of the Bedouin of Arabia. For those wanting to head back to Ouarzazate from here, the best route is west, along a starkly beautiful and very rough track to **Foum Zguid** ⓫, another frontier town with a strong military presence. There are several cafés and craft shops scattered around the centre of town. From Foum Zguid, take the R111 to **Tazenakht** and on to Ouarzazate or Marrakech – a much quicker drive than the long way back via Zagora.

Valley of Kasbahs: The Dadès

Stretching away east of Ouarzazate is the **Dadès Valley**, a magical landscape of oases, gorges, rose gardens and innumerable mud-brick *ksours* – hence its popular nickname, the '**Valley of Kasbahs**'. Some 40km (25 miles) from Ouarzazate, on the N10, is the fairy-tale settlement of **Skoura** ⓬, with weathered pisé villages half

Camel riding at Erg Chebbi dunes.

Moroccan camels.

buried amidst endless palm groves which meander for over 20km (12 miles) down the valley – a perfect place to hole up for a few days in one of the various up-market boutique hotels and maisons d'hôte hidden away amidst the trees.

At the end of the valley, some 75km (47 miles) beyond Skoura, is the town of **Boumalne Dadès** ⑬, which has a souk on Wednesdays and is a centre for roses and their associated perfume industry.

Boumalne is also the place to hire guides for treks through the two dramatic gorges that bisect the mountains nearby. Water flows into the Dadès Valley from high in the Central High Atlas, bursting out of the mountains through the spectacular **Dadès Gorge** ⑭ and the parallel **Todra Gorge** ⑮ slightly further down the valley, both of which become raging torrents in spring when the snow thaws on the Atlas.

Of the two gorges, the Dadès is longer and perhaps the more beautiful, with sheer-sided walls rising up to 1,000 metres (3,280ft) canyon in

places. The Todra Gorge was once populated by Jews, who still remember Todra in a popular Hebrew folksong. Both canyons also offer some of the best bird-watching in Morocco.

Exploring the gorges

It's possible to drive right through both the Dadès and Todra gorges – the road is sealed through the Dadès Gorge as far as Msemrir, though beyond there you'll need a 4x4. Beyond Boumaine turn onto the R704 to Aït Arbi, which has the ruins of a kasbah, entering the vertiginous Dadès Gorge outside Aït Oudinar. After a ford to the east bank, the piste has been blasted from sheer cliffs.

Further inside the gorge, **Msemrir** boasts a colourful Saturday market and serves as the historic meeting place between two of the region's major nomadic tribes, the Haddidou and Merghad. Beyond Msemrir, the road (now dirt) begins a long crawl up to the Ouerz pass reaching, after just over a kilometre a prominent right-hand fork at point 1996, where there is a survey pillar and signpost.

Dadès Gorge.

From here, the piste curves east between stark escarpments to reach the Ouguerd Zegzaoune pass in an empty area of rocky badlands.

A longer descent and another fork south deposits you in **Tamtattouchte** on the seasonal Temda stream, the chief feeder to the gorge lower down and the site of several *marabouts*. The road then winds south, entering the upper Todra Gorge after around 5km (3 miles). Floods sometimes close the canyon to vehicles. Parts of the piste have been raised above the riverbed, first on the west side and latterly in the main gorge on the east side, which begins just after the tight bend at point 1599. Though less forbidding than the Dadès, the rock walls of the Todra Gorge soar 400 metres (1,300ft), and the defile at its narrowest point is impressive. Gardens, small fields, date palms and fig trees presage the magnificent oasis of **Tinerhir** (20km/12 miles from Tamtattouchte), noted for its gold and jewellery workshops, castellated buildings and decayed palace.

The Ziz and the Tafilalt valleys

Continuing along the N10 highway east of **Tinerhir**, the road traverses arid hills to arrive at the crossroads settlement of **Er Rachidia**, a modern town and the regional seat of government. A few kilometres south of here is the **Source Bleue de Meski,** head of the other great valley of the south, the **Ziz**. Once an idyllic oasis, the clear pools have been cemented and a characterless café has done its best to destroy what atmosphere remains. Walk a little way downstream, however, and the landscape opens out into a vista of picturesque villages and hills.

After Meski, the Ziz Valley appears, a great scar cutting through barren hills. The drive to Erfoud is spectacular, as the road first descends from the plateau to the sheer-sided valley floor and then winds its way through a string of villages at the heart of the **Tafilalt**, as the area is known. The people here are very different from the communities inhabiting the Dadès and the Drâa to the west. The home territory of the ruling Alaouite

Tomb of Moulay Ali Sherif in Rissani.

Ziz Valley landscape.

FACT

Travel through the south in October and you will find the date harvest in full swing. Each tree produces between 100 and 200kg (220–440lbs).

dynasty, the Tafilalt is an isolated Arab community, whose roots in the valley are far older than those of the Berber tribes surrounding them today. They inhabit impenetrable villages of covered and winding alleys.

The town of **Erfoud** ⑯, like Ouarzazate, is another colonial creation, established by the French in the 1920s, with streets laid out in a grid – but pleasant nonetheless, and well set up for tourists. A date festival is held here each autumn (see page 319).

Rissani ⑰, at the end of the Tafilalt, is located on the site of another former trading crossroads, and home to Morocco's most African market. Rissani is also said to be the site of one of the world's largest date palmeraies, with some 4 million trees and more than 100 varieties of dates. Like Tamegroute, the city is also an important religious centre, based on the tomb of Moulay Ali Sherif, the founder of the ruling Alaouite dynasty. Behind are the ruined remains of the Alaouite Ksar Akbar, while still more isolated adobe villages and *zaouias* dating as far back

as the 13th century can be found in the surrounding countryside.

Close to Rissani lies **Sijilmassa**, founded by an Arab general at the beginning of the 8th century. At its peak in the Middle Ages it developed into a fabulously wealthy city that dominated the south of Morocco, gaining its wealth through the all-important trans-Sahara trade. Little now remains of the once glorious city bar a couple of gateways and the distintegrating remains of a few other unidentifiable mud-brick structures – an evocative, if enigmatic, sight.

East of Erfoud and Rissani are the dunes of **Erg Chebbi**, often referred to as Merzouga after the small village and military outpost located near their southern limit. The dunes here are the highest in Morocco and regularly host film crews shooting on location, though they are less spectacular than the Erg Chigagga and much more crowded. On a clear day, it is possible to see the snowcapped M'Goun massif – more than 150km (93 miles) away – from the summits of the dunes. If you want to experience the dunes

Inside the tomb of Moulay Ali Sherif.

in relative peace, it is advisable to avoid the well-worn track leading to the cluster of small cafés at the dropping-off point for the tourist convoys. Camping among the dunes is also possible – most hotels in Merzouga can arrange this.

Eastern outposts

Between Er Rachidia and the Algerian border crossing at Figuig are 400km (250 miles) of gravel plain, with little to relieve the eye, save the occasional palm plantation in the Oued Guir, a scattering of *ksars*, a few military outposts and the mountains in the distance.

At the end is the remote and rarely visited settlement of **Figuig**, an oasis of date palms and gardens. Separate communities, barricaded within now-crumbling *ksars*, fought each other for lack of other enemies until the French provided them with a common foe. Figuig was once a staging post on the overland route to Mecca and also supported a significant Jewish population until the 1950s, although today most of the town's inhabitants are soldiers.

The Jebel Siroua

South of Aït Benhaddou, the N10 climbs between the Anti-Atlas and the volcanic peaks of the **Jebel Siroua**, a high, sparsely populated plateau, roasting in summer and heavy with snow in winter. It is a harsh and remote range, dominated by old volcanic plugs, of which Mount Siroua at 3,304 metres (10,837ft) is the highest. Few people come here to trek, and those who do usually come in late spring or autumn to avoid the extremes of weather. The most popular access routes to the high peaks are from the south, where the road passes fields of saffron and runs through the carpet-weaving villages of the Siroua Berbers.

Along the way the road passes through **Tazenakht**, a market for carpets. Further west is **Taliouine**, whose main claim to fame is its saffron, with an associated festival to mark the harvest every year in October. Just before

Taliouine, a huge rambling ruin appears: another Glaoui kasbah. It is still inhabited by descendants of the Glaoui's servants, who will happily guide you through the ruins.

For those with time to spare, but little inclination to hike, a tarmac road cuts into the Siroua from Taliouine to **Askaoun**, an uninspiring government centre in the middle of one of the most beautiful and unspoilt parts of the Atlas. From Askaoun a road turns west to Aoulouz, back on the N10, while a spectacular track north heads towards the peaks of the Atlas then swings east, away from the Tifnout Valley, joining the Tizi N'Tichka road at Agouim – a long and arduous drive for which you'll need a four-wheel-drive vehicle and a local guide.

To Taroudant

The journey on to Agadir from Taliouine enters the Sous Valley, a huge fertile river plain. The city of **Taroudant** 🔞 sits, like a miniature Marrakech, in the heart of the valley, surrounded by pink walls. Centuries ago Taroudant was a staging post for

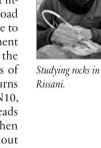

Studying rocks in Rissani.

Ziz Valley.

On Location

Some of Hollywood's most famous movies were filmed in Morocco, using the country's dazzling landscapes as some of the most iconic backdrops in movie history.

The film most often associated with Morocco is the Bogart–Bergman classic *Casablanca*. However, like many other films made at the time, it was entirely filmed on a back lot in Los Angeles. Yet Morocco has been a real destination for filmmakers since the very beginning of cinema.

Way back in 1897, the Lumière brothers shot *Le Cavalier Marocain* on location. Marlene Dietrich also made her US debut in 1930 with a film called *Morocco* in which her lingering screen kiss with another woman before striding off into the desert dressed in full tuxedo and high heels shocked audiences at the time. The Marx brothers also came to Morocco to make *A Night in Casablanca* in 1946, and Hitchcock made good use of Marrakech's mystery in the opening sequence of *The Man Who Knew Too Much*, while David Lean's

Atlas Film Studios, Ouarzazate.

Lawrence of Arabia (1962) was filmed in the desert south of Ouarzazate.

Other film classics that have taken advantage of Morocco's sumptuous landscapes are Orson Welles's *Othello* (1952), shot in Essaouira, El Jadida and Ouarzazate, John Huston's *The Man Who Would Be King* (1975), and *The Sheltering Sky*, directed by Bertolucci (1990).

More recently, the Hollywood blockbusters *Spy Game, Black Hawk Down, Gladiator, Hidalgo, The Mummy* and *Sahara*, along with *Sex and the City 2, Prince of Persia, Inception* and Oliver Stone's *Alexander the Great* and Ridley Scott's *Kingdom of Heaven*, were all partly filmed here.

Home-grown industry

Much of this success is attributed to the energy of the Centre Cinématographique Marocain (www. ccm.ma), the country's film commission. Set up during the Protectorate period, the CCM licenses the industry, approves scripts and issues filming permits. In a country known for its over-large bureaucracy, it is an enthusiastic and efficient organisation run by people who are filmmakers themselves.

Mohammed VI has also encouraged the industry, and on several occasions has lent the Moroccan armed forces to help make films requiring thousands of extras. Shooting facilities include two studios in Ouarzazate and one in El Jadida, with two of the largest sound stages outside of Hollywood. The Moroccan actor Jamal Debouzze, after his success as the comical architect in *Asterix and Cleopatra*, starring Gerard Depardieu, has used his wealth and position to make Marrakech a second centre of film in Morocco. The city also now hosts a major annual international film festival (en.festivalmarrakech. info), which has attracted film giants from Martin Scorsese to Sigourney Weaver.

It is not just Morocco's stunning scenery and improving infrastructure that attract producers. There is a wealth of skilled technicians and talented craftsmen, who can turn their hands to producing costumes, props and scenery of all types. In *Kundun*, Moroccan craftsmen not only built replicas of Tibetan temples but also made most of the costumes and props. Moroccan film production companies have sprung up in Marrakech, Casablanca and Rabat, and film lighting hire is available. Thousands of Moroccans are now employed as technicians, assistant producers, directors, designers and actors. The industry is creating real employment opportunities and making a significant contribution to the economy.

dynasties on the road to power, and also served as a temporary seat of government before the capture of Marrakech itself. In 1912, it was also the stronghold of El Hiba, the 'Blue Sultan', whose short-lived revolt against the French Protectorate ended in his bloody expulsion at the hands of High Atlas Berbers allied to the colonial power.

Few monuments to the city's rich history now remain, apart from the walls, which still follow their Almoravid plan, but it is still a charming and peaceful place to visit. The **Palais Salam Hotel** (see page 308) is worth a visit, even if you are not staying there. Converted from the 19th-century palace of the then pasha, the hotel's public rooms maintain some of their original splendour and the ground-floor rooms enclose small, luxuriant gardens of which the towering banana trees form the crowning glory. About the only other historical site in the town is the impressive **Kasbah Gate** in the eastern side of the walls.

Taroudant's chief attraction, however, is its marvellous souk, now attracting increasing numbers of tourists (including regular coach parties from Agadir). Prices and hassle have increased accordingly, but the small scale of the souk and the distinctive crafts on offer still make it an enjoyable and easy place through which to wander.

South of Taroudant

From Taroudant, route R109 climbs the Anti-Atlas massif of Jebel Aklim to the town of Irherm, a small market and administrative centre at one time noted for its silversmiths. The road beyond descends spectacularly, through striated hills and huge valleys (dwarfing what villages there are) to **Tata** ⓳, an oasis on the edge of the Algerian Sahara and a base from which to explore the stunning surrounding areas, including the beautiful Akka Oasis, with its dozens of ksars and *mellahs* at **Tagadirt**, and the rock art at Oum el Alek, Foum el Hassan and Aït Herbil.

West of Tata, the road arrives at Goulimime, gateway to the deep south and the Western Sahara (see page 284).

Rose water.

The walls of Taroudant.

Red cliffs on a beach near Sidi Ifni.

AGADIR AND THE DEEP SOUTH

Agadir, Morocco's 'playground resort', is also a springboard for expeditions into the Anti-Atlas and along the coast to Goulimime, the gateway to the Western Sahara.

The modern city of **Agadir ❶** is something of an anomaly: Morocco's premier beach resort, attracting thousands of international tourists every year and looking more like something from the Spanish Costa del Sol rather than anything Moroccan. The original city was largely destroyed by an earthquake in 1960s and rebuilt around a spacious modern grid system. It subsequently developed into Morocco's most important port and the country's leading (in fact, only) package-tourism destination. Despite its modernity and lack of historic monuments, Agadir is a pleasant and enjoyable city to visit, as well as offering an ideal base from which to venture into Morocco's deep south.

Rising from the ashes

During the night of 29 February 1960, an earthquake destroyed Agadir. The quake's epicentre hit the old medina with devastating effect. The town had for centuries been a prosperous fishing port and a market centre for the valley of the River Souss, which runs out to sea to the south. But on the morning of 1 March, most of the town was turned to rubble: some 15,000 people died and 20,000 were made homeless as 3,650 buildings were destroyed. Agadir had effectively to be rebuilt from scratch.

Modern Agadir was conceived as a showcase for the new country. A modern port, administration centre and new tourist complex were built in stages, a process that has taken many years and is still continuing today. New residential quarters have spread out from the city centre and a toll motorway opened between Agadir and Marrakech, cutting what used to be a four-hour drive down to just two hours. The predominantly Berber city is also home to an impressive university that has been instrumental in a

Main Attractions

Agadir
Imouzzer des Ida Outanane
Taghazoute
Tafraoute
Tiznit
Sidi Ifni
Goulimime
Tarfaya
Laâyoune
Dakhla

Sidi Ifni's school.

TIP

Beach and poolside reading can be picked up at the Crown English Bookshop (8 Avenue Moulay Abdellah), which also exchanges second-hand books.

revival of Amaziah (Berber) culture (see page 64).

Fishing is another major industry – the city claims to be the largest sardine fishing port in the world. Within the port itself there is a yacht mooring and a good restaurant, while in the nearby square from late morning until late evening in summer (early evening in winter) tightly packed stalls serve inexpensive, freshly grilled seafood. Invisible around the headland are the heavier industrial docks.

Sunshine and nightlife

For tourists, however, the city's prime attraction is its 10km (6 miles) of broad sandy beach and an average of 300 days of sunshine a year. In summer Agadir is cooler than the interior of the country, while the winter climate is often sunny and mild with temperatures in the mid-20s Centigrade (upper 70s Fahrenheit). The beach is huge and impeccably clean. Lining its promenade are hotels, beach clubs, bars, cafés and restaurants. At the centre of the bay is a ridge of rocks, exposed at low tide, that shelters much

of the beach from Atlantic breakers and makes for safe swimming most of the time (flags provide warnings of dangerous conditions).

At the northern end of the beach is Agadir's billion-dollar Marina d'Agadir, lined with apartments, shops and restaurants.

Inland, between Boulevard du 20 Août and Boulevard Mohammed V is a wedge of tourist shops, hotels and apartments, stuffed with restaurants, cafés, pubs and fast-food outlets. Similar tourist complexes have sprung up along the beach front, especially to the south around the Sofitel. Most of the larger up-market hotels have private beaches, with loungers and parasols on the beach in front of the hotel. There's plenty of nightlife, too, with casinos, terrace cafés, live music and cabarets. Some of the most popular places include Bar Fly on Boulevard du 20 Août and So club at the Sofitel.

Exploring the city

The best view of the city is from the kasbah Ⓐ on the hill that dominates

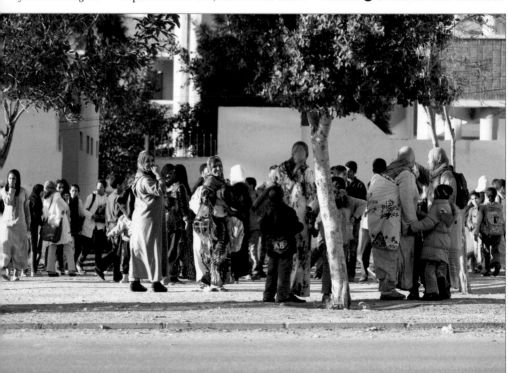

Picking up the kids from school in Agadir.

the northern end of the bay. It's a long walk, although the road gives superb views down onto both the fishing and industrial ports as it winds around the hill, before turning back on itself to overlook the beach and the city. The kasbah itself is the one historic monument left in the town, built in the mid-16th century by Saadian Sultan Mohammed ech Cheikh; an inscription ('God, King, Country') over the entrance in both Dutch and Arabic dates from a mid-18th-century restoration. In an expanse of green below the kasbah is the **Ancienne Talborjt,** which is the site of old Agadir before it was destroyed in the earthquake.

Another place of interest is the **Vallée des Oiseaux ❸ (Valley of the Birds**; daily 11am–6pm), a park-cum-zoo between Hassan II and Avenue du 20 Août, with various aviaries and animals in pens, including a group of Moroccan moufflon, a cross between a goat and a sheep. Outside town, on the Inezgane road, is the **Medina d'Agadir,** a modern but traditionally constructed Berber village, housing a collection

of handicraft shops and some busy traditional craft workshops making everything from doors to mosaic tables and floors for architectural projects around the country. On Boulevard Hassan II is the **Musée du Patrimoine Amazigh (Museum of Berber Art**; Mon–Sat 9.30am–12.30pm, 1.30–5.30pm), showcasing Berber arts and crafts, including a collection of silver jewellery put together by Bert Flint, responsible for Marrakech's Maison Tiskiwin.

Umbrellas on Agadir beach.

Sporting Agadir

Agadir's good sports facilities include four excellent golf courses, the Royal (www.royalgolfagadir.com), the Soleil (www.golfdusoleil.com), Golf de l'Océan (see page 322) and the Dunes (www. clubmed.fr), the last run by Club Med but open to non-residents. There are also a number of possibilities for horse

Agadir beach.

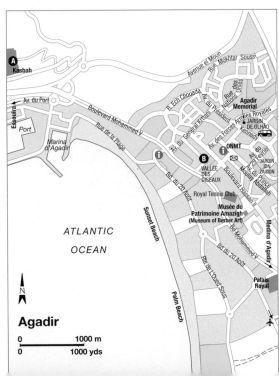

riding – try Amoudou Cheval (amo-doucheval.com), who can arrange two-hour to day-long trips along the beach and in the mountains, as well as camel rides.

Numerous agencies in Agadir offer sea fishing expeditions and boat trips as well as excursions into the countryside around town, including day trips into the Atlas Mountains in four-wheel-drive vehicles. Most good hotels can arrange all these things for you or at least recommend a good tour company or guide. If you want more independence, car and motorcycle hire is available from various operators on boulevards Mohammed V or Hassan II.

There are dozens of beach activities to be had, including sailing (from the yacht club in the old port; tel: 0528-82 41 98), jet-skiing, bodyboarding, windsurfing and surfing and paragliding (all of which can be rented at several spots along the beach). Dynamic Loisirs (tel: 0528-31 46 55; www.dynamicloisirs.com), just outside Agadir in Douar Tamghart, operates a surf school and provides board rental as well as

The spelling of place names varies.

quad bikes and simple accommodation at reasonable rates.

Around Agadir

Twelve kilometres (7 miles) north of Agadir is a signposted turning to **Imouzzer des Ida Outanane ❷**, a spectacular drive through the so-called Paradise Valley, a palm-lined gorge with cascading springs, ending in the prettily sited village.

A little beyond the turning for Imouzzer is the smaller resort of **Taghazoute ❸**, which began as a sleepy fishing village and has grown in popularity over the years. It has one of Morocco's best surfing beaches and has long been popular with independent travellers. Today, there are a number of guesthouses and apartments to rent. On the beach front, Surf Maroc (tel: +44 20 8123 0319; www.surfmaroc.co.uk) has rooms and a surf school.

As you leave Agadir heading south, the real Morocco crowds back around the roadside. For the first few kilometres, you're still in the estuary plains of the River Souss: flat fertile land where trees line the road and villages

are rows of small, cell-like shops in arcades where metalworkers labour next door to butchers. The road skirts the town of **Inezgane**, southern Morocco's most important fruit and vegetable market, and splits into three in the centre of **Aït Melloul** One road leads up the River Souss, westwards to Taroudant and the High Atlas, a second road runs south to Tiznit, and a third crosses the mountains to Tafraoute. The fastest way to reach Tafraoute is actually to take the wider, straighter road via Tiznit, although the narrower, more direct road is the more interesting and scenic.

Both routes pass through the arid mountains of **Anti-Atlas**, the range's final flourish before it subsides finally into the sands of the Sahara, offering constant surprises en route, such as the curious sight of the town of **Aït Baha**, a jumbled cluster of pink, box-like modern buildings, invisible until you top a mountain ridge.

The landscape around **Tafraoute** ➍ itself is startling, dominated by the Jebel Lekst, a jutting ridge of pink granite looming out of the crumbly sandstone. Below it, thousands of date palms spread out across the **Ameln Valley**, dotted with villages in assorted earth colours – umber, pink, red and yellow ochre. This remote area is unexpectedly prosperous, partly due to its fertility but mostly because many local men tend to seek their fortunes in the cities. This is a superb area to explore or to camp out in for the night thanks to the grandeur of the mountain scenery and the 1,000-year-old lifestyle in the villages. Interesting villages to explore include **Oumesnat** (northeast of Tafraoute), **Agard Oudad** (south) and **Adai** (southwest). In early spring the hillsides are covered with almond blossom.

A few kilometres south of Tafraoute the road to Tiznit passes through a landscape of huge weathered granite boulders in weirdly contorted shapes. To the left is a signpost to **Les Roches Bleues**, a surreal area of huge boulders painted by Belgian artist Jean Vérame and a team of Moroccan firemen in an intense Fauvist blue, dotted with occasional splashes of red, green, purple and black – the colours are now

Agadir marina.

Berber jewellery.

Tafraoute.

to legend the town is named after a prostitute, a certain Lalla Tiznit, the 'Lady of Tiznit'. The good lady decided eventually to reform her ways and turned towards God, who rewarded her by causing a miraculous freshwater spring, the Source Bleu (next to the Grand Mosque), to appear beside her home.

Tiznit is also famous for its silver jewellery, introduced to the town by Jewish artesans brought here by Hasan I in the 1880s; pieces are sold in the *souk des bijoutiers* (jewellers' market) just inside the walls, a short walk from the main square. Here you can watch the jewellers work delicate silver filigree into swords and daggers, as well as heavy Berber bracelets and necklaces. Also worth seeing is the minaret of the Grand Mosque, with its curious wooden perches, also found in the southern Saharan town of Agdz in Niger.

somewhat faded, but the site retains an outlandish kind of magic when seen against the endless landscape of ochre desert and rock beyond.

Walled city

Six kilometres (4 miles) of four-square ramparts wrap around **Tiznit ❺**, established (despite its venerable appearance) as recently as 1882 by Hassan I as an outpost from which to subdue the rebellious local tribes – according

Deserted terrain

Moving on south, sharp, contoured valleys divide mountain sides covered with green stubble that looks smooth

from a distance, but turns out, on closer inspection, to be a mass of nobbly boulders and ground-hugging cacti. Barbary figs (prickly pears) and low, bushy argan trees grow in deeper soil. The argan, *argania spinosa*, is unique to Morocco and grows only along its southwestern seaboard. It produces a fruit like an olive, which is pressed for oil (see box). The goats like these trees too, and they can often be seen in the branches, nibbling the leaves.

South of the mountains around Tiznit is where the Sahara really begins, sometimes unnerving in its sheer scale and lack of any human reference point. Mountains resembling frozen sand dunes poke up from the horizon; others, with dark patterns, look as if a dry brush laden with dark-green paint has been drawn over a light-brown background.

As an alternative to travelling straight on to Goulimime, a pretty secondary road heads west back towards the coast, coming first to **Mirleft ⑥**. This is a small, sleepy town that only really comes alive in the months of July and August, when Moroccans and tourists come to enjoy the beaches around town, the most impressive of which is **Sidi Mohammed,** a small sandy bay dominated by rocky outcrops eroded into caves and arches. The town – with tourist shops, a few restaurants, a bank and most of the places to stay – is set back from the beach, on the main road.

Sidi Ifni

The road continues southwards from here, never going very far from the coast and running across the tops of cliffs, until it arrives at **Sidi Ifni ⑦**. A Spanish enclave until 1969, Sidi Ifni is an extraordinary place, full of striking Art Deco colonial architecture and with a kind of run-down charm, as if time has stood still. The focus of the town is the old Plaza España, which is dominated by the ruined governor's mansion. Off on the seaward side, next to the old church, is the Hotel Bellevue, which has spectacular views over the Atlantic. From the square a grand, operatic sweep of steps runs down to the surf-battered beach.

Stones of argan berries are used to make argan oil.

ARGAN OIL

The stones of the argan berries form the basis of a traditional oil, made by what must be one of the most labour-intensive extraction processes in existence. It requires 30kg (66lbs) of berries and eight hours of intensive manual labour to produce 1 litre (2.25 pints) of oil. The work is done entirely by women.

The fruit is collected during the summer months, when it is sun-dried and stored. The dried flesh of the fruit is then removed, to be used as animal fodder, and the stones cracked open to remove the almond-like nut inside. This is then roasted and ground in a small stone hand mill. The milled nut residue is also used as high-quality animal feed.

The decanted oil is not only used for cooking but also as a valuable local medicine, treating everything from stomach ailments to heart failure, poor blood circulation and even fertility problems. In the West it is gaining popularity as a cosmetic product.

The oil is sold throughout the region – mainly by women's cooperatives – on its own or mixed with ground almonds (in a kind of Moroccan peanut butter called *amalou*), and you will probably see it being sold on roadsides. However, because of its high value, it is difficult to guarantee that the oil you buy is really pure and not mixed with olive or sunflower oil.

Sidi Ifni architecture.

Date palms are common in the deep south.

Far off, visible through the sea spray, stand the remains of a *téléférique* tower that the Spanish used for hauling goods up to the town from a safe deep-water anchorage in the late 1960s, when land approaches to Sidi Ifni were blockaded by the Moroccans. Across the river is the *marabout* complex where the local *moussem* is held in summer.

From Sidi Ifni the road winds through hills of argan trees to Goulimime. A few kilometres before the town a 20km (12-mile) piste leads to the impressive **Fort Bou Jerif** (www.boujerif.com), once a Foreign Legion outpost, now a comfortable *auberge* and campsite that has become a major staging post for four-wheel-drive vehicles on the road south. Run with military efficiency by a French couple, it is well signposted and there is little chance of getting lost among the winding dusty tracks that lead to it.

Further along the River Noun are the ruins of a 14th-century Portuguese fort and a track that comes out on the coast at Foum Assaka, the start of the impressive **Plage Blanche**, a huge series of white beaches and dunes that run down to the mouth of the River Drâa. Another, more difficult access to the dune area is possible at **Aoreora,** via a piste 72km (45 miles) south of Goulimime.

Goulimime

The town of **Goulimime** ❽ (some signposts say 'Guelmim'), despite its romantic desert reputation as the 'Gateway to the Sahara', has very little to write home about. It is primarily an administrative centre and its chief claim to fame is as the venue of a camel and livestock market every Saturday morning – although this is now mainly run for the benefit of coach parties ferried in from Agadir. Goulimime is also touted as the place to see 'blue men', or Tuareg (see page 288), although most of the hustlers offering tourists the chance to meet Tuareg are best avoided.

The town is also close to a group of oases, and you will have no trouble finding somebody to take you out to one or all of them.

Tan Tan

On the road south, the occasional con-voy of monstrous trucks heading to the city of Laâyoune and garrisons in Dakhla forces oncoming vehicles half off the road. Tabletop mountains sur-rounding Tan Tan (a further 125km/78 miles south of Goulimime) look no more substantial than sandcastles. **Tan Tan ⑨** is made up of custard-yellow buildings. The turquoise dome of a mosque stands out, visible from the edges of the basin in which the town sits. There is a military feel to the place: lots of flags, men in uniforms and garrison compounds. There are a few basic places to stay.

The sea is 25km (16 miles) away at **Tan Tan Plage,** a wild stretch of beach where the desert meets the sea and an exhilarating drive, as the tarmac road meanders in and out from the coast, occasionally dusted over with blown sand. The beach is lined with an incongruous assortment of small, elaborate seaside bungalows in a neo-Moorish style, while the wind whips creamy spray from Atlantic breakers before they hit a crescent beach of

sand, layered rock and the odd boul-der. During the week at least, nothing much stirs apart from boys mussel-hunting in rock pools.

Heading south of Tan Tan Plage towards Tarfaya, the crumbling table-land comes to an abrupt end, and then gives way to unstable cliffs. Flocks of seagulls congregate on certain stretches of road; beside it are Land Rovers, swathed in nets and wearing fishing rods like huge antennae, and

Petrol station.

Tiznit.

fishermen casting from the cliffs. At times, the road swoops down into a valley of brackish water. Here and there are desert cafés painted green or white or yellow, one-storey concrete cabins whose cheery colours seem to underline their isolation.

A whole village of cafés has grown up in **Sidi Akhfennir**, 100km (62 miles) north of Tarfaya, at the base of a headland pitted with gaping caves. This is a useful petrol stop: you can rely on getting petrol around every 100km (62 miles) from Tan Tan to Laâyoune. But you cannot rely on French or English being spoken, and it helps to know the Arabic for water as well as please and thank you (see page 334).

At the Caidat of Sidi Akhfennir, get permission to visit the most notable of the estuaries that bisect the route south. **Khan N'fiss** is a wildlife reserve and wonderful wild campsite. The estuary is huge, bounded by emerald-green marshes, silken white dunes and populated by a few fishermen, outnumbered by flocks of flamingos, cormorants and even the odd osprey.

Sidi Ifni market stall.

Beyond the dunes on the north bank is a vast beach, wild, remote and scattered with the flotsam of the Atlantic. Harsh, semi-arid plains alternate with shifting sand dunes, looking (deceptively) as cosy as any seaside version.

The journey south is eerily quiet, and other vehicles become quite an event. North of the little Spanish-influenced port of Tarfaya, the spooky mood is enhanced by the hulks of abandoned ships and large fishing boats leaning half-grounded just offshore. They're too recent to look like wrecks, and some seem as if they're only resting, but they're definitely dead. The local authorities have helpfully installed a plaque identifying each of the wrecks and the dates when they ran aground.

South to Tarfaya

Tarfaya ⑩ has lost much of its passing trade since the road south now bypasses the port. However, it is worth a visit as it has had an intriguing history and still exudes a certain sleepy charm. It was established initially as a trading post by a determined

TRAVELLING IN WESTERN SAHARA

The reason for the military lorries and surfeit of troops from Tan Tan southwards is political. It was from Tan Tan that troops, followed by King Hassan II and 350,000 unarmed Moroccans, waving flags and copies of the Qur'an, marched to claim Moroccan sovereignty of the then-Spanish Sahara in 1975. The anniversary of the Green March is celebrated as a national holiday every 6 November; posters and postcards commemorate the event in bold green and red. Morocco is today obliged by the United Nations-brokered ceasefire to limit its standing army in the south to 140,000 men. Foreigners are allowed to travel freely through the region, although since 2010 rising tensions have made the situation increasingly uncertain for casual visitors (particularly if you're heading for Laâyoune). There is a small risk of being caught up in clashes between local Saharawis and Moroccan government forces, while you will also have to negotiate roadblocks en route south, run by the Gendarmerie Royale. The police are particularly suspicious of anyone connected with the media or with aid organisations – journalists may be turned back. Attempts to visit refugee camps around Laâyoune will also raise suspicion, while you should avoid pointing your camera at any of the region's military installations or at anything else of a sensitive political nature. Keep your passport to hand, and exercise discretion.

although undoubtedly eccentric Scotsman called Mackenzie in the late 19th century. Mackenzie built a fort-like outpost on a tiny rocky island, which he inevitably called Port Victoria. He eventually sold out to the then-Sultan Moulay Hassan for a fantastically large sum of money, although not before trying to raise a consortium to build a trans-Saharan canal.

The port next hit the headlines during World War I, when the Spanish caught a German submarine unloading arms to supply the Blue Sultan's resistance to the colonists. That galvanised the Spanish to settle the site as Villa Bens. Their garrison buildings have since been taken over by the Moroccan military, but an abandoned theatre still stands next to a small overgrown square. The town is also famous for its association with the French pilot and writer Antoine de Saint-Exupéry (author of *Night Flight* and *The Little Prince*, amongst other titles), who stopped regularly in Tarfaya during his mail flights from France to Senegal in the 1920s. The small **Musée Antoine de Saint-Exupéry**

(Mon–Fri 9am–noon, 2–4pm) on Avenue Mohammed V contains some interesting exhibits covering the history of the Service Aéropostale, which Saint-Exupéry helped to pioneer.

Tarfaya today is mostly a small fishing and administrative port, which also exports sand for the otherwise rocky beaches of the Canary Islands. If you are planning to stay the night here, don't expect to find anything but the most basic accommodation.

Laâyoune

Western Sahara proper (there is no official border) begins just south of Tarfaya. The animation and size of **Laâyoune** ⓫ jolt the senses after the denuded bleakness of the desert. Passing through two police checkpoints and a huge ornate gateway, and crossing the Green March bridge, you realise that Laâyoune has been designed as a city of the desert. Since the Green March and King Hassan's return visit 10 years later, a lot of money has gone into making the city an emblem of the 'benefits' that Morocco can give to the Sahrawi people. But nothing

Sidi Ifni.

Meet the Blue Men

The Tuareg, or 'Blue Men', present one of the most iconic – and impossibly romantic – images of the Saharan desert regions.

Any trip south of Agadir is likely to involve an encounter with *un homme bleu*, a blue man of the Sahara, or Tuareg, as they are properly called – one of those romantic desert nomads depicted in Hollywood epics as blue-turbaned aristocrats mounted on pure-white camels. It was a blue man that swept Kit (played by actress Debra Winger) to safety and desert madness in Bertolucci's 1990 film *The Sheltering Sky*.

But though you might *think* you're meeting a blue man, in truth, he is probably fake. Southern Morocco only brushes the Sahara, a desert that spans the width of Africa, but Moroccans make the most of it – especially when there are tourists to satisfy. In the town of Goulimime, one of the places where the blue men traditionally came to sell camels, the promise of nomads draws Saturday coach tours from Agadir, the day when the weekly camel

Tuareg and camels in the Western Sahara.

market is held. Alas, most of the traders are not real blue men at all but townspeople intent on making a profit.

Authentic desert nomads

Desert nomads still operating as such are found further south and east. Real blue men, though fallen upon hard times, are not particularly interested in entertaining tourists, and their pride is legendary. Wyndham Lewis, who visited the region and recorded his adventures in his book *Filibusters in Barbary*, published in 1932, said: 'At their feet you may look. A downcast eye, fixed upon the exceedingly filthy blue feet belonging to these lords, will not attract a bullet.'

Blue men belong to the Tuareg tribes, which spread through Mauritania, the Western Sahara, southern Algeria and southwest Libya. Physically, they are unusually tall, with a regal demeanour emphasised by flowing robes; their headdress wraps over the nose and chin to keep out sand-laden winds.

Traditionally it was the dye in their robes that imbued the skin with its indigo hue. In the 15th century an enterprising Scottish cloth merchant is supposed to have travelled to Agadir and introduced a dark-blue coloured calico, which was greatly admired. The fact that its dye rubbed off on the skin was the cloth's main attraction. Before buying, a tribesman would test the cloth between wet thumb and forefinger to ensure the dye came off well.

Tuareg culture

The Tuareg are associated with a rich intellectual heritage that values literature and poetry. The women are known for *guedra*, an erotic dance performed on their knees. The shows performed for Westerners' benefit tend to be fairly sedate affairs, but at one time the *guedra* was the speciality of nomadic prostitutes.

Such vestiges of their culture apart, the nomads' traditional way of life has eroded fast, due to improved methods of transport in the Sahara, the breakdown of the traditional status quo, and severe droughts that have destroyed many of their traditional grazing areas. Many nomads have congregated in the towns, picking up odd jobs here and there, abandoning their culture and leading a sedentary life. The Maghrebi governments have more pressing problems than the protection of endangered minorities, and the blue men of the Sahara have had to be pragmatic in order to survive.

can escape the fact that Laâyoune is the main city of occupied Western Sahara. If you are in any doubt, the refugee camps on the fringes of town are a reminder.

There is no medina, and the huge modern square, the **Place du Méchouar**, is not the focus it sets out to be. The real animation of Laâyoune is in street after street of shops and markets selling daily produce and livestock. For visitors, Laâyoune puts on its best face in the **Hotel Parador**: a mock castle enclosing a series of lush courtyards and shallow pools and one swimming pool; there's Arab decor and green trellises throughout. The alternative is the **Sahara Line Hotel**, mostly booked out by groups or by the UN on their mission to organise the seemingly never-to-happen referendum. These two hotels both serve alcohol, but otherwise the entire town is dry. One of the best restaurants in town is **Le Poissonière**, on Boulevard de Mekka.

Big plans are afoot for the development of tourism in the Sahara, but they still have a long way to go. Trips to the sand sea, an area of shifting dunes, are easy to organise, and are occasionally laid on (together with folklore displays, camel rides and dromedary kebabs). Regular visitors to the region are from the expatriate community in the nearby Canary Islands, who use regular flights to Laâyoune as an easy way of complying with Spanish immigration laws. **Laâyoune Plage**, 20km (12 miles) west, is attractive chiefly because it is so empty. The city also has a large fishing port, much visited by foreign fishing fleets. A trip to Laâyoune can be fascinating, but come for the pleasure of the trip rather than the town. It is also worth keeping an eye on travel advice for the region.

Phosphate mines

Inland from Laâyoune the road runs alongside the deep wadi, **Saguia el Hamra**, before cutting through inhospitable desert, past old earthen defences built by the Moroccan army against the Polisario, towards **Smara** and **Boukra**, once the largest phosphate mine in the world. Halfway along, the road comes up alongside

FACT

Laâyoune was the scene of brutally repressed demonstrations in 1999 that hastened the departure from government of Driss Basri, Morocco's hard-line Minister of the Interior. Basri was fired by King Mohammed VI after more than 20 years in the position under Hassan II.

Agadir transport.

the forlorn-looking Boucraa conveyer belt, trundling the now uneconomic phosphate for more than 100km (62 miles) across the stony ground from the mine to loading piers on the coast near Laâyoune port. It also has the unusual distinction of being the longest conveyor belt in the world.

The mine itself can be found down a turning before Smara. If you make it to the mine, you will find a surprisingly green oasis and a comfortable club set up by the engineers, which serves very good food using fresh vegetables grown in their own gardens. The mine itself is a huge open pit, surrounded by spoil heaps, excavated by the mother of all Tonka toy diggers that amazingly moves on compressed air-powered skids.

Smara is mostly a military garrison today, but was once the centre of the desert empire of Sheik Ma el Ainin, who was a hero of the Moroccan resistance against France, and was the father of El Hiba, the Blue Sultan. Today little is left of Ma el Ainin's town except the mosque and a few roofless black-stone walls, but once it was an impressive stronghold built with the help of craftsmen from the north of Morocco. The site was sacked by French forces in 1913 and occupied by the Spanish in 1934, as the still-used beehive barracks testify. If you've had enough of the desert at this point, the R101 from Smara to Tan Tan offers an alternative to the coast road. Be sure to fill up with fuel though, as the one petrol station on the way is often empty.

Paradise lagoon

Past Laâyoune, Dakhla (Ad Dakhla) is a serious 500km (300-mile) drive across barely inhabited desert. The road passes **Boujdour**, on the coast, 89km (55 miles) south of Laâyoune. It is then a very long drive to **Dakhla** , the last town before Mauritania. After the vast emptiness that has preceded it, Dakhla seems positively metropolitan, although its few cafés and hotels are basic and usually quiet.

The real draw here is the stunning beach and lagoon on a spit of sand stretching 40km (25 miles) off the coast. This untamed, sun-bleached, windblown place has become a mecca for serious kite- and windsurfers, who come for the perfect conditions: near-constant sunshine, a calm lagoon and fierce winds. Scattered on the dunes around the lagoon are funky guesthouses and camps to service the growing number of independent travellers and sporting enthusiasts who are flocking here every year – local operators include Windfish Pro (www.dakhlakitesurfhotels) and Club Mistral (www.club-mistral.com). At certain times of year, whales and sea lions can be spotted off the coast.

The road to **Nouakchott** in Mauritania is open in both directions. If you are planning to continue your drive south, Mauritanian visas, though cheaper from the embassy in Rabat, are usually available at the border. However, it is essential to check up-to-date travel advice for Mauritania before embarking on the journey.

Tiznit craftsman.

Aerial view of Dakhla.

INSIGHT GUIDES TRAVEL TIPS
MOROCCO

ACCOMMODATION

EATING OUT

ACTIVITIES

A – Z

LANGUAGE

TRANSPORT

GETTING THERE AND GETTING AROUND

GETTING THERE

By air

Principal Airlines

Royal Air Maroc (www.royalairmaroc. com) is the national airline and operates services between cities in the US, Western Europe, the Middle East and Asia and destinations all over Morocco.

Casablanca is the main hub for Moroccan air services. **Direct Royal Air Maroc** (RAM) flights connect the city with major cities across the country, and with London, Paris and many other European, African and Middle Eastern cities. There are also direct RAM flights to Casa from New York and Montréal, and one-stop flights via New York from Seattle, San Francisco, Los Angeles, Tampa, Orlando and Washington. **British Airways** (www.ba.com) also has direct flights from London to Casablanca.

Marrakech is also well connected, and is where the majority of tourist visitors arrive. There are direct budget flights from London with **easyJet** (from Gatwick; www.easyjet.com), **Ryanair** (from Luton; www.ryanair. com), and **Thomson** (from London Gatwick, Manchester, Birmingham and Bristol; www.thomsonfly.com), as well as British Airways (from Heathrow). Additionally, the city has good RAM connections to numerous other European cities. Ryanair also has flights from London to **Fez**, which is also connected by RAM and easyJet to Paris and Marseilles. **Agadir** has direct flights to London (with British Airways and Thomson) and Manchester (with Thomson). **Tangier**

is linked to London, Paris and other European cities by RAM. Alternatively, it may be worth investigating flights to Gibraltar or even Málaga (from where you must take a bus to the ferry in Algeciras). Ferries leave throughout the day.

Other Moroccan airports receiving international flights (mainly with RAM from France) include Rabat, Laâyoune, Ouarzazate, Oujda, Al Hoceima and Nador.

There is no departure tax when leaving Morocco.

Airports

Morocco has 12 airports (www.onda. ma) handling varying numbers of international flights. The country's principal airport is in the commercial capital of Casablanca, although many tourists fly into Tangier, Marrakech, Agadir, Essaouira and Fez.

Agadir

El Massira airport (AGA, tel: 0288-39112; www.agadir-airport.com) is situated 21km (13 miles) east of Agadir. Package holiday-makers on charter flights are met by bus for the 20-minute trip into town. Independent travellers must take a *grand taxi* (rates are fixed at 200dh); to cut costs share with other travellers and arrange a group before approaching a driver. There is also a local bus (No. 22, 4dh); the stop is a short walk from the terminal and it arrives at the town of Inezgane, just outside Agadir, from where taxis or local buses can be taken into the city.

Casablanca

Mohammed V International Airport (CMN, tel: 0522-53 90 40; www.onda. ma) lies 30km (19 miles) south of

the city. There is a rail link between the airport and central Casablanca (40dh), with connections to Rabat; trains run hourly 6am–8pm to Casa Port (more convenient for the city centre) and take 40 minutes, and 6am–10pm to Casa Voyageurs, taking 30 minutes. Check www. oncf.ma for up-to-date timetables. A shuttle bus runs between the airport and the CTM bus station downtown (hourly service, journey time 40 minutes). *Grands taxis* (see page 295) are also available and cost 300dh (or 350dh at night).

Essaouira

Mogador airport (ESU; tel: 0524-47 67 04) is 16km (10 miles) from town. Bus No. 5 (10dh) runs roughly every two hours from the airport into town; alternatively, most hotels can arrange a pick-up for around 280dh and there are also taxis available (around 200dh).

Tangier train.

Marrakech airport.

Fez

Fez-Saïss Airport (FEZ; tel: 0535-67 47 12) lies some 15km (9 miles) south of central Fez. An airport shuttle bus (20dh) runs every half hour or so from the airport to the train station, taking about 30 minutes; alternatively, taxis are available for a fixed fare of 120dh.

Marrakech

Menara airport (RAK; tel: 0524-44 79 10; http://marrakech.airport-authority.com) is about 3km (2 miles) southwest of the city. The taxi drivers at the airport here are reputedly crooked. Taxi fares to the centre of town are officially set at an already steep 70dh, or 100dh to outlying areas like the palmery (with a 50 percent increase from 9pm to 6am), although drivers may try for anything up to 200dh. Always agree the fare before getting in. A shuttle bus (20dh) also runs between the airport and Jemaa el Fna, departing every 30 minutes between around 6am and 9pm. Alternatively, local bus No. 11 runs every 20–30 minutes to the Djemaa el Fna.

Tangier

Ibn Battouta (Boukhalef) airport (TNG; tel: 0539-39 36 49) is 11km (7 miles) southwest of the city. If you are not on a charter flight, which is usually met by a bus, you will have to take a taxi. A *grand taxi* should cost around 200dh for the whole vehicle and takes about 30 minutes: to share the cost with other travellers,

arrange a group inside the airport and agree the fare with the driver before getting in.

By Sea

Numerous ferries connect various places in Morocco (mainly Tangier, but also Ceuta, Melilla and Nador) with various cities in Spain, as well as Gibraltar, France and Italy. The main ferry companies are Trasmediterranea acciona (www.trasmediterranea.es/en) and Balearia (www.balearia.com), although it's often easier to buy tickets through one of the numerous travel agents in Algeciras, Gibraltar and other departure points. All ferries take cars.

The most popular crossing is between **Algeciras** in southern Spain across the Strait of Gibraltar to **Tangier** (around 2.5 hours by ferry; departures every 60–90 minutes; tickets cost around €30). Ferries are particularly busy in July and August, when it's best to book in advance, especially if you're taking a car over. Passport control takes place on board the boat; you must have your passport stamped before disembarking. There are also faster hydrofoil services to Tangier from **Algeciras**, as well as from **Gibraltar** and **Tarifa** – around an hour from Algeciras and Gibraltar, and just 35 minutes from Tarifa. On the downside – departures are less frequent, tickets are more expensive than on normal ferries, and hydrofoils don't run if the sea is too rough.

Another popular route is from Algeciras to the Spanish enclave of **Ceuta** – a shorter crossing, although Ceuta is obviously much less well connected with the Moroccan rail and road network than Tangier. There are also longer crossings from Málaga and Almeria to Melilla (around eight hours).

Finally, there are car ferries run by the **Grand Navi Veloci** (www.gnv.it/en/) from **Sète**, in southern France, to Tangier (35 hours) and **Nador** (30 hours).

GETTING AROUND

City transport

In cities the easiest way to get around is in *petits taxis* (they cannot pass the city limits): small saloon cars with a different livery in each town. These are generally cheap (usually under 30dh for most short city trips), although it's essential to agree on a fare before you set off unless you can get the driver to agree to use the meter (assuming it's working). It's a good idea to ask at your hotel what the latest going rate is for a particular trip so you know what to aim for when bargaining.

Larger *grands taxis* (Mercedes cars, usually painted a light beige or white) are also available in all towns and cities. They can either be shared or hired for exclusive use. The prices of *grands taxis* are higher than *petits taxis* but should be no more than 30–40dh for a short inner-city journey. *Grands taxis* can also be hired for longer trips to other towns or to places in the surrounding region (such as into the High Atlas from Marrakech).

In **Marrakech** (and also in Taroudant), glossy horse-drawn carriages, or **calèches** hang out around the centre touting for custom – although these are now aimed mainly at tourists looking to see a few sights in style, rather than as a practical means of getting from A to B. Official rates are posted inside the vehicle, but you'll have to bargain hard to get a reasonable fare and are unlikely to get the driver to agree to the official posted rates.

By air

Internal flights operated by **Royal Air Maroc** (www.royalairmaroc.com) connect Casablanca with eleven cities around the country, including Laâyoune and Dakhla . The advantages of flying are clear-cut: speed and reliability: the journey from Dakhla to Tangier, for example, can be done in just a couple of hours by air, compared with around three days by road – although obviously you'll pay a lot more than you would by bus or train.

By car

Morocco has one of the best road systems in Africa, with 1,420km (880 miles) of relatively cheap toll motorways (autoroutes). The main autoroute runs from Tangier in the north, along the Atlantic Coast to Rabat, Casablanca and El Jadida. There are also branches of the motorway system running inland from Rabat to Meknes and Fez, and inland from Casablanca to Settat and Marrakech.

If driving yourself, always drive defensively. Driving standards are erratic and accident rates high (at least compared with Europe). Be particularly wary of *grand taxis* on inter-city routes, whose drivers often fly along at dangerously high speeds.

Drivers must be over 21. If taking your own vehicle, the European Insurance Green Card is required and you will also need the registration document. Few British insurers are willing to cover cars in Morocco, so if your insurer doesn't issue Green Card insurance for Morocco your best bet is to purchase cover from Assurances Aux Frontières at the Tangier port or other places of entry. Your own national licence is valid, but it does

no harm to carry an International Driving Permit as well (it has French and Arabic translations), available from motoring organisations. An international customs carnet is required for caravans. Always take your passport with you.

The old system of giving priority to the right *(priorité à droite)* is still generally in force. This means that traffic going onto a roundabout has priority over the traffic already on the roundabout. However, junctions increasingly have give-way signs indicating priority. Major roads are well surfaced, minor ones good with lapses (some treacherous potholes) and mountain roads often not as bad as you'll have been led to expect.

Fuel *(essence* or, more likely, *super* for petrol/gas; *gas-oil* for diesel) is available in towns and along the highway, but fill up before striking out on a long journey away from main roads. Many petrol stations sell lead-free *(sans plomb)*, especially Afriquia. Petrol prices are generally significantly cheaper than those in the UK and other countries in Europe (around 11dh for a litre of unleaded). Parking in towns of any size costs a few dirhams, collected by an official attendant.

Car hire

The major international hire companies are all represented in Morocco, and it is possible to make arrangements to pick up a vehicle at any of the airports and also in the *villes nouvelles*, where there are also local companies that will undercut the rates of the major companies. This will be useful for short rentals (which

Orientation

Most major urban centres in Morocco offer an archetypal tale of two cities, consisting of a pair utterly contrasting districts: a traditional old medina, on the one hand, and a European-style *ville nouvelle* (new town) built by the French during the colonial period on the other. Entering the average medina for the first time is often a bewildering experience. These are usually surrounded by ramparts and entered through grand gateways, within which you'll discover a disorientating maze of narrow streets and souks in which it's all too easy to become instantly disoriented – and sometimes hopelessly lost. Both Marrakech and Fez medinas now feature plenty of helpful signs pointing you in the direction of the nearest landmark, though in other places signage is generally minimalist or nonexistent and you may have to appeal to a local to show you back to a convenient landmark. At the other extreme is the typical *ville nouvelle* – usually planned and laid out by the French, with grand, straight avenues (the main avenue often named after Mohammed V) and connecting squares and roundabouts. Roads are generally clearly signed, and even if they're not, the simplicity of the basic layout makes it difficult to get lost.

are proportionately more expensive): but for a rental lasting the whole trip, it may be cheaper to organise a car before you depart – on a special **holiday tariff** – either online when booked together with a flight and/ or accommodation, through a travel agent or direct with one of the major companies.

Car-hire prices are usually quoted exclusive of a 19 percent government tax: be sure this has been added to the price that is agreed. Remember that the international companies have a better network of offices if anything goes wrong. For gruelling itineraries with a lot of mountain driving, consider hiring a larger and sturdier car. Toyota Land Cruisers for more adventurous routes can be hired locally, often with a chauffeur. If you are planning on doing a lot of exploring on smaller roads and pistes, remember that some are passable only in a 4x4.

Driving in Zagora.

Agadir
Avis: El Massira airport
Tel: 0528-82 92 44
Budget: Al Massira Airport
Tel: 0528-83 91 01
Europcar: corner of Boulevard Giraud
and Boulevard Mohammed V
Tel: 0528-84 02 03
Hertz: Bungalow Marhaba,
Avenue Mohammed V
Tel: 0528-84 09 39

Casablanca
Avis: 19 Avenue de L'Armée Royale
Tel: 0522-31 24 24
Europcar: Complexe des Habous,
Avenue des F.A.R.
Tel: 0522-31 37 37
Hertz: 25 Rue Oraibi Jilali
Tel: 0522-48 47 10

Fez
Avis: 50 Boulevard Chefchaouni
Tel: 0535-62 69 69

Hiring a guide

Local guides – both official and
unofficial – can often be found
hanging around the entrances
to medinas across the country.
Unofficial guides may be students,
professional hustlers or even small
boys chancing their luck – and
all are generally best avoided.
Some are persistent, rarely taking
your first no for an answer. The
government has clamped down
on these so-called *faux guides*
in recent years, and if they are
caught by the police they are liable
to be thrown in prison. However,
economic necessity forces
many young men to try their luck
regardless.

   Official guides are a completely
different proposition. All are
licensed (ask to see their photo ID)
and can provide rewarding tours,
steering you to places you might
otherwise miss and protecting
you from other sources of hassle
en route. Always agree a fee in
advance however. The rate for
official guides (hired at the tourist
office or your hotel) is around
150dh for half a day.

   At some point almost all guides
(even official ones) will most likely
try to steer you into a least a
couple of shops, where he will earn
commission on what you spend. If
you are not interested in shopping,
make this absolutely clear
before setting out – and don't be
surprised if they still ignore this
request at some point in your tour.

Fez–Saiss Airport
Tel: 0525-62 69 69
Budget: Fes-Saiss airport
Tel: 0535-03 09 21
Europcar: 45 Avenue Hassan II
Tel: 0535-62 65 45
Hertz: 1 Rue Kissariat de la Foire
Tel: 0535-62 28 12

Marrakech
Avis: Marrakech Menara airport
Tel: 0524-43 31 69
Budget: Marrakech Menara airport
Tel: 0524-37 02 37
Europcar: 63 Boulevard Zerktouni
Tel: 0524-43 12 28
Hertz: 154 Boulevard Mohammed V
Tel: 0524-43 99 84

Tangier
Avis: 54 Boulevard Pasteur
Tel: 0539-93 46 46
Boukhaif Airport
Tel: 0539 39 30 33
Budget: Boukhaif airport
Tel: 0539-06 09 51
Europcar: 87 Boulevard
Mohammed V
Tel: 0539-94 19 38
Hertz: 36 Avenue Mohammed V
Tel: 0539-32 21 65

Websites
Avis: www.avis.com/car-rental/
location/MA
Budget: www.budget.com
Europcar: www.europcar.com/car-
MOROCCO.html
Hertz: www.hertz.ma

Local transport

By bus
Morocco is covered by a well-
developed network of bus services
linking all major towns – generally a
bit cheaper than trains, although also
slower and generally less comfortable.
The main inter-city company is
CTM (www.ctm.ma), which runs
comfortable buses across the country,
while services are also operated by
various smaller local companies –
although these might be less reliable.
Timetables for CTM buses can be
found on their website but should be
taken with a pinch of salt, since most
buses tend to stop frequently en route
to pick up and set down passengers.
Faster and more luxurious express
services are operated by **Supratours**,
which also ply the Southwest and
North coasts (where the railway
doesn't run): these cost 50 percent
more than regular bus fares.

   Most large cities have acquired a
new, centralised bus station in the

last few years. These are equipped
with efficient information centres that
can advise on routes and timetables.
In **Fez**, the main bus station is outside
Bab el Mahrouk.

   In **Meknes**, most buses leave
and depart from the station outside
Bab Khemis, but limited delivery and
pick-up continues at Bab Mansour.

   In **Marrakech**, the main bus
station is next to the Bab Doukkala,
on the edge of the medina. However,
the Supratours buses go from next to
the railway station.

   In **Casablanca** the CTM bus
station is off Avenue des F.A.R.

   In **Rabat** the main bus station is
situated 2km (1 mile) away from the
centre of town, in Place Zerktouni.

By grands taxis
These are large cars, usually
Mercedes, which rattle along with
up to six passengers on routes from
town to town, charging a fixed price.
They will leave when they are full.
It's possible to charter an entire taxi,
but make sure you know the going
rate. The fare is a bit more than
the bus, but the journey is much
quicker – although kamikaze drivers
can sometimes make for a rather
stressful experience. In remote
areas, Land Rovers often replace
taxis, and open trucks act as local
buses.

By train
Faster and more comfortable than
buses, Morocco's excellent rail
network (www.oncf.ma) extends from
Tangier in the north to Marrakech
in the south, and links up with
Safi, El Jadida, Casablanca, Rabat,
Tangier, Fez, Meknes and Oujda.
First-class carriages usually have
air conditioning. Travellers under
the age of 26 can use Eurotrain or
InterRail passes on Moroccan trains.
Even if you don't have a card, prices
are cheap (for example: Tangier to
Marrakech costs 310dh first class,
205dh second class). Plan your
journey in advance (timetables are
available on the website, although
it's worth double-checking in
person just in case they've recently
changed). It can be worth travelling
first class at busy times and on
popular routes, as it's the only way
to guarantee having a seat. Train
stations are usually found near the
centre of the *ville nouvelle*. Be sure
to get out at the right station: for
example, in Rabat you will probably
want Rabat Ville, not Rabat Agdal;
likewise you will need Meknes, not
Meknes Amir Abdelkader.

ACCOMMODATION

HOTELS, RIADS, AUBERGES AND TENTED CAMPS

Accommodation in Morocco varies widely and, apart from the large chain hotels and tourist resorts, most places do not have official star ratings. This does not mean, however, that they are not good quality. Many guesthouses and *maisons d'hôte* in places like Marrakech, Fez and Essaouira are of a four- or five-star standard and, though they may not have certain amenities like televisions, minibars and telephones, they are often much more characterful.

Bear in mind that prices fluctuate significantly between high and low seasons, and it is always worth asking about discounted rates during low seasons. During peak periods in the most popular destinations, booking ahead is essential. Marrakech, the High Atlas and the southern and desert regions are most popular over Easter, Christmas and New Year. July and August are very busy on the Mediterranean and Atlantic coasts, when much of Morocco as well as France and Spain take their summer holidays. During the Gnaoua World Music Festival in Essaouira and the World Sacred Music Festival in Fez (both in June) accommodation is extremely hard to find.

HOTEL STANDARDS

Hotel standards vary hugely. There are many truly luxurious five-star hotels, renowned for their character and style – notable examples include La Mamounia and the Royal Mansour, the Sofitel Fès Palais Jamaï in Fez, El Minzah in Tangier and La Gazelle d'Or in Taroudant. Hotels at the next level down (the equivalent of a four-star hotel) are usually excellent, albeit without the film star glamour of the most up-market places – though the lack of glitz is compensated for by considerably lower room rates. If the hotel in this range is a boutique hotel, such as a riad or *maison d'hôte*, expect more character, and perhaps fewer amenities but all the usual elements of a four-star hotel including excellent food and professional service.

At three-star levels, you can expect a reasonable restaurant and bar, en suite facilities in all rooms and sometimes a pool. Rooms will usually be modern and clean but can often lack character. Budget hotels at the higher end have private facilities in most (but not all) rooms, sometimes a modest bar and restaurant, but rarely a pool, and at the bottom of the scale – in hostels and very basic budget hotels – quality varies wildly. Expect shared facilities, a basic restaurant/café (if any at all) and no amenities such as air conditioning.

RIADS, AUBERGES AND MAISONS D'HÔTE

Smaller hotels – riads, *auberges* and *maisons d'hôte* – are almost always the most charming places to stay in Morocco, full of character and authenticity, with personal service and very good food. Several agencies advertise selections of riads on the internet, and mainstream travel agencies can fix up accommodation in *maisons d'hôte*. Some of the more established agencies specialising in renting rooms or entire houses in the medina are www.hipmarrakech.com, www.ilove-marrakesh.com and www.boutiquesouk.com.

TENTED CAMPS

In recent years, several luxury 'boutique' tented camps in the Saharan dunes of the Erg Chigagga have opened, offering one of the most extraordinary and romantic experiences in Morocco.

The following are a selection of the very best. All offer a high standard of accommodation and excellent service, plus activities such as camel treks into the dunes during your stay. All are eco-conscious and ensure that impact on the desert landscape is kept to a minimum. Some (such as **Camps Nomades**) have started schemes that benefit the local communities and enable visitors to learn a little bit about desert nomadic life. Due to the time it takes to reach the Erg Chigagga (three hours in a 4x4 from M'hamid) and because it is worth spending time in these magical places, most of the camps require a two-night minimum stay.

Camps Nomades Dunes Camp, Erg Chigagga
Tel: 0524-43 48 08
www.camps-nomades.com
$$$$
Dar Ahlam (Le Campement), Maison des Rêves
Tel: 0145-44 16 79 (Paris office)
www.maisondesreves.com
$$$$
Dar Azawad Dune Camp, Erg Chigagga
Tel: 0524-84 87 30
www.darazawad.com
$$$
Erg Chigagga Luxury Camp
Tel: 0524-31 39 01
www.desertcampmorocco.com
$$$$

TANGIER

Hotel Continental
36 Rue Dar el Baroud
Tel: 0539-93 10 24
www.continental-tanger.com/fr
Overlooking the revamped port area
and Straits of Gibraltar, this was
once Tangier's most fashionable
hotel, where Degas used to paint
and Bertolucci filmed scenes from
The Sheltering Sky. Full of faded,
old-world charm – although
renovations have brightened up
some of the rooms considerably.
$$

Dar Nour
20 Rue Gourna, Kasbah
Tel: 0662-11 27 24
www.darnour.com
The oldest maison d'hôte in town,
built into the ramparts of the
kasbah and situated opposite the
house of Moroccan literary legend
Mohammed Choukri. Owned and run
by an architect, a journalist and an
archaeologist, whose love for Tangier
is evident in the service and decor.
$$$

El Minzah
85 Rue de la Liberté
Tel: 0539-33 34 44
www.leroyal.com/morocco/thecomplex.asp
A short walk from the Grand Socco,
this is Tangier's most luxurious and
iconic hotel, once a clandestine
refuge for spies and expats, and still
full of period atmosphere. Rooms,
arranged around a lovely courtyard,

come with attractive Moorish
decor, and facilities include a pool,
wellness centre and no less than five
restaurants and bars. **$$$$**

Le Mirage
Les Grottes d'Hercule
Tel: 0539-33 33 32
www.lemirage.com
Exclusive, luxurious hotel, an old-
school hang-out for expats, sprawling
over the cliffs near the Caves of
Hercules on Cap Spartel, a few
kilometres west of Tangier, and with
stunning views of the coast. Worth
going for a drink even if you aren't
staying there. **$$$$**

Hotel el Muniria
1 Rue Magellan
Tel: 0539-93 53 37
www.hotelelmuniria.com
A legendary hotel for Beat fans –
this is where William Burroughs
wrote The Naked Lunch. Now faded,
but a decent budget option, with the
popular Le Tangerine pub below.
$

Hotel Nord-Pinus
11 Riad Sultan, Kasbah
Tel: 0661-22 81 40
www.nord-pinus-tanger.com
Chic, minimalist riad situated at
the highest point in the kasbah and
partly resting on the ramparts. It has
just four suites, one double room
and a 'kasbah house', all elegantly
decorated with antique fabrics and
handmade Moroccan tiles. **$$$$**

Hotel Rembrandt
Avenue Mohammed V
Tel: 0539-93 78 70
www.hotelrembrandt.ma
This large 1950s stalwart remains a
good option in the heart of the Ville
Nouvelle. Rooms are ordinary, but
there's a decent bar (sometimes
with piano player) overlooking
the garden, good restaurant and
outdoor pool, with views of the
distant bay. **$$**

La Tangerina
19 Riad Sultan, Kasbah
Tel: 0539-94 77 31
www.latangerina.com
Beautifully restored kasbah riad with
magical views from its roof terrace
across the Bay of Tangier. The ten
rooms are set around a central
courtyard and decorated in chic
Moroccan and colonial European
designs, and there's also a decadent
hammam. **$$**

Villa Josephine
231 Rue Mesmoudi
Tel: 0539-33 45 35
www.villajosephine-tanger.com
One of the most magical places
to stay in the city. Situated on the
Old Mountain, this idyllic colonial
villa – built by Times journalist
Walter Harris and the last summer
residence of the Glaoui family – is a
nostalgic, and luxurious, step back
in time to the golden era of Tangier.
$$$$

THE RIF

Al Hoceima

Suites Hotel Mohammed VI
Place Mohammed VI
Tel: 0539-98 22 33
www.hotelsuitesmohammedv.com
Within walking distance of the
main square and the beach, this
former government-run hotel
has now been given a thorough
makeover, with smart modern
rooms overlooking the sea, plus
restaurant, bar and gym.
$$$

Hotel Villa Florido
Place du Rif
Tel: 0539-84 08 47
www.florido.alhoceima.com
Elegant old Art Deco hotel, dating
from 1929, with plenty of period
character combined with modern
amenities (including free Wi-fi and
gym), all at very competitive rates.
$

Chefchaouen

Casa Perleta
68 Avenue Hassan II
Tel: 0539-98 89 79
www.casaperleta.com
Eight beautifully designed rooms
(some with mountain views) in an
enchanting Andalusian-style house,
set around a pretty little patio with
fountain. Staff are extremely helpful,
and there's also Wi-fi and central
heating for chilly nights. **$$**

Dar Echchaouen
Ras el Maa
Tel: 0539-98 78 24
www.darechchaouen.ma
Comfortable hotel with pleasantly
rustic rooms (some featuring
wooden ceilings and tadelakt
showers), backed up by helpful
service and an enticing pool to cool
off in after a day exploring.
$$

Dar Gabriel
Bab Souk
Tel: 0539-98 92 44
www.dargabriel.com
A stunning and excellent-value riad
with seven gorgeous bedrooms, a
sitting room with open fire and a
roof terrace with chill-out area and
views over the Rif Mountains.
Welcoming hosts and delicious
Moroccan food. **$$**

PRICE CATEGORIES

Price categories are for a double
room with bath (if available) per
night in high season:
$ = up to 350dh
$$ = 350–750dh
$$$ = 750–1,250dh
$$$$ = over 1,250dh, though it can
be a lot more.

Dar Meziana
7 Rue Zagdud
Tel: 0539-98 78 06
www.darmezianahotel.com
Away from the bustle of the
medina, this riad is a haven of
peace, with attractive rooms and a
pretty breakfast terrace. Staff are
immensely knowledgeable and
helpful in arranging tours. **$$**

Hostal Guernika
49 Rue Onssar
Tel: 0539-98 74 34
Run by an artistically inclined
Spanish woman, this is one of the
town's top budget options, with
excellent-value rooms (all with
showers) and sweeping views from
the terrace. **$**

Lina Ryad & Spa
Avenue Moulay Hassan I,
Medina
Tel: 0645-06 99 03
www.linariad.com
Opened in 2013, this superb riad is
done out in classic shades of blue
and white. Spacious rooms come
with mountain or medina views and
facilities include a beautiful indoor
pool, traditional hammam and idyllic
little spa. **$$$$**

M'diq

Golden Beach Hotel
Route de Ceuta
Tel: 0539-97 50 77
www.golden-beachotel.com
One of several resort-style hotels
now spreading along the white
sands between Ceuta and Tetouan,
this pleasant four-star offers a nice
spot for some downtime on the
beach, with neat rooms, attractive
seafront gardens and a big pool.
$$$

Dar Gabriel in Chefchaouen.

Oujda

Ibis
Place de la Gare
Tel: 0532-11 02 80
www.ibishotel.com
Modern chain hotel with comfortable
rooms, a swimming pool, restaurant
and bar. Rates vary but are often
excellent value, and the location next
to the railway station couldn't be
more convenient. **$$**

Hotel Royal
13 Boulevard Mohammed Zerktouni
Tel: 0536-68 22 84
Comfortable and well-run budget
hotel in a good central location.

Rooms are clean and well-furnished,
and come with either bath or shower
– excellent value for money. **$**

Tetouan

Blanco Riad Hotel
25 Zankat Zawiya Kadiria
Tel: 0539-70 42 02
www.blancoriad.com
One of the most charming places
to stay in Tetouan, with cosy and
prettily decorated rooms set around
a beautifully restored 18th-century
courtyard. Service is excellent, with
experienced staff on hand to help
with tours and local advice. **$$**

THE NORTHWEST COAST

Asilah

Berbari
Dchar Sidi Ghanem, Cercle de Tnine Sidi el
Yamani
Tel: 0660-29 54 54
www.berbari.com
A gorgeous country house 7km (4
miles) outside Asilah. Lovingly built
from natural materials, there are just
seven rooms, decorated in warm,
rustic colours and full of character. **$$**

Hotel Patio de la Luna
12 Rue Zellaka
Tel: 0539-41 60 74
www.patiodelaluna.com
Quaint little Spanish-owned
guesthouse, just outside the medina
walls facing Bab Kasaba, with

accommodation in eight simple but
characterful rooms. Closed 15 Jan–1
Apr. **$$**

Larache

Hotel Espana
6, Rue Hassan II
Tel: 0539-91 31 95
www.hotelespanalarache.com
Old colonial hotel overlooking the
town's central square. Touches of
original character survive, although
most rooms have been nicely
renovated and upgraded, offering
comfortable lodgings at competitive
rates. **$**

La Maison Haute
6 Derb Ben Thami

Tel: 0655-34 48 88,
http://lamaisonhaute.free.fr
Well located just inside the market of
Soco Chico, this traditional Hispano-
Moorish house has wonderful views
over the medina and sea with well-
furnished, if slightly faded rooms. **$$**

PRICE CATEGORIES

Price categories are for a double
room with bath (if available) per
night in high season:
$ = up to 350dh
$$ = 350–750dh
$$$ = 750–1,250dh
$$$$ = over 1,250dh, though it can
be a lot more.

RABAT

Hotel Majestic
121 Avenue Hassan II
Tel: 0537-72 29 97
www.hotelmajestic.ma
Reliable budget hotel opposite Bab el Had, at the junction of the medina and Ville Nouvelle, offering bright and comfy en-suite rooms at very competitive rates. **$**

The Repose
17 Zankat Talaa, Salé
Tel: 0537-88 29 58
One of the few places to stay in Salé, this wonderfully elegant riad offers five-star service and is also very child-friendly. The owners live on site and provide invaluable local knowledge. Discounts for booking online. **$$$**

Riad Kalaa
3–5 Rue Zebdi
Tel: 0537-20 20 28
www.riadkalaa.com
Beautifully restored 19th-century riad in the medina, just a few steps from the ramparts and sea. The decadent rooftop pool has sweeping views, and there's also a hammam

and spa. **$$$**

Le Pietri Urban Hotel
4 Rue Tobrouk
Tel: 0537-70 78 20
www.lepietri.com
Funky modern boutique hotel in the Ville Nouvelle with cool rooms and the inviting little Le Bistrot du Pietri bar-restaurant. One of the first Moroccan hotels to be awarded the Le Clef Verte for its eco-friendly credentials. **$$$**

La Tour Hassan
26 Rue Chellah
Tel: 0537-23 90 00
www.latourhassan.com
One of the best hotels in Rabat with sumptuous rooms and lavish Moroccan styling, lovely gardens and pool, a beautiful little spa and fitness centre, and the excellent L'Impérial in-house restaurant. **$$$$**

Villa Mandarine
19 Rue Ouled Bousba
Tel: 0537-75 20 77
www.villamandarine.com
Situated in the heart of a vast

orange grove, this luxury villa has 27 rooms overlooking a hibiscus- and bougainvillea-filled courtyard. Inside, the walls are covered with art and there are plenty of private places to eat and relax. **$$$$**

Fresh style at The Repose, Salé.

CASABLANCA AND SOUTH OF CASABLANCA

Casablanca

Hotel Astrid
12 Rue 6 November
Tel: 0522-27 78 03
Email: hotelastrid@hotmail.com.
Excellent little budget hotel right in the heart of downtown with old-fashioned but cosy rooms, friendly service and a surprisingly peaceful atmosphere given the very central location. **$$**

Barceló Casablanca
139 Boulevard d'Anfa
Tel: 0522-20 80 00
www.barcelocasablanca.com
Part of the reliable Barceló chain, this comfortable hotel offers a good base in the heart of modern Casablanca, with chic modern rooms and good Spanish and Moroccan cuisine at the in-house Tubkal restaurant. **$$$**

Hotel and Spa Le Doge
9 Rue Docteur Veyre
Tel: 0522-46 78 00
www.hotelledoge.com
Five-star elegance in what was a 1930s townhouse in a peaceful and attractive part of town renowned for its Art Deco architecture, with plenty of luxury and personality. **$$$$**

Hyatt Regency
Place des Nations Unies
Tel: 0522-43 12 34
www.casablanca.regency.hyatt.com
Conveniently located right in the centre of town, with all the amenities of a modern five-star hotel including a big pool, fitness centre, several up-market restaurants and the swanky SixPM Lounge Bar. **$$$$**

Ibis Moussafir
Boulevard Bahmad
Tel: 0522-40 19 84
www.ibishotel.com
Conveniently located right next to the train station, and just a few minutes by tram to the centre of downtown. Rooms are simply furnished, but cosy and well equipped. Rates vary, although it's usually one of the best deals in town. **$$**

Le Royal Mansour Méridien
27 Avenue de l'Armée Royale
Tel: 0522-45 88 88
www.leroyalmansourmeridien.com
The swankiest and most characterful of the city's many chain hotels, with plush rooms and lavish Moroccan-style suites. There's also a fitness centre and spa (but no pool) and the atrium courtyard is a pleasant place for a drink or a coffee. **$$$$**

El Jadida

Mazagan Beach Resort
Mazagan
Tel: 0523-38 80 00
www.mazaganbeachresort.com
Massive luxury resort hotel (as featured in *Sex & the City 2*), with 500 rooms and 11 restaurants and bars set in vast grounds around a spectacular, palm-studded pool. Plenty of facilities for children as well as a spa, casino and golf course. **$$$$**

Pullman Mazagan Royal Golf & Spa Hotel
Route de Casablanca, Km 7
Tel: 0523-37 91 00
www.accorhotels.com
Just north of El Jadida, this luxury oceanfront five-star (formerly the Sofitel Royal Golf) boasts plenty of amenities including tennis courts, pool, hammam, nightclub and several restaurants, plus an 18-hole golf course next door. **$$$$**

Riad Soleil Orient
131 Derb el Hajjar
Tel: 0523-35 02 42
www.riadsoleilorient.com
A pretty riad *maison d'hôte* in the medina of El Jadida. There are just six rooms facing the tranquil

courtyard shaded by fig and banana plants, and delicious breakfasts and dinners are served on request. **$$$**

Oualidia

L'Hippocampe
Oualidia Plage
Tel: 0523-36 60 09
www.hippocampeoualidia.com
A charming and popular bungalow-style hotel nestled in flower-filled gardens on the lagoon. Rooms

are simple but the restaurant is good and activities include good birdwatching and surfing. **$$$$**

Hotel-Restaurant l'Initiale
Oualidia Plage
Tel: 0523-36 62 46
Intimate beachfront guesthouse with just a handful of neat and colourful rooms, plus an excellent restaurant (licensed) serving up top-notch seafood and friendly and helpful staff. **$$**

La Sultana
Parc à Huîtres No. 3
Tel: 0524-38 80 08
www.lasultanahotels.com
A member of the Small Luxury Hotels of the World, set on the edge of Oualidia's lovely lagoon and with just 11 beautifully decorated rooms, making it feel almost like a private home. Facilities include a wonderful restaurant serving fresh fish and oysters, plus a hammam and spa. **$$$$**

THE SOUTHWEST COAST

Essaouira

Auberge Tangaro
Four km (2 miles) south of Essaouira, on the way to Diabet
Tel: 0524-78 47 84
www.aubergetangaro.com
Located a few kilometres outside Essaouira, this recently renovated hotel offers a marvellously oceanfront retreat a short drive from the city, with 18 bright and attractively decorated rooms set in lovely gardens with Atlantic views. **$$**

Dar Loulema
2 rue Souss, Medina
Tel: 0524-47 53 46,
www.darloulema.com
All is light and calm in this stunning 18th-century riad, located just off the ramparts. The rooms are named after places in Morocco and decorated accordingly, and fantastic food is available on request. **$$$**

Heure Bleue
2 Rue ibn Batuta
Tel: 0524-78 34 34
www.heure-bleue.com
This colonial gem is the most up-market place to stay in town, and one of the most beautiful, with sumptuous rooms, an exquisite roof terrace with pool and bar

overlooking the bay, and a fine-dining restaurant serving traditional and contemporary Moroccan fare. **$$$$**

Madada Mogador
5 Rue Youssef el Fassi
Tel: 0524-47 55 12
www.madada.com
Ultra-chic riad on the edge of the medina. Most of the (large) rooms have a private terrace overlooking the port and are decorated in a cool contemporary style. **$$$**

Ocean Vagabond Guest House
4 Boulevard Lalla Aicha
Tel: 0524-47 92 22
Email: hotel@hoteloceanvagabond.com
A good choice if you don't fancy staying in the medina, and close to the sea, so a good place to arrange water sports. Rooms are comfortable and stylish, and there's a nice little garden with a small pool and a good restaurant. **$$$**

Riad Chbanate
179 rue Chbanate
Tel: 0524-78 33 34
www.riadchbanate.com
Plush modern riad arranged around a deep central courtyard with spacious rooms gorgeously decorated in traditional Moroccan style, plus an excellent little restaurant. **$$$$**

Riad Nakhla
12 Rue d'Agadir
Tel 0524-47 49 40
Email: riad-nakhla@essaouiranet.com.
Excellent-value riad in a very central location, offering mid-range comforts at budget prices. Rooms, set around a shady courtyard, are attractively decorated with traditional fabrics and furnishings, and breakfast is served on the breezy rooftop terrace with sweeping sea views. **$**

Villa Maroc
10 Rue Abdellah Ben Yassine
Tel: 0524-47 61 47
www.villa-maroc.com
Superb, atmospheric hotel, one of Essaouira's finest, with a variety of individually designed rooms and suites set around two courtyards, plus good Moroccan food and a terrace with wonderful sea views. **$$$**

Hotel Villa Soleil
Sidi Kaouki Beach
Tel: 0670-23 30 97
www.hotelvillasoleil.com
Peaceful little hotel on Sidi Kaouki Beach, popular with windsurfers and surfers. The simple but charming rooms all come with their own private patio, and there's also excellent food and a warm welcome from the Belgium owners. **$$**

FEZ AND REGION

Fez

The growth in riad *maison d'hôte* accommodation has spread from Marrakech to Fez, offering more authentic and characterful options than the hotels in the *Ville Nouvelle*.

Dar Hafsa
Derb Sidi Safi, Souiket Ben Safi,
Talaa Sghira
Tel: 0535-63 67 02
www.darhafsa.com

Good-value riad accommodation near Talaa Sghira, with friendly owners and cosy, slightly kitsch rooms in an old nineteenth-century townhouse. **$$**

Dar Melody
18 Rue Laalouj,
Saffah
Tel: 0535-71 13 43
www.darmelody.fr
A simple but lovely place to stay in the heart of the medina, with

knowledgeable and welcoming French hosts who will pick you up and take time to show you around the medina. **$$**

Dar Seffarine
14 Derb Sbaa Louyate
Tel: 0671-11 35 28
http://darseffarine.com
Occupying an ancient riad in the Seffarine quarter at the heart of Fez el Bali, this intimate, stunningly decorated boutique hotel has just

Riad Tizwa, Fez.

six charming rooms – while larger groups (maximum 12 people) might consider renting the riad in its entirety. **$$$**

La Maison Bleue
33 Derb Miter
Tel: 0535-74 18 39
www.maisonbleue.com/riad-maison-bleue
Antique-filled suites and rooms in the former mansion of one of Fez's leading families. Facilities include all you would expect from a luxury hotel, with an up-market restaurant, spa and hammam, intimate lounge and bar, gym and idyllic pool in the centre of a leafy courtyard. **$$$$**

Riad 9
9 Derb Lamsside
Tel: 0535-63 40 45
www.riad9.com
Bijou 18th-century riad in the heart of Fez el Bali, lovingly restored by its designer owner. Accommodation is in three large suites set around a central courtyard, and there is also a cool rooftop terrace with great views, plus excellent food and superb hosts who know every inch of Fez. **$$$**

Riad el Bartal
21 Rue Sournas
Tel: 0535-63 70 53
www.riadalbartal.com
Built in the early 20th century by a family of weavers, this tranquil riad features a cool, leafy courtyard, cosy living room with fireplace, a mix of magical rooms and suites, plus wonderful Fassi food. **$$$**

Riad le Calife

19 bis Derb el Ouarbiya, El Makhfia, Medina
Tel: 0535-76 26 08
www.riadlecalife.com
One of the most highly rated of Fez's ever-expanding number of luxury riads, at a surprisingly affordable price. Lovingly decorated rooms are set around a leafy central courtyard, and there's also excellent food, enjoyable cooking lessons on demand, and superb city views from the rooftop terrace. **$$$**

Riad Laaroussa
3 Derb Bechara
Tel: 0674-18 76 39
www.riad-laaroussa.com
A breathtaking 17th-century riad that took two years to restore. Accommodation is in four bedrooms and four suites, all individually decorated in traditional Moroccan style, and there's also a hammam, spa, fantastic food and cookery lessons with the resident chef. **$$$$**

Riad Louna
21 Derb Sarraj,
Talaa Sghira
Tel: 0535-74 19 85
www.riadlouna.com
Gorgeous Belgian-owned riad hotel with stylish rooms set around a magnificent courtyard filled with orange and apricot trees. Dinner provided on request, and cookery classes can also be arranged. A bargain at current rates. **$$$**

Riad Mabrouka
25 Derb el Miter

Tel: 0535-63 63 45
www.ryadmabrouka.com
Eighteenth-century riad renovated in traditional style, with eight large suites and a beautiful garden complete with an enticing plunge pool. Staff can also arrange biking, hiking and horse riding in the surrounding countryside. **$$$**

Riad Norma
16 Derb Sornas,
Ziat
Tel: 0535-63 47 81
www.riadnorma.com
French-owned riad with seven good-sized rooms arranged around a pleasant courtyard garden with plunge pool. There's also excellent food, while various activities including golf and horse riding can be arranged. **$$$**

Riad Tizwa
15 Derb Guebbas
Tel: +44 7973-115 417 (UK)
www.holidayfes.com
One of the best-value places to stay in town, in a peaceful and pretty riad in the heart of the medina. The nine double rooms come with air

conditioning and iPod docks, and there's a huge courtyard and terrace for meals and sunbathing. **$$**
Royal Mirage
Avenue des FAR
Tel: 0535-93 09 09
www.royalmiragehotels.com
Less character than many other places in town, but with clean rooms,

good service and a child-friendly atmosphere, while the *Ville Nouvelle* location offers a good alternative if you don't fancy staying in the medina. **$$$$**
Sofitel Fès Palais Jamai
Bab Guissa
Tel: 0535-63 43 31
www.sofitel.com

Opulent 19-century palace hotel with beautiful gardens and views of Fez – it's well worth spending a bit extra for a room with a medina view. There's also excellent Moroccan food in the El Fassia restaurant, as well as a good French restaurant for those tired of tagines. **$$$$**

MEKNES AND REGION

Meknes

Hotel Majestic
19 Avenue Mohammed V
Tel: 0535-52 20 35
Situated in the *Ville Nouvelle*, this good-value hotel dates back to the 1930s and still has a touch of character. Bedrooms are large and mostly come with private bathrooms, but try to avoid the noisy rooms at the back of the hotel facing the station. **$**
Palais Didi
30 Derb Hammam Moulay Ismail
Tel: 0535-55 85 90
www.palaisdidi.com
A beautiful *maison d'hôte*, once the palace of a descendant of Moulay Sulaiman, now restored in traditional Moroccan style with a grand courtyard – a romantic place to have dinner at night – and magnificent town views from its terrace. **$$$**

Ryad Bahia Tiberbarine
Medina, nr Place el Hedim
Tel: 0535-55 45 41
www.ryad-bahia.com
Intimate riad just off Place el Hedim in the thick of the medina action, brimful of traditional Moroccan character and with an excellent restaurant and friendly and informative hosts. **$$$**
Riad Felloussia
23 Derb Hammam Jdid
Tel: 0535-53 08 40
www.riadfelloussia.com
A low-key riad in the heart of the medina, with some of the best views in Meknes and four colourful suites carefully decorated with Moroccan and African arts and crafts. Staff are very helpful and will arrange excursions into the surrounding region and to Volubilis, Moulay Idriss and Azrou. **$$$**
Riad Lahboul
6 Derb Ain Sefli

Tel: 0535-55 98 78
www.riadlahboul.com
Beautifully restored traditional Moroccan guesthouse, ideally situated on the edge of the medina. The seven simple but inexpensive and tastefully decorated rooms come with air conditioning and Wi-fi, and staff can organise cooking, dancing and music workshops, as well as wine-tasting tours at nearby vineyards. **$$**

Moulay Idriss

Dar Zerhoune
45 Derb Zouak
Tel: 0642-24 77 93
http://buttonsinn.com
A charming little *dar* – one of the nicest places to stay in Moulay Idriss. Trips to Volubilis, visits to the nearby Roman hot springs and riding picnics in the countryside can all be arranged. **$$**

THE MIDDLE ATLAS

Azrou

La Perle d'Azrou
Ait Ameur ou Ali, 7km (4 miles) from Azrou
Tel: 0610-13 59 15
www.laperledazrou.com
Idyllic farmstay on the outskirts of Azrou, set amongst orchards and woodlands with sweeping views over the surrounding countryside. Accommodation is in neat and colourful rooms, while activities include trekking, fishing and horse riding, plus relaxing massages. **$$**

Ifrane

Hôtel des Perce Neige
3 Hay Riad, Rue des Asphodelles
Tel: 0535-56 63 50
Simple but comfortable mid-range option. Rooms all come with TV and bathrooms, and there's Wi-fi in the lobby and decent food in the in-house restaurant (licensed). **$$**

Hotel Mischliffen
Avenue Hassan II (Ifrane–Fez road)
Tel: 0535-56 66 07
Renovated in 2010 and now the top place to stay in Ifrane, this huge hotel-cum-ski lodge on a hill overlooking Ifrane resembles a little bit of Switzerland in the heart of Morocco, with wooden decor reminiscent of an alpine chalet, luxury fittings throughout and a pair of pools. **$$$$**

Immouzzer du Kandar

Le Gîte du Lac Dayet Aoua
Km 7, D'Imouzzer d'Ifrane
Tel: 0535-61 05 75
www.gite-dayetaoua.com
Cosy and affordable chalet-style guesthouse around 7km (4 miles) out of Immouzer on the road to Ifrane, offering a range of activities including horse riding, canoeing and guided mountains walks. **$**

Hôtel des Truites
Avenue Mohammed V
Tel: 0535-66 30 02
www.lestruites.com
Simple but comfortable and very affordable rooms in an old family-run hotel. The cosy bar–restaurant has a good reputation for its locally sourced food, including Atlas trout. **$**

Cascades d'Ouzoud

Riad Cascades d'Ouzoud
Tanant-Azilal, Ouzoud

PRICE CATEGORIES

Price categories are for a double room with bath (if available) per night in high season:
$ = up to 350dh
$$ = 350–750dh
$$$ = 750–1,250dh
$$$$ = over 1,250dh, though it can be a lot more.

Tel: 0662-14 38 04
www.ouzoud.com
Attractive guesthouse with simple
but attractively decorated rooms
and stunning views from its terrace
over the surrounding hills. Also does
delicious country food – worth a
visit for lunch if visiting the nearby
waterfalls. **$$$**

Sefrou

Dar Attamani
414 Bastna
Tel: 0535-96 91 74
www.darattamani.com
A lovely and intimate 100-year-old
maison d'hôte with just five afforable
rooms (or sleep on the terrace in
summer for just €10) and lots of
private places to relax dotted about.
Exceptional service, good food and
trips into the region can be arranged.
$$

La Mamounia.

MARRAKECH

Marrakech has the most diverse
range of accommodation in Morocco,
from charming little guesthouses to
hip boutique riads to luxury resorts
and large chain hotels. Despite this
plethora of rooms, it is still essential
to book in advance, especially over
Christmas, New Year and Easter. If
you arrive without a hotel booking
and have difficulty finding a room, try
the streets off Avenue Mohammed V
in Gueliz, where there are many two-
and three-star hotels, or the narrow
lanes immediately south of the
Jemaa el Fna and east of Rue de Bab
Agnaou, dotted with dozens of basic
little guesthouses.

Medina and Gueliz

Dar Attajmil
23 Rue Laksour
Tel: 0524-42 69 66
www.darattajmil.com
Magical riad, set around a leafy
courtyard. Owned by an Italian lady
who has excellent advice on things
to do in Marrakech and surrounding
areas. Four individually decorated
en suite rooms. Cooking classes
available. **$$$**

Dar el Souk
56 Derb Jdid
Tel: 0524-39 15 68
www.darelsouk.com/riad
Located in a great part of the
medina just steps from Jemaa el
Fna, this immensely popular flower-
filled riad has individually decorated
rooms with private outside seating
areas, plus terrific views from the

two cushion-covered roof terraces.
$$$

Dar Soukaina
19 Derb el Farrane
Tel: 0524-37 60 54
www.darsoukaina.com
Blissfully peaceful, simply decorated
little riad with charming rooms
set around two lovely courtyards
shaded by a huge orange tree, plus a
secluded roof terrace and Berber tent.
Dinner available on request. **$$**

Dar Tchaikana
25 Derb el Ferrane
Tel: 0524-38 51 50
www.tchaikana.com
It's all about attention to detail at
this super-stylish and consistently
recommended riad. The staff are as
welcoming and discreet as the decor,
and the food is excellent. **$$$**

Hotel Essaouira
3 Sidi Bouloukate
Tel: 0524-44 38 05
One of the best of the dozens of little
guesthouses dotting the honeycomb
of alleys south of the Jebel el Fna,
with ultra-cheap rates and attractive,
simple accommodation in a pretty
riad. Friendly and spotlessly clean
with a great roof terrace. **$**

Les Jardins de la Medina
21 Derb Choutka
Tel: 0524-38 18 51
www.lesjardinsdelamedina.com
Large and luxurious riad on the
southern edge of the Kasbah, with
lush gardens and a beautiful pool,
plus a good restaurant and in-house
cooking school. **$$$$**

La Maison Arabe
1 Derb Assehbe
Tel: 0524-38 70 10
www.lamaisonarabe.com
Beautiful riad hotel, full of antiques,
with elegant rooms and lots of cosy
places to sit. There's also a fine-
dining Moroccan restaurant and one
of the city's best cookery schools,
plus spa and pool. **$$$$**

La Mamounia
Avenue Bab Jdid
Tel: 0524-38 86 00
www.mamounia.com
The Grand Old Lady of Marrakech,
between the medina and Gueliz,
combining old-world-style with
modern five-star luxuries. All rooms
have a view of the magnificent
gardens and Atlas Mountains,
and there are four restaurants
– Moroccan, Italian, French and
seafood – five bars, spa and casino
(www.grandcasinomamounia.com).
$$$$

Riad 72
72 Arset Awsel
Tel: 0524-38 76 29
www.riad72.com
Perfectly designed boutique riad
close to Bab Doukkala, with just four
grand rooms. The roof terrace is one
of the highest in the medina and
has wonderful views and complete
privacy. **$$$**

Riad el Fenn
Derb Moullay Abdullah Ben Hezzian, Bab el
Ksour
Tel: 0524-44 12 10
www.riadelfenn.com

Decadent bohemian luxury, spread over four riads knocked into one, with 21 uniquely designed suites, three pools, a bar and two restaurants, The spectacular roof terrace with plunge pool lies in the shadow of the Koutoubia Mosque, and there's also a spa, library, movie room and organic garden. **$$$$**

Riad Porte Royale
84 Derb el Maada, Diour Jdad
www.riadporteroyale.com
Lovingly restored by an English writer, Riad Porte Royale provides a calm oasis in the spiritual heart of the medina, filled with antiques and textiles from all over the world and with a pretty tiled plunge pool in the courtyard. **$$$**

Royal Mansour
Rue Abou Abbas el Sebti
Tel: 0524-80 80 80
www.royalmansour.com
One of the most spectacular – and spectacularly expensive – hotels in the country, built by Mohammed VI to celebrate the very best in Moroccan design and craftsmanship. Accommodation is in one of 53 private riads, each with its own plunge pool and sitting room, and there's exceptional dining at one of the three restaurants, with almost 100 chefs in attendance. **$$$$**

Hotel Sherazade
3 Derb Jemaa
Tel: 0524-42 93 05
www.hotelsherazade.com
Delightful, low-priced riad just south of Jemaa el Fna, run by helpful multilingual staff. There are 22 rooms, some with shared bathroom and lovely roof terraces. **$$**

La Sultana
403 Rue de la Kasbah
Tel: 0524-38 80 08
www.lasultanamarrakech.com
Luxury hotel next door to the Saadian Tombs in the southern medina, full of opulent orientalist touches. There is a jacuzzi on the roof, a delicious pool in the courtyard, and every corner of the hotel evokes the grandeur of Imperial Marrakech. **$$$$**

Tlaatawa Sitteen
63 Derb el Ferrane
Tel: 0524-38 30 26
Great budget option run by a charming Moroccan family. The traditional riad houses six simple but stylish rooms with shared *tadelakt* (lime plaster) bathrooms, and dinner is available on request. **$**

Hotel Toulousain
44 Rue Tarik Ben Ziad, Gueliz
Tel: 0524-43 00 33
www.hoteltoulousain.com

Long-running budget hotel in the heart of the Ville Nouvelle. Simple, good-value rooms (some with shared bathroom) are set around a pair of attractive courtyards, and the peaceful atmosphere and friendly staff offer a welcome respite after a day navigating the souks. **$**

Villa des Orangers
6 rue Sidi Mimpoun
Tel: 0524-38 46 38
www.villadesorangers.com
Although situated in the heart of the medina, this lovely old riad feels almost like a country villa, complete with an incredible terrace pool and a wonderfully lush courtyard garden – as well as two further pools, spa and hammam. Very expensive. **$$$$**

Further afield

Amanjena
Route de Ouarzazate, Km 12
Tel: 0524-39 90 00
www.amanjena.com
One of Marrakech's ultimate luxury hotels, with palatial pavilions and villas in crisp modern Moroccan design set among beautiful gardens. There's also seriously good food in Thai and Spanish restaurants, spa, library and a huge, decadent pool. **$$$$**

Beldi Country Club
Route du Barrage, Km 6
Tel: 0524-38 39 50
www.beldicountryclub.com
A wonderful retreat, set in extensive rose gardens 15 minutes outside Marrakech. Rooms are decorated in rustic style and there's a wonderful pool and great artisanal workshops in the attached 'souk' where you can buy pottery, linens and carpets. **$$$$**

Les Deux Tours
Douar Abiad, Palmeraie
Tel: 0524-32 95 27
www.les-deuxtours.com

Riad el Fenn, Marrakech.

One of the oldest and most beautiful hotels in the Palmeraie. Built by Tunisian architect Charles Boccara as his private home, the gardens are jungly and beautiful, the pool sublime and the rooms all unique (some have their own private pool). Understated luxury in a wonderfully romantic setting. **$$$$**

Jnane Tamsna
Douar Abiad, Palmeraie
Tel: 0524-32 84 84
www.jnanetamsna.com
Set in stunning organic gardens, Tamsna has 24 secluded and sumptuous suites, set in three houses, which really feel like your own private home. The living spaces are filled with wonderful art and books and the home-grown food is delicious. **$$$$**

Ksar Char Bagh
Djnan Abiad, Palmeraie
Tel: 0524-32 92 44
www.ksarcharbagh.com
This exquisite hotel, set in large, pristine gardens, has some of the best food in Marrakech and one of the most decadent hammams – not to mention its very own London black cab, a 34-metre (112ft) heated pool, a wonderful library with over a thousand books. **$$$$**

La Pause
Douar Lmih Laroussiene, Commune Agafay
Tel: 0661-30 64 94
www.lapause-marrakech.com
Idyllic retreat 40 minutes from Marrakech, in the heart of the beautiful Agafay Desert. There is no electricity here, just a few romantic Berber tents and a pool shaded by olive trees. Activities can be arranged including mountain biking, horse riding, camel bivouac treks and 'cross-country' golf. **$$$**

THE HIGH ATLAS

Kasbah Tamadot in the High Atlas.

Asni

Kasbah Tamadot
Route d'Imlil
Tel: 0524-36 82 00
www.kasbahtamadot.virgin.com
Richard Branson spotted this hilltop kasbah while hot-air ballooning here. He subsequently bought the property and transformed it into a luxury retreat with gorgeous Arabian Nights-style suites and very up-market Berber tents, plus spa, guided treks and day trips to Marrakech. $$$$

Imlil

Douar Samra
Tamatert, Imlil
Tel: 0524-48 40 34
www.douar-samra.com
Tranquil Berber lodge 2km (1 mile) up a dirt track from Imlil, with cosy rustic rooms, a tree house, traditional wood-burning hamman and stupendous views over the Atlas Mountains. $$

La Kasbah du Toubkal
Tel: 0524-48 56 11
www.kasbahdutoubkal.com
This stunning kasbah hotel has a variety of accommodation and is the best place to base yourself for treks up Jebel Toubkal. It's also run in partnership with the local Berber community, meaning that a percentage of all fees goes to the village association. $$$$

Ouirgane

Au Sanglier Qui Fume
Tel: 0524-48 57 07
www.ausanglierquifume.com
Characterful *auberge* with a hugely popular restaurant serving Franco-Moroccan cuisine – in the summer on a vine-shaded terrace, in winter in a cosy dining room. Lots of activities are on offer – from mountain biking to boules. $$
Chez Momo
Tel: 0524-48 57 04

www.aubergemomo.com
Beautiful hotel in traditional Berber style, set in olive groves by the river, and with lovely gardens offering fantastic views of the lake. There's also a small pool, good food, and trekking can be arranged. $$$
Domaine de la Roseraie
Taroudant Road, Km 60
Tel: 0524-43 91 28
www.laroseraiehotel.com
A great escape, folded into the mountains, with rose garden, pool and stunning views. Accommodation is in a mix of bungalows and apartments, and horse riding and trekking are available. $$$

Oukaimeden

Chez Juju
Oukaimeden
Tel: 0524-31 90 05
www.hotelchezjuju.com
This wonderful chalet-style lodge is the nicest place to stay in Oukaimeden with charming rooms and a wonderful restaurant serving warming casseroles – always full on snowy weekends. $$$

Ourika

Kasbah Bab Ourika
Tel: 0668-74 95 47
www.kasbahbabourika.com
Set in landscaped gardens on its own hilltop, with 360-degree views, this idyllic kasbah hotel has luxurious rooms and a wonderful pool. Lots of activities available, including trekking, skiing, mountain biking and various day-trips. $$$$

THE SOUTH

Erfoud

Auberge Derkaoua
Route Dunes de Sable et Merzouga
Tel: 0661-34 36 77
www.aubergederkaoua.com
Southeast of town, en route to the Merzouga Dunes, this complex of bungalows, rooms and tents is a haven of good food, charm and peace. $$

M'hamid

Dar Azawad
Douar Ouled Driss
Tel: 0524-84 87 30
www.darazawad.com
Just outside M'hamid, edging the first dunes of the Sahara, this is a great base for exploring Erg Chigagga,

offering beautifully decorated air-conditioned rooms plus pool and restaurant. Dar Azawad also runs a stunning luxury tented camp in the dunes. $$

Ouarzazate

Le Camp de l'Oasis
Tel: 0524-43 48 08
www.camps-nomades.com
Attractive tented camp in the heart of an ancient oasis in the shadow of the Atlas, 45 minutes from town. The tents are romantic, the simple food wonderful and the staff passionate about the region. $$
Dar Daif
Talmasla

Tel: 0524-85 49 47
www.dardaif.ma
Rambling, rustic and eco-friendly kasbah-style hotel on the outskirts of town overlooking the palmeraie, nicely decorated with local crafts. There's also a private hammam,

PRICE CATEGORIES

Price categories are for a double room with bath (if available) per night in high season:
$ = up to 350dh
$$ = 350–750dh
$$$ = 750–1,250dh
$$$$ = over 1,250dh, though it can be a lot more.

TRANSPORT

ACCOMMODATION

EATING OUT

ACTIVITIES

A – Z

LANGUAGE

and a wide range of activities and tours. **$$**

Skoura

Kasbah Ait Ben Moro
Tel: 0524-85 21 16
www.kasbahaitbenmoro.com
Atmospheric accommodation in an imposing old towered kasbah, with wonderful views over the sprawling Skoura oasis and traditional interiors featuring cool stone floors and Berber textiles. **$$$**

Taroudant

Dar Zitoune
Boutarial el Berrania
Tel: 0528-55 11 41
www.darzitoune.com
Modern hotel offering a range of bungalows, suites and luxurious Berber-style tents set in lovely gardens, plus a great pool, jacuzzi, hammam and spa. **$$$$**

La Gazelle d'Or
Route d'Amezgrou
Tel: 0528-85 20 39
www.gazelledor.com
Stunning luxury retreat just outside the medina, with chic pavilions decorated in cool contemporary Moroccan style and set amidst tranquil gardens. There's also a spa, and food comes straight from the hotel's organic farm.

Very expensive. **$$$$**
Palais Salam Hotel
Boulevard Moulay Ismail
www.hotel-palais-salam-taroudant.com
Historic four-star in a converted former palace built into the town walls, set amidst luxuriant gardens and with a pair of pools. **$$$**

Riad Maryam
140 Derb Maalem Mohamed
Tel: 0666-12 72 85
www.riadmaryam.com
Popular guesthouse with eight rooms around a shady courtyard in an old 19th-century house. Good local food, and the helpful Moroccan owners can arrange local excursions. **$$$**

AGADIR AND THE DEEP SOUTH

Agadir

Hotel Atlantic
Ave Hassan II
Tel: 0528-84 36 61,
www.atlantichotelagadir.com
Appealing three-star resort with attractive rooms and more facilities than you'd expect at the price including a private section of beach, spa and a pretty little pool. **$$**

Riad Villa Blanche
Baie des Palmiers, Bensergao
Tel: 0528-21 13 13
www.riadvillablanche.com
One of the top hotels in town, this beautiful boutique riad-style hotel is set close to the beach, with 28 rooms, pool, spa and library. **$$$$**

Hotel Riu Tikida Beach
Chemins des Dunes
Tel: 0528-84 54 00
www.riu.com
Huge resort-hotel, with well-equipped modern rooms and private beach, plus numerous activities and facilities including a spa, golf course and popular nightclub. A minumum three- or five-night stay often applies. **$$$$**

Hotel Sindibad
Place Lahcen Tamri
Tel: 0528-82 34 77
Inexpensive and well-run hotel overlooking a lively central square (about 20 minutes to the beach) with 55 air-conditioned rooms, plus

PRICE CATEGORIES

Price categories are for a double room with bath (if available) per night in high season:
$ = up to 350dh
$$ = 350–750dh
$$$ = 750–1,250dh
$$$$ = over 1,250dh, though it can be a lot more.

restaurant and a small rooftop pool. **$**
Sofitel Agadir Thalassa Sea & Spa
Baie des Palmiers, Cité Founty P5
Tel: 0528-38 80 00
www.sofitel.com
Enormous modern five-star resort right on the beach, with all amenities imaginable, including a private beach, one of Morocco's largest swimming pools and an attractive thalassotherapy centre. **$$$$**

Dakhla

Ocean Vagabond
PK 27 route d'El Argoub
Tel: 0613-03 78 61,
www.oceanvagabond.com
At the foot of Dakhla's sand dunes, with accommodation in chic wooden huts, and water coming from naturally warm springs. Meals are served, and a range of water sports are available. **$$$**

Immouzer des Ida Outanane

Hôtel des Cascades
Tel: 0528-21 88 08
www.cascades-hotel.net
Attractively old-fashioned hotel in a fine location high above Paradise Valley at the start of a 4km (2-mile) path down to the splendid Immouzer Des Ida Outanane waterfalls. Facilities include a lovely pool, and there are great views from all 27 bedrooms. **$$**

Laâyoune

Hotel Nagjir Ville
Place de La Resistance
Tel: 0528-89 41 68
www.hotel-nagjir.com
One of the more reliable of Laâyoune's small and overpriced selection of hotels – the building's ugly and the decor is dated, but it's at least clean and comfortable, and

with above-average service at a reasonably sensible rate. **$$**

Mirleft

Les 3 Chameaux
Tel: 0528-71 91 87
www.3chameaux.com
Wonderful converted hilltop fort overlooking the Atlantic with huge rooms, pleasant public areas and great food. There's also a pool and hammam, and treks, horse riding and various water sports can be arranged. **$$$$**

Sidi Ifni

Xanadu
5 Rue el Jadida
Tel: 0528-87 67 18
www.maisonxanadu.com
A chic, tranquil *maison d'hôte*, just 10 minutes from the beach. The five rooms are brightly coloured and spacious and there's a lovely terrace for breakfast and communal dinners in the evening. **$$**

Tafraoute

Hôtel Les Amandiers
Tel: 0528-80 00 08
www.hotel-lesamandiers.com
Kasbah-style hotel in a wonderful location above town. Rooms (all en-suite) could do with an upgrade, but rates are very reasonable, and there's also a restaurant, bar and pool. **$$**

Tan Tan

Hotel Afra
Avenue Biranzarane
Tel: 0528-76 50 16
www.hotelafra.ma
Basic, but perfectly clean and welcoming hotel in the centre of town with 30 comfy, competitively priced rooms and a decent restaurant. **$**

EATING OUT

RECOMMENDED RESTAURANTS, CAFÉS AND BARS

WHERE TO EAT

Morocco is home to one of the world's classic cuisines – although most actual Moroccans tend not to eat out, meaning that the majority of more upscale restaurants are mainly aimed at – and patronised by – tourists. Excellent Moroccan restaurants can be found in all major towns and cities, while there are almost as many fine-dining French restaurants – and lots of places offer a mix of Moroccan and French dishes, with maybe a few other Italian or pan-European style offerings thrown in for good measure. There are decent restaurants in all the big hotels, although many of the very best places to eat are found either in independent restaurants or in up-market riads, offering a winning combination of superb food in an unforgettably romantic setting. Some places also preserve a traditional Arabian-style dining arrangement, with low banquette seats set against the wall, and even lower tables – fun, if not always terribly comfortable.

It's generally a good idea to book at more up-market places. Most serve alcohol, although it's never cheap.

Eat like the locals

Food stalls in places like the Jemaa el Fna in Marrakech, Place el Hedim in Meknes and around the western end of the medina in Rabat are always a good option, with crowds of locals (and tourists), great billowing clouds of smoke and an array of stalls selling everything from sheep's heads to snails. Standards of hygiene may make some visitors nervous, but trade is reassuringly brisk and the food is usually safe to eat, though be more wary during the very hot months of July and August. Elsewhere, cheaper eating options are often restricted to uninspiring shwarma stalls and cafés selling slices of pizza or rotisserie chicken.

Menu decoder

The following are the staples of Moroccan menus.

Briouats: deep-fried parcels of flaky pastry containing spiced meat, fish or cheese.

Brochettes: cubes of meat on skewers, most often lamb or beef.

Couscous: a huge bowl of steamed semolina grains with vegetables, chickpeas and meat – usually mutton or chicken – but sometimes fish. It's supposed to be eaten using your fingers, but spoons are generally provided. It is more of a domestic meal than a meal eaten out, and if you are invited to a Moroccan home you are most likely to be given this. Traditionally it is eaten on Fridays.

Djej: chicken. A favourite chicken dish is *djej mqualli*, chicken tagine with preserved lemons and green olives.

Harira: thick, spicy, sometimes creamy soup, based on lamb and pulses. It's often offered as a starter, but it is filling enough to be a meal in itself. During Ramadan it is served daily to break the fast, often with milk and dates.

Hout: fish. On menus, you will often find this under its French names – *loup de mer* (bass), *rouget* (red mullet), merlan (whiting), *thon* (tuna).

Kefta: meatballs flavoured with coriander and cumin. A popular and quick standby, it is sometimes served with eggs in a tagine.

Khobz: bread for mopping up *harira* or tagines; the traditional flat, round loaves are ideal. Fairly dry, with a grainy texture. Leftover bread is made into breadcrumbs and combined with honey, flaky pastry and nuts to make sweets.

Mechoui: whole lamb, spit or oven roasted. *Mechoui* is usually found only on special occasions or in the more traditional restaurants where it often needs to be ordered in advance, though there are places that sell it year-round.

Merguez: spicy beef or lamb sausages, often served with harissa sauce.

Pastilla: classic Moroccan pie, with meat encased in layers of flaky *warkha* pastry, often dusted with sugar or cinnamon – a traditional delicacy. Pigeon meat is traditionally used, although nowadays chicken (or even fish) is often substituted.

Tagine: Morocco's signature dish, cooked in a distinctive conical tagine vessel and comprising a stew of meat (usually beef, lamb or chicken) or fish with vegetables, spices and perhaps fruits and nuts, slowly cooked on a bed of oil in an earthenware pot. Popular versions include beef with almonds and quinces, lamb with apricots, and chicken with lemons and olives.

TRANSPORT

ACCOMMODATION

EATING OUT

ACTIVITIES

A – Z

LANGUAGE

TANGIER

As well as the restaurants listed below, many of Tangier's popular beach bars have restaurants, and also provide changing facilities and sunbeds (for around 50dh a day). Fans of the British playwright Joe Orton may want to visit the **Windmill**, frequented by Orton during his stays in Tangier but pretty sedate in its current incarnation.

Anna e Paolo
77 Avenue du Prince Héritier
Tel: 0539-94 46 17
Cosy, family-run, family-friendly traditional Italian restaurant with a wonderfully relaxed atmosphere and all the simple Italian favourites, from carpaccio to squid risotto and pizza. Excellent value for money. **$$**

Casa d'Italia
Palais des Institutions Italiennes (Palais Moulay Hafid)
Tel: 0539-93 63 48
Wonderfully nostalgic Italian restaurant in a faded palace, much loved by Tangier's expats. Serves basic but delicious home-made Italian favourites and excellent pizzas both inside and on the simple terrace. **$$**

Chez Abdou
Forêt Diplomatique, Km 17 Route de Larache Rabat
Tel: 0533-31 91 86
The best-kept secret in Tangier and beloved lunchtime refuge for Tangier's expats, Abdou's is a riot of pastel colours and crazy sculpture, set on a sweeping stretch of beach. It serves up some of the most fantastic fresh seafood anywhere in Morocco, at some of the cheapest prices. Justifiably packed at weekends. **$$**

Darna
9 Rue el Boughaz
Tel: 0539-33 35 58
Darna (meaning 'house'; www.darna

maroc.org) is an organisation that houses street children and women in need and teaches them all the skills necessary to reintegrate into society. Their restaurant is situated in an attractive courtyard; it serves good and very reasonably priced meals, and there's also a shop selling clothing and other items produced by the Darna women. **$**

Le Fabrique
7 Rue d'Angleterre
Tel: 0539-37 40 57
Next to Tangier's Great Mosque on a quiet side street, this immensely popular, crisply modern restaurant with split-level dining serves up delicious French food with a subtle Asian twist. **$$$$**

El Korsan
Hotel Minzah, 85 Rue de la Liberté
Tel: 0539-33 34 44
Tangier's most lavish Moroccan restaurant serves excellent traditional Moroccan food. There are stunning views of the Straits of Gibraltar through huge windows, and live music some evenings. **$$$$**

Le Nabab
4 Rue el Kadiria
Tel: 0661-44 22 20
One of the most popular Moroccan restaurants in town, in a restored riad with an elegant *Thousand and One Nights* design and a menu of fine modern Moroccan cuisine, such as lamb and artichoke tagine. **$$$**

Ô Saveur
15 Rue Boubana, at the junction with Rue Cavendish
Tel: 0539-94 96 60
Just outside town in what feels like a villa in the south of France, a French husband-and-wife team have created a magical oasis serving delicious salads, risottos, fish and wonderful desserts. The interior is almost as

lovely as the garden. **$$$**

Le Pagode
3 Rue el Boussouri
Tel: 0539-93 80 86
A refreshing alternative to endless tagines and couscous, this good Chinese restaurant in the heart of town serves up classic Chinese dishes in a pleasant ambience. **$$**

Le Relais de Paris
Complexe Dawliz, 42 Rue Hollande
Tel: 0539-33 18 19
Excellent French brasserie (plus bar lounge) with wonderful views of the Straits of Gibraltar from its terrace and good old-fashioned French cuisine, from foie gras to sirloin steak. **$$$**

Le Restaurant
Hotel Club Le Mirage, next to the Caves of Hercules
Tel: 0539-33 33 32
www.lemirage.com
Situated in the five-star Mirage Hotel, on the edge of a cliff overlooking a huge sweep of beach, this glamorous restaurant – a reminder of the glory days of Tangier – has stunning views and excellent French food to match. **$$$$**

Le Salon Bleu
71 Rue Amrah, Kasbah
Tel: 0662-11 27 24
www.facebook.com/salonbleutanger
Opposite the Kasbah Museum is this charming little blue-and-white restaurant spread over multiple floors, including a breezy roof terrace with sea views. Simple but delicious Moroccan food with some Mediterranean additions. **$$**

Essential ingredients.

THE RIF

Al Hoceima

Fish stalls
Behind the bus station
The best budget eating option in Al Hoceima, these busy snack bars close to the bus station serve inexpensive plates of freshly barbecued fish and brochettes. **$**

Club Nautique
Port d'Al Hoceima
Tel 0539-98 14 61
Attractive harbour restaurant with port views and fresh fish straight out

of the boat grilled for you on request – and the terrace bar is a nice place for a drink even if you're not eating. **$$**

Chefchaouen

Aladdin
17 Rue Targi
Tel: 0539-98 90 71
www.aladinchefchaouen.com
Homely restaurant with indoor and outdoor seating and a good selection of traditional Moroccan favourites.

Slightly pricier than other nearby places, although the views from the upstairs terrace compensate. **$$**

La Lampe Magique
17 Rue Targui
Tel: 0539-98 90 71
Purple walls, red cushions, low tables and candles everywhere – this is definitely one of the most colourful and exotic places to eat in town. The food isn't amazing, but the views are great and the prices very cheap. **$**

Restaurant el Mokhtar
Avenue Moulay Abderahmane Chrif
Tel: 0661-59 54 91
Friendly place serving simple but good-value salads, tagines, omelettes, sandwiches and fresh juices – and as popular with locals as with tourists. **$**

Tissemlal Restaurant
Casa Hassan, 22 Rue Targui
Tel: 0539-98 61 53
www.casahassan.com/en/tissemlal-restaurant
Pleasant Moroccan restaurant off the main square, serving tasty Moroccan staples at reasonable prices. Eat in the restaurant downstairs (comprising several rooms, plus fireplace) or

Ideal barbecue food.

on the upstairs terrace, prettily illuminated with lanterns and candles after dark. **$$**

Tetouan

Palais Bouhlal
48 Jamaa el Kebir

Tel: 0670-85 95 63
Situated behind the Great Mosque in the medina, the plush Palais Bouhlal serves decent tagines, couscous and *pastilla* in an Arab-Andalusian house. Favoured by tour groups, who are often entertained by musicians. **$$**

NORTHWEST COAST

Asilah

Casa Garcia
Rue Moulay Hassan Ben el Mehdi
Tel: 0539-41 74 65
Popular and long-established restaurant on the corniche serving up good Spanish-style fish and seafood dishes including a memorable paella. **$$**

Restaurante Oceana Casa Pepe
8 Plaza Zalaka
Tel: 0539-41 73 95
One of the best of several fish restaurants clustered outside the medina gates, dishing up simply cooked sardines, squid, swordfish,

prawns and sole served with bread and salads. Tables are set out on the pavement in summer. Licensed. **$$**

Restaurant Yali
Avenue Hassan II
Tel: 0539-04 32 77
One of a row of bustling cafés along this section of street, Yali is uninspiring but serves decent, simple food – omelettes, tagines, couscous and fish – at good cheap prices. Excellent for a quick lunch stop and people-watching. **$**

Restaurant de la Place
7 Avenue Moulay Hassan Ben, Al Mehdi
Tel: 0539-41 73 26

Serving fish, seafood and traditional Moroccan cuisine, this is a popular place in the summer, when the outside seating is always full, and there's a cosy candlelit interior for the evenings or winter days. No alcohol. **$$**

Larache

El Khozama
114 Avenue Mohammed V
Tel: 0539-91 44 54
One of the best of Larache's unremarkable selection of restaurants, serving seafood and meat dishes, with a lunchtime menu and à la carte in the evenings. **$$**

RABAT

Le Bistrot du Pietri
4 Rue de Tobrouk
Tel: 0537-70 78 20
www.lepietri.com
A lovely brasserie, popular with locals for its good Moroccan and European food. There's live jazz on Tuesdays, Fridays and Saturdays, and it's also a nice place for a drink. **$$**

Dinarjat
6 Rue Belgnaoui, Medina
Tel: 0537-70 42 39
www.dinarjat.com

Excellent traditional Moroccan food – *pastilla*, tagines, couscous and brochettes – in a beautiful old 17th-century house, with Andalusian music adding to the restaurant's refined atmosphere. **$$$**

Le Grand Comptoir
279 Avenue Mohammed V
Tel: 0537-20 15 14
www.legrandcomptoir.ma
This stylish 1930s Art Deco 'Parisien brasserie' bar-restaurant serves good classic French dishes and is one of

Rabat's favourite places to see and be seen with live music in the lounge bar from Thursday to Saturday. **$$$**

PRICE CATEGORIES

Prices refer to the cost of a meal per person, excluding alcohol (if available):
$ = under 100dh
$$ = 100–200dh
$$$ = 200–350dh
$$$$ = more than 350dh

TRANSPORT

ACCOMMODATION

EATING OUT

ACTIVITIES

A – Z

LANGUAGE

Le p'tit beur (Dar Tagine)
8 Rue Damas
Tel: 0537-73 13 22
One of the best traditional
restaurants in town, with (as its
name suggests), excellent tagines,
pastilla and couscous, while the

waiters double as musicians,
providing a discreet oud and drum
accompaniment when not serving
food. **$$**

Villa Mandarine
19 Rue Ouled Bousbaa, Souissi
Tel: 0537-75 20 77

www.villamandarine.com
Some way from the centre of town
in the pleasant garden suburb of
Souissi (Agdal), but worth the taxi fare
for the chance to sample a refined
French-Moroccan menu in a beautiful
mansion. **$$$**

CASABLANCA AND SOUTH OF CASABLANCA

Casablanca

A Ma Bretagne
Boulevard de la Corniche, near the Koubba
of Sidi Abderrahman around 5km (3 miles)
from the city centre
Tel: 0522-36 21 12
Sometimes claimed to be the best
restaurant in Morocco, overseen
by André Halbert, one of just three
maitre cuisiniers de France currently
working in Africa. The main focus is
on fish and seafood, backed up by
a fine wine list and served in a chic
dining room designed by Philippe
Starck protégé Brigitte Martinez with
breezy ocean views. **$$$$**

La Bavaroise
131 Rue Allal Ben Abdallah, behind the
Central Market
Tel: 0522-31 17 60
Stately old French-style restaurant
opened in 1968 and still claiming to
serve the best beef in Morocco, along
with various other meat and fish
dishes, plus oysters. Closed Saturday
lunchtime and all day Sunday. **$$$**

Chez Paul
Corner of boulevards Anfa and Moulay
Rachid
Tel: 0522-36 42 42
An offshot of the well-known French
chain, this stylish café-cum-*patisserie*
occupies a fine old Art Deco villa
and its garden. Good selection of
sandwiches and cakes, and a popular
destination for Sunday brunch. **$**

Al Mounia
95 Rue du Prince Moulay Abdallah, off the
Boulevard de Paris
Tel: 0522-22 26 69
Set in a beautiful walled garden and
richly tiled dining room, this is one of
the city's best places for traditional
Moroccan cuisine, serving sumptuous
tagines, *pastillas* and the like. Closed
on Sunday. **$$$**

Port de Pêche
Tel: 0522-44 13 90
Popular, no-frills little fish restaurant
down at the port with a basic choice
of fried or grilled fish, shrimps and
paella, served in huge portions and
with cheap – if rather rough – local
wine to wash it down with. **$**

Rick's Café
248 Boulevard Sour Jdid

Tel: 0522-27 42 07
American Kathy Kriger recreated this
courtyard café, set into the walls of
the medina, to replicate the famous
café from *Casablanca*. International
menu, nostalgic pianist. Surprisingly
easy to miss. **$$$**

La Sqala
Boulevard des Almohads
Tel: 0522-26 09 60
Popular and atmospheric café-
restaurant serving good Moroccan
food, with seating scattered in and
around a courtyard garden tucked
in behind a section of the old city
ramparts. **$$**

El Jadida

Restaurant du Port
Port d'el Jadida
Tel: 0523-34 25 79
Situated beyond the barrier in the
fishing port, this licensed restaurant
specialises in seafood from the
nearby fish market, with good
service and ambience, and views
in summer of local daredevil kids
jumping off the town ramparts.
Closed Sunday. **$$**

Oualidia

Hôtel Restaurant L'Initiale
Hôtel L'Initiale, Oualidia Plage
Tel: 0523-36 62 46
A bustling restaurant on the beach,
part of the Hôtel L'Initiale. Friendly

Rick's Café in Casablanca.

Moroccan fast food.

service, reasonable prices and
fantastic fish and seafood. And it's
licensed. **$$**

L'Ostréa II
Parc à Huitres No. 7
Tel: 0523-36 63 24
Peaceful seafood restaurant on the
lagoon, with a beautiful waterfront
terrace and surrounded by oyster
beds. Needless to say, oysters are
their speciality, along with market-
fresh lobster, crab, salmon and so
on. **$$**

THE SOUTHWEST COAST

Essaouira

Food Stalls
Place Moulay Hassan
Located near the port, Essaouira's popular food stalls (grillades) offer just-caught fish and seafood at bargain prices, including crab, sea urchin, langoustine, sole and shark. Pick your fish, have it weighed to determine the price and then grilled in front of you. **$**

Chalet de la Plage
Boulevard Mohammed V
Tel: 0524-47 59 72
Large portions of good French and international food at reasonable prices. The emphasis very much on fish – the bouillabaisse is very good, as are the sea urchins, when in season. It is possible just to drink at the bar and eat tapas. Very busy at weekends. **$$**

Elizir
1 Rue d'Agadir
Tel: 0524-47 21 03
Wonderfully quirky Moroccan restaurant in the heart of the medina decorated with Art Deco flea-market finds and adorned with an eclectic mix of artwork. The short but satisfying menu features a range of fish, pasta and authentic tagines. Open evenings only; reservations advised. **$$$**

Ferdaouss
27 Rue Abdesslam Lebadi
Tel: 0524-47 36 55
Tucked away down a side alley off the main drag, this little restaurant offers a taste of proper Moroccan home cooking amidst Essaouira's cosmopolitan culinary scene, with traditional couscous dishes and tagines, served sizzling dramatically to your table. **$$**

Laayoune
4 bis Rue el Hajjali
Tel: 0524-47 46 43
Very popular and excellent-value Moroccan restaurant, serving mainly tagines and couscous dishes (including good set menus), with traditional seating on low banquettes around candlelit tables. **$**

Restaurant d'Orient and d'Ailleurs
Rue Touahen 67 bis
Tel: 0524-47 59 77
www.dorientetdailleurs.com
Suave French-owned restaurant with a neat little dining room and (as its name suggests) superior Moroccan and European cuisine, including good-value set menus. Closed Saturday. **$$**

La Table Madada
7 Rue Youssef el Fassi (opposite the Madada Mogador hotel)
Tel: 0524-47 21 06
www.letablemadada.com
Built into the walls of the medina, this chic restaurant (formerly known as After 5) is one of the best in town, serving up top-notch Moroccan food using the freshest ingredients. There's also live music on Friday and Saturday, and good cookery classes. Open evenings only. **$$$**

Taros Café
Place Moulay Hassan, above Café-Restaurant Marrakech (entrance around the side of the building)
Tel: 0524-47 64 07
www.taroscafe.com
This popular bar-restaurant serves excellent Moroccan–French food with a twist. Seating is on a fabulous roof terrace-cum-bar with a relaxed, sunset-in-Ibiza atmosphere, a very mellow soundtrack and sweeping views over the sea and the square. **$$**

Triskala
Rue Touahen
Tel: 0655-58 51 31
Bustling Spanish-run café-restaurant in the shadow of the ramparts, occupying an atmospheric little vaulted dining room and serving up a short but excellent selection of daily-changing specials, beautifully presented and at giveaway prices. There's not much space, however, so arrive early or reserve. Open evenings only; closed Sunday. **$**

Fresh seafood in Essaouira.

FEZ AND MEKNES

Fez

Al Fassia
Sofitel Fès Palais Jamaï, Bab Guissa
Tel: 0535-63 43 31
www.sofitel.com
Set in one of Fez's most beautiful hotels, Al Fassia is one of the top Moroccan restaurants in town. Eat reclining on a velvet banquette inside the extravagantly decorated dining room – part of the original 1879 palace – or on the terrace outside, and there's also regular live Andalusian music and belly dancers. Open dinner only. **$$$$**

Café Clock
7 Derb el Magana, off Talaa Kbira
Tel: 0535-63 78 55
Popular café-cum-art gallery in a cavernous old courtyard house serving snacks, salads and light Moroccan and Mediterranean meals – try the camel burgers. Also runs good cookery classes. **$**

Restaurant Dar Hatim
19 Derb Ezaouia Fandak
Tel: 0535-666 52 53 23
A little gem tucked away in the heart of Fèz el Bali – the owner can arrange to have you collected you from your lodgings and guided to the restaurant, which is in his own small courtyard house, beautifully decorated. The fantastically good traditional Moroccan meals are home cooked by his mother and wife, and diners are often given a tour of the house as part of a meal. **$$**

La Maison Bleue
2 Place de L'Istiqlal
Tel: 0535-74 18 43
www.maisonbleue.com

PRICE CATEGORIES

Prices refer to the cost of a meal per person, excluding alcohol (if available):
$ = under 100dh
$$ = 100–200dh
$$$ = 200–350dh
$$$$ = more than 350dh

TRANSPORT

ACCOMMODATION

EATING OUT

ACTIVITIES

A – Z

LANGUAGE

Grilled meat in Meknes.

Up-market restaurant in an exclusive riad close to Bab Boujeloud, with a romantic atmosphere, live music and excellent, if pricey, Moroccan food. Reservations strongly recommended. **$$$$**

Medina Café
6 Derb Mernissi
Tel: 0535-63 34 30
Long-running café right next to Bab Boujeloud, consistently popular for its good, reasonably priced food and attractive decor. Better value than the nearby cluster of touristy places just inside the Bab Boujeloud entrance to the medina. **$$**

La Mezzanine
17 Ksbat Chams
Tel: 0535-63 86 68
Not far from Bab Boujeloud en route to Fez el Jedid, this hip modern venue offers an unlikely contrast with the nearby medina, serving up good tapas and contemporary French and Moroccan food. The chic roof terrace is a popular place for a (pricey) drink, especially after dark. **$$$**

Najmat Souafine
9 Oued Souafine
Tel: 0535-63 31 49
Cosy restaurant beautifully located in a former mill beside the river, *looking a bit like an old French wine cellar*. The emphasis is on fresh, seasonal, light food with a daily-changing menu offering contemporary versions of Moroccan (and a few Mediterranean) classics. **$$**

Palais de Fez
16 Rue Boutouil-Kairouyine (opposite the Kairouyine Mosque)
Tel: 0535-76 15 90
www.palaisdefes.com
In the deepest depths of the medina, this riad restaurant offers superb Fassi fare in an authentic setting – choose between the Moroccan-style dining room and rooftop terrace with magical views. Food features spectacular salads and excellent tagines and *pastilla*. Pricey, and service can be slow, but well worth waiting for. Live music. Licensed. **$$$**

<h3>Meknes</h3>

Collier de la Colombe
67 Rue Driba
Tel: 0535-55 50 41
Signs at the far end of Place Lalla Aouda direct you to this modern restaurant with stunning views from its dining room and outdoor terrace. Fresh Atlas Mountain trout and succulent *pastilla* are the specialities, along with plenty of other traditional Moroccan fare. **$$**

Le Dauphin
5 Avenue Mohammed V
Tel: 0535-52 34 23
Up-market French-style restaurant serving up a good selection of Moroccan and French meat and seafood, with seating either indoors in the attractive tiled dining room or in the tranquil garden. Licensed. **$$**

Marhaba Restaurant
23 Avenue Mohammed V
Tel: 0535-52 16 32
Extremely popular, this delightful little place serves excellent tagines, delicious *harira* soup, *brochettes* and other simple Moroccan favourites to a mainly local crowd, all at bargain prices. **$**

Restaurant Omnia
8 Derb Ain el Fouki
Tel: 0535-53 39 38
Tucked away just inside the entrance to the medina, this lovely family-run restaurant serves inexpensive and mouth-watering Moroccan specialities (along with some lesser-known recipes) in charming, traditionally decorated surroundings. **$$**

Restaurant Riad
Riad Meknes, 79 Ksar Chaacha-Dar Kebira
Tel: 0535-53 05 42
www.riadmeknes.com
Below the ramparts of the medina, beyond Place Lalla Aouda, this gorgeous garden restaurant in the attractive Riad Meknes is a good place for classic Moroccan specialities like *pastilla* and *mechoui*, along with the inevitable tagines and couscous. **$$$**

<h3>PRICE CATEGORIES</h3>

Prices refer to the cost of a meal per person, excluding alcohol (if available):
$ = under 100dh
$$ = 100–200dh
$$$ = 200–350dh
$$$$ = more than 350dh

MARRAKECH

Marrakech offers arguably the best choice of places to eat in Morocco, reflecting the presence of both wealthy Moroccan and expatriate communities and the large numbers of visitors. The options in Marrakech are endless and cater for every taste and budget. Like most places in Morocco, bear in mind that all but the high-end restaurants in the medina will only take cash. Most places in Gueliz (the *Ville Nouvelle*) take cards.

Medina

Food Stalls
Jemaa el Fna
Marrakech's iconic food stalls come alive at sunset and serve anything from grilled sheep heads and snails to delicious *merguez* sausages and *brochettes*. All places have menus with fixed prices (most mains around 30dh), although be aware that you'll

Aubergine salad.

often be charged extra for things like bowls of olives or bread which might appear to be free. Popular with both Moroccans and tourists, dinner here is accompanied by one of the greatest spectacles in the world. **$**

Café Arabe
184 Rue el Mouassine
Tel: 0524-42 97 28
www.cafearabe.com
Serving both Italian and Moroccan food, this popular restaurant has seating both in a courtyard and on a stunning roof terrace with superb medina views. A great place to stop for lunch or for a romantic dinner. **$$$**

Café des Epices
75 Rabha Kedima
Tel: 0524-39 17 70
www.cafedesepices.net
The best place in the medina to watch the world go by, with a laid-back atmosphere, good music, great

mint tea and a limited but delicious lunch menu, plus free Wi-fi. **$**

Chez Chegrouni
Jemaa el Fna
Tel: 065-47 46 15
One of the most popular spots on Jemaa el Fna, this old favourite serves simple but good quality Moroccan food at inexpensive prices, and there are also great views if you can bag on of the tables overlooking the square. **$**

Dar Moha
81 Rue Dar el Bacha
Tel: 0524-38 64 00
www.darmoha.ma
Set around a romantic pool in a beautiful villa that once belonged to French fashion designer Pierre Balmain and serving modern, inventive Moroccan cuisine – an amazing feast of flavours. **$$$$**

Dar Yacout
79 Sidi Ahmed Soussi
Tel: 0524-38 29 29
Enjoyable riad restaurant, expensive and unashamedly touristy, but with exquisite decor, terrific ambience and good live music. Food features a huge selection of classic Moroccan dishes, superbly cooked and presented. Booking essential. Closed Sunday. **$$$$**

Un Déjeuner à Marrakech
2–4 Place Douar Graoua
Tel: 0524-37 83 97
A café, tea salon and patisserie in the heart of the medina that is a firm local and tourist favourite. The food (from spinach and ricotta pies to hamburgers, club sandwiches and salads) is gorgeous, excellent value and great for vegetarians. Sit on the roof terrace if you can. **$**

Le Foundouk
55 Souk Hal Fassi Kat Bennahid
Tel: 0524-37 81 90
www.foundouk.com
A lovely medina restaurant offering up-market French and Moroccan cuisine in an attractively restored *foundouk* just north of the Medersa Ben Youssef. Closed Monday. **$$$**

Gastro MK
14 Derb Sebaai
Tel: 0524-37 61 73
www.maisonmk.com/gastro.htm
Top-notch Moroccan–French fusion cuisine showcased in a fabulous five-course tasting menu featuring fine-dining versions of local classics like chicken pastilla alongside contemporary European-style

dishes. Bookings essential. Closed Wednesday. **$$$$**

Pepe Nero
17 Derb Cherkaoui
Tel: 0524-38 90 67
www.pepenero-marrakech.com/en/contact.html
Top-rated restaurant specializing in a mix of classic Moroccan cuisine alongside tempting Italian dishes – mechoui, tagines, and fine homemade pastas – backed up by a quality wine list. Closed Monday. **$$$**

Terraces des Epices
15 Souk Charifia Sidi Abdelaziz
Tel: 0524-39 59 04
www.terrassedesepices.com
The sister establishment to Café des Epices, this fabulous roof-terrace restaurant serves excellent *tagines* and *couscous* dishes alongside light European meals, plus a good dessert selection. **$$**

Le Tobsil
22 Derb Moulay Abdellah Ben Hessaien
Tel: 0524-44 40 52
Lavish, daily-changing Moroccan set menus served in a beautiful riad lovingly restored by its French owner. Tricky to find, and reservations recommended so that staff can guide you to the restaurant. Closed Tuesday. **$$$$**

Villa Flore
4 Derb Azzouz
Tel: 0524-39 17 00
www.villa-flore.com
Part of a riad hotel, serving up good up-market Moroccan food given a French makeover, with the emphasis on fresh, seasonal local ingredients. Lighter and less expensive meals and snacks also available at lunchtime. **$$$**

Gueliz

L'Avenue
Corner of Route de Targa and Rue du Capitaine Arigui

Tel: 0524-45 89 01
www.lavenuemarrakech.com
High-quality French and Italian cuisine at this swanky bar-restaurant with big chandeliers, leather armchairs and plenty of wine glasses everywhere. **$$$$**

Bagatelle
103 Rue Yougoslavie
Tel: 0524-43 02 74
One of Marrakech's oldest restaurants, this attractively old-fashioned Parisian-style establishment was founded in 1949 and remains popular with locals and expats for its good, solid French food in convivial surroundings. **$$**

Café du Livre
44 Rue Tariq ibn Ziad (next to the Hôtel Toulousain)
Tel: 0524-43 21 49
Marrakech's first and only literary café, popular with expats and serving good breakfast, lunch and light dinners. The menu includes salads, sandwiches and bistro fare, backed up by a good drinks selection and proper pots of tea. Free Wi-fi and an interesting library of books to browse. **$$**

Al Fassia
55 Boulevard Zerktouni
Tel: 0524-43 40 60
www.alfassia.com
Excellent restaurant with a beautiful garden courtyard and a good menu of classic Moroccan dishes. Booking recommended. Closed Tuesday. **$$$**

Casanova
221 Avenue Yacoub el Mansour
Tel: 0524-42 37 35
One of the best Italians in Marrakech, offering a wide range of regional specialities (with wines to match) served either in the old-fashioned dining room or lovely garden. **$$$**

Le Comptoir Darna
Avenue Echouada
Tel: 0524-43 77 02
www.comptoirmarrakech.com
Excellent modern Moroccan and international cuisine in one of the most chic spots in town. Elegant belly dancing after dinner and a lively bar upstairs. **$$$$**

Grand Café de la Poste
Corner of Avenue Imam Malik and Boulevard el Mansour Eddhabi
Tel: 0524-43 30 38
The heart of the city's social scene for decades, set in the stunning colonial Art Deco post office, and with a wonderful bar upstairs. Food is French brasserie-style, with some Moroccan additions. **$$$**

Katsura
Rue Oum Errabia
Tel: 0524-43 43 58
Arguably the best Asian restaurant in town and good value too, serving delicious sushi, maki and other Japanese specialities along with Thai curries, soups and stir-fries. **$$**

Kechmara
3 Rue de la Liberté
Tel: 0524-42 25 32
Fashionable international restaurant in the heart of the Ville Nouvelle. Always packed at lunchtime on the roof terrace and in the evening, when there's a DJ most nights. Good-value lunchtime set menus. **$$**

Further afield

Le Flouka
Barrage Lalla Takerkoust
Tel: 0664-49 26 60
www.leflouka.com
A 40-minute drive from Marrakech at the edge of Lake Takerkoust in the shadow of the Atlas. Good hearty French food, much of it grilled, and served at tables set under shady trees and umbrellas next to the water. **$$**

THE HIGH ATLAS

Ouirgane

Au Sanglier Qui Fume
Tel: 0524-48 57 07
www.ausanglierquifume.com
A roadside *auberge* beside the lake in Ouirgane, which serves homely French and Moroccan cooking (including mechoui, and Berber bread cooked in a traditional tanourht oven) in the garden in summer and in a cosy restaurant inside in winter. Popular at weekends. **$$**

L'Oliveraie de Marigha
Marigha (3km/2 miles north of Ouirgane)

Tel: 0524-48 42 81
www.oliveraie-de-marigha.com
Notable more for its beautiful garden and swimming pool than the food, but still a great place for an open-air lunch and an escape from the city. **$$**

Ourika

Auberge le Maquis
Aghbalou
Tel: 0524-48 45 31
www.le-maquis.com
Neat little country restaurant specializing in traditional Moroccan

fare, including lots of fruity tagines (with figs, prunes, apricots and so on), plus Berber, Belboula and Fassi-style couscous dishes. Licensed. **$$**

PRICE CATEGORIES

Prices refer to the cost of a meal per person, excluding alcohol (if available):
$ = under 100dh
$$ = 100–200dh
$$$ = 200–350dh
$$$$ = more than 350dh

THE SOUTH

Ouarzazate

Chez Dimitri
22 Ave Mohammed V
Tel: 0524-88 73 46
Open since 1928, Dimitri's has
a French Foreign Legion feel,
complete with a large old-fashioned
bar, chunky wooden furniture and
military memorabilia on the walls. At
dinner there is usually a *table d'hôte*
menu as well as *à la carte*, with
choices including hearty casseroles,
often featuring rabbit or lamb.
$$

La Kasbah des Sables
195 Hay Aït Ksif
Tel: 0524-88 54 28
www.lakasbahdessables.com
Romantic restaurant in a gorgeously

restored old kasbah on the eastern
edge of town. Food is a mix of
modern Moroccan and European,
well prepared, and very reasonably
priced. **$$**

Le Relais de Saint Exupéry
13 Boulevard Moulay Abdellah
Tel: 0524-88 77 79
www.relais-ouarzazate.com
The top restaurant in town, overseen
by French chef and slow-food
enthusiast Jean-Pierre, and serving
excellent and inventive French-
and Moroccan-inspired cuisine.
Licensed. **$$**

Taroudant

Restaurant L'Agence
Boulevard Prince Heritier Sidi Mohamed

Tel: 0528-55 02 70
Easy to miss if you're not looking for
it, this pretty little restaurant scores
highly for its welcoming atmosphere
and above-average Moroccan
cooking. No alcohol. **$$**

Zagora

Hotel La Fibule du Draa
Route de M'hamid
Tel: 0524-84 73 18
A traditional Moroccan restaurant
in a pleasant hotel at the southern
end of town. All the classic
Moroccan dishes are on offer,
served at low tables in the vast
dining area or around the lovely
pool. **$$**

AGADIR AND THE DEEP SOUTH

Agadir

Agadir thinks of itself as a
cosmopolitan resort, and this
is reflected in the restaurants,
including several lovely waterside
establishments down in the modern
marina. It's also a great place for
fish, and for inexpensive dining you
can't do better than take a seat at
one of the makeshift stalls inside
the port where a plate of fried
squid, prawns and sardines costs
around 50dh.

Les Blancs
Marina d'Agadir
Tel: 0528-82 83 68
On the edge of the beach and in front
of the marina, this great restaurant
offers Spanish and Mediterranean

Moroccan coffee.

food including good tapas and various
paellas, plus home-made ice cream.
$$$

Da Rugantino
Complexe el Moggero
Tel: 0528-84 14 25
This seafront restaurant serves
reliable Italian food and fish dishes,
with friendly service and a pleasant
terrace from which to watch the world
go by. **$$**

La Madrague
Marina d'Agadir
Tel: 0528-84 24 24
Superbly situated on the sparkling
marina of Agadir, this elegant
restaurant serves fish, seafood and
Mediterranean cuisine, with French
wines. **$$$$**

Le Jardin d'Eau
Boulevard du 20 Août
Tel: 0528-84 01 95
www.jardindeau.com
Good international and Moroccan
food in an attractive restaurant
with tiled floors and wicker chairs
indoors, a large terrace and pretty
garden outside. Gets lively during
regular theme nights, including
salsa nights and 'soirées orientales'.
$$

Mimi La Brochette
Rue de la Plage
Tel: 0528-84 03 87
At the north end of the beach, Mimi's
cooking is a real treat, with Jewish,
French and Spanish influences and
a large menu including the best
brochettes (kebabs) in town. **$$**

Le Quai
Marina d'Agadir

Tel: 0661-60 58 22
Another of the chic modern
restaurants down at the Agadir
marina (with a large outdoor
terrace), this calm, minimalist place
serves up excellent Mediterranean
food, with an emphasis on fish.
$$$

La Scala
Rue Oued Sous
Tel: 0528-84 67 73
Good French restaurant specialising
in fish and seafood dishes
featuring locally caught salmon,
sea bream, oysters and so on,
along with excellent steaks, plus a
spacious terrace outside. Bookings
recommended. **$$$**

Yacht Club
Port d'Agadir
Tel: 0528-84 37 08
Romantic modern restaurant
overlooking the sea and specialising
in simple but excellent fish and
seafood – salmon, sea bream,
lobster and so on – fresh out of the
boat. Licensed. **$$$**

Tafraoute

Restaurant La Kasbah
Rue Aguerd-Oudad
Tel: 0672-30 39 09
One of the best of Tafraoute's
modest selection of restaurants,
serving good Moroccan cuisine
including their signature kalia
– a southern Moroccan speciality
featuring richly spiced, slow-cooked
lamb. Licensed. **$$**

ACTIVITIES

FESTIVALS, NIGHTLIFE, SHOPPING, SPORTS AND ACTIVITIES, HAMMAMS AND EXCURSIONS

FESTIVALS

The staple of festival life is the *moussem:* a local festival (or pilgrimage) in honour of a local holy man, though some are on a much larger scale, with ceremonial dancing and *fantasias* (displays of horsemanship). There are also folklore and harvest festivals in almost every village in Morocco, ranging from the Almond Blossom Festival of Tafraoute to the Date Festival in Erfoud. Music festivals are becoming increasingly popular – and incredibly numerous and varied, from the hugely popular Gnaoua World Music Festival, held in Essaouira (see page 175), to the Fez Festival of World Sacred Music (see page 198) and the lively Mawazine Music Festival in Rabat (see page 75), at which big-name international artists perform.

Moroccan festivals often provide the visitor with the best possible way to experience genuine Moroccan folk music, such as the music of the Gnaoua (see page 75), and

Marrakech dancers.

dance, like the Berber women's guedra dance, away from a tourist-oriented environment. They are also the cultural heart of Moroccan life, preserving traditions and passing them on for the next generation.

The *fantasia* is the most exciting of all Moroccan traditions, a breathtaking display of horsemanship. Charging horsemen perform daring manoeuvres and acrobatics, sometimes to the accompaniment of gunfire.

Calendar of events

The following is a list of all the major festivals, *moussems* and public holidays in Morocco. Exact dates should be confirmed in advance, as they change from year to year, with the exception of a few fixed national holidays. Note that most shops, banks and public offices are closed on public holidays. For details of Ramadan in Morocco, see page 331.

Islamic festivals

The major nationwide religious

festivals run according to the Islamic calendar, meaning that their dates according to the western calendar change constantly, falling approximately 11 days earlier year on year.

Mouloud (Milad un Nabi) National holiday commemorating the birth of the Prophet. 2 Jan 2015.

Eid ul Fitr Festival celebrating the end of Ramadan. 17 July 2015.

Eid al Adha Held 70 days after Eid ul Fitr, the 'Feast of the Sacrifice' commemorates the willingness of Abraham to sacrifice his own son, Isaac, according to the command of god. 5 Oct 2014.

Fatih Muharram (Islamic New Year) 25 Oct 2014.

January

New Year's Day Public holiday. 1 January.

Independence Manifesto Day Public holiday commemorating the manifesto demanding Morocco's independence from France. 11 January.

February

Almond Blossom Festival Tafraoute, southeast of Agadir, celebrates the almond harvest, with music, dance and a souk.

March

Salé *Moussem* Festival in honour of *marabout* Sidi Abdallah Ben Hassan.

Marathon des Sables This desert marathon (www.marathondessables.co.uk) is an extreme endurance test: six days on foot over 200km (124 miles) of desert.

Rose Petal Festival A beautiful festival in El Kelaa M'Gouna (near Ouarzazate) celebrating the local rose harvest.

April

Printemps Musical des Alizés d'Essaouira Five days of classical music in Essaouira (www.printemps musicaldesalizes.com), with concerts by top European performers. Late April/early May.

International Magic Festival Marrakech holds the largest magic festival in the world, with artists from all corners performing for four days.

Transahara Music Festival A trance music festival (www.nomadstribe.com) in the Sahara near Erfoud.

Festival of Sufi Culture Celebration of Sufi mysticism in Fez with music and dance.

May–June

Labour Day National public holiday. 1 May.

Mawazine Music Festival Rabat hosts Morocco's biggest music festival (www.festivalmawazine.ma) featuring big international artists.

June

Fez Festival of World Sacred Music (www.fesfestival.com). See page 198.

Benamar, Goulimime *Moussem* Festival commemorating Sidi M'Hamed featuring a large camel market; is both a religious and trading occasion.

Festival of Cherries Sefrou hosts another colourful harvest festival.

Gnaoua World Music Festival Essaouira is firmly on the cultural map with this weekend of fantastic Gnaoua and African music (www. festival-gnaoua.net/en/), which attracts thousands of people.

Desert Symphony Festival Ouarzazate. Featuring artists from Morocco and other countries, such as Mali, Mauritania and Senegal.

International Arts Festival Asilah's popular arts festival, attracting local and international exhibitors.

July

Marrakech National Festival of the Popular Arts Five-day event with fortune-tellers, artists, musicians, dancers and theatre troupes from across Morocco performing at various locations around the city. (www.marrakechfestival.com).

Moussem of **Outa Hammou** Chefchaouen's religious festival celebrating the life of this holy man.

Feast of the Throne A national celebration of the king's coronation. 30 July.

August

Moussem of Dar Zhirou Rabat.

Moussem of Setti Fatma Ourika Valley (near Marrakech).

Oued Ed Dahab Day Public holiday commemorating the return of the southern province of Oued Ed Dahab from Spanish control in 1979. 14 August.

Revolution Day A national holiday commemorating the revolution of 1953 and also the king's birthday, which falls on 21 August. 20 August.

September

Boulevard des Jeunes Musiciens Festival Casablanca's popular music festival (www.boulevard.ma), featuring Moroccan musicians.

Moussem of Moulay Idriss II Fez hosts Morocco's largest *moussem*, attracting thousands of pilgrims to the saint's tomb.

Imilchil Marriage Festival Now a world-famous event, where men and women from different tribes in the region can meet and become engaged.

Tanjazz Tangier's small but perfectly formed jazz festival (www.tanjazz.org).

National *Fantasia* **Festival** Meknes holds a *fantasia* on an epic scale.

October

Taliouine Saffron Festival Annual celebration of the saffron harvest in the southern town of Taliouine.

November

Date Festival A *moussem* in Erfoud to celebrate the date harvest, so important in Morocco.

Green March Public holiday commemorating the anniversary of Morocco's 'march' into Western Sahara in 1975. 6 November.

Independence Day Public holiday celebrating the day Morocco gained independence from France in 1956. 18 November.

December

International Film Festival Marrakech's glitzy film festival (www.festivalmarrakech.info), with screenings and plenty of Hollywood movie stars.

NIGHTLIFE

Marrakech is arguably Morocco's premier destination for nightlife, and with the best bars, clubs and music, the fun continues until about 4am. Many clubs, such as Theatro (www.theatromarrakech. com) and the So Night Lounge (www.

soloungemarrakech.com) are found in hotels (Es Saadi and Sofitel respectively) and most of the bars and newer up-market clubs are in Hivernage (Le Comptoir Darna; comptoirmarrakech.com/en) or just outside (Pacha; www.pachamarrakech. com) and fall either into the Moroccan cabaret or Western club categories. However, late-night lounge bars and restaurants such as the busy Jad Mahal (www.jad-mahal.com) are becoming increasingly popular. It also must win the prize for most exciting city at night with the most Moroccan feel with the activity on the Jemaa el Fna that can keep going until dawn.

Resort nightlife is restricted to Tangier, Casablanca and its outskirts (Ain Diab and Mohammedia) and Agadir (where it is, in fact, fairly subdued).

Tangier still lays claim to being the city that keeps the latest hours, and this is certainly true in July and August. As well as late bars and hotel discotheques, the kitsch-but-fun Morocco Palace (11 Avenue Prince Moulay Abdellah) offers belly dancing and disco dancing well into the early hours. Some of the beach bars also offer nightlife.

Casablanca has a cosmopolitan and sophisticated nightlife scene that includes international live music, late-night eating and nightclubs. Most of the clubs are along the corniche.

Bars

Bars are a late 20th-century addition to Moroccan nightlife, and not always a happy one. It's as though they are symbols of the clash between Islamic Morocco, with its tradition of total abstinence from alcohol, and Moroccan modernity, with its liberal, urban, Westernised way of thinking. Bars can be loud and intimidating (especially for women) or furtive and uneasy, and, in the case of local dive bars, often male-dominated, though some of them (particularly in more relaxed Tangier) have a certain appeal. **Hotel bars** are a different matter, but can be expensive and often characterless.

The best bar scene is found in Tangier and Marrakech.

Gambling

Marrakech There are casinos in the Mamounia and Es Saadi hotels. The Mamounia casino is the more sophisticated, with a dress code if you want to get past the slot machines. The casino of the Hotel es Saadi just has slot machines.

Tangier and Agadir have, respectively, Mövenpick in Malabata, built around a huge casino, and the Casino La Mirage in Valtour Village.

Folklore and fantasias

In up-market touristy restaurants, the most common evening entertainment is a combination of a Moroccan meal and a display of folkloric dancing and/or traditional music – oud players, Gnaoua singers and so on. Although these performances sometimes have a rather packaged feel, they can be genuinely enjoyable, and the music is sometimes of a very high quality.

The early evening in any town or city is vibrant as everyone comes out to shop and meet up. Evening street life is notably exciting in **Marrakech**, where the celebrated Jemaa el Fna whirls with dancers, snake-charmers, traders, beggars, magicians and musicians. Have plenty of change in your pocket while you watch the performers: a contribution is expected from everyone, visitors above all.

Nightclubs

Nightclubs (often with belly-dancing shows) in tourist centres and cities are aimed at tourists, the Westernised urban population and visiting Gulf Arabs intent on letting their hair down. Most, though not all, nightclubs are found in hotels.

SHOPPING

Shopping in Morocco is becoming increasingly sophisticated – particularly in Marrakech and Casablanca. However, it is still largely based on traditional handicrafts, of which carpets, ceramics, jewellery and brass work are the most popular and which are largely found in Morocco's famed souks. Bargaining or haggling is absolutely essential. To bargain well you need to know something about the object you are buying – its quality or age and its market value. When it comes to haggling, the general rule of thumb is to offer half of what the seller initially quotes as the price and go from there. Be prepared to take your time over any negotiations – it is not unusual to sit down and drink tea with the owner, especially if buying something expensive like a carpet. Strong bargainers will be prepared to walk away from a purchase, in the hope that a counter-offer will be made – sometimes in the street. Tactics and strategies on both sides

Berber jewellery, Tiznit.

(incredulous laughter, walking towards the door) are all part of the process of arriving at a mutually acceptable price, though it never helps to be rude. Always keep your sense of humour. When bargaining, never offer a price for something unless you are willing to buy it.

Increasingly, however, as Moroccan and Morocco-based designers become better known, visitors are interested in seeking out contemporary Moroccan design. **Mia Zia** clothing (www.miazia.eu), for example, commands high prices in Europe but is designed and made in Morocco by an expatriate Frenchwoman. The beautiful high-end fashion of designer **Noureddine Amir** is also sought after, as are the wonderfully intricate lanterns made by **Yahya Creation** (www.yahya-group.com).

Modern Moroccan furniture and textiles are rarely seen on sale in the *souks* of Marrakech or Fez, not least because they would be spotted and copied within a matter of days. To find such items, you need to venture out to the up-market designer shops in the new parts of towns or, better still, track down the designers themselves, often in the industrial quarters, where many of them have showrooms.

A good example is **Akkal** in the industrial quarter of Marrakech. Originally just the showroom of a ceramics company, it has grown to become one of the smartest designer shops in the city, despite the fact that it is never going to attract any passing trade. Many of these showrooms keep collections of business cards of like-minded craftspeople and designers, and it is not uncommon to see shoppers touring from one showroom to another.

Marrakech has seen a boom in boutique clothing, design and interiors shops and western chain outlets (Zara, Mango). With a few exceptions, all are found in Gueliz, but the medina, too, has seen its fair share of boutique souk shops, such as KifKif, selling everything from vintage kaftans to select finds from around the country.

Antique shops can be found throughout the souks of Fez, Essaouira and Marrakech. Beware of items made to look like antiques and be prepared for steep prices. Marrakech has a particularly good flea market – Souk el Khemis – which has fabulous things from Victorian prams to Sixties plastic furniture.

Most tourist towns and cities will have large emporiums, or *ensembles artisanaux*, which sell jewellery, crafts, carpets and local products. These places are rather soulless and quality is variable, but prices are fixed.

What to buy

The traditional crafts of Morocco still make the best bargains. First and most prominent of the handicraft traditions are **carpets and rugs**, hand-knotted and in some cases, still coloured with vegetable dyes. Designs (apart from the Turkish-inspired patterns of Rabat carpets) are predominantly in traditional Berber tribal style. Their colours and symbolic motifs enable experts to pin down not only the area in which a carpet was produced but sometimes the tribe or even family that made it. Top-quality carpets sell for thousands of dirhams; more affordable and easily portable are Berber rugs, kilims or blankets. Try the small country souks around Marrakech.

Edibles are a popular purchase. As well as spices, nuts, herbs, olives and Moroccan sweets, possible buys include argan oil, produced in the southwest. It is sold, either on its own or mixed with ground almonds (a nut butter called *amalou*). Because of its high value, it is difficult to guarantee that the oil has not been mixed with olive oil. One way of being sure that the oil you buy is 100 percent pure is to buy from one of the women's cooperatives organised by the Projet Conservation et Développement de l'Arganeraie, which markets its oil to supermarkets under the name Cooperative Tissaliwine and has the EU-approved certificate of producing an organic product.

Leather goods are widespread, from unpolished leather bags and belts to distinctive pointed slippers

Marrakech souks.

(babouches) and ornate pouffes, studded and dyed. Some leather goods are finished in a style closer to Italian designer luggage. In all cases, price should go hand in hand with quality, so check workmanship and the quality of the leather before buying.

Jewellery is available for sale everywhere, although one of the best places to buy it is in Tiznit's famous silversmiths' souk and in the souks of Taroudant, Essaouira and Marrakech. Dull silver is the basic material: heavy but beautifully decorated bracelets, delicate filigree rings, chunky necklaces of semi-precious stones (or occasionally of plastic, for the unwary) are most commonly found. Slightly more unusual, and sometimes antique, are decorated daggers, scabbards, or Qur'an boxes, covered with silver-wire decoration. The fastenings are often a weak point. Beware, too, of silver-plating masking what the Moroccans call b'shi-b'shi – meaning rubbish.

Woodwork such as boxes and turned containers made of thuya, a lavishly grained, aromatic wood that grows only on the Atlantic Coast, is what Essaouira is famous for. Elaborately painted wood is also a Moroccan tradition: look for ornate painted mirror frames and hanging wall shelves of all sizes.

Marquetry is another traditional craft: wooden furniture, ornaments, chess sets and small wooden boxes made in cedar, thuya and oak, as well as boxes and mirror frames inlaid with camel bone. Many wooden goods are inlaid with veneers or mother of pearl. Often the quality of finish is less than ideal: hinges are points to watch. The woodworkers' ateliers under the ramparts at Essaouira are an ideal place to buy (and to watch the manufacturing process).

Metalwork ranges from copper or brass items such as trays with fine, ornate hammered designs (which,

along with a small folding wooden stand, make attractive tables) to wrought-iron and pierced copper or brass lanterns, mirror frames and tables with tiny hand-carved zellige-tile inlaid tops. There is also custom-made, contemporary designer furniture which is in good supply in Marrakech's ironworkers' souk near the Medersa Ben Youssef.

Pottery ranges from the rough earthenware of household pots and crocks to gaudy (and predominantly tourist-orientated) designs and beautiful blue and white, green or coloured ceramics from the main pottery centres of Safi, Fez, Meknes and Salé. Marrakech and Fez both have extensive pottery souks. The more refined, detailed (and expensive) pieces usually come from Fez, while Safi is famous for its dark-green-coloured pieces. In Marrakech you can find almost anything, including modern takes on traditional designs.

Perfume is loved by Moroccans of both sexes. Western brands are admired, but traditional scents, such as musk, orange flower, patchouli and amber, remain popular and are usually found in pure essential oil form in the spice souks and apothecaries of most medinas. Incense is used in the home on special occasions and for perfuming clothes.

Where to shop

The following list contains the best places to shop in the main cities, especially for quality Moroccan crafts, furniture, clothing and antiques.

Agadir

Argan House, 30 Rue Moulay Idriss – a lovely place, selling argan oil cosmetics and essential oils.

Casablanca

Artisanat Fenouche, 33 Boulevard Moulay Abderrahmane – designer

accessories such as purses, belts, shoes, jewellery and local crafts.
Coté Créateurs, 7 Rue Ahmed Charci, Quartier Vélodrome – presents, souvenirs and designer furniture.

Fez

Au Petit Bazaar de Bon Accueil, 35 Talaa Seghira, Fez el Bali – a treasure trove of jewellery, vintage carpets, pottery and metalwork.
Boutique Majid, Abdelmajid Rais el Fenni, 66 Rue des Chrétiens – antique jewellery, carpets, chests and embroidery.

Marrakech

Akkal, 322 Sidi Ghanem Industrial Zone, Route de Safi – a range of designer ceramics, from tagine pots to vases.
Bazaar du Sud, 117 Souk des Tapis, medina – as good a place as any to start haggling over rugs in the Criée Berbère carpet souk, offering a range of carpets and kilims, both old and new, from across the country.
Beldi, 9–11 Rue Laksour, medina – super-stylish kaftans, off-the-peg or tailor-made.
Ben Rahal, 28 Rue de la Liberté, Gueliz – up-market collection of museum-quality Moroccan carpets and kilims.
Darkoum, 5 Rue de la Liberté, Gueliz – three floors of antique (and very expensive) artefacts including stunning tribal African pieces from Gabon, the Congo, Cameroon and elsewhere.
Ensemble Artisanal, Avenue Mohammed V, Gueliz – vast emporium of Moroccan crafts with set prices.
Jamade, Rue Riad Zitoun el Jdid, Medina – quirky contemporary collectibles from local artisans including brightly coloured pottery and jewellery.
Kaftan Queen, Angle Rue Mohammed V and Rue Mohammed El Beqqal, Gueliz – chic, minimalist kaftans and lovely linen, plus children's clothes.
KifKif, 8 Derb Laksour, medina – entertaining selection of unusual, specially commissioned contemporary Moroccan handicrafts, quite unlike anything you'll find in the souks – think unusual handbags made from recycled flour sacks, plus funky jewellery and clothes.
La Lampe d'Aladdin, 70 bis Souk Semmarine – one of the most up-market of the myriad shops crammed in along Souk Semmarine, selling top-quality Moroccan artefacts

including antique jewellery and superb original paintings, with prices to match.

L'Orientaliste, 11 & 15 Rue de la Liberté, Gueliz – interesting little shop with a colourful selection of unusual collectibles, including original artworks, glassware and assorted bric-a-brac.

Moro, 114 Place de la Fontaine, Mouassine, medina – fantastic finds and bespoke creations from around Morocco, such as wedding blankets, kaftans, notebooks and more.

El Nour, 57 Rue Laksour, medina – a non-profit organisation producing beautiful handmade traditional Moroccan embroidery, created by disadvantaged women and girls.

Scènes de Lin, 70 Rue de la Liberté, Gueliz – fine linen and superior embroidered kitchen- and homeware.

Rabat

Alchimies, 5 Rue el Mari, Quartier Tour Hassan – top-quality traditional crafts, furniture and gifts.

Ensemble Artisanal, Boulevard Tariq el Marsa – fixed prices on a range of traditional crafts and jewellery.

Marylin Bottero, Complexe 2 des Potiers d'Oulja, www.marylinebottero. com – the atelier of a French potter, with some interesting pieces.

Tangier

Bazaar Tindouf, 72 Rue de la Liberté (opposite El Minzah hotel) – antiques, pottery, lamps, jewellery and much more.

Boutique Majid, Rue Les Almohades (www.boutiquemajid.com) – rare Moroccan antiques.

Ensemble Artisanal, Corner Rue Beligique and Rue Ensallah. Government emporium showcasing full range of local crafts at fixed prices.

Madini, 5 Boulevard Pasteur and 14 Rue Sebou, Kasbah – famous perfumerie selling traditional and modern fragrances.

SPORTS AND OUTDOOR ACTIVITIES

Fishing

The **fly fisher's** choice is wide: fishing in isolated streams and pools of the Middle and High Atlas, or casting into custom-stocked lakes (most of them in the Middle Atlas) where the permits are expensive and the catch weighed before leaving. Trout fishing is popular in Morocco, to the extent that the rivers and lakes that are easily reached have been overfished.

Specialist Tours

Complete Morocco Morocco specialists offering a huge range of bespoke tours – everything from trekking, camel treks, skiing and water sports through to dance and music workshops and wine tasting. Tel: +44 1225 706 665 (UK), www.completemorocco.com

Epic Morocco Specialist adventure operator offering small-group trekking, mountain-biking and other holidays. Tel: +44 20 8150 6131 (UK), www.epicmorocco.co.uk

Exodus Travels Provides a comprehensive adventure programme in Morocco Tel: + 44 20 8675 5550 (UK), www.exodus.co.uk

Explore Worldwide Experienced pioneers in original small-group adventure holidays, including ascents of Jebel Toubkal and Bedouin trails in the Sahara. Tel: +44 845 013 1537 (UK) www.explore.co.uk

Journey Beyond Travel Tailor-made quality Moroccan holidays, including cultural tours, trekking and desert expeditions.

Tel: +44 20 8123 8708 (UK) www.journeybeyondtravel.com

Naturally Morocco Specialist operator specialising in tailor-made riad and kasbah accommodation, and with strong responsible tourism credentials. Tel: +44 1239 710 814 (UK) www.naturallymorocco.co.uk

Saddle Skedaddle Mountain-biking and road-cycling tours in the Moroccan south. Tel: +44 191 265 1110 (UK) www.skedaddle.co.uk

Specialist Morocco Tailor-made Moroccan itineraries specialising in guided tours and treks, with an up-market emphasis. Tel: +44 20 7193 2461 (UK), +1 877 293 2854 (US) www.specialistmorocco.com

Splash Morocco Adventure Tours Rafting specialist, but also offering lots of other adventure tours including trekking, mountain biking, canyoning, kitesurfing, windsurfing and ballooning. Tel: +44 7780 465 905 (UK), 0618-96 42 52 (Morocco) www.moroccoadventuretours.com

How not to lose your rug

Beware of buying anything that can't be carried away. Many traders will offer export facilities (eg for large carpets) and, although there are no customs formalities to be met, the shipping of goods could take months. There is little comeback against a souk trader who has been paid in cash and fails to deliver.

Coarse fishing: lakes and reservoirs of the Middle Atlas are the most popular setting for coarse fishing, around Azrou, Ifrane and Immouzer du Kander in particular, and in the reservoir of Ben el Ouidane. Species include some of the world's largest pike, as well as black bass and perch.

Permits are required for trout and coarse fishing and are usually available locally (through hotels or tourist offices).

Sea fishing is rich, too, and does not require a permit. From massive sea bass off Dakhla and Laâyoune in the south, to the summer visits of tuna north of Casablanca and swordfish off Tangier, fish are populous and varied. Bream, mackerel and sardines are also common. The Mediterranean and the South Atlantic coasts are the most fruitful: deep-sea fishing from boats is relatively easy to arrange, and spear-fishing with aqualung is possible with a permit.

Golf

Golf is very big business in Morocco, and the country boasts an astonishing number of golf courses, including numerous world-class venues created by some of the world's leading designers and former players. The following are just a few of the best – for fuller listings, see www.moroccogolf.com.

Lessons and caddies are available at all courses. Some courses require a handicap card. The country's main golf tournament is the Hassan II Trophy (Hassan II was a very keen golfer), which is held in March in Agadir.

Exclusive Golf Tours are specialists in golfing holidays in Morocco (tel: +44 870 870 4700; www.exclusive golf.co.uk).**Agadir**

Golf de l'Océan Opened in 2010, this modern course comprises a trio of nine-hole courses: 'Dunes', 'Garden' and 'Desert', laid out on a varied terrain. Tel: 0528-27 35 42, www.golf delocean.com.

Beach football in Essaouira.

Chemin de l'Oeud Souss Bensergao. Tel: 0528-82 41 46, www.golfdelocean.com.

Casablanca

Royal Golf Mohammedia Dating back to the 1920s and formerly the premier golfing venue in the country, with an 18-hole links-style course laid out alongside the Atlantic coast. Boulevard Lice d'Anfa. Tel: 022-36 10 26, www.rgam.ma.

Essaouira

Golf de Mogador Oceanfront 18-hole course designed by Gary Player and opened in 2010, set amidst sandy coastal scrub and dunes and offering a series of challenging par 3, 4 and 5s. Tel: 0524-47 92 30, www.golfdemogador.com.

El Jadida

El Jadida Royal Golf Opened in 1993, this is the second of El Jadida's pair of top-notch golf venues, with an 18-hole course overlooking a sweeping Atlantic bay. Hotel Pullman Mazagan Royal Golf & Spa, Route de Casablanca Km 7. Tel: 0523-37 91 00, www.pullmanhotels.com.

Mazagan Opened in 2009, this modern links course (the longest in the country) was designed by Gary Player for billionaire South African hotel mogul Sol Kerzner and is every bit as spectacular as you'd expect.

Golf information

For more information on courses and facilities, contact:
The Royal Moroccan Golf Federation (*Fédération Royale Marocaine de Golf*)
Royal Dar es Salaam Golf Club
Rabat
Tel: 0537-75 56 36

Mazagan Beach Resort. Tel: 0523-38 33 00, www.mazaganbeachresort.com.

Marrakech

Al Maaden Golf Resort State-of-the-game course, opened in 2010 to a design by Kyle Phillips, with unusual water features designed to evoke the atmosphere of a Moroccan garden. Sidi Youssef Ben Ali. Tel: 0524-40 13 50, www.almaaden.com.
Amelkis One of the older of Marrakech's ever-proliferating number of golf complexes, and still one of the best, opened in 1995 as an 18-hole course, with a new nine-hole Green course added in 2009. Km 12, Route de Ouarzazate. Tel: 0524-40 44 14.
Le Palmeraie Golf Club Originally opened in 1992 to a Robert Trent Jones design, with a further nine holes added in 2008.
Tel: 0524-36 87 66, www.palmeraiemarrakech.com.

Rabat

Royal Dar es Salaam One of Africa's top golfing venues, designed for King Hassan II in 1971 by Robert Trent Jones, this extravagant complex comprises three courses:

Paraglider landing on Legzira beach, Agadir.

two 18-holes (Red and Blue) and an easier nine-hole Green. Tel: 0537-75 58 64, www.royalgolfdaressalam.com.

Helicopter flights

Voyage to Morocco 43 Ave Hassan II, Marrakech. Tel: 0661-20 99 46. www.voyagetomorocco.com. Offers several helicopter tours of varying lengths.

Hiking and trekking

Several adventure tour operators run hiking holidays in the Atlas and Anti-Atlas Mountains that come with guides and porters. However, it is possible to devise your own hikes in situ, especially in the Toubkal National Park south of Marrakech. Unless you are a very experienced (and properly equipped) mountain hiker, hire a local guide and pack mules and follow the standard routes, and also read the advice given on page 98.

Reputable guides and operators will always publish a fixed price list for services, accommodation and sometimes food, though these may be negotiable when business is quiet. Good springboards, where hiking has been turned into an important local industry, are Imlil, Oukaimeden and Tabant. Basic accommodation on hikes is found in mountain refuges (usually run by the Club Alpin Français, www.caf-maroc.com) or in the homes of locals.

Recommended companies include:
Exodus Trekking tours focused on the Atlas mountains, including Mount Toubkal winter and summer ascents. Tel: +44 845 564 4753 (UK), www.exodus.co.uk.
KE Adventure Travel A range of tours including summer and winter hikes through the Atlas and Anti-Atlas, and camel treks in the Sahara. Tel: +44 1768 773 966 (UK), www.keadventure.com

TRANSPORT

ACCOMMODATION

EATING OUT

ACTIVITIES

A – Z

LANGUAGE

Ramblers Holidays Ltd Options include walking in southern Morocco and the Atlas Mountains.
Tel: + 44 1707 331 133 (UK)
www.ramblersholidays.co.uk
Responsible Travel Various treks in the Atlas mountains, including dedicated hikes with local Berber nomads.
Tel: +44 1273 823 700, www.responsibletravel.com
Walks Worldwide Tailor-made walking tours.
Tel: +44 845 301 4737 (UK)
www.walksworldwide.com

Horse riding

Another popular activity is **riding** – either mule-trekking in rugged mountain terrain, or galloping on horseback along the sandy beaches of the coast. You can hire horses in Essaouira and Agadir for beach or countryside rides. Treks into the High Atlas – either on horses or mules – can be arranged from a few hotels in the region, such as the **Club Equestre** at La Roseraie in Ouirgane, near Marrakech.
Club Farah is based in Meknes and offers horse-riding trips across Morocco: Club d'Equitation Farah, Renate Erroudani, BP 597, Meknes. Tel: 0535-54 88 44, www.clubfarah.com.
L'Atlas à Cheval organises riding holidays at its ranch 26km (16 miles) from Marrakech: 932 Résidence el Massar, Route de Safi, Marrakech. Tel: 0524-33 55 57.
Ranch de Diabet offers horse and camel rides on the beach and to attractions in the Essaouira area. Tel: 0524-47 63 82, www.ranchdediabat.com.
Unicorn Trails is a UK-based outfit offering horse-riding tours in Agadir, Essaouira, Marrakech and Skoura. 21 The Acorn Centre, Chestnut Avenue,

Royal Golf Club at Meknes.

Biggleswade, Beds, UK. Tel: +44 1767 600 606 (UK), www.unicorntrails.com.

Hot-air ballooning

Largely based out of Marrakech, you can now go hot-air ballooning over this amazing city and the surrounding countryside. A number of tour operators can arrange trips, including the following two specialist outfits:
Ciel d'Afrique Imm. Ali, Appt. 4, 2ème étage, Avenue Youssef Ben Tachfine, Marrakech, tel: 0524-43 28 43, www.cieldafrique.info.
Marrakech by Air 184 Lala Haya, Marrakech, tel: 0652-12 97 21, www.marrakechbyair.com.

Paragliding

Marrakech is the main centre for this sport, which takes place in the foothills of the Atlas.
Passion Paragliding Paragliding holidays in Morocco. Tel: +44 20 8123 7427 (UK) or 0658-36 19 53 in Morocco, www.passionparagliding.com.

Skiing

The peculiarity of the High Atlas climate enables the tourist board to boast of Marrakech being a base from which you can go skiing in the morning and sunbathe in the afternoon, which is, technically, true – if there is snow. The ski resort of Oukaimeden (2,650 metres/8,700ft), an hour's drive southeast of Marrakech, expects snow from December to April, but this is not to be relied on, and often, when there is a large amount of snow, the pistes aren't groomed, so conditions can be dangerous. There are several drag (button) lifts and the highest chair lift in North Africa. Skis and boots can be hired at the bottom of the piste. The other resort, Mischliffen, is

reached through cedar forests from Azrou or Ifrane: the setting – a mini Switzerland in Africa – rather than the skiing is the main attraction here and mainly draws wealthy Moroccans.

Water sports

Morocco has 2,000km (1,250 miles) of Atlantic coastline, with hundreds of outstanding beaches and dozens of water sports on offer, from wind- and kitesurfing to surfing, jet-skiing and sailing. Two of the most popular resorts are Agadir and Essaouira, and the whole stretch of coastline between Agadir and Oualidia has stunning beaches, as does the Northern Atlantic Coast, south of Tangier. For sea swimming, do not venture out of your depth anywhere on the Atlantic Coast: the undertow can sweep you out to sea in a matter of minutes. Taghazoute, Essaouira and Dakhla have international reputations for their surfing, windsurfing and kitesurfing. Sailing and scuba-diving are both available in Agadir.
Club Mistral (www.club-mistral.com) in Essaouira rents wind- and kitesurfing equipment and regular surfboards.

Whitewater rafting

In spring, when the snows melt, and in late autumn, when rains fall, the rivers of the High and Middle Atlas quickly swell. Good rafting is to be had on the Ahansal and Ourika rivers in the High Atlas, and (more demanding) the Oum er Rbia River in the Middle Atlas. Several adventure tour operators now include rafting in their programmes. Specialist operators include:
Morocco Rafting Whitewater rafting and kayaking on the Ahansal and Ourika rivers. Tel: +44 1226 740 400 (UK), 0672-88 25 29 (Morocco), www.rafting.ma.
Splash Morocco Adventure Tours Whitewater rafting specialist, offering trips on the N'Fiss, Ourika and Ahansal rivers. Tel: +44 7780 465 905 (UK), -0618-96 42 52 (Morocco), www.moroccoadventuretours.com.
Water by Nature Worldwide rafting specialist, offering Atlas Mountains rafting and kayaking trips. Tel: +44 1226 740 144 (UK), +1 303-261 8896 (US), www.waterbynature.com.

HAMMAMS/SPAS

The art of the hammam (steam bath/bathhouse) is an ancient and integral part of Moroccan life where water, which is considered sacred, and

Hard-going cycling in the Atlas mountains.

cleanliness are essential elements of Islam. The hammam is where people go to socialise, gossip, make connections, do business and even arrange marriages. There are one or more hammams in the medina of most towns and cities. Some are basic and others are hundreds of years old and full of character. Many hotels and *maison d'hôtes* have hammams and spas or will be able to arrange for a visit to one nearby.

Entry to a local hammam (strictly segregated) usually costs around 10dh. Leave your things in the changing room and take toiletries into the first 'warm' room. This is where you acclimatise to the heat and can collect buckets to fill with water – one cold and one hot. Once accustomed to the heat, move into the second 'hot' room to let your pores open and breathe. Move back to the warm room for your cleanse.

In most hammams, you can have a massage and a gommage (scrub) done for you by an attendant for a few extra dirhams. If it all gets too much, just say 'shwiya afak' (gently, please). At the end of it all, you'll look like and feel as good as a shiny newborn baby. The best selection of hammams, and more up-market hammam-style spas, can be found in Marrakech. These include:

Les Bains de Marrakech 2 Derb Sedra, tel: 0524-38 14 28, www. lesbainsdemarrakech.com. A riad in the kasbah that is entirely devoted to luxurious indulgence. This serene place – all muted colours, warm wood, candles and exotic scents – is a blissful escape.

Hammam Dar el Bacha 20 Rue Fatima Zohra. The city's largest traditional hammam, and a good place to soak with the locals, if you don't mind the slightly rough-and-ready facilities.

Hammam de la Rose 130 Dar El Bacha, www.hammamdelarose.com. Up-market spa-style hammam offering a range of bespoke massages.

EXCURSIONS

There are, of course, an infinite number of touring routes and excursions throughout Morocco that could be contrived, and the main text of this book should help in the planning of a suitable itinerary. Below, however, are lists of the must-see excursions and routes radiating from the most popular holiday centres.

From Agadir

The mountain villages and scenery around **Tafraoute** (150km/95 miles) southeast; the fishing and surfing villages of **Mirleft** and **Sidi Ifni** south of Tiznit and, for those wanting to venture further south, **Western Sahara**.

From Marrakech

The pass roads through the High Atlas of **Tizi N'Test** (to the south) and **Tizi N'Tichka** (to the southeast); the highest peak of Morocco, **Jebel Toubkal**, due south, visible for miles around, and climbable from Imlil; the **southern valleys** of oases and kasbahs, east and south of Marrakech and reached via Ouarzazate, 204km (126 miles) from Marrakech – specifically the **Drâa Valley**, the **Dadès Valley** and the **Todra Gorge**.

Birdwatching

Morocco lies under one of the two major migratory routes for European birds wintering in Africa. Storks, ibis and flamingos are seen in the wetlands of river estuaries and coastal lagoons. Eagles and falcons sometimes wheel high in a semi-desert sky. Several tour companies offer birdwatching holidays; their expertise will help determine the place and time to go. Mid-October is one of the best times, and March to May is also good.

Particularly good areas include: **Oualidia**, where the lagoons and salt pans attract flamingo, black-winged stilt, avocet, Audoin's and Slender-billed gulls; the islands off **Essaouira**, where a colony of Eleonora's falcon breed; **Oued Massa** for crested coot, Pale

The really dedicated will press further east into the **Sahara** to watch sunrise over the magnificent dunes of **Erg Chigagga** or **Erg Chebbi**. Via Beni-Mellal (200km/124 miles northeast), you can reach the reservoir at **Bin el Ouidane** and the waterfalls at **Ouzoud**. There is also the old Portuguese fishing port of **Essaouira** situated two hour west.

From Meknes or Fez

The cedar forests around **Azrou** and **Ifrane** (80km/50 miles and 60km/37 miles south of Fez); the **Kandar massif** (30km/19 miles south of Fez); the holy city of **Moulay Idriss** and the nearby Roman ruins of **Volubilis** (30km/19 miles north of Meknes); the end of the Middle Atlas Mountains to **Taza**, and further east, the end of the Rif massif at the **Beni-Snassen** Mountains.

From Rabat

Head inland! There are only coastal towns to visit closer than Meknes: **Salé**, Rabat's other half; **Casablanca** (90km/56 miles) and **El Jadida** (187km/117 miles).

From Tangier

The market town of **Tetouan** and the pretty houses at **Chefchaouen** and **Ouezzane** are in the foothills of the Rif. **Asilah** is a good place to head on the west coast. You might also try a day trip to **Gibraltar** or the Spanish enclaves of **Ceuta** and **Melilla**.

crag martin, osprey and the rare Bald ibis; the **Souss Valley** for Moussier's redstart, Bush and Great grey shrike, Lanner falcon and Chanting goshawk; the **Anti-Atlas** for Long-legged buzzards, Cream-coloured courser and Black wheatear; **Jebel Saghro** for Desert sparrow, Trumpeter bullfinch, Brown-necked raven, Rat-rumped wheatear and larks. For packages, try: **Birdfinders** Eleven-day tours starting in Marrakech and taking in both mountain and desert environments. Tel: +44 1258 839 066 (UK), www.birdfinders.co.uk. **Naturetrek** Birdwatching and botanical tours in southern Morocco or the High Atlas Mountains. Tel: +44 1962 733051 (UK), www. naturetrek.co.uk.

A – Z

A HANDY SUMMARY OF PRACTICAL INFORMATION

A

Admission charges

Visits to most of Morocco's monuments and museums are subject to an admission charge. This is normally a small fee of about 10–30dh (75p–£2.25/$1.20–3.60), with the exception of the Hassan II Mosque in Casablanca, where the charge is currently 120dh (£9/$14.50), which includes a guided tour. The guide chapters in this book state where entry fees are charged, while in many other places even where official entrance charges aren't levied it's customary to tip guardians and caretakers who show you around.

B

Budgeting for your trip

Morocco is not as cheap as it once was, but you can still count on enjoying a cheaper holiday than in most European countries. Here are some guideline prices:
B&B for two in a comfortable (but not luxurious) *maison d'hôte*: 600dh (£45/$72)
Three-course meal with wine for two in a medium-priced city restaurant: 500dh (£38/$60)
Daily (economy model) car rental: 300dh (£22/$36)
Litre of petrol: 11dh (80p/$1.30)
Litre bottle of mineral water: 5dh (37p/$0.60)
Bottle of local beer (33cl) in three-star hotel: 35dh (£2.60/$4.20)
Airport transfer. **Agadir**: taxi 200dh (£15/$24). **Casablanca**:

train 40dh (£3/$4.80), bus 20dh (£1.50/$2.40), taxi 300dh (£22/$36). **Fez**: taxi 120dh (£9/$14.50), bus 20dh (£1.50/$2.40). **Marrakech**: taxi 70dh (£5.25/$8.50). **Tangier**: taxi 200dh (£15/$2.4).
Bicycle and moped hire: rates are negotiable, but average around 100dh a day.
Motorbike hire (125cc) costs from 200dh (£15/$24) a day.
Buses: city buses have a flat fare of 3dh (22p/$0.36).
Long-distance coach (CTM), one-way: Casablanca–Marrakech 80dh (£6/$9.60); Marrakech–Ouarzazate 80dh (£6/$9.60).
Taxis: cross-town trip in a petit taxi about 10–15dh (75p–£1.10/$1.20–1.80), depending on time of day.
Trains (www.oncf.ma): adult single, second-class Tangier–Rabat 90dh (£6.75/$10.80); Rabat–Fez 76dh (£5.80/$9.40); Rabat–Marrakech 112dh (£8/$13). First-class is about 30 percent more.

Business travellers

Those visiting Morocco on business are well catered for in the larger cities with a range of hotels offering conference facilities and internet access for guests. Casablanca is by far the most important commercial centre in Morocco; it's where most large Moroccan companies have their headquarters, and there is a sprinkling of regional offices of multinational companies in the city as well. Casablanca, more than anywhere else in Morocco, keeps a more European timetable. Elsewhere, Marrakech is the main centre in Morocco for conferences and trade fairs.

C

Children

Moroccans adore children, and they are welcome everywhere, at any time of the day or night. However, few cities have attractions specifically aimed at children.

The most obvious kids' attraction in Morocco is the beach. Agadir is easily the best set-up place for families and children, while Essaouira also has plenty to offers, especially for old kids, with boat rides, camel treks, water sports and lots of other activities. The big resort hotels in Agadir (and sometimes in other parts of the country) also often have a good programme of child-oriented entertainment.

Away from the coast, things become more challenging. Marrakech, with its nightly circus-cum-fair on the Jemaa el Fna, horse-drawn carriages, colourful souks and great hotel pools is one possibility, while desert trips (perhaps with some camel- or horse riding thrown in) out into the Saharan dunes or less strenuous mountain walks might appeal to active and adventurous older children. Other adventurous possibilities include hot-air balloon trips from Marrakech and whitewater rafting trips in the mountains.

Eating out can be problematic, particularly if your child has narrow tastes. However, a daily diet of omelette/chicken and chips can be reasonably nutritious when supplemented by fresh fruit, yoghurts and fresh fruit milkshakes. Preprepared baby foods can also be found, although usually only in larger shops and supermarkets.

If you buy milk to give to babies, you should boil it first or buy UHT milk, which is widely available. Formula is available from most good pharmacies.

Nappies (diapers) and baby wipes are sold in many of the larger grocer's and in most pharmacies. 'Pull-ups' (trainer pants) are much more difficult to obtain, so bring these with you.

Climate

Three types of climate hold sway in three distinct regions. The coastal regions have warm, dry summers, are wet for the rest of the year and mild in winter: the coast is drier south of Agadir, where it is free of Atlantic depressions in winter (Agadir itself has a well-protected climate, with a narrow range of temperatures, but in common with the rest of the Atlantic Coast, cold offshore water can cause cloud and fog.) The mountains get hot, dry summers and very harsh winters; parts of the High Atlas are under snow well into the summer. The remainder of the country has a continental climate, getting hotter and drier in summer to the south, but moderated by the sea to the west.

In the inland Sahara very dry, hot summers give way to warm, sunny days and cold (sometimes frosty) nights in winter.

All of which means that there's no single 'best time' to visit Morocco – when you come will depend largely on what you want to do. Summer can be wonderful in the mountains when the snows have finally melted but murder in the desert, with temperatures rising into the 50C°s. Winter can be wonderfully mild in the desert, while the mountains are buried under several feet of snow. Away from the high mountains and the Saharan south, most of the country is generally most pleasant to visit in spring and autumn (roughly Mar–May and Sept–Oct, although, obviously, exact times vary, with temperatures rising as you head further south and inland).

What to wear

Dress for comfort, not for fashion. Light-coloured, lightweight cottons are advisable in summer. In winter, dress in layers, taking some warm clothes and a waterproof. Hotels are rarely dressy, although some four- and many five-star hotels have formal restaurants in which men will feel more comfortable in a jacket and women in a smartish dress. When touring or sightseeing, let tact and discretion be your guide: keep skimpy clothes for the beach and remember that jewellery and fine clothes are the mark of a wealthy tourist in a poor country; expensive bags or cameras may also attract more attention than you would like.

From June to September the days are always hot, but evenings on the coast and in the north can be cool, so take a jacket or sweater. Also pack long-sleeved tops, a sunhat and sunblock. During the rest of the year a light jacket and a raincoat or umbrella will come in handy, while a warm coat for cold desert nights is essential. Modest clothing should be worn when visiting mosques and other Islamic monuments and in the medinas of towns, which are more conservative than the Villes Nouvelles. Women should cover shoulders and avoid wearing short or revealing clothing. You will not only be treated with a great deal more respect, but will find that your trip is far more enjoyable and relaxing. Scantily dressed women are unlikely to be seriously bothered, but will be stared at. Topless sunbathing is very rarely permitted even in private hotel grounds, and never on public beaches.

Crime and safety

Crime against tourists is not common, but neither is it unknown. Any guide in the packed souks of Fez and Marrakech will advise you to hold tightly to your bag. What tends to be most intimidating, especially in the imperial cities, is harassment from faux guides (literally, false guides) who try to force their services on you. The government has steadily clamped down on them for many years now and it is technically illegal to hassle tourists, so the problem has been dramatically reduced. The best way to deal with them if you don't want their help is to decline firmly but with good humour. Above all, don't become aggressive or confrontational. (See page 297.)

Avoid wearing expensive-looking jewellery, or carrying too much money: use hotel safe deposit boxes. If you're on the move, use a secure pocket or money belt rather than a shoulder bag for valuables; if you do use a bag, sling the strap over your head, not just your shoulder.

In the highly unlikely event that

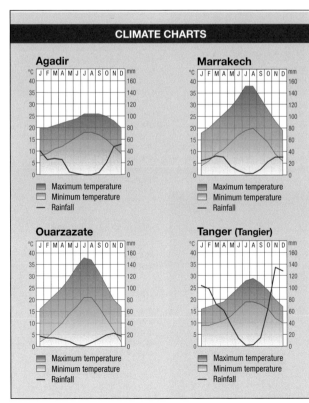

CLIMATE CHARTS

Agadir

°C / J F M A M J J A S O N D / mm

- Maximum temperature
- Minimum temperature
- Rainfall

Marrakech

°C / J F M A M J J A S O N D / mm

- Maximum temperature
- Minimum temperature
- Rainfall

Ouarzazate

°C / J F M A M J J A S O N D / mm

- Maximum temperature
- Minimum temperature
- Rainfall

Tanger (Tangier)

°C / J F M A M J J A S O N D / mm

- Maximum temperature
- Minimum temperature
- Rainfall

TRANSPORT ACCOMMODATION EATING OUT ACTIVITIES A – Z LANGUAGE

you are attacked, don't put up a fight: better to lose money than risk being hurt. If driving, don't leave bags visible in the car, always lock your vehicle and leave it empty overnight. Better still, do as the locals do and have a *gardien* watch over it (5–10dh for short stays; 10–20dh for the night).

Loss of belongings

If any of your belongings have been stolen, a police report must be made. Do not be put off by hotel staff if they advise otherwise; insurance companies invariably require a local police report before they will entertain a claim for theft. If tour company representatives are on hand, they may be able to help, and should certainly be informed.

If your belongings do not arrive at the airport, it is the responsibility of the airline: ask for a Property Irregularity Form to fill in. Many travel insurance policies will then allow reasonable expenses on clothes and other essentials.

Customs regulations

When you arrive you will be given an official form to fill in, stating profession, address(es) in Morocco and length of stay. Each time you register at a hotel you are required to fill in a similar form, which is submitted to the police.

Customs procedure on entry will vary according to point of arrival.

Allowances

You can take any amount of foreign currency into or out of the country, but must declare on entry amounts over the value of 15,000dh. It is illegal to import or export more than 1,000dh.

Mausoleum of Mohammed V, Rabat.

You are allowed to bring with you personal effects including jewellery, cameras, electronic equipment and phones. Foodstuffs and medicines in reasonable quantities for personal use may also be imported.

Duty-free allowances permit the import of 250 grams of tobacco or 200 cigarettes or 25 cigars; one litre of wine plus one litre of spirits; 150ml of perfume and 250ml of eau de cologne.

Extensions of stay

Contact the local police department well in advance if your stay is likely to exceed 90 days. Proof of funds will be required, along with reasons for staying. It is easier, at least in the north, to leave Morocco inside the 90-day period, and re-enter on a fresh visa.

Pets

An international health and inoculation certificate and a certificate of anti-rabies vaccination are both needed to take pets into Morocco. These will need to be certified by your nearest Moroccan embassy or consulate.

D

Disabled travellers

Facilities for disabled travellers in Morocco are minimal. Only a few top-end hotels have specially adapted rooms, and many cheaper hotels do not have lifts, and so may have limited accessibility Public transport is also difficult to use for those with impaired mobility – hiring a car is far preferable – while the narrow, crowded and irregular roads of a typical Moroccan medina also provide significant challenges, and visitors in wheelchairs are likely to be the object of many curious stares. The easiest plan of action is to arrange your journey in advance with a reputable tour agent – try www. moroccoaccessibletravel.com, who run dedicated accessible tours across the country.

E

Electricity

Most of the country's supply is rated 220 volts, but some places have a 110-volt supply; sockets and plugs are of the continental European type, with two round pins.

Embassies and consulates

Embassies are found only in the capital, Rabat; elsewhere there are consulates.
Australia: The Canadian Embassy (below) provides consular services to Australians.
Canada: 13 bis Rue Jaâfa as Sadik (BP 709), Agdal, Rabat, tel: 0537-68 74 00, www.canadainternational.gc.ca.
Ireland: 57 Boulevard Abdelmoumen, Rue Salim Cherkkaoui, Résidence Al Hadi noºB, ème Ètage, Casablanca, tel: 0522-27 27 21.
South Africa: 34 Rue des Saadiens, Quartier Hassan, Rabat 10100, tel: 0537-68 91 59.
UK: 28 Avenue S.A.R. Sidi Mohammed Souissi, 10105 (BP 45) Rabat, tel: 0537-63 33 33, www.ukin morocco.fco.gov.uk.
US: 2 Avenue Mohammed el Fassi, Rabat, tel: 0537-76 22 65, http:// morocco.usembassy.gov.
8 Boulevard Moulay Youssef, Casablanca, tel: 0522-26 45 50.

Emergency numbers

Police (police secours): 19
Fire services (pompiers): 15
Ambulance (SAMU): 15

Etiquette

It is worth bearing in mind a few simple guidelines when it comes to etiquette in Morocco. As it is forbidden for non-Muslims to enter virtually all mosques, it is also considered rude to peer inside mosques and religious buildings, especially during prayer times. For those mosques (Hassan II, Tin Mal) and medersas that can be visited, dress modestly, with arms and legs covered. Similarly, to avoid unwanted attention, women in particular should dress modestly in medinas, where sensibilities are more traditional. If invited to the home of a Moroccan, it is customary to bring a small gift (a box of patisserie is always appreciated). Always use your right hand for eating (the left is considered unclean).

G

Gay and lesbian travellers

Morocco no longer offers visitors the free and easy attitude it once did towards homosexuality. What Moroccan law describes as an 'unnatural act' between two persons of the same sex is punishable by imprisonment (from six months to three years) and by fines, although the law is only loosely enforced, and you're unlikely to run into trouble assuming you're discreet. It's also not generally a problem for same-sex couples to share a hotel room, although again discretion is the order of the day.

H

Health and medical care

Aids

Morocco has relatively low reported rates of HIV infections, although the conservative nature of Moroccan society means that many cases go unreported. For tourists, it's worth noting that one of the country's major HIV hotspots is the resort of Agadir.

Most Moroccan pharmacies now stock disposable needles, and clinics and hospitals are usually reliable: check with a consulate or embassy if you are in doubt over treatment. It is possible to buy medical kits containing sterile hypodermic needles and plasma, which can be carried in case of an emergency.

Common ailments

Stomach upsets are the most common ailment: diarrhoea remedies or relief will come in handy. To cut down on the chances of getting an upset stomach, avoid food that has been left standing or has been reheated, and use bottled water in remote areas.

The next most common cause of

illness is usually sunstroke, especially when combined with alcohol; light cotton clothing, moderate exposure and protective lotions all reduce the risk of **sunstroke**.

Medical services

There are private clinics in all main towns, along with government hospitals in many. Consulates will have details of English-speaking doctors, as will tour company representatives and staff at hotels. Be sure to come to Morocco with full medical insurance, including cover for repatriation. All services will be charged for immediately, except in cases of extreme need or emergency. Ask for and keep receipts.

Pharmacies in towns sell many kinds of medicines and contraceptives (usually, only sanitary towels are found in medina pharmacies; tampons are found in all Ville Nouvelle pharmacies). Medicines can be expensive: aspirin, insect-bite cream and stomach settlers are best bought at home and taken with you. There is at least one all-night pharmacy in each major town. Most pharmacies post the address of the all-night pharmacy on their doors. They are also published in most newspapers.

Vaccinations and protection against malaria

No vaccinations are required by the Moroccan government for entry into the country, unless you have come from a recognised infected area (eg a yellow fever, cholera or smallpox zone). For your own safety, however, inoculations against typhoid, polio, cholera and tetanus are advised

Catching up with the news.

by some doctors, especially if you are travelling in remote areas in the south, where a course of malaria tablets is also advised. There is a very limited malaria risk in Chefchaouen province, but anti-malarial drugs are not recommended, only the use of a good insect repellent.

Some protection against hepatitis may be useful if travelling in remote country areas. Injections of immuno-globulin give protection for about four weeks. Contact with standing fresh water (swimming or paddling in river valleys and lagoons) may carry the risk of bilharzia, which is caught from flatworms living inside freshwater snails, so take local advice. Rabies is present: seek medical advice immediately if you are bitten.

I

Internet

Levels of internet access in Morocco are on a par with those you'd expect in Europe or North America. There are plenty of internet cafés in all towns and cities (usually charging around 10dh an hour). Wi-fi is also available in the majority of hotels (even budget places) as well as many cafés. Access in most places is usually free.

L

Left luggage

For a small charge, luggage may be left at railway stations or offices of the Compagnie de Transport Marocain (CTM): it should be safe.

M

Maps

The reliable maps produced by European companies are: Hallwag (1:1,000,000), Lascelles (1:800,000) and Michelin Maroc (1:1,000,000). Also good is the companion fold-out map to Insight Pocket Guide: Morocco, which contains town plans of major towns as well as a clear country map, and Insight Fleximap: Morocco (1:1,600,000), which is laminated and hard-wearing.

Large-scale topographical maps of the Atlas are difficult to obtain. In Morocco try the shop at 31 Avenue Hassan I, Rabat, or the Hotel Ali in Marrakech on Rue Moulay Ismail just south of the Jemaa el Fna. Maps can also be ordered online via sites such as www.mapsworldwide.com and www. stanfords.co.uk in the UK, and www. chesslerbooks.com in the US. Maps of Toubkal National Park are available at Imlil and Asni.

Media

Newspapers and magazines

Educated Moroccans are avid readers, and the country has a healthy selection of newspapers and magazines. The French *Le Monde* is printed and distributed in Morocco, while local French-language papers include the left-leaning *L'Opinion* and the strongly royalist *Le Matin du Sahara*. Weekly news magazines include the outspoken *Telquel* and *Le Journal*. The two main French-language financial papers are *L'Economiste* and *La Vie Eco*. *Femmes du Maroc*, *Citadine* and *Ousra* are the main French-language women's glossies. *Marrakech Mag* is a glossy magazine covering fashion and culture.

Listing magazines and city newspapers also exist, such as *Clips Essaouira* and *Le Tribune de Marrakech*, both of which can be found in most hotels and restaurants in each town. International newspapers and magazines are found in the larger hotels and magazine kiosks in the cities. English-language newspapers are usually no more than a day old in the main cities.

Radio and television

Moroccan TV consists of two channels, of which the stupefying TVM (the original government-run channel) is under pressure to make itself more interesting. 2m, originally a private channel that went bankrupt and was taken over by the government, has kept its editorial independence and is considered much better. Satellite

Moroccan dirhams.

television is common in homes and hotels across the country.

RTM runs a radio station which broadcasts daily programmes in English, Spanish and Berber as well as the more usual Arabic and French. It is complemented by Median (Radio Mediterranée Internationale), which broadcasts from Tangier to the whole of the Maghreb. Radio 2m is a music station, broadcasting in the capital area and Marrakech. With a short-wave radio you will be able to pick up the English-language broadcasts of the BBC World Service and Voice of America.

Money

The Moroccan dirham (dh) is divided into 100 centimes (often called francs). In rural areas people often count in rials – which no longer exist (20 rials = 1dh). Recent official rates have hovered around £1 = 13dh, US$1 = 8dh. Check the Bank of Morocco official rate card, which is available at all money-exchange desks in hotels and banks.

You are not allowed to import or export more than 1,000 Moroccan dirhams. Visitors can import as much foreign currency (in cash or traveller's cheques) as they wish.

ATMs

There are numerous ATMs accepting foreign cards in all Moroccan towns and cities – although most are concentrated in more modern urban areas, typically the Ville Nouvelle, rather than medinas.

Traveller's cheques

Traveller's cheques are becoming increasingly difficult to exchange in Morocco, and often attract sizeable commissions when they are. ATMs are now the most reliable and inexpensive way of getting cash during your

stay. Most ATMs are located outside banks and are accessible 24 hours, although obviously it's worth taking care when withdrawing sums from machines in quiet areas after dark.

Credit cards

Credit cards are accepted in many three-star and above hotels, the more expensive restaurants, most petrol stations and most car-hire firms – but it's wise to check in advance.

Money transfer

Western Union money transfer is the quickest way (four hours) of obtaining money from abroad. Western Union has offices in major cities and also operates through Atijari Wafabank and the post offices.

O

Opening hours

Business hours in Morocco are very variable, but typical times are:
Banks: Monday–Friday 8am–noon and 2–4pm.
(during Ramadan, 9am–2 or 3pm).

Many major branches of banks now incorporate money-exchange kiosks (with separate entrances) that have longer opening hours and are open over the weekend.
Offices: Monday–Thursday 8.30am–noon and 2.30–6pm, Friday 8.30am–noon and 3–6.30pm (during Ramadan, 9.30am–3 or 4pm).

Government offices close early on Friday and many private businesses open on Saturday morning.
Post offices: Monday–Friday 8.30am–4.30pm (though some close for lunch), Saturday 9am–noon (during Ramadan, 9am–2 or 3pm).

Many post offices have a desk selling stamps that is open through lunch time and into the early evening. Larger post offices have a telephone section that keeps longer hours (there are also many late-night téléboutiques).
Shops: Monday–Saturday 9am–12.30pm and 2.30–8pm (shops in medinas may keep shortened hours during Ramadan, possibly not opening until the afternoon and staying shut all day Friday, but staying open later in the evenings).

Some shops close on Friday (the Muslim holy day). In the villes nouvelles, shops often close on Sunday. Other shops remain open throughout the week. Generally, Western shops in the Villes Nouvelles will keep similar opening hours to

those in Europe, opening a bit later in the morning but without closing for lunch.

P

Postal services

In the past, visiting a post office in Morocco could take hours. Today both the post office and Maroc Telecom (the telephone company) have become a lot more efficient and easy to use.

The post office now has a separate *Post Rapide* service for national and international express parcel services. Stamps are widely available from tobacconists *(tabac)*.

Post office.

Public holidays

There are two sets of holidays, religious and secular: the former based on the Muslim (lunar) year (and therefore movable), and the other on the Western (Gregorian) calendar.

Religious holidays are as follows. For exact dates – they get earlier by 11 days each year (12 in a leap year) – consult the Tourist Office.

Muslim holidays

These religious holidays are observed by most businesses.

Edi ul Fitr (Aid es Seghir) Marking the end of Ramadan.

Eid ul Adha (Aid el Kebir) Feast of the Sacrifice; 70 days after Ramadan.

Islamic New Year (Fatih Muharram)

Mouloud (Milad un Nabi) The Prophet's birthday.

State holidays

New Year's Day – 1 January
Independence Manifesto Day – 11 January
Labour Day – 1 May
Feast of the Throne – 30 July
Oued Ed Dahab (Reunification Day) – 14 August
Revolution Day – 20 August
Green March – 6 November
Independence Day – 18 November

R

Religion

Morocco is a Muslim country but is very tolerant of other religions. Christians account for about 1 percent of the population; there are Roman Catholic churches in most large towns and Anglican churches in Tangier, Rabat and Casablanca. Jewish synagogues can also be found in the main cities. Alcohol is not restricted by law (except during Ramadan), and many European habits of government and administration are followed. For example, New Year's Day is a holiday and Sunday is the closing day for offices and larger shops. It is generally only in souks that shops close for Friday afternoon prayers.

Nonetheless, Morocco is a Muslim country, for all its compromises with Western calendars and customs, and never more obviously than during the holy month of Ramadan, when all Moroccans observe the daily fast.

Islam in the countryside is a peculiarly Moroccan hybrid – the faith of the Arabs adapted by the Berber tribes. There is more emphasis on individuals and saints than rigid Islamic codes would sanction.

In the city, the minarets of the mosques are a constant visible reminder of faith, and the call to prayer is heard five times a day. The mosque – and the wisdom and learning traditionally associated with it – are (often literally) central to town and city life. Qur'anic schools and conclaves of Islamic scholars reinforce orthodoxy, the most important tenet being that there is no God but God and Mohammed is his Prophet. There are no priests, no intermediaries: in praying five times a day, the Muslim is talking directly to God. At the same time, even without priests, centres of religious devotion have immense influence – and power. The king is the country's spiritual leader, so never make jokes about the monarch.

The first and most visible element of rural Islam is the popularity of the marabout or local saint – visible, because the countryside is dotted with small white buildings with domed roofs. Each is the tomb of a local holy man; the tomb itself sometimes known as a marabout (otherwise called a *koubba*). Around these local saints, cults of devotion have grown up over centuries.

Rich cults have *zaouia* – educational colleges that were set up next to the marabout in the same way as a mosque set up a medersa – but as an alternative to the city-based orthodoxy taught at the mosque. Every cult has its *moussem* – an annual festival in honour of the saint.

Ramadan

The ninth month of the Muslim calendar was the one in which God revealed to Mohammed the truths, which were written as the Qur'an. In remembrance of this and in obedience to one of Islam's 'five pillars', Muslims must observe a fast during the hours of daylight (see page 63). Non-Muslims are not required to observe the fast, but abstinence from smoking, eating and displays of physical affection in public is tactful. Travelling in Morocco during Ramadan can be both rewarding and tricky, but knowing a few basic rules will help make things much easier. In most major towns and cities and especially in rural areas, everything will shut down around half an hour before the breaking of the fast, at sunset, and it will also be impossible to find taxis at this time and for about an hour after sunset. Most places catering to tourism will remain open. Be aware that sensitivities can be more pronounced during this sacred month, so dressing and behaving appropriately is important. If you are ever invited to break the fast with a Moroccan, accept – but be prepared for a long night of eating ahead of you.

S

Smoking

Smoking is virtually a Moroccan pastime, and there are no restrictions on smoking in restaurants or cafés. For women smokers, it is worth bearing in mind that Moroccan women almost never smoke in public.

Students

There are few official discounts available to students in Morocco.

T

Tax

Quoted hotel rates usually include VAT (TVA in French), but other local taxes – Taxe Promotion Touristique (TPT) and Taxe de Séjour (TS) – may add between 10dh and 30dh per night.

Telephones

There are three main licensed telecommunications companies in Morocco: Maroc Télécom, Meditel and Inwi. Domestic and international telephone calls can be made from phone boxes *(cabines)* on the street, or in a main post office. Most take phone cards, available from post offices, tobacco shops and some grocery stores. Private payphone booths *(téléboutiques)* are widespread and efficient; they cost little more than a payphone on the street. There are many public telephones that also accept prepaid cards.

Most Moroccans, of course, have mobile phones, but Morocco's ubiquitous and extremely useful téléboutiques are still widely used by locals and by visitors who don't want to pay a fortune in mobile phone bills. Sim cards issued by the major mobile telecoms providers are readily available if you want to take advantage of local call rates.

Telephone codes

0522: Zone of Casablanca

You'll see private payphone booths everywhere.

0523: Zone of Settat (includes Azzemour, Azilal, Beni Mellal, El Jadida, Ksiba, Mohammedia).
0524: Zone of Marrakech (includes Demnate, El Kelaa Mgouna, Ouarzazate, Oukaimeden, Safi, Tinerhir, Zagora).
0528: Zone of Laâyoune (includes Agadir, Guelmime, Sidi Ifni, Tafraoute, Tan Tan, Taroudant and Tiznit).
0535: Zone of Fez (includes Erfound, Er Rachidia, Guercif, Ifrane, Khenifra, Meknes, Moulay Idriss, Rissani, Sefrou).
0536: Zone of Oujda (includes Figuig, Nador and Saida).
0537: Zone of Rabat (includes Khenitra, Moulay Bousselham, Ouezzane, Skhirate, Souk el Arba, Temara).
0539: Zone of Tangier (includes Al Hoceima, Asilah, Chaouen, Larache, Tetouan).

Telephoning home

Most exchanges are now automatic, and direct dialling abroad is now the rule. Dial 00 for an international call, wait for a second dial tone, and then dial the country code. The codes are as follows:
Australia: 61
Belgium: 32
Canada: 1
Denmark: 45
France: 33
Germany: 49
Great Britain: 44
Ireland: 353
New Zealand: 64
Portugal: 351
Spain: 34
United States: 1

Time zones

Moroccan time is the same as Greenwich Mean Time. Daylight Saving Time (DST, one hour ahead of GMT) is traditionally used during the summer between roughly late April and early October, although to confuse matters further DST is cancelled during the month of Ramadan, when the country reverts to GMT.

Tourist offices

Outside Morocco

Canada: Place Montreal Trust, Suite 2450, 1800 Avenue McGill College, Montreal QC H3A 3JS
Tel: +1 514 842 8111
Great Britain: 205 Regent Street, London W1B 4HB
Tel: +44 20 7437 0073
US: Suite 1820, 104 W 40th Street, New York 10018
Tel: +1 212-221 1583

In Morocco

National Tourist Offices (Office Nationale Marocain du Tourisme, ONMT) are often complemented by a municipal Syndicat d'Initiative. Both can give out maps, advice and provide guides, but the ONMT are usually better staffed. Most offices are open Mon–Sat mornings from 8am.
Agadir: Immeuble Ignouan, Avenue Mohammed V
Tel: 0528-84 63 77
Casablanca: 55 Rue Omar Slaoui
Tel: 0522-27 11 77
Fez: Syndicat d'Intiative, Place Mohammed V
Tel: 0535-62 34 60
Marrakech: Place Abd el Moumen Ben Ali
Tel: 0524-43 61 79
Meknes: Place de l'Istiqlal
Tel: 0535-52 44 26
Ouarzazate: Avenue Mohammed V
Tel: 0524-88 24 85
Rabat: Corner of Rue Oued Makhazine and Rue Zalaka, Agdal
Tel: 0537-67 40 13
Tangier: 29 Boulevard Pasteur
Tel: 0539-94 80 50
Tetouan: 30 Avenue Mohammed V
Tel: 0539-96 19 15

Tour operators

The Moroccan National Tourist Office (www.visitmorocco.com) provides a comprehensive list of tour operators. Here is a selection:

TRANSPORT

ACCOMMODATION

EATING OUT

ACTIVITIES

A – Z

LANGUAGE

Internet café.

General

Abercrombie & Kent Tailored luxury holidays in Essaouira, Marrakech, Fez, the desert and the High Atlas.
Tel: 0845 485 1529
www.abercrombiekent.co.uk
Club Med All-inclusive activity and family holidays in Agadir and Marrakech.
Tel: 0845 163 7888
www.clubmed.co.uk
Natural Morocco Moroccan specialists offering a wide range of bespoke tours with accommodation in riad or kasbah-style locations.
Tel: 0845 345 7195
www.naturallymorocco.co.uk
The Ultimate Travel Company Bespoke trekking, cultural and beach holidays across Morocco.
Tel: 020 3582 1287
www.theultimatetravelcompany.co.uk
Voyages Jules Verne Comprehensive programme of group tours throughout Morocco.
Tel: 0845 166 7003
www.vjv.com

V

Visas and passports

Holders of full British passports and holders of valid US, Canadian, Irish, Australian, New Zealand or Scandinavian passports need no visa for a stay of up to three months. Make sure that the expiry date of your passport is not less than six months after your departure to Morocco,

otherwise you may be refused entry. Crossing the border from Morocco (Western Sahara) into Mauritania is relatively straightforward, though you may have to wait for a few hours. Visas are needed and can be obtained from the Mauritanian Embassy in Rabat. The border crossing between Morocco and Algeria has been closed since 1994 with no sign of reopening.

W

Websites

www.visitmorocco.com National Tourist Office (in English).
www.morocco.com Includes hotel booking and travel tips.
www.hipmarrakech.com Good list of riads and a restaurant guide.
www.ilovemarrakech.com Online travel guide.
www.bestrestaurantsmaroc.com Restaurant listings.
www.morocco-holidays-guide.co.uk Listings (sites, hotels) for the major cities.
www.riadzany.blogspot.co.uk Interesting 'View from Fez' blogspot.
www.moroccanfood.about.com Moroccan recipes galore.

Weights and measures

Metric measures are used throughout Morocco: distances are in metres and kilometres, quantities in litres and weights in grams and kilograms, etc.

To convert = multipy by
Kilometres to miles = 0.621
Metres to feet = 3.28
Kilograms to pounds = 2.204
Grams to ounces = 0.035
If this all sounds like too much maths, it helps to remember that a kilometre is just over half a mile, a metre is roughly the same as a yard (3ft), a kilogram is just over two pounds, and 100 grams is a bit less than a quarter of a pound.

What to bring

Bring any prescription medicines you may need, and a spare pair of glasses (if you wear them). Remember that the sun can be fierce in summer, so it's a good idea to bring a hat, sunglasses and sunblock (although these items can be purchased once you arrive).

Women travellers

Women travelling alone or with female friends often complain of unwanted attention from Moroccan men – although contrary to popular belief, Western women are no more likely to attract attention of this nature than Moroccan women. Although hard to avoid completely, a few simple common sense measures can keep the problem to a minimum. Dressing modestly is the most important of these. Short (above-the-knee) skirts or shorts and vest tops are best left at home; and assuming a confident manner on the streets can help deter all but the most persistent males.

LANGUAGE

UNDERSTANDING THE LANGUAGE

Arabic is Morocco's official first language, although many people speak dialects of the Berber language, especially in and south of the High Atlas. Moroccan Arabic is unlike other forms of Arabic, so Arabic phrasebooks are not always completely reliable (although classical Arabic speakers will be understood). The easiest way to communicate for most Westerners is to use French, the second language, commonly used alongside Arabic on signposts, menus and in shops. English, German and Spanish are also understood in many hotels or souks – or wherever tourists are found.

It's very useful to have a few words of Arabic as a matter of courtesy, and to establish friendly relations. Some useful words are listed below; an accent shows the stressed syllable.

MOROCCAN ARABIC WORD AND PHRASES

In conversation

Hello *Márhaba, ahlan*
(reply) *Márhaba, ahlan*
Greetings *As-salám aláykum* (peace be with you)
(reply) *Waláykum as-salám* (and to you peace)
Welcome *Áhlan wasáhlan*
(reply) *Áhlan wasáhlan*
Good morning *Sabáh al-kháyr*
(reply) *Sabáh al-kháyr*
Good evening *Masá al-kháyr*
(reply) *Masá al-kháyr*
Good night *Tisbáh al-kháyr* (wake up well)
(reply) *Tisbáh al-kháyr*
Good bye *Máa Saláma*
How are you? *Káyf hálak?* (to a man)/*Káyf hálik?* (to a woman)
Well, fine *Al-hámdu li-llá*

Please *min fádlak* (to a man)/*min fádlik* (to a woman)
After you *Tafáddal* (to a man)/*Tafáddali* (to a woman)/*Afáddalu* (to more than one)
Excuse me *Samáhli*
Sorry *Áfwan or mutaásif* (for a man)/*Áfwan or mutaásifa* (for a woman)
Thank you (very much) *Shúkran (jazilan)*
Thank you, I am grateful *M'tshakkrine*
Thanks be to God *Al-hámdu li-llá*
God willing (hopefully) *Inshá allá*
Yes *Náam or áiwa*
No *La*
Congratulations! *Mabrúck!*
(reply) *Alláh yubárak fik*
What is your name? *Sh'nnu ismak?* (to a man)/*Sh'nnu ismik?* (to a woman)
My name is... *Ismi...*
Where are you from? *Min wáyn inta?* (for a man)/*Min wáyn inti?* (for a woman)
I am from... England *Ána min Ingíltra*
Germany *Ána min Almánia*
the United States *Ána min Amérika*
Australia *Ána min Ustrália*
Do you speak English? *Tkellem Inglisi?*
I speak... *Kan tkellem*
English *Inglisi*
German *Almámi*
French *Fransáwi*
I do not speak Arabic *Ma kan tkellemichi Arabíya*
I do not understand *Ma báfham*
What does this mean? *Shka te ani?*
Repeat, once more *Sh'hal*
Do you have...? *Ándkum...?*
Is there any...? *Kayn...?*
There isn't any... *Ma kaynsh...*
Never mind *Ma'alésh*
It is forbidden *Mamnú'a*
Is it allowed...? *Masmúh...?*
What is this? *Sh'nnu hádha?*

I want *Baghi*
I do not want *Ma baghish*
Wait *Istánna* (to a man)/*Istánni* (to a woman)
Hurry up *Yalla/Bi súra'a*
Slow down *Shwáyya*
Finished *Baraka*
Go away! *Imshi!*
What time is it? *Adáysh as-sáa?*/*Kam as-sáa?*
How long, how many hours? *Sha'al?*

General

embassy *sifára*
post office *máktab al-baríd*
stamps *tawábi'a*
bank *bank*
hotel *otél/fúnduq*
museum *máthaf*
ticket *tadakir*
ruins *athár*
passport *jiwáz as-sáfar*
good *m'zayn*
not good, bad *mashi m'zayn*
open *maftúh*
closed *múghlk*
today *al-yáum*
tonight *el barah ghadda*
tomorrow *búkra*

Arabic pronunciation

í as in **see**
ya as in **Soraya**
ai as in **eye**
ay as in **may**
aw as in **away**
dh as in **the**
gh as in **mirage**
kh as in the Scottish **loch**
' (an apostrophe) indicates a glottal stop.
Double consonants: Try to pronounce them twice as long.

Eating/drinking out

restaurant *máta'am*
fish *sámak/hout*
meat *láhma*
milk *halíb*
bread *khúbz*
salad *saláta*
delicious *záki*
coffee *káhwa*
tea *shái*
cup *kass*
with sugar *bi súkkar*
without sugar *bla sukkar*
wine *sh'rab*
beer *bíra*
mineral water *mái ma'adaniya*
glass *kass*
bottle *karaa*
I am a vegetarian *Ána nabbáti* (for a man)/*nabbátiya* (for a woman)
the bill *al hisáb*

Getting around

Where...? *Wáyn...?*
street *shária*
car *sayára*
taxi *táxi*
shared taxi *servís*
bus *tobis*
aeroplane *tayára*
airport *matár*
station *mahátta*
to *íla*
from *min*
right *yamín*
left *shimál*
straight *dúghri*
behind *wára*
near *karíb*
far away *ba'id*
petrol, super *benzín, benzín khas*

Numbers

zero *sifir*
one *wáhad*
two *itnín*
three *taláta*
four *árba'a*
five *khámsa*
six *sítta*
seven *sába'a*
eight *tamánia*
nine *tísa'a*
ten *áshara*
eleven *hidáshar*
twelve *itnáshar*

Shopping

market *súq*
shop *dukkán*
money *fulús*
cheap *rakhís*
expensive (very) *gháli (jídan)*
receipt, invoice *fatúra, wásl*

Days of the week

Often used to identify towns and villages, which are named after the day of their weekly souk: thus Souk-Tnine is the town that has a market on Monday. The days are numbered from Sunday, with the exception of Friday, the day of Muslim worship, which has no number.
El had the first day: Sunday
At tnine the second day: Monday
At tleta the third day: Tuesday
El arba the fourth day: Wednesday
El khemis the fifth day: Thursday
Aj djeema day of mosque or assembly: Friday
As sebt the sixth day: Saturday

How much does it cost? *Adáysh?/Bi-kam?*
What would you like? *Sh'nou khsek?*
I like this *Baghi hádha*
I do not like this *Ma baghish hádha*
Can I see this? *Mumkin ashúf hádha?*
Give me *A'atíni*
How many? *Kam?*

Looking for a room

a free room *ghúrfa fádia*
single room *ghúrfa munfárida*
double room *ghúrfa muzdáwija*
hot water *mái skhoon*
bathroom, toilet *hammám, tuwalét*
shower *dúsh*
towel *foota*
How much does the room cost per night? *Sha'al el bit allayla?*

Emergencies

I need help *Bídi musáada*
doctor *doct/Bídi musáada*
hospital *mustáshfa*
pharmacy *saidalíya*
I am ill, sick *Ána marídh* (for a man)/*Ána marídha* (for a woman)
diarrhoea *ishál*
operation *amalíya*
police *shúrta*
lawyer *muhámmi*
I want to see *Ba'ghi anshoof*

Glossary

agadir fortified granary
agdal garden
aït community
el Andalus Muslim Spain
bab gate
baraka blessing (often considered magical)
bled el makhzen land of government
bled es siba land of dissidence
caid district judge
djemma assembly, but also mosque
djinn spirit
Fassi person from Fez
fondouk lodging house with stables
Hajj the pilgrimage to Mecca
hammam steam bath
horm sanctuary
imam prayer leader
jebel mountain
koubba white, domed building containing the tomb of a saint
ksar (ksour) fortified pisé building or community (plural)
l'tam veil
Maghreb collective name for Morocco, Algeria and Tunisia
makhzen government
marabout saint
Marrakchi person from Marrakech
mechouar square, assembly area
medersa (madrassa) Islamic college and living quarters for students (plural)
medina old town
mellah Jewish quarter
mihrab niche indicating direction of Mecca in mosque
minaret tower of mosque
Moriscos Muslim refugees from Spain in 15th century
moujehaddin Islamic soldiers engaged in Holy War
Moulay indicates descendancy from the Prophet
Mouloud Prophet's birthday
moussem religious festival
msalla prayer area
muezzin caller to prayer
oued river
pisé mud and rubble
quibla direction of Mecca in a mosque
shereef ruler who is descendant of Prophet
Shia branch of Islam which recognises Ali as the successor to Mohammed
shouaf fortune teller
stucco elaborate plaster work
Sufi religious mystic
Sunni orthodox Muslim
tabia mud used in pisé architecture
tizi mountain pass
zaouia religious fraternity
zellige elaborate tile mosaics

FRENCH WORDS AND PHRASES

How much is it? *C'est combien?*
What is your name? *Comment vous appelez-vous?*
My name is... *Je m'appelle...*
Do you speak English? *Parlez-vous anglais?*

I am English/American *Je suis anglais(e)/américain(e)*
I don't understand *Je ne comprends pas*
Please speak more slowly *Parlez plus lentement, s'il vous plaît*
Can you help me? *Pouvez-vous m'aider?*
I'm looking for... *Je cherche...*
Where is...? *Où est...?*
I'm sorry *Excusez-moi/Pardon*
I don't know *Je ne sais pas*
No problem *Pas de problème*
Have a good day! *Bonne journée!*
That's it *C'est ça*
Here it is *Voici*
There it is *Voilà*
Let's go *On y va/Allons-y*
See you tomorrow *A demain*
See you soon *A bientôt*
Show me the word in the book *Montrez-moi le mot dans le livre*
yes *oui*
no *non*
please *s'il vous plaît*
thank you *merci*
....(very much) *(beaucoup)*
you're welcome *de rien*
excuse me *excusez-moi*
hello *bonjour*
OK *d'accord*
goodbye *au revoir*
good evening *bonsoir*
here *ici*
there *là*
today *aujourd'hui*
yesterday *hier*
tomorrow *demain*
now *maintenant*
later *plus tard*
this morning *ce matin*
this afternoon *cet après-midi*
this evening *ce soir*

On arrival

I want to get off at... *Je voudrais descendre à...*
What street is this? *A quelle rue sommes-nous?*
How far is...? *A quelle distance se trouve...?*
Validate your ticket *Compostez votre billet*
airport *l'aéroport*
train station *la gare*
bus station *la gare routière*
Métro stop *la station de Métro*
bus *l'autobus/le car*
bus stop *l'arrêt*
platform *le quai*
ticket *le billet*
return ticket *aller-retour*
hitchhiking *l'autostop*
toilets *les toilettes*
This is the hotel address *C'est l'adresse de l'hôtel*

I'd like a (single/double) room... *Je voudrais une chambre (pour une/deux personnes)...*
...with shower *avec douche*
...with a bath *avec salle de bain*
...with a view *avec vue*
Does that include breakfast? *Le prix comprend-il le petit déjeuner?*
May I see the room? *Je peux voir la chambre?*
washbasin *le lavabo*
bed *le lit*
key *la clé*
elevator *l'ascenseur*
air conditioned *climatisé*

On the road

Where is the spare wheel? *Où est la roue de secours?*
Where is the nearest garage? *Où est le garage le plus proche?*
Our car has broken down *Notre voiture est en panne*
I want to have my car repaired *Je veux faire réparer ma voiture*
the road to... *la route pour...*
left *gauche*
right *droite*
straight on *tout droit*
far *loin*
near *près d'ici*
opposite *en face*
beside *à côté de*
car park *parking*
over there *là-bas*
at the end *au bout*
on foot *à pied*
by car *en voiture*
town map *le plan*
road map *la carte*
street *la rue*
square *la place*
give way *céder le passage*
dead end *impasse*
no parking *stationnement interdit*
motorway *l'autoroute*
toll *le péage*
speed limit *la limitation de vitesse*
petrol *l'essence*
unleaded *sans plomb*
diesel *le gasoil*
water/oil *l'eau/l'huile*
puncture *un pneu crevé*

Shopping

Where is the nearest bank (post office)? *Où est la banque/Poste?*
I'd like to buy *Je voudrais acheter*
How much is it? *C'est combien?*
Do you take credit cards? *Est-ce que vous acceptez les cartes de crédit?*
I'm just looking *Je regarde seulement*
Have you got...? *Avez-vous...?*
I'll take it *Je le prends*
I'll take this one/that one *Je prends celui-ci/celui-là*

What size is it? *C'est de quelle taille?*
size (clothes) *la taille*
size (shoes) *la pointure*
cheap *bon marché*
expensive *cher*
too much *trop*
a piece *un morceau de*
each *la pièce (eg oranges, 15F la pièce)*
bill *la note*
chemist *la pharmacie*
bakery *la boulangerie*
bookshop *la librairie*
grocery *l'alimentation/l'épicerie*
tobacconist *tabac*
markets *le marché*
supermarket *le supermarché*

Sightseeing

town *la ville*
old town *la vieille ville*
town hall *hôtel de ville*
hospital *l'hôpital*
staircase *l'escalier*
tower *la tour*
museum *le musée*
exhibition *l'exposition*
tourist information office *l'office de tourisme/le syndicat d'initiative*
free *gratuit*
open *ouvert*
closed *fermé*
every day *tous les jours*
all year *toute l'année*
all day *toute la journée*
swimming pool *la piscine*

Dining out

breakfast *le petit déjeuner*
lunch *le déjeuner*
dinner *le dîner*
meal *le repas*
first course *l'entrée/les hors d'œuvre*
main course *le plat principal*
made to order *sur commande*
drink included *boisson compris*
wine list *la carte des vins*
the bill *l'addition*
fork *la fourchette*
knife *le couteau*
spoon *la cuillère*
plate *l'assiette*
glass *le verre*
napkin *la serviette*
ashtray *le cendrier*
Can you recommend a good restaurant? *Pouvez-vous recommander un bon restaurant?*
I'd like to reserve a table for two *Je voudrais réserver une table pour deux personnes*
We have a reservation *Nous avons réservé*
The bill, please *L'addition, s'il vous plaît*

FURTHER READING

FICTION

The Sand Child, by Tahar Ben Jelloun. A haunting novel, which radically challenged Arab traditions of gender and society and Islamic law, by Morocco's foremost novelist.
This Blinding Absence of Light, by Tahar Ben Jelloun. An immensely powerful novel, based on the true story of a political prisoner who managed to survive incarceration in an underground prison in the Moroccan desert.
The Spider's House, by Paul Bowles. The extraordinary story of an American expat in Fez during the period leading up to Moroccan independence in 1956.
The Sheltering Sky, by Paul Bowles. Familiar to many through the film adaptation by Bernardo Bertolucci, this is Bowles's most famous existentialist work. Other books by Bowles set in Morocco include **Without Stopping** and **Let it All Come Down**.
For Bread Alone, by Mohammed Choukri. Harrowing autobiography of Choukri's harsh childhood in the slums of Tangier.
Hideous Kinky, by Esther Freud. Humorous novel about a young girl's adventures with her hippie mother in Morocco in the 1960s.
M'Hashish, by Mohammed Mrabet. A classic little book on hashish, by one of Morocco's foremost writers.

FOOD AND COOKING

The Food of Morocco, by Tess Mallos. A culinary tour of Morocco and an exploration of Moroccan cooking, from *briouats* to tagines.
The Momo Cookbook, by Momo Mazouz. Wonderful cookbook combines poetic portraits of Morocco with 90 delicious recipes.

HISTORY

Lords of the Atlas, by Gavin Maxwell. Compelling story of the Glaoui dynasty in the last two centuries.
The Conquest of Morocco, by Douglas Porch. French adventurism and Moroccan history at the end of the 19th century.
North Africa: A History from the Mediterranean Shore to the Sahara, by Barnaby Rogerson. Definitive and readable history of North Africa – Libya, Tunisia, Algeria and Morocco.

PHOTOGRAPHY/ART

Living in Morocco: Design from Casablanca to Marrakech, by Lisl and Landt Dennis. Sumptuous exploration of Morocco's decorative and folk arts.
Morocco: A Sense of Place, by Cécile Tréal and Jean-Michel Ruiz. An evocative blend of travel writing and photography.
The Berbers of Morocco, by Alan Keohane. Impressive photographic study of the Berbers of Morocco by a longtime Morocco resident.

Send Us Your Thoughts

We do our best to ensure the information in our books is as accurate and up-to-date as possible. The books are updated on a regular basis using local contacts, who painstakingly add, amend and correct as required. However, some details (such as telephone numbers and opening times) are liable to change, and we are ultimately reliant on our readers to put us in the picture.

We welcome your feedback, especially your experience of using the book "on the road". Maybe we recommended a hotel that you liked (or another that you didn't), or you came across a great bar or new attraction we missed.

We will acknowledge all contributions, and we'll offer an Insight Guide to the best letters received.

Please write to us at:
**Insight Guides
PO Box 7910
London SE1 1WE**
Or email us at:
insight@apaguide.co.uk

TRAVEL LITERATURE

Morocco: The Traveller's Companion, by Margaret and Robin Bidwell. The classic literary guide to Morocco.
Marrakech, The Red City, by Barnaby Rogerson (ed.). Compendium of literary extracts from writers ranging from Elias Canetti to Edith Wharton.
The Last Storytellers, by Richard Hamilton. Magical collection of folktales handed down by the legendary – and fast-disappearing – storytellers of Jemaa el Fna.
Morocco That Was, by Walter Harris. Account of the end of feudal Morocco and the beginning of French rule from London *Times* correspondent.
A Year in Marrakesh, by Peter Mayne. An engrossing account of Mayne's year in Marrakech.
The Caliph's House, by Tahir Shah. Best-selling story of Shah's move to Casablanca to restore a jinn-haunted caliph's house in the suburbs of the city.
In Arabian Nights, by Tahir Shah. Tahir Shah's fascinating account of a journey across Morocco in search of the story inside him.
Valley of the Casbahs, by Jeffrey Tayler. A delightful account of Tayler's journey along the Drâa Valley by foot and camel.
In Morocco, by Edith Wharton. Compelling account of Wharton's travels through Morocco at the time of the French Protectorate.

WOMEN

Beyond the Veil, by Fatima Mernissi. Acclaimed exploration of the position of women in Islam by Morocco's preeminent feminist.
Dreams of Trespass, by Fatima Mernissi. The story of Mernissi's fascinating childhood, in a harem in Fez in the 1940s.
Stolen Lives, By Malika Oufkir. Fascinating true story by the daughter of the leader of the failed coup against Hassan II in 1971 and the price she paid for her father's actions.

CREDITS

Insight Guide Credits

Distribution

UK
Dorling Kindersley Ltd
A Penguin Group company
80 Strand, London, WC2R 0RL
sales@uk.dk.com

United States
Ingram Publisher Services
1 Ingram Boulevard, PO Box 3006,
La Vergne, TN 37086-1986
ips@ingramcontent.com

Australia and New Zealand
Woodslane
10 Apollo St, Warriewood,
NSW 2102, Australia
info@woodslane.com.au

Worldwide
Apa Publications GmbH & Co. Verlag
KG (Singapore branch)
7030 Ang Mo Kio Avenue 5
08-65 Northstar @ AMK
Singapore 569880
apasin@singnet.com.sg

Printing
CTPS-China

www.insightguides.com

Project Editor
Tom Stainer
Series Manager
Rachel Lawrence
Author
Gavin Thomas
Picture Editor/Art Editor
Tom Smyth/Shahid Mahmood
Map Production
Original cartography Berndtson &
Berndtson, updated by
Apa Cartography Department
Production
Rebeka Davies

Contributors

Insight Guide: Morocco was
commissioned by **Tom Stainer** and
edited by **Alyse Dar**. This edition was
updated by **Gavin Thomas**, a
freelance travel writer specializing in
Asia and Arabia who has also
contributed to numerous other Insight
guides including books on Oman,
Dubai and the UAE, Sri Lanka and
India. A regular visitor to Morocco for
over 15 years, he has now travelled
across the country from the
mountains of the Rif to the southern
Saharan oases. Previous contributors
include **Dorothy Stannard, Tatiana
Wilde, Alan Keohane, Barry Miles,
Rosemary Bailey, Stephen Ormsby-
Hughes, Anne Lambton, Nicholas
Shakespeare, John Offen** and
David Herbert.

About Insight Guides

Insight Guides have more than
40 years' experience of publishing
high-quality, visual travel guides. We
produce 400 full-colour titles, in both
print and digital form, covering more
than 200 destinations across the
globe, in a variety of formats to meet
your different needs.

  Insight Guides are written by
local authors who use their on-the-
ground experience to provide the
very latest information; their local
expertise is evident in the extensive
historical and cultural background
features. All the reviews in **Insight
Guides** are independent; we strive
to maintain an impartial view. Our
reviews are carefully selected to
guide you to the best places to stay
and eat, so you can be confident that
when we say a restaurant or hotel is
special, we really mean it.

Legend

City maps

- Freeway/Highway/Motorway
- Divided Highway
- Main Roads
- Minor Roads
- Pedestrian Roads
- Steps
- Footpath
- Railway
- Funicular Railway
- Cable Car
- Tunnel
- City Wall
- Important Building
- Built Up Area
- Other Land
- Transport Hub
- Park
- Pedestrian Area
- Bus Station
- Tourist Information
- Main Post Office
- Cathedral/Church
- Mosque
- Synagogue
- Statue/Monument
- Beach
- Airport

Regional maps

- Freeway/Highway/Motorway (with junction)
- Freeway/Highway/Motorway (under construction)
- Divided Highway
- Main Road
- Secondary Road
- Minor Road
- Track
- Footpath
- International Boundary
- State/Province Boundary
- National Park/Reserve
- Marine Park
- Ferry Route
- Marshland/Swamp
- Glacier
- Salt Lake
- Airport/Airfield
- Ancient Site
- Border Control
- Cable Car
- Castle/Castle Ruins
- Cave
- Chateau/Stately Home
- Church/Church Ruins
- Crater
- Lighthouse
- Mountain Peak
- Place of Interest
- Viewpoint

INDEX

Main references are in bold type

INSIGHT GUIDES

INSPIRING YOUR NEXT ADVENTURE

Insight Guides offers you a range of travel guides
to match your needs. Whether you are looking for
inspiration for planning a trip, cultural information,
walks and tours, great listings, or practical advice, we
have a product to suit you.

www.insightguides.com